CW01203573

Edward, Lord Hawke.

THE LIFE

OF

EDWARD LORD HAWKE

ADMIRAL OF THE FLEET, VICE-ADMIRAL OF GREAT BRITAIN,
AND FIRST LORD OF THE ADMIRALTY FROM 1766 TO 1771.

WITH SOME ACCOUNT

OF

*THE ORIGIN OF THE ENGLISH WARS IN THE REIGN OF
GEORGE THE SECOND, AND THE STATE OF THE
ROYAL NAVY AT THAT PERIOD.*

BY

MONTAGU BURROWS,

CAPTAIN, R.N. (RETIRED LIST),
AND
CHICHELE PROFESSOR OF MODERN HISTORY IN THE UNIVERSITY OF OXFORD.

LONDON:
W. H. ALLEN & CO., 13 WATERLOO PLACE.
PUBLISHERS TO THE INDIA OFFICE.

1888.

(All rights reserved.)

LONDON:
PRINTED BY W. H. ALLEN AND CO., 13 WATERLOO PLACE.

PREFACE AND DEDICATION.

THE Life of Admiral Lord Hawke, which I here present, with no little diffidence, to the reader, is in the first place due to a conviction long ago formed, and strengthened by time, that a great man had, by no fault of his own, been accidentally placed in the pages of history far below his proper level. Anyone may observe that the notices of Lord Hawke's career, when placed side by side with the undoubted facts and results of his services—services which have scarcely been surpassed by those of even our greatest admirals—are uniformly meagre and inadequate. It is impossible to avoid the inference that it would have been otherwise had there ever existed anything like a Life or Memoir of the man. Scores of naval officers, avowedly inferior to him in merit and importance, have had that advantage.

It is possible that this conviction might never have borne fruit had it not been for a friendship formed in early life at sea, with a descendant of the Admiral, the late Commander Bladen Edward Hawke.

This officer, the only member of the family who had ever embarked in the profession in which the fortunes of the House had been founded,* gave high promise of displaying a character worthy of his descent; but his opening career was cut short by a paralytic seizure. For thirty-two years he lingered on in this incapable condition, exhibiting to the last the indomitable spirit, the cheerful patience, and the indefatigable energy in doing good to his fellow-creatures which might, had his life been otherwise ordered, have issued in noble deeds for the public service of his country. By his wish I took up the subject, and to his memory I dedicate the book.

I have to thank Lord Hawke for kind encouragement, Frances Lady Hawke, for the loan of the family papers and official books, and J. K. Laughton, Esq., Lecturer in Naval History at the R. N. College, Greenwich, not only for pointing out sources of information, but for valuable hints and corrections. To him the profession anxiously looks for a new and detailed History of the Royal Navy. I have also had the advantage of being allowed to make use of the intelligent experience of my oldest friend, Admiral Chads, who shared with me in early life the friendship of Bladen Hawke. Neither of my kind critics will, of course, expect to find their opinions entirely reflected in these pages.

---

* His nephew, the Hon. Stanhope Hawke, has recently followed his example.

Finally, I must not omit to mention the ever-ready assistance which I have received at the Public Record Office from Alfred Kingston, Esq., and, at Deptford, from F. H. Miller, Esq., of the Victualling Yard, to whose immediate care the earlier Records of the Royal Navy are entrusted.

MONTAGU BURROWS.

OXFORD, *January* 1883.

NOTE.—The frontispiece is engraved from the original picture at Womersley Park (near Pontefract), of which the picture in the "Painted Hall," Greenwich, is believed to be a copy.

TABLE OF CONTENTS.

CHAPTER I.

INTRODUCTION.—PART I.

Lord Hawke's claim to greatness.—His place in Naval History.—The English wars inevitable . . . . . p. 1

CHAPTER II.

INTRODUCTION: PART II.—THE ORIGIN OF THE ENGLISH WARS IN THE REIGN OF GEORGE THE SECOND.

Burke on the Spanish War.—Position of Sir Robert Walpole.—The Opposition.—The Peace of Utrecht.—Idea of restoring Gibraltar.—Gibraltar and Portobello.—Hosier's expedition.—"Hosier's Ghost."—The first "Family Compact."—Success of Fleury's policy.—Origin of the West Indian disputes.—Claim of the "Right of Search."—History of the Treaties.—Practice of smuggling.—The Assiento Treaty.—Mutual exasperation.—Resolutions of Parliament.—Walpole's resistance.—Arguments of the Opposition.—The Satires of the time.—Declaration of War.—Burke's assertions.—Depression of the nation.—Contemporary feeling.—A war of self-defence . p. 7

CHAPTER III.

INTRODUCTION: PART III.—THE STATE OF THE BRITISH NAVY IN THE REIGN OF GEORGE THE SECOND, WITH ESPECIAL REFERENCE TO LORD HAWKE'S PLACE AMONGST HIS CONTEMPORARIES.

The English and the Dutch.—Soldiers and Sailors.—Absence of great officers.—Fighting in line.—Indecisive combats.—Progress of Naval Tactics.—Hawke's predecessors.—His special merit.—Political position.—The "Father of the British Navy."—Byng and Wager.—Norris and Haddock.—Vernon and Ogle.—Lord Anson.—Sanitary state of the Navy.—The treatment of seamen.—Inferiority of English ships and guns.—Superiority of English seamen.—Systems of Tactics.—State of the Navy illustrated.—Enforced respect for the Flag.—History of the claim.—The King's own Captain . . p. 60

CHAPTER IV.

EARLY HISTORY AND SERVICES OF LORD HAWKE.

Parentage.—First going to sea.—Early obscurity.—West Indian experience.—Marriage.—Colonel Bladen. — Colonel Bladen's letters.—Captain of the "Portland."—Rotten ships.—Dismasted in a hurricane.—Barrow upon Hawke . . p. 109

CHAPTER V.

HAWKE'S SHARE, AS CAPTAIN, IN THE BATTLE OF ADMIRAL MATHEWS, OFF TOULON.—1744.

The Press-gang.—Sickness of pressed men.—Before the battle.—European international relations.—French policy.—Mathews and Lestock.—Abortive proceedings.—Battle off Toulon.—Hawke and the "Poder."—Lestock's behaviour.—Mathews' errors.—Courtmartial on Mathews.—A multitude of Courts-martial.—Captain Richard Norris.—Mathews' treatment of Hawke.—Employment in Mediterranean . . . p. 132

CHAPTER VI.

BATTLE WITH THE FRENCH OFF USHANT.—1747.

Anson's battle.—Sir Peter Warren.—Hawke made an Admiral.—Conduct as to the Galleons.—Letters to Warren.—The British Squadron.—Description of the battle.—State of the victors.—His own share in the combat.—Fine conduct of the French.—The size of the French ships.—Courtmartial on Fox.—Honours conferred on Hawke.—Member for Portsmouth.—Warren and Billingsgate.—Admiral Boscawen.—Chatham and the Naval Heroes.—Naval Uniform.—Peace due to naval victories . . . . p. 169

CHAPTER VII.

SIR EDWARD HAWKE'S POSITION DURING THE PEACE AND AT THE OPENING OF THE SEVEN YEARS' WAR.—CONDITION OF THE GOVERNMENT.—1748-1755.

French policy during the Peace of Aix-la-Chapelle.—War in the Colonies.—Duke of Newcastle.—Hawke and Byng.—Byng's character.—The crisis.—The Royal Marines.—Alliances and preparations.—Hawke the leading Admiral.—Boscawen in America . . . . p. 210

CHAPTER VIII.

HAWKE'S POSITION IN RELATION TO ADMIRAL BYNG.—COURT-MARTIAL ON BYNG.—1756, 1757.

Secret Instructions.—Justification of them.—William, Duke of Cumberland.—Hawke's first quarrel with the Admiralty.—

Ministerial incapacity.—Byng's action off Minorca.—Fury of the English people.—Bad treatment of Byng.—Fall of Newcastle and Anson.—Byng's Courtmartial.—Forbes and Temple West.—The King's conduct.—Hawke and Pitt.—Hawke's spirited conduct in the Mediterranean.—Strain on his health.—Gloomy close of 1756 . . . . p. 233

CHAPTER IX.

THE ROCHEFORT EXPEDITION.—1757.

Pitt's Dictatorship and war policy.—Hawke's responsibility.—Anson reinstated.—Secret Instructions.—Delays.—Transports.—Pitt urges haste.—Hawke's private memoranda.—Wolfe's criticisms.—Admiral Knowles.—Hawke's Despatch.—Account of Rochefort.—Howe attacks Fort of Aix.—Landing-place found.—Councils of War.—Landing impossible.—Expedition relinquished.—Fury of English people.—Court of Enquiry and Courtmartial.—Pitt's anger.—Hawke's character unshaken.—Gloomy retrospect of 1757.—Men rally round the old King . . . . p. 280

CHAPTER X.

THE DESCENTS ON FRANCE IN 1758.

Brighter prospects of 1758.—Boscawen, Amherst, and Wolfe.—Capture of Cape Breton.—Hawke again at Rochefort.—Destroys the enemy.—Second quarrel with the Admiralty.—Resigns.—The Admiralty explain.—Their mistake repeated in later times.—Serious illness of Hawke.—Disaster at Saint Cas.—Pitt's success balanced . . . . p. 336

CHAPTER XI.

THE BLOCKADE OF BREST.—1759.

The officers of the fleet.—Edward, Duke of York.—Rules of the blockade.—Hawke's praise of Captain Hervey.—Neutrals.—Boot-hose-topping.—Struggle with Bureaucracy.—Boscawen's victory off Lagos.—Improvements in gunnery.—The plot thickens.—Blockade tells on the officers.—Scene between Pitt and Newcastle.—The enemy caught at last . . p. 361

CHAPTER XII.

THE BATTLE OF QUIBERON.—1759.

Hawke's Despatch.—The judgment of history.—A calculated venture.—The Chaplain's narrative.—Contemporary criticism.—Fine spirit in the fleet.—French Commanders.—The Duc d'Aiguillon.—Fleet half-starved.—Rejoicings in England.—Inadequate reward to Hawke.—Consequences of his victory.—Poetical effusions.—"The Great Fifty-nine" . . p. 393

CHAPTER XIII.

LAST SERVICES.—1760–1771.

Keppel and Hodgson at Belleisle.—George II. and Louis XV. compared.—Hawke's "Inactivity."—The new Spanish War.—Last sea service.—Spanish Colonies shattered.—Anecdote of Hawke.—Death of Anson and Boscawen.—Ranke on the foundation of the British Empire.—Sir Charles Saunders.—Sir George Pocock.—Hawke First Lord of the Admiralty.—Keppel and Rodney.—Lord Howe.—Attacks upon Hawke.—Walpole's criticism.—Sandwich's Administration.—The King's Letters.—Naval First Lords or Civilians? . p. 430

CHAPTER XIV.

PEERAGE, RETIREMENT, AND DEATH.—1776-1781.

Delay of Hawke's Peerage.—His interest in Keppel's action.—The battle discussed.—Keppel's letter to Lord Hawke.—Palliser made a scapegoat.—Memorial of the twelve Admirals.—Lord Rockingham's letter.—The Whig ladies.—Palliser's mistakes.—Lord Hawke's letters to Admiral Geary.—His letter to Admiral Barrington.—His death.—His character . p. 472

INDEX AND ERRATA . . . . p. 499

THE LIFE OF LORD HAWKE.

CHAPTER I.

INTRODUCTION.—PART I.—LORD HAWKE'S CLAIM TO GREATNESS.

AT this distance of time it is impossible to put the subject of our memoir into intelligible connection with the history of his country without glancing back at that history during the period of his career; nor can the respective merits of naval officers be estimated by a bare and simple comparison of their services. Such a method is ridiculous. The circumstances of the times when they performed their exploits, the condition of the naval service in their age, as compared with its previous and subsequent condition, and especially the point of development at which naval tactics had arrived, the advance which had been made by foreign navies in comparison with our own,—all this, and a great deal more, it is necessary to consider if we are to form anything like a correct judgment. The history of a country's military or naval forces is only a reflex of its own history. The spirit which animates those forces at any period is the direct index of the national spirit. Even in the most splendid national annals it will not be found invariably that the prevailing spirit of a people is "*dulce et decorum est pro patria mori.*" To analyse and detect the influences which have at different times created or impaired that high standard is the province of history.*

Here, of course, the briefest sketch must suffice, and the reader's patience must be requested while he is detained for a few pages from the life of our hero. But, indeed, throughout this book, and not only in the introductory chapters, its plan will be seen to include, along with the incidents of a noble life, a full view of the circumstances by which it was surrounded, and a sufficient sketch of the chief figures in the Government and in the naval service to bring out the full character of the man whom we shall try to understand. No life can be really separated from its times. In this case it is a chief factor in the whole course of events.

From a naval point of view it is not too much to say that we shall find, on a full consideration of the

---

* An attempt of this sort has been recently made by the writer in the pages of the "Quarterly Review," under the headings "Balance of Power" and "The Rise of the Modern British Empire." Both of these have been reprinted, along with a treatise by the writer on the "Foreign Policy of Great Britain during the Reign of George III.," under the title "Imperial England" (Cassell, Petter, and Galpin, 1880).

subject, that we are dealing with the man who was the parent of the modern British navy, in a sense which can be attributed to no one else; and we shall trace in his manly character the highest type to which the thorough, old-fashioned British seaman and gentleman had attained. We shall identify him as the admiral who broke through with success, and upon a uniform plan, the antiquated traditions which had hampered his gallant predecessors, and as the author of the new system of resting satisfied with nothing short of destroying the enemy whenever and whereever he could be found, instead of parting with him after indecisive combats sustained according to the then received principles of naval warfare.

It will be necessary in the cause of fair play to challenge some opinions which come to us with authority. Presumptuous as it may seem, we shall have to break a lance with Burke on the origin of the war with Spain in 1739. We shall also see that great as was the influence of the immortal Chatham in arousing the nation to a sense of its mighty destinies, not only was Hawke's share in the process by which Chatham attained his success in founding the British Empire far greater than is usually supposed, but, also, contrary to the received opinion, that the brilliant examples of the true old British spirit which, before Chatham appeared on the scene, Hawke himself set, entitle him to a place of his own, quite independent of the career of the great Minister.

Lastly, though the reader will hardly find himself at liberty to dispute the verdict of poetic genius recorded by Campbell when he singled out the two most eminent of all naval heroes,—

> "Where Blake and mighty Nelson fell
> Your manly hearts shall glow";

he will not be called upon to assign our hero a place below anyone else—unless it be Rodney; and he will be summoned to recognise as witnesses not only Hawke's actual services—the conditions under which they were rendered being taken into account—but also the estimation in which those services were held at the time, and their critical character in relation to the safety and welfare of Great Britain.

A word must be said in this Introduction on the sense in which the writer desires to be understood in speaking of the struggle between England and her enemies. So much has happened since those times, and France, as well as Spain, have for so many years —one might say generations—been friends and allies of this country, that to some it may seem ungracious to descant upon the victories won at their expense, and to revive the memory of quarrels which have so long vanished away. If this feeling is entertained at all it should not pass without notice, but it ought surely to be reckoned a symptom of hyper-sensibility.

The wars which are now to be noticed were a struggle for trade, commerce, and colonial development, and this necessarily involved a struggle for national existence. The exclusive ideas of Spain on these points, inherited from the days of her brilliant discoveries and conquests, could not possibly, as we shall see, have been dissipated except by war. Great

Britain had her rights as well as Spain, and they were not confined to herself alone.

France, on the other hand, under Louis XIV. and Louis XV., believing herself to have found, through the Bourbon connection with the crowns of Spain and Naples, an opportunity to establish a colonial empire on the basis of that connection, and, therefore, in necessary antagonism to her ancient rival, had a perfect right to adopt that policy; and there were many indications of its probable success. That the English, after the exhausting wars of William and of Anne, and amidst the difficulties of a disputed Succession, should shrink as long as possible from such a conflict, should gradually gather resolution from the contempt to which they found themselves exposed by such conduct, and at last should enter on the strife with a vigour which issued in success, was surely the most natural thing in the world, being simply, in that age, a question of self-preservation. Considering the relations which had existed for centuries between the two great Powers on either side of the British Channel, the reciprocal threats and dangers of invasion, and the numerous parts of the world in which their respective interests could not but clash, it was a struggle on which neither could enter without an inward certainty—however necessary a truce might be—that neither could emerge out of it till the battle was fought out.

It does not come within the limits of this book to discuss the later issues of the conflict, its renewal in connection with the revolt of the American colonies, and again through the French Revolution; but in the two wars (which in reality were but one) now before us, if it is impossible to trace the combat with cosmopolitan nonchalance, it will at least be seen that full credit is given to the high qualities of both the national enemies, and that the disadvantages under which they laboured in naval warfare are faithfully pointed out. This last is a circumstance which is too often forgotten. It greatly enhances the merit of that fortitude which so nobly bore up under unparalleled reverses, while at the same time it detracts, to precisely the same extent, from the credit due to the victors. However, they have enough glory, and to spare.

CHAPTER II.

INTRODUCTION.—PART II.—THE ORIGIN OF THE ENGLISH WARS IN THE REIGN OF GEORGE THE SECOND.

To the English war with Spain, which broke out in 1739, was soon added a war with the close ally and protector of that Power, France. It had, indeed, been from the commencement, virtually and covertly, a war with the two combined Powers and their allies. This is in many respects the most important as well as arduous conflict in which Great Britain ever engaged; for in the course of twenty-four years it issued in the foundation and establishment of the British Empire. It is also the one conflict which has been most uniformly misrepresented.

The opening of this war, which must be here treated as continuous, though broken for a while by a sort of truce, was signalised by one of the most bitter Parliamentary contests ever known in English history; but the nation had fully and irrevocably made up its mind, and when it had once embarked on the course into which it believed itself to have been forced, all questions as to the justice of the cause were forgotten. Nor were those questions, to any extent, or in any public way, revived till some sixty years later, when Burke, in his famous "Thoughts on a Regicide Peace," composed with the fullest power of his trained rhetorical genius, conceived the idea of heightening the effect of the arguments he triumphantly employed for the purpose of exciting his countrymen to bear up against revolutionary France, by painting that war as one of righteous principle, which was to be gloriously contrasted with the war of 1739. The earlier war he held up to obloquy as a war of "extreme injustice" and of "plunder." By thus going out of his way he did in reality weaken a strong case; but men's minds were too full of the tremendous present to trouble themselves about antiquarian questions; and it would have been rash to challenge the authority of the British Cicero, when he declared that he had made an accurate study of the subject, and had based his epithets on the candid confessions "of many of the principal actors" against Sir Robert Walpole, and "those who principally excited the clamour" which brought on the war.

Such words from such a man, backed by such authority, do not fall to the ground. Two years later they were quoted with approval by Coxe, in his standard work the "Life of Sir Robert Walpole," no doubt in perfect good faith; but it cannot escape observation that they were extremely welcome to Walpole's able apologist. In our own day they have been taken for established truth by no less an authority than the late Lord Stanhope, who, as "Lord Mahon," proved himself by far the most eminent of our modern historians for the period in question. It is not, then, wonderful that Burke's dictum should have been almost universally received by all the later compilers and essayists, whose name is legion, and that the people of Great Britain should still gather their notions of these events tinted by the hues which the great painter had thrown over the picture.

Thus the question of fact has a most real bearing on our present subject. Was the British Empire founded on injustice and the hope of plunder? It is at the commencement of this war that we first hear of Hawke's exploits; at the close of it he is the real head of the British navy. Was he, were the other great officers of whom we are justly proud, was Chatham, were his associates in triumph, animated, more or less unconsciously, by the principles which are alleged to have dictated the war? *Hoc Ithacus velit.* The subject is at least worth consideration. Is there anything connected with the past and future of Great Britain much more deserving of attention?

Even the most vehement admirers of Sir Robert Walpole's long pacific administration will admit that it was only successful up to a certain point. If they are candid, they can scarcely refuse their assent to the proposition that his administration, unbroken in its continuance, unrivalled in duration, was the true parent of the momentous war which brought it to an end. Bred in the grand school of Somers and

Halifax, Godolphin and Marlborough, trained to office from the very opening of his Parliamentary life, a financier of the highest ability ever witnessed before the days of the younger Pitt, urged to the most strenuous exertion by his undying rivalry with Bolingbroke, the one man he had to fear, and whose return to power he took care to prevent, Walpole towered above his contemporaries at a height and for a length of time, quite unapproached by any statesman of modern English history. Chatham's glorious, but wayward and eccentric, career offers no parallel in this respect, and the magnificent position of his son was balanced by that of Fox. No one saw more clearly than Walpole the need of a pacific policy if the principles of the Revolution of 1688 were to prevail, if the Hanoverian Succession was to be maintained, and if the Constitution in Church and State was to hold its own against the incessant intrigues of Jacobites and Jesuits, home conspiracies and foreign combinations. With a standing army so small that it hardly deserved the name, without even a militia, with a people riotously impatient of taxation, and only sullenly obedient to an unpopular but necessary dynasty, with the smouldering ashes of the old war ready at any moment to burst into flame abroad, what a consummate statesman was required! And Walpole was consummate. His business-like and yet most persuasive oratory, the incarnation of common sense, never exerted for mere show, always penetrating to the very bottom of the subject in hand, was accompanied by a practical dexterity in dealing with the governing elements of the nation, perfect in its kind, and not too scrupulous as to the means employed. Well informed of all that was passing in the Continental courts, and associated with a kindred genius in the great Minister, Fleury, who governed the French nation as he himself did the English, his foreign policy was for a long time apparently successful; and the delicate relations between the English and Hanoverian interests were so adjusted by him as to make him the absolutely necessary Prime Minister to two successive sovereigns, neither of them by any means easy to manage under the exceedingly difficult circumstances of their royal position.

But the great statesman's vision began, as time went on, to be clouded by the atmosphere in which he had enshrouded himself. What seemed so sensible, so necessary for the very existence of the nation, did in reality, when too prolonged, carry with it national dishonour and disgrace. What had been for a time a wise retirement from the active part which England, in the full vigour of the Revolution movement and during the reign of Queen Anne, had taken in Continental affairs, began to exhibit the fatal symptoms of feebleness and decrepitude. Naval demonstrations lost, after too frequent a repetition, their old effects, allies their confidence, enemies their dread. The nation was believed to have forfeited, in its eager pursuit of wealth, its ancient title to a leading place in European affairs. The representatives of the very interests for the sake of which the policy of peace and retrenchment had been adopted, began to assume a hostile attitude towards their old favourite when they found his policy issuing in national degradation, and injuriously reacting upon their own prosperity. To adopt the fine words of the present poet laureate, men saw with dismay the greatness of the England of William and Anne, of Marlborough and Somers, visibly breaking down "through craven fears of being great." An "inordinate ambition"[*] blocked up every avenue by which the association with himself of able men, on equal terms, might have enabled the great Minister to comprehend the true wants and the real mind of the people whose government he had so long monopolised.

It was necessary to premise as much as this, which is indeed nothing but simple fact. The difficulties we have to face begin with the details of the process by which Walpole's successful administration changed to one of failure and misfortune.

It was in consequence of the isolated position deliberately assumed by the Minister that the powerful Opposition, which in its earlier stage, under the auspices of Pulteney and Bolingbroke, took the name of the "Patriots," and, later on, was identified with the name of the first William Pitt, its child and product, came to represent all those vigorous political elements of national life which Walpole was holding down with the strong hand. They were sure to triumph in the end. From the year 1727, when, after the death of

---

[*] Stanhope's "History of England," vol. ii. p. 75.

George I., he may be said to have commenced the second portion of his premiership, the national discontent began to show itself in an organised form. For the interpenetration of the domestic with the foreign causes of that discontent the reader must turn to the periodical literature of the day, and more especially to the "Craftsman," the able organ of the two statesmen named above, and in some respects the precursor of the "North Briton" and "Junius's Letters" of the next reign. It is here, and in the Parliamentary debates of the period, that he will find what we may look for in vain when we study the digests of the history of that time, constructed at a later date. It is here that he will trace the immediate springs of action out of which arose the mighty movement which has placed Great Britain in her present position. Allowance must of course be made for the bitter ingredient of political strife to be found in those turbid waters; but it may not be amiss to remark that the tendency of our own philosophical age has been to throw too much discredit on the value of the opposition to Walpole because of that heat and bitterness; and too much demand has been made upon our sympathies for the great statesman, battling in his old age, singly and with unfailing courage, against the whole army of his political opponents, to the disparagement of the cause for which they contended, and the fatal obscuration of the principles which were most assuredly at stake.

It is in this spirit that our leading historians have made light of the persistent efforts of the Spaniards to recover Gibraltar, as if they had never fairly forfeited it, and of their high-handed behaviour towards our trade in the West Indies, as if we had only ourselves to thank for the treatment we received. It is thus they have considered it a sufficient reply to the complaints of our merchants, that they were founded on what Burke long afterwards scoffed at as the "fable of Jenkins' ear," have failed to appreciate the perilous significance of Fleury's success in filling the thrones of Europe with the Bourbon princes, and have ascribed to mere greed and turbulence what, as we shall see, was in reality an unerring instinct of sound policy, demanding that the people who had once been great should be governed on the simple principles by which the independence of all States ever has been, and always must be, preserved.

There are two main grounds of quarrel leading up to the Spanish war of 1739,—the occupation of Gibraltar by the English, and their claim to share in the trade of the Spanish West Indies. To the last may be added their claim to certain special trading rights in the so-called Spanish seas with which the Spaniards themselves had no claim to interfere. The actual quarrel arose out of the West Indian claims, but behind them loomed plainly and unmistakably the frowning Rock of Gibraltar. We must, therefore, first entrench ourselves at the Pillars of Hercules.

Gibraltar, taken during the war of the Spanish Succession by Sir George Rooke, and Minorca, taken by Sir John Leake, were the sole acquisitions carried off by Great Britain at the Peace of Utrecht in 1713, the sole compensation for the thousands of men and millions of money she had expended in obtaining, as people often said, kingdoms for other princes, but which the terms of that Peace rightly described as the means of averting " the great danger which [under Louis XIV.] threatened the liberties and safety of all Europe from the too close conjunction of the kingdoms of Spain and France."

We must stop somewhere, and therefore the arguments which fully justify the deliberate policy, above stated, of our great English sovereigns and statesmen will be here omitted.* It is enough to remark that the importance of these acquisitions, insignificant as they appeared to the critics of the day, the mere barren and ridiculous result of the victories of Marlborough and Eugene, of Peterborough, Stanhope, and Galway, turned out to be far greater than those critics supposed, as measured not only by their subsequent usefulness to the safety and progress of British trade, but by the persistent efforts of France and Spain to recover them. It was not so at first with these countries. At the time of the Peace, so low had they been brought by the victories of Great Britain and her allies, that they could hardly believe their eyes and ears when they found the Tory Government of Queen Anne acceding to such easy terms. As, however, the memory of the conditions on which these places had been conceded, and of the British sacrifices which they represented, became dim in the

---

* See " Imperial England."

eyes of Spanish patriotism, the position of the victors on the impregnable rock grew to be intolerable; nor, though France put a better face on it, could she digest the painful fact any better than Spain.

With France it was not indeed, as with Spain, a matter of wounded pride; but it was a standing injury to her strategical position; and all the more distressing, since one of the few abiding advantages of Louis XIV.'s grand but unfortunate policy had been to establish Toulon as a powerfully fortified naval arsenal. These two English acquisitions, but especially Gibraltar, were thus to France a most palpable grievance. Not only were they the sure guarantee of an independent British commerce with Italy, Africa, and the Levant, and an efficient means of protecting that commerce against what were then its terrible enemies, the Algerine and other Turkish "rovers,"—thus becoming the station-points for British men-of-war, unwelcome intruders into those inland waters; they were of infinitely more importance than this. Gibraltar, with Port Mahon as its support, was in the exact position to cut off, whenever war broke out, all communication between the southern ports of France and her western sea-board.

Spain was equally cloven in two. Gibraltar, jutting out into the sea at her southernmost point, barred the way between her eastern and western ports, and stood sentinel over queenly Cadiz, the emporium of all the wealth of Spanish America. With such a station for her ships, England was in a position to suck away the sole remaining nourishment of the old imperial trunk.

Spain, however, being already in decay, was willing at times, under the pressure of adverse circumstances, to forget the affront; but her more powerful neighbour, still keenly reckoning on a glorious maritime future, would never allow her to forget it. She was ever standing by, reminding her of the disgrace she had suffered, and offering to support her in her efforts to recover her lost possessions. In vain was Spain forced to confirm the tenure of the obnoxious intruders by repeated treaties. The same causes continued to act; the same fretful disgust betrayed itself over and over again. It was perfectly natural.

But it is not so easy to comprehend at first sight how the Government of England could forget, or make light of, conquests of such vital importance; for, as a matter of fact, both George I. and his ministers did beyond question commit themselves more than once to the policy of restitution; and in justice to Walpole it must be said that it was before he came into power. The excuse for them is that they knew better than anyone else the perils which beset the Hanoverian Succession, and the delicate relations in which Hanover stood to the nations by which it was surrounded. During the panic of 1715, for instance, George I., little understanding what he was doing, went so far as to offer of his own accord the restitution of Gibraltar. His Prime Minister, Lord Stanhope, urged it as a means of making an arrangement with Alberoni, the aggressive Prime Minister of Spain, in 1718. The short war of that latter year, caused by the enterprise of the rash cardinal, did indeed annul what had passed; and the Quadruple Treaty confirmed the English tenure; yet after all this we find King George I., in 1721, actually promising once again to restore it "at the first favourable opportunity, with consent of my Parliament, upon the footing of an equivalent." Happily that equivalent was never settled; still less did "my Parliament" ever dream of giving its consent. The people of England, whatever their Government might devise for them, had never for a moment lost sight of their true rights and interests. No change of dynasty was to affect these. If the new king had no love for Marlborough, the people never forgot what he had done for them. It was of him, not of the actual captor, Rooke, that the people were reminded by their prize; it was the pledge left them by his great services. They were clearly right. The Spaniards on the other hand expressed a natural, but unreasonable, feeling. They forgot that it was as a virtual portion of France that their pride and their interest had alike suffered.

The general and violent indignation of the English people as soon as ever these secret proposals became known, made, of course, the consent of Parliament impossible. How was the feeling aggravated by the humiliation to which their country was subjected by the arrogant language of the Spanish Court, not unjustly exasperated at finding that the English king and minister had encouraged hopes which were absolutely chimerical! "Either give up Gibraltar," cried the haughty Spanish queen, their virtual sovereign, "or relinquish your trade to the Indies and Spain."

The English people had no idea of giving up either. Both rights had been honourably won; both had been secured by repeated treaties; they knew the value of both; the expense of keeping Gibraltar, reckoned at £50,000 a year, was insignificant; they were not in a humour to listen with patience to such language. But what were their feelings when, in 1726, Spain translated its words into action, and actually, without any Declaration of War, laid siege to the English stronghold! At any rate, all idea of a compromise was now at an end for evermore.

And here the two causes of quarrel meet and overlap. The danger to Gibraltar was less than was expected; a rash general knocked his head against the Rock as others had done before, and were to do again. But the people looked to their Government in vain for any adequate display of spirit in replying to this unheard-of insult. What was Walpole's idea of the best means of convincing Spain that such insults were not to escape unpunished? It was to stave off a war by a demonstration against their West Indian settlements, to send out a naval force which was on no account to assume a too hostile attitude, for fear of giving too serious a cause of offence. A wellproved admiral, Hosier, was despatched with a fine fleet to Portobello with orders not to attack the place, not to take the rich galleons which were lying there ready to sail for Spain, but to blockade them in port, and so derange for a time the Spanish finances. This was, no doubt, very disagreeable to Spain, but it was also very costly to ourselves. If it was galling to the Spanish Government to find that their supplies could be stopped, and that they had no fleet ready to prevent the stoppage, it was also gratifying to feel that this was the worst the supposed mistress of the seas could do, and that it was only a temporary infliction.

But how about the cost and the humiliation to those who inflicted the punishment? The sad story has left an indelible mark on English history, and it need not be repeated. Never was such a blunder made by even the most incompetent Government. The fleet of old ships, worn out during a long Peace, might have performed their service well enough had they been despatched straight against the enemy. As it was, fretting at enforced inaction, kept cruising, for ever cruising, off a petty fortress which Vernon afterwards took with six ships, in the deadly Gulf of Mexico, under such wretched arrangements for our sailors as prevailed in those days, it came to this:—twice over were nearly the whole of the crews of the fleet destroyed by fever—for the ships had been manned afresh at Jamaica—the fine old admiral's corpse was given to the sharks, as well as his successor's, and along with them, those of ten captains, fifty lieutenants, and on the whole between 3,000 and 4,000 inferior officers and seamen: the ships rotted to pieces, and the entire armament dissolved away, at a cost of men and money equal to at least three general actions such as in those days were fought at sea. It is not surprising that the catastrophe sank deep into the souls of Englishmen, and was never forgotten.

Twelve years later Glover's celebrated ballad sounded the knell of Walpole's administration.*

The scene of the quarrel, thus hopelessly embittered,

---

* This noble ballad, which came out just after the capture of Portobello, has been so entirely forgotten, and is now so difficult of access, that it may be acceptable in a note.

Hosier's Ghost.

As near Portobello lying
    On the gently swelling flood,
At midnight with streamers flying
    Our triumphant navy rode;
There while Vernon sat all-glorious
    From the Spaniard's late defeat;
And his crews with shouts victorious,
    Drank success to England's fleet:

On a sudden shrilly sounding
    Hideous yells and shrieks were heard;
Then, each heart with fear confounding,
    A sad troop of ghosts appeared,
All in dreary hammocks shrouded
    Which for winding-sheets they wore,
And with looks by sorrow clouded,
    Frowning on that hostile shore.

On them gleamed the moon's wan lustre
    When the shade of Hosier brave
His pale bands was seen to muster
    Rising from their watery grave.
O'er the glimmering wave he hied him
    Where the "Burford" reared her sail,
With three thousand ghosts beside him,
    And in groans did Vernon hail:—

"Heed, oh heed our fatal story,
    I am Hosier's injured ghost,
You who now have purchased glory
    At this place where I was lost!

was now transferred to the West Indies; but the historical sequence of events, as here recounted, forbids us to separate for a moment the two grand

> Though in Portobello's ruin
>   You now triumph free from fears,
> When you think on our undoing
>   You will mix your joy with tears.
>
> "See those mournful spectres sweeping
>   Ghastly o'er this hated wave,
> Whose wan cheeks are stained with weeping,—
>   These were English captains brave.
> Mark those numbers, pale and horrid,—
>   Those were once my sailors bold.
> Lo! each hangs his drooping forehead
>   While his dismal tale is told.
>
> "I, by twenty sail attended,
>   Did this Spanish town affright;
> Nothing then its wealth defended
>   But my orders not to fight.
> Oh! that in this rolling ocean
>   I had cast them with disdain,
> And obeyed my heart's warm motion
>   To have quelled the pride of Spain!
>
> "For resistance I could fear none,
>   But with twenty ships had done
> What thou, brave and happy Vernon,
>   Hast achieved with six alone.
> Then the Bastimentos never
>   Had our foul dishonour seen,
> Nor the sea, the foul receiver
>   Of this gallant train had been.
>
> "Then, like thee, proud Spain dismaying,
>   And her galleons leading home,
> Though condemned for disobeying
>   I had met a traitor's doom,

causes of the war from one another. It is true that the Treaty of Madrid, in 1729, professed to replace both nations on their old footing, as it existed before all these things had happened; but the Gibraltar dispute only slept awhile, to be renewed again and again, till Eliott and Rodney, in 1782, gave the final lesson to the combined forces of France and Spain.

To have fallen, my country crying,
'He has played an English part,'
Had been better far than dying
Of a grieved and broken heart.

"Unrepining at thy glory
Thy successful arms we hail,
But remember our sad story
And let Hosier's wrongs prevail.
Sent in this foul clime to languish,
Think what thousands fell in vain,
Wasted with disease and anguish,
Not in glorious battle slain.

"Hence with all my tribe attending
From their oozy tombs below,
Through the hoary foam ascending,
Here I feed my constant woe:
Here the Bastimentos viewing,
We recall our shameful doom,
And, our plaintive cries renewing,
Wander through the midnight gloom.

"O'er these waves for ever mourning
Shall we roam deprived of rest,
If to Britain's shores returning
You neglect my just request;
After this proud foe subduing
When your patriot friends you see,
Think on vengeance for my ruin,
And for England shamed in me."

The dexterity of Walpole in negotiating the above Treaty has been praised; but it was one of those diplomatic successes that merely skin over a wound, which, if treated properly at first, might have been soon cured. And this will be the place to notice a secret cause of inflammation to which the wound was exposed, and which Walpole was the last to believe, however strongly it had been suspected by the simpler instincts of the English people. Relying on his skilfully organised relations with France established through Fleury, and very much also through the ability of his own brother Horace, he lost sight of the real tendency of French feeling in the matters which appeared externally to affect Spain alone. He was consequently duped by his ally, whose profound policy it was, under cover of peace with England, to gain gradually and noiselessly for France all that she could have gained by war; and part of this policy was to encourage Spain without seeming to do so. Hence, no doubt, the grandiose language of the Spanish Court, and its rash challenge to Great Britain; and hence the secret Treaty of 1733, the importance of which in the development of the Spanish war of 1739 cannot be overrated, and yet which has remained a secret, not only to Walpole and the English of his day, but down to our own times.

Until quite of late years the "Family Compact" between France and Spain has been simply identified with the year 1761, when the French, almost destroyed under the successful administration of Pitt, again persuaded Spain to make common cause with them,

and thus added one more to the injuries by which, through that connection, Spain has lost her place as a Great Power. Twenty-eight years previously to that well known "Family Compact" of the House of Bourbon, the series of such Compacts did in reality begin. The Court of France, finding, by the events of 1726 and the years following, that Spain, with all the will in the world to stand out against Great Britain, was too conscious of her naval inferiority to take the active measures which were necessary in order to cripple the English trade, entered into a secret engagement with Spain, to the following effect :—
"Whenever it seems good to both nations alike, the abuses which have crept into commerce, especially through the English, shall be abolished; and if the English make objection, France will ward off its hostility with all its strength by land and sea." And this Compact was made during a period of intimate and ostentatious alliance with England itself! "Thus," says Ranke, "the policy against which William the Third had called on England and Europe to arm, and which even the Tory ministers had thought to hinder in the Treaty [of Utrecht] by a total separation of Spain from France, at last came into existence."*

The hostile movements of Spain in the West Indies were based on this Compact, of which the English had no knowledge, except by its fruits; and those were visible both in Europe and the West Indies. The

---

* Ranke's "History of England," Oxford edition, vol. v. p. 398.

most public and notorious effect was displayed in the former. The general tranquillity of Europe, which the skill of the English and French ministers had kept virtually intact for twenty years, was broken in 1734—the very year after the secret Compact had been formed—by the union of France, Spain, and Sardinia against the Emperor, and their success in placing the Spanish Charles upon the throne of Naples and Sicily. Great Britain helplessly looked on, while her faithful ally, the Emperor, was overpowered. Holland had more excuse for non-interference.

The House of Bourbon now reigned supreme over the whole west of Continental Europe; the two great peninsulas of Spain and Italy which commanded the Mediterranean were in the same hands; the continued tenure of the obnoxious outposts by the English wore now, of course, year by year, a still more intolerable aspect; and the resolute policy of France to use the Spanish alliance for the purpose of pushing forward the colonial empire which she was bent on acquiring, not only began to show itself in the formation of forts and settlements along the rear of the English colonies in North America, but in fresh enterprises which threatened the English possession in India.

The next year, 1735, placed France on a still loftier pinnacle. With consummate sagacity the ablest Fleury devised to complete, in the Treaty of Vienna, the sweeping achievements of French policy, by securing the provinces of Lorraine and Bar, which sent the so-called France at last ren-

laid a sure foundation for an inevitable wa
withdrawing his country from her accustome
in Continental affairs, and by allowing her
insulted and betrayed, he had encouraged
nation like Spain, which must have collapsed
been treated with becoming spirit, to carry in
defiance still further; and in the complicated
items of the trade between the two countries
West Indies and Spanish America, there was
abundance of occasions for the display of th
spirit which rapidly developed in both nations

The unsatisfactory manner in which th
Indian quarrel has been treated in modern
renders unavoidable the notice of a few deta
though, like the question of Gibraltar, it only
of consequence in the reign of George I., i
must be traced back, however briefly, much f
It was the defeat of the Spanish Armad
first broke down those exclusive pretensions
in the New World, to which her discove
conquests, the successful enterprise of her
and the dream of a Papal gift, had giv
Under the eye of Elizabeth, the naval chi
England, with their "*Afflavit Deus et dissipa*
pierced through and through the pasteboar
work of the giant which had so long a
humanity; and though Englishmen had indeed
begun to found colonies in North America, t
now a fresh start; and, what is of importanc
survey, the English introduced a new kind of

... Europeanise the whole of North America.
... agricultural and Anglo-constitutional
... wholly different in kind from the Spanish
...," the Spanish mining settlements, or
... governments of conquered tribes, and
... ... of Greece and Rome.
... the West Indies, indeed, the system
... ... English had, to their shame,
... ... assimilated the colonists
... ... before the close of the
... ... the hardy settlers of the
... ... already spreading far into
... ... their bread with the
... ... the deep-sea fisheries
... ... sea with their trading
... ... gave the tone to all the
... ...
... ...

laid a sure foundation for an inevitable war. By withdrawing his country from her accustomed place in Continental affairs, and by allowing her to be insulted and betrayed, he had encouraged a weak nation like Spain, which must have collapsed had she been treated with becoming spirit, to carry insult and defiance still further; and in the complicated regulations of the trade between the two countries in the West Indies and Spanish America, there was a rich abundance of occasions for the display of the bitter spirit which rapidly developed in both nations.

The unsatisfactory manner in which the West Indian quarrel has been treated in modern histories renders unavoidable the notice of a few details; and though, like the question of Gibraltar, it only became of consequence in the reign of George I., its origin must be traced back, however briefly, much further.

It was the defeat of the Spanish Armada which first broke down those exclusive pretensions of Spain in the New World, to which her discoveries and conquests, the successful enterprise of her people, and the dream of a Papal gift, had given rise. Under the eye of Elizabeth, the naval chivalry of England, with their "*Afflavit Deus et dissipati sunt*," pierced through and through the pasteboard framework of the giant which had so long affrighted humanity; and though Englishmen had indeed already begun to found colonies in North America, there was now a fresh start; and, what is of importance to our survey, the English introduced a new kind of colony, destined to Europeanise the whole of North America. This was the agricultural and Anglo-constitutional settlement, wholly different in kind from the Spanish "Plantations," the Spanish mining settlements, or the Spanish governments of conquered tribes, and more like the ancient colonies of Greece and Rome. In the islands of the West Indies, indeed, the system of slave-labour which the English had, to their shame, done so much to propagate, assimilated the colonists to those of Spain; but long before the close of the seventeenth century it was the hardy settlers of the North American coasts, already spreading far into the interior,—men who earned their bread with the sweat of their brows, or made the deep-sea fisheries their home, or covered the sea with their trading vessels,—it was these men who gave the tone to all the English of the New World, and suffered with rugged impatience the insulting conduct of a people for whom they could have but little respect, and the restrictions upon trade which such a people pretended to enforce.

Nor should it be forgotten, in tracing the quarrels of the eighteenth century, that even in the West Indies the English had already had to bear their part in connection with the European wars of the previous age, and that men like the two Christopher Codringtons, lords of rich sugar islands, and each in succession "Governor-General of the Caribbean seas," had, in the reigns of William and Anne, led great expeditions against the French, and cultivated with some success a military spirit among the planters;

while the undaunted Benbow had, so late as 1698, taught the Spaniards that they might easily try the temper of the English too far.

Let us also remember that the theory of maritime freedom was steadily advancing along with the civilisation of the age; and however the English might resist at home the claims of Grotius for the Dutch, it is not to be supposed that the doctrines of the "Mare Liberum" were unheeded in their equally direct application to Spain and the American waters. Add to these considerations that the French and Dutch had also, in the seventeenth century, settled in the West Indies and on the adjacent coasts. Thus it is plain that any practical operation resulting from the old Spanish theory that the American coasts and seas were exclusively their own, must have appeared to the English and the English colonists an absurd, insane, and most injurious anachronism. The nations of Europe were inextricably mixed up together within narrow seas; and each of those nations, as yet in the infancy of the colonising process, looked with more than a parental eye on its promising progeny. How could constant smuggling and everlasting disputes fail to arise under such circumstances between Spain and the new comers? Nothing but the most liberal policy between States which were in real accord at home, could possibly have kept the peace. We have seen how far removed from such a state of things was the condition of Europe during Walpole's so-called pacific administration.

It was with these colonists quite as much as

with the English people themselves—with a body so numerous, so active, and so self-reliant, it was with that English flag, the honour of which had been carried so high that the claim for an ancient mode of paying it respect had led to a bloody war,—that Spain, a power no longer of first-rate rank among maritime nations, resolved to deal as if she were undisputed mistress of the ocean. What must have been the feelings of such men, both at home and abroad, when they found the Spaniards presuming to exercise the "Right of Search" on the high seas upon English vessels proceeding on their legitimate traffic from one English colony to another! What must they have felt when they were perfectly aware that no such "Right" existed by treaty? What when they found this practice become customary, without their own Government interfering to prevent it? It was even stated over and over again, though perhaps never proved, that the Spanish guarda-costas which exercised this search, and which, not being regular men-of-war, were not to be trusted with such a delicate commission, had actually sailed into English ports and carried off English merchant vessels under the eyes of English men-of-war. At any rate the instances of their barbarous treatment of Englishmen caught smuggling, were numerous and undoubted, even if we count the shaving off of Captain Jenkins' ear to be a "fable"; yet, if we may judge by the histories of those times, it was fully believed for fifty years. What must have been the opinion of these men upon a state of "peace" gained on such terms, and of a minister who, upon each occasion of complaint, minimised the affront, and provoked fresh insolence by the betrayal of a pusillanimous dread of giving offence! War was horrible enough. Peace was divine. But was this the way to secure peace? Did any nation ever yet succeed in retaining its independence by allowing injury and insult to pass unnoticed? These very just and natural sentiments by degrees extended themselves to the whole nation, and at last forced Walpole himself to demand categorical redress. Was this a war of " plunder and extreme injustice " ?

But, perhaps, it may be thought that too much has been taken for granted. It was a long time ago, and the reader must bear with a little explanation. Let us come to the grounds on which the Spaniards claimed their Right of Search. Let us suppose for a moment a British minister so hampered by the circumstances of his country as to be forced for years to connive at what ought to have been peremptorily stopped under penalty of instant war. It will not be difficult to show that the treaties under which the right was claimed gave no countenance whatever to the mode in which, encouraged by France, Spain was now exercising it, and also that the system of "smuggling" on which that mode was pretended to be justified, had itself a considerable amount of moral justification.

The hollow nature of the Spanish claim was identified with its origin. Spain, for more than a century, not unlike the modern Chinese under similar circumstances, was afflicted with a peculiar sort of blindness.

She affected not to see, not to be conscious of, the settlements which were being made by other European nations on the shores of that New World she fondly called her own. The defeat of the Armada was far from opening her eyes. It was not till the year 1667 that, stung by the depredations which had been made on her colonial merchandise by British colonists, who, like the poet's maiden, "felt their life in every limb," and had entered fully into the national hostilities with Spain during the Commonwealth, that she condescended, even tacitly, to recognise their existence. In the Treaties of that year and of 1670 are laid the bases of the subsequent intercourse. It was the reign of Charles II., and the attitude of the two nations had changed since Cromwell's time. The ambitious hostility of Louis XIV., coinciding with the recent evidence of a serious power for mischief in the British colonies, was drawing Spain and England together in unwonted alliance. Hence favourable conditions of trade, and specially of West Indian trade, were at last granted, and expressions used which, whether intentionally or not, were open to more than one construction.

The first Treaty began by referring to the Treaty of Munster in 1648, by which the Dutch (long before the English) had been admitted to commercial privileges; these were now to be extended to the English; but there is nothing whatever here which throws light on any claim to the Right of Search. Indeed it was by no means clear that the privileges which the Spaniards afterwards held to apply to European ports alone, did not, by the terms of this Treaty, apply to their colonies. In the second Treaty the restrictions which provided that there should be no mutual trade in the colonies without special licence, were not far separated from the Fifteenth Article, which declares that "liberty of navigation ought in no manner to be disturbed where nothing is committed against the genuine sense and meaning of these Articles." The Right of Search is here, for the first time, definitely mentioned, but it is carefully guarded from abuse, and specifically stated to apply only to a search for arms, ammunition, and soldiers. Even this was, it seems, intended to apply principally to the prohibition of English ships from supplying the States of Barbary with military stores.* Yet it was the Spanish interpretation of this one Article, in the times of which we are now speaking, to mean the right of search for contraband *merchandise* in American waters, and there, not only when "close to the ports," but out of sight of land, in the open sea, which formed the *casus belli* in 1739! This illegal system of search, exercised, as has been seen, with insult and indiscretion, as well as barbarity, had resulted in seizures which Spain herself admitted to amount to the value of £200,000, more than half a million of our present money.

Let us next inquire how the system of English "smuggling" had grown to proportions so great as to lead the Spanish Government to imagine they had

---

* Coxe's "Walpole," vol. i. p. 557.

a right to press the interpretation of the treaties to such an unwarrantable length. The process can easily be traced.

During the whole reign of Charles II., and even to the close of the century, the same spirit which had dictated the unwonted liberality of the Spanish Treaties, derived from the dread of France and the friendship with England, operated in the direction of an entire relaxation of those treaties, a relaxation which grew into custom, and, of course, became associated with an idea of right. "A flourishing, although illicit, trade was, by the connivance and indulgence of Spain, carried on between the English and Spanish plantations" *; nor was it till the accession of Philip of Bourbon to the Spanish throne, in 1700, that any change took place; nor scarcely even then—for Spain was torn to pieces by the Succession war— till the Peace of Utrecht (1713).

A new system of relations was now adopted, a system of definite and absolute restriction, which, after the lapse of three generations of mutual intercourse, virtually amounting to free trade, it was absolutely impossible to work. That it should have been acceded to by Queen Anne and her Tory ministers is not usually, though it well might be, charged among their faults. They might, perhaps, be excused on the ground of a sanguine hope that the new plan would be suffered to bear as lax an interpretation as the old. The sequel proved them to be entirely in error.

---

* Coxe's "Walpole," vol. i. p. 558.

Philip V. was a Frenchman, but he became a thorough Spaniard. On the points of quarrel before us, his sympathies flowed from both sides in a direction against the English; and the old friendliness between Spain and England had been extinguished in the late war, with its disastrous result to Spain of the capture of Gibraltar and Minorca. Here was his opportunity. By the Treaty of Utrecht the old permission to trade by licence had been annulled, and the famous "Assiento Treaty" had taken its place. This was a contract with the English South Sea Company for supplying the Spanish Colonies with a certain number of negroes, and to it was attached the privilege of annually sending a single ship of a certain burden, laden with European merchandise, to Spanish America. The negro clause does not affect our argument; but was the other to be literally interpreted? The Spanish Government would have been wise had they reflected upon the impossibility of undoing the work of their predecessors, and, by a mere edict from the mother country, reversing a stream which had been so long running in one direction; but under the circumstances it was perfectly natural that such reflections should find no place. The effect is described by Coxe in the following words:—

> The letter of the American treaty was now followed, and the spirit by which it was dictated abandoned. Although England still enjoyed the liberty of putting into Spanish harbours for the purpose of refitting and provisioning, yet they were far from enjoying the same advantages of carrying on a friendly and commercial intercourse. They were now watched with a scrupulous

jealousy, strictly visited by guarda-costas, and every efficient means adopted to prevent any commerce with the colonies, excepting what was allowed by the annual ship.*

It was not, therefore, surprising that British merchants and colonists, considering the trade as theirs by long prescriptive right, and not a matter of indulgence, adopted, *in concert with the Spanish colonists*, all sorts of petty methods of evasion. They—

continually put into the Spanish harbours, under pretence of refitting and refreshing, and in many places almost publicly disposed of European merchandise in exchange for gold and silver. Other vessels sailing near their ports and harbours were repaired to by smugglers, or sent their long-boats towards the shore, and dealt with the natives. The Spaniards complained that the "Assiento annual ship" was followed by several other vessels which moored at a distance, and, as it disposed of its cargo, continually supplied it with fresh goods; that by these means and by the clandestine trade which the English carried on, they almost supplied the colonies; and the Fair of Panama, once the richest of the world, where the Spaniards were accustomed to exchange gold and silver for European merchandise, had considerably fallen; they monopolised the commerce of America.†

It is obvious that as there were two parties to these transactions, the attempt to interfere with what both people were alike resolved to have, was as hopeless as to fill the cask of the Danaids. The confusion into which matters fell is well described in Lord Hervey's Memoirs:—" The Spaniards had often seized ships which were not smuggling; and many of the Spanish governors connived at the English smug-

---

* Coxe's "Walpole," vol. i. p. 559.
† *Ibid.*, vol. i. p. 560.

glers for money. Thus merchants were often secure in ports where they ought not to have found any [security], and insecure on the seas."* The Spanish-American coast was open for hundreds of miles; there were but few settlements; the hope of profit, the sense of danger, the love of adventure, and the belief that right was substantially on their side, produced, of course, the effect of stimulating this "illicit" commerce in exact proportion to the severity of the means adopted for putting it down; and it must be noticed here that there had been more than one short interval, even since the Treaty of Utrecht, when Spanish quarrels with France had, for a time, again produced a relaxation of the restrictions imposed by that Treaty, and given rise to a variety of misconstructions of the same nature as those already mentioned. Thus failure after failure, dating from the year 1727, when the siege of Gibraltar and the blockade of Portobello had exasperated both nations, only made Spain more obstinate, and blinded her as to the true nature of the means to which she now resorted. The "Craftsman," in 1729, by no means exaggerated the English sentiment when it said—

It looks, indeed, as if all the Powers of Europe, both friends and foes, were confederated against us, and resolved to unite their endeavours to deprive us of all our trade at once.†

As the English placed their own interpretation on past treaties, on their relaxations, and on their own "customary rights," so their opponents on the treaty-

---

* Vol. ii. p. 485. † Vol. iv. p. 196.

MUTUAL EXASPERATION.

right of Search. It was indeed, as now applied, a pure invention. Lord Chatham, in 1770, quoted with approval the following remark of Lord Granville :—

In all the negotiations which preceded the Convention our Ministers never found out that there was no ground or subject for any negotiation; that the Spaniards had not a right to search our ships; and when they attempted to regulate them by treaty, they were regulating a thing which did not exist.[*]

So matters went drifting on. At length it became clear that nothing short of an entire concession of the trade on the part of Spain could avert war. The despatch of the English Ambassador in Spain, Mr. Benjamin Keene, on whom the chief burden of dealing with the complaints on both sides fell, puts the case as fairly as it could be put from the technical point of view, independently of any questions of prescriptive rights[†] or moral obligation, questions nevertheless of the highest moment in adjusting the blame attributable to either party.

"Upon the whole," says Keene, writing on December 13th, 1737, "the state of our dispute seems to be that the commanders of our vessels always think that they are unjustly taken if they are not taken in actual illicit commerce, even though proofs of their having loaded in that manner be found on board of them; and the Spaniards, on the other hand, presume that they have a right of seizing not only the ships that were continually trading

---

[*] Parliamentary Debates.

[†] "The English traders regarded the extension of their business as hitherto allowed, a possession honestly won, looked upon all interference with it as an unjustifiable act of violence, and claimed the assistance of Government against it."—Ranke's "History of England," Oxford edition, vol. v., p. 398.

in their ports, but likewise of examining and visiting them on the high seas, in order to search for proofs of fraud which they have committed; and till a medium be found out between these two notions, the Government will always be embarrassed with complaints, and we shall be continually negotiating in this country for redress without ever being able to procure it."

Keene's despair was only too well justified. In that very year the affair had indeed reached its climax.

It has not been thought necessary to notice in this rapid sketch the abortive attempt to deal with the quarrel by the Treaty of Seville in 1729. We have seen that in this treaty Spain engaged to establish the *status quo ante*. She professed to replace the West Indian trade on its previous footing, restoring all captures, and making compensation for the loss sustained by British merchants. But in point of fact the Treaty only supplied occasion for further interminable quarrels, too tedious to relate, as to the sums due from either party; and to all the causes of difference, which admitted at any rate of some dispute, had recently been added one which admitted of none, and yet produced exactly the same high-handed action on the part of Spain as the rest. This was the double right of the British to cut logwood in the Bay of Campeachy, and to collect salt at the island of Sal Tortugas. This right had always been taken as implied in the various treaties, and rested upon precisely the same grounds as that by which the British held the island of Jamaica, or any other settlement in those seas. It was now not only questioned, but the British salt-fleet had been actually attacked by two Spanish ships of the line, and only saved by the brilliant courage and conduct of the single British ship, the "Scarborough," of twenty guns, Captain Thomas Durell, in charge of the convoy. This fine officer gallantly employed his colossal enemies so long that thirty-two out of thirty-six vessels made their escape, as he himself also did, after seeing his convoy in safety.

In short, for some time not a year had passed without a series of the most bitter complaints from British merchants, often no doubt exaggerated, but in the main well founded, and emphasised in Parliament by the "Patriots," after the bitterest fashion. Yet, was it possible to call too loud for reparation? The English people were becoming furious. "*Patientia læsa vertit in furorem.*" Their attitude was not at all unlike that of one of their own mastiffs, chained up by a servant, and lashed to fury by the provocations of house-breakers who knew it would not be let loose. Their instinct told them there was something wrong, and that if the country was to be preserved they must be allowed to get free. Walpole, the timid servant, was doing his very utmost to keep them quiet; yet a well-meaning servant and no traitor, quite aware of the danger, and only daunted by the attitude of the burglars. A careful study of the Parliamentary debates of 1737 and 1738 reveals the English minister in the disgraceful attitude of an apologist for the grievous wrongs which he himself admits his country to have sustained, on the confessed ground that it would not be safe to resent these wrongs. And yet such was his command of Parliament,—we need not stop to inquire how obtained,—that it took two whole years to destroy his authority, and to force him to recognise, in the only way now left, the outraged dignity of the people of England.

Thus the scene of the last Act shifts from the West Indies to the House of Commons. Not that the complaints against the Spaniards had been hitherto unheard in Parliament. A continuous dropping fire had been long levelled at Walpole; as in 1732, when Sir Wilfrid Lawson led the attack upon Government for not having resented what were officially styled the Spanish, "depredations," but which the public called "piracies." In the year 1737 these complaints culminated in the famous "Petition of West India Merchants" to that House. The petitioners insisted that :—

for many years past their ships have not only been frequently stopped and searched, but also forcibly and arbitrarily seized upon the high seas, by Spanish ships fitted out to cruise, under the plausible pretence of guarding their own coasts; that the commanders thereof, with their crews, have been inhumanly treated, and their ships carried into some of the Spanish ports and there condemned with their cargoes, in manifest violation of the treaties subsisting between the two crowns; that the remonstrances of His Majesty's ministers receive no attention at Madrid, and that insults and plunder must soon destroy their trade.

They conclude by demanding full satisfaction, and insist for the future that no British vessel be detained or seized upon the high seas by any nation on any pretext whatever.

Next year several still stronger petitions formed the basis of the debates in Parliament. The principal one took a historical survey of the subject, reminding the House of its own futile proceedings in having frequently acknowledged the justice of the British complaints, and again "addressed the Crown" for satisfaction. It contained the following remarkable passage:—

> The Spaniards have paid so little regard to His Majesty's most gracious endeavours, that they have continued their depredations almost ever since the Treaty of Seville, and, more particularly last year, have carried them to a greater height than ever, they having arbitrarily seized several ships with their effects, belonging to His Majesty's subjects, on the high seas, in the destined course of their voyages to and from the British colonies, amounting to a very considerable value; and that the captains or masters of some of the said ships were, according to the last advices of the petitioners, and are (as the petitioners believe) at this time, confined by the Spaniards in the West Indies, and the crews are now in slavery in old Spain, where they are most inhumanly treated.

In spite of his well-drilled majority it was impossible for Walpole to prevent the House from coming, under the influence of Barnard, Wyndham, and Pulteney, to Resolutions which endorsed the petitions. In this memorable debate he was forced to admit " that our merchants have fully proved their losses, and that the depredations that have been committed are contrary to the law of nations, contrary to the treaties subsisting between the two Crowns; in short, that they are everything bad, and without the least pretence or colour of justice." The very words which he prevailed on the House to substitute for those originally proposed were the strongest condemnation of the policy he had been so long pursuing; and, as far as the rights of the case are concerned, they may—considering the quarter from whence they come—be taken to sum up the whole :—

That the freedom of navigation and commerce which the subjects of Great Britain have an undoubted right to by the law of nations, and which is not in the least restrained by virtue of any of the treaties subsisting between the Crowns of Great Britain and Spain, has been greatly interrupted by the Spaniards under pretences altogether groundless and unjust. That before and since the execution of the Treaty of Seville and the declaration made by the Crown of Spain pursuant thereunto, for the satisfaction and security of the commerce of Great Britain, many unjust seizures and captures have been made, and great depredations committed by the Spaniards, which have been attended with many instances of unheard-of cruelty and barbarity. That the frequent applications to the Court of Spain for procuring justice and satisfaction to His Majesty's injured subjects, for bringing offenders to condign punishment, and for preventing the like abuses for the future, have proved vain and ineffectual; and the several orders, or "cedulas," granted by the King of Spain for restitution and reparation of great losses sustained by the unlawful and unwarrantable seizures and captures made by the Spaniards, have been disobeyed by the Spanish governors, or totally evaded and eluded. And that these violences and depredations have been carried on to the great loss and damage of the subjects of Great Britain trading to America, and in direct violation of the treaties subsisting between the two Crowns.

Will it be believed that a prime minister of England, who persuaded the House to adopt such language, should, in the very speech with which he introduced it, still recommend a continuance of the timid forbearance hitherto displayed? It was no longer a question of fact. The House had examined the petitioners' witnesses, and reported that they had proved their case; it was only a question of how to deal with the facts. Yet Walpole still harps on his old string. He is still bent on " obtaining satisfaction and full reparation by peaceable means," and declares that " we ought not to involve the nation in a war from the event of which we have a great deal to fear." "Some branches of our Spanish and Mediterranean trade might, if the war should be of any duration, be irrecoverably lost,"—a doctrine he had still more clearly expressed in a former speech when he told the House that " it may sometimes be for the interest of a nation to pocket an affront," and when he shadowed forth the dangers which a war with Spain would bring on " from other potentates of Europe"; since "if the Spaniards had not private encouragement from Powers more considerable than themselves they would never have ventured on these insults and injuries which have been proved at your bar."*

Sir William Wyndham had no difficulty in deducing a different moral from the Premier's " long account of the late treaties between Spain and us, whence it appeared that we had been for above twenty years not only negotiating, but actually concluding treaties in vain, and without the least effect"; and he carried

---

* Machiavelli's authority has been deservedly diminished by the modern growth of political science; yet there are many passages which never grow old. On such questions as the above he tells the simple truth when he says:—"Dangers that are seen afar off are easily prevented; but protracting till they are near at hand, the remedies grow unseasonable, and the malady incurable. The Romans never swallowed an injury to put off a war; for they knew that war was not avoided but deferred thereby, and commonly with an advantage to the enemy."

the House with him when he denounced the system of "fitting out formidable squadrons without proper instructions for enabling them to follow words with blows." Sir John Barnard repelled the Minister's argument for peace, derived from the respect obtained by the country through former wars, by referring to the common facts of English history, which showed how the two great Edwards, Henry V., and Elizabeth, had each been succeeded by a sovereign who brought the nation into contempt. Pulteney, with all the thunder of his eloquence, insisted that the time for "reparation had long passed away," and that "the suffering our American trade to be ruined was not the way to protect our Spanish, Italian, and Turkish merchants"; which argument Mr. Plumer followed up by remarking that "the more our trade decays the less will be our power to assist ourselves, the less ready will be our neighbours to assist us"; and that "every British subject ought to choose to live upon bread and onions rather than see the House of Bourbon giving law to Europe," for "an open and declared war was better than a cruel and contemptuous peace." Wyndham had on another occasion, in the same spirit, laid down the law of difference between public and private insults:—"When the insult or attack appears from the very nature of it to have been committed by public authority, satisfaction ought not to be sued for by ambassadors; it ought to be immediately taken by fleets and armies, properly instructed for that purpose."

Equally significant passages might be quoted from

the debates in the House of Lords. In the present day they appear like mere commonplaces. But if we are to make any attempt to assign its true character to the war, the only way is to show the extreme difficulty which such commonplaces found in making their mark on the conduct of the British Government, thus tenaciously clinging to peace at any price. Some impression at any rate was made on this occasion, for the "gracious answer" from the Crown was an echo of the Addresses from both Houses of Parliament.

And yet will it be believed that even in May of this year, when the subject came once more before Parliament, the Minister announced his intention to oppose any Bill "which may tend to plunge this nation into a ruinous and perhaps doubtful war," and openly propounded it as his opinion that "we were not a match for the Spaniards and French too"? To which Pulteney replied that he hoped the time had not arrived when it might be said, "your seamen are to be enslaved, your merchants plundered, and your trade ruined, because if you take one step to prevent it France will interpose." "We have already been insulted by our enemies; we shall soon be despised by our allies: we shall be considered as a nation without rights, or, what is the same, without power to assert them." "Every petty people, every nest of pirates, every combination of encroaching traders, will without scruple plunder a nation that sits down tamely under the grossest injuries, and, instead of punishing, caresses the robber."

Again the House "addressed the Crown" in becoming terms, and the expressions used by the famous Speaker, Onslow, on the occasion, are germane to our purpose :—" To encourage the Spaniards," said this truly representative Whig statesman, " to rummage our ships, is to give them a right to the sovereignty of the seas, as it was always deemed by Great Britain; and was never allowed by any of Your Majesty's predecessors."

Again a " gracious answer," in precisely the same sense as the Address, issued from the Crown; and again, what?—a "Convention of Pardo" (so named from the King of Spain's palace), one of those expedients on which the Minister seemed to live from year to year. This was a mere disgraceful compromise in which the honour of the country was sacrificed to Spain; the word "satisfaction" for wrongs done is studiously omitted, the payments which had been previously agreed upon by way of compensation for Spanish "depredations," juggled away; and the vital question of the Right of Search wholly evaded. It was not even mentioned! Well might Sir Thomas Sanderson observe in the House, that Spain, instead of giving us reparation, had obliged us to give her a general release.

This final blunder sealed the fate of the Minister. The whole country now turned against him, for he had been convicted out of his own mouth. It was no personal question, no division of Whig and Tory. Nor is there much solid ground for attributing, as Burke has attributed, the universal feeling of the nation to the literary skill of certain writers of prose and poetry. They expressed what was already a deep and wide-felt national grievance: the people were thankful for any spokesman. They recognised the prose of Bolingbroke and the verses of Pope and Thompson, Johnson and Glover, just as they did the oratory of Pulteney, Carteret, Wyndham, Barnard, and even the rough, seamanlike harangues of Vernon, as the language of Englishmen; and when a nation has made up its mind against the policy of a once favourite minister, it is time for that minister to retire. Walpole failed to perceive what was so obvious to everyone else. Unfortunately for himself and his reputation to all time, he took the fatal course of attempting to put in practice the policy forced upon him by his opponents; thus retaining his great place as if he were the only person who could govern the country; a plausible policy,—for when a man has been virtually sole governor of a country for many years, it is quite true that the vacancy caused by his retirement is sure to be disastrously felt—but a policy which is equally certain to drag after it many worse consequences than it can possibly obviate.*

---

* The best proof that Burke was wrong in attributing so large a share in producing war to the poets of the day is to be found in the fact that the only men who really made their mark, Pope and Dr. Johnson, did not publish till 1738, the year after the whole country had been aroused by the West Indian petition and the debates in Parliament. Glover's "Hosier's Ghost" did not, of course, appear till Portobello had been taken. The passages from Pope and Johnson are here transcribed. The other minor writers are Glover in his "Leonidas," a poem which

A fatality pursued him. Even when he had made up his mind to become the mere agent of the Opposition, he showed to the last his entire misapprehension of the true state of affairs. The Spanish Government, having most unwillingly signed the Convention,

---

no one could ever have read through unless he had already been in a very excited frame of mind; Nugent, in his "Odes to Mankind and to Lord Pulteney"; Thompson in his "Britanni," his "Liberty," and his "Tragedy of Agamemnon"; Mallet, in his "Mustapha"; and Brooke in his "Gustavus Vasa." Pope's lines occur in his "Satires and Epilogue":—

"And own the Spaniards did a waggish thing,
Who cropt our ears and sent them to the king."

Again:—

"Nay, hints 'tis by suggestion of the Court
That Spain robs on, and Dunkirk 's still a port."

Johnson's lines occur in his "London," an imitation of the "Third Satire" of Juvenal:—

"Struck with the seat that gave Eliza birth,
We kneel and kiss the consecrated earth,
In pleasing dreams the blissful age renew,
And call Britannia's glories back to view,
Behold her cross triumphant on the main,
The guard of commerce and the dread of Spain,
Ere masquerades debauched, excise opprest,
Or English honour grew a standing jest."

Again:—

"Here let those reign whom pensions can incite
To vote a patriot black, a courtier white,
Explain their country's dear-bought rights away,
And plead for pirates in the face of day."

Again:—

"But lost in thoughtless ease and empty show,
Behold the warrior dwindled to a beau,
Sense, freedom, piety, refined away,
Of France the mimic, and of Spain the prey."

proved at once, by its conduct, that there was no intention whatever of keeping it; but no Declaration of War came from England. An order for reprisals was thought sufficient. This, however, was soon seen to be a wholly untenable position; and at last the momentous document, so long delayed, went forth to the world. That Declaration of War, issued by Walpole on October 15th, 1739, contains the best commentary on his own repeated defence of his policy of peace. It pronounced that "the treaties had been habitually violated"; the claims of Spain to the Right of Search were stated to be "unwarrantable, groundless, dangerous, and destructive to England and her colonies"; British subjects had been treated with great "cruelty and barbarity"; "exorbitant duties and impositions had been laid upon trade"; "ancient and established privileges had been broken"; and "the late Convention manifestly violated." War was declared "to vindicate our undoubted rights, and secure to our loving subjects the privileges of navigation and commerce to which they are justly entitled."

After such an exhibition of the absence of self-respect it was impossible that the country could, for

---

Again:—
"Has heaven reserved, in pity to the poor,
No pathless waste or undiscovered shore,
No secret island in the boundless main,
No peaceful deserts yet unclaimed by Spain?"

But none of these found so much favour with the vulgar as the famous line, ascribed to Atterbury, and at this time reproduced:—
"The cur-dog of Britain and spaniel of Spain."

any length of time, confide the conduct of the war to its long-accustomed chief. It is beyond the scope of this Introduction to detail the painful process by which he was at length hurled from power, or to deal with his character further than as it bears on the war which Burke pronounced to have been "a war of plunder and extreme injustice." The above simple statement of facts impels us for once to desert the leadership of the greatest of political writers. If we may venture to say so, his error seems to be due to his fixing his attention on only one cause of the quarrel between Spain and England, and of that complicated question observing one side alone; whereas we have seen that the issues, as Walpole himself only too well understood, were much larger and deeper.

The best excuse that the great Minister ever ventured to make for himself was that his advice and his policy were the best under the circumstances. If, on a general survey of the whole, we can honestly endorse that opinion, we must at least admit that its result was disastrous. There is nothing new in such political lessons. It turned out, as it often has turned out in other cases, that Great Britain had bought peace for a short time at the cost of a future struggle for existence. It is true that out of this struggle arose the modern British Empire. But what a tax upon the three generations, on whom it devolved to build up and defend that Empire, was levied by the peaceable generation which reposed its confidence for so many years in Sir Robert Walpole! Each has its own duty assigned to it; if neglected, the debt has still to be paid.

But though the sketch has now been brought down to the opening of the grand drama in which Hawke was to play one of the most important parts, it is still necessary to notice the greatest difficulty of all in discussing Burke's judgment on the justice of the Spanish war. Not only did he, writing in 1796, condemn it in the terms which have been mentioned; not only did he sacrifice Walpole's character by condemning him for allowing himself, against his better judgment, to "daub false colours over the war," but he declared, as already said, that he had conversed with "many of the principal actors against that minister, and with those who principally excited that clamour, and found that none of them, no, not one, did in the least defend the measure, or attempt to justify their conduct." What an extraordinary statement is this! We have seen the value of Burke's conclusion; let us beware how we take the authority upon which he supports it at more than it is worth. What a prodigious tax, for example, would it be upon our veneration for Burke if he called upon us to believe that the first William Pitt ever made such a confession!—the man whose glorious career opened with the debate on the Convention of Pardo, and the whole of which was identified with the principle of supporting British independence against France and Spain; but perhaps he is not included, for Burke only speaks of "many of the principal actors," and if not included, we need not trouble ourselves too much about the rest.* No doubt some of the "principal actors" were originally governed by party spirit in the first place, and, not having a clear conscience in the matter, forgot in later times how much ground they really had for their action. We know that they were all, as well as Burke himself, ignorant of the existence of the all-important Family Compact of 1733, and therefore liable to give Spain too much credit for her professions of fairness and desire for peace. We may dismiss these witnesses.

Above all, we may fairly join issue with the great orator as to the attribution of conscious falsehood —for it comes to that—to Sir Robert Walpole. Burke supposes him to have deliberately, and against his own opinion, "adopted very nearly the sentiments of his adversaries," though, if he had followed his own conscience, he might have defended himself "on the reason and justice of his cause." Now, with all the Minister's faults, there is no ground for such a tremendous accusation. Nothing can be plainer to the student of the debates as well as of the treaties themselves, than that Walpole was forced into every one of his admissions by the weight of testimony, that he most reluctantly made those admissions, and that he used the whole weight of his "influence" to diminish the cogency of the inferences which he knew, as well as anyone, must necessarily be drawn from them. Burke's explanation is inadmissible. The

---

* Lord Chatham's speech, quoted above, of itself shows he had not changed his mind.

key to the whole of Walpole's later failures and disgrace is, as stated at the outset, to be found in the success which had deservedly attended his early administration, and, in the later part of it, his monopoly of the Government, which prevented him from understanding the changes of the times.

If it were worth while to speculate any further on the reasons which operated in causing " many of the principal actors " against Walpole to change their minds about the war, and Burke to form his unfavourable opinion of it, we might call to mind the exceeding gloom and depression which fell upon the nation soon after its commencement, and which scarcely lifted till Pitt threw over the scene the illumination of his glory. This period synchronised with the most impressionable part of Burke's life, a period when Englishmen looked about regretfully for such a leader as even Walpole, with all his faults, had been, and were slow to understand that they had the greatest statesman of his century rising to power in their very midst. The "ringing of bells" for joy at the war was soon, as Walpole predicted, succeeded by "wringing of hands." The ecstatic burst of national delight at Vernon's success was the one short-lived moment of exultation, to be succeeded by many a bitter disappointment. The very next year after the war commenced saw France abetting Spain. Three years later Prussia ranged herself on the same side. In 1744 the mask was dropped, and open war commenced with the enemy whom Walpole had, unlike an Englishman, dreaded. This he only just lived to see.

What a dreary history is that of the succeeding administrations! What a state of naval anarchy did Mathews' action off Toulon reveal! What millions appeared to be wasted on the Continent, with little more result than to prove the innate courage of British soldiers! How disgracefully was England governed when the Rebellion of 1745 broke out! * What a confession of weakness was embodied in the Peace of Aix la Chapelle, even though victory had at last shone upon the fleets of Anson and Hawke! What a painful period of half peace, half war succeeded that so-called Peace! And how hard it was to convince the nation that nothing could possibly restrain their enemies from attempting to recover the position they had held under Louis XIV., but a desperate struggle for supremacy! It was twenty years before victory decisively declared itself on the English side. This was not much perhaps for the founding of an empire; but during the extreme tension of the process how

---

* The lively and bitter pen of Horace Walpole has drawn the picture of England shortly before the Rebellion of 1745:— "You may judge of our situation by the conversation of old Marshal Belleisle. He has said for some time that we were so little capable of making any defence that he would engage with 5,000 scullions of the French army to conquer England. When he was told of the taking of Cape Breton, he said he could believe that, because the ministry had no hand in it. We are making bonfires for Cape Breton, and thundering over Genoa, while our army in Flanders is running away and dropping to pieces by detachments, taken prisoners every day, while the King is at Hanover, the Regency at their country seats, and not above fourteen or fifteen ships at home."—Letters to Horace Mann, vol. ii. p. 62 (July 26, 1745).

many a philosophic mind must have had its misgivings, and brooded with sad reflections over what may easily have come to be reckoned the madness of the people who provoked the conflict! We might carry our speculations on the influences which led to Burke's statement down to a later date. Those of his informers who lived on to the date of the struggle with the American Colonists, and the alliance with them of France and Spain, which seemed as if it would overwhelm the new empire, may well have cursed the part they played in bringing on the original war, and forgotten its justification. What a sea of difficulties disclosed itself as the consequence!

One thing, however, is certain. The misgivings impressed upon Burke found no expression in the military and naval histories of the last century. It is not easy to find them in contemporary history of any kind. No suspicion of the justice of the cause ever oozes from the pen of those who have handed down the deeds of the British heroes of the war. Still less, we may be sure, did these heroes themselves ever harbour such a thought. Absolved by their profession from the duty of criticising their superiors, they threw themselves into the conflict with much the same spirit as animated the heroes of the later French war, who believed that, in the internecine conflict with the forces of the French Revolution, they were piercing the dragon with the spear of St. George, a chivalry banded together in a holier cause than that of the Crusades.

Let us, then, transport ourselves back to the

opening of this war with Spain, and if we feel we may fairly acquit the nation of embarking in it after the fashion of pirates, out of a hope of "plunder," and fully aware of its "extreme injustice," let us ask ourselves what must have been their sentiment when France—first covertly, and then openly—appeared on the scene. With that country they had had no quarrel. In order to keep at peace with it, their Government had thrown overboard nearly all its ancient traditions, and borne, with a strange equanimity, insults from Spain which at any other period would have produced instant war. What had this nation with which the English were so anxious to keep at peace, to do with the Anglo-Spanish quarrel in the West Indies? It had no common ground whatever in the complaints made by the Spaniards, whether just or not; from the English point of view they ought rather to have sided with England against Spain; and if they retained a grudge in the matter of Gibraltar and Minorca, these had never been French territory. They were simply the price the French had made another nation pay for the miseries which Louis XIV., the common aggressor and tyrant of Europe, their own sovereign, had brought upon the world.

The French policy was natural enough; but it was not the less galling to the men whose memory of the times of William and of Anne had not even yet been obliterated. Nor did it mitigate their resentment to find, as the true nature of the war developed itself, that the cause of the Pretender had once more, under the influence of his special friend, Cardinal Tencin, become the leading factor in the French counsels; and that the old insolent pretension to force a Popish sovereign on their country, so far from being abandoned, was now to be enforced by the bayonets of the chief General in Europe, Marshal Saxe. That one consideration alone was felt to be sufficient. Take them altogether,—observe the whole course of France and Spain in union,—and what remains of the allegation that it was, on the part of England, a war of " plunder and extreme injustice " ?

It was a war of self-defence, a just and necessary war, just politically and morally, a war only too long delayed, a war which was of the most real value not only to Great Britain but to the world.

CHAPTER III.

INTRODUCTION.—PART III.—THE STATE OF THE BRITISH NAVY IN THE REIGN OF GEORGE THE SECOND, WITH ESPECIAL REFERENCE TO LORD HAWKE'S PLACE AMONGST HIS CONTEMPORARIES.

IN estimating the rank held by a British admiral amidst the roll of his peers before and after his time, the circumstances attending his first appearance are of the greatest moment. Hawke came prominently before his country at the precise period when a long peace had prevented the formation of any large number of officers of a high type, and when for nearly a century there had been no instance of a consummate commander such as Blake had been, and Rodney and Nelson were destined to be. It seems so strange that a long interval of this sort should have occurred, that a few preliminary words are necessary to account for the fact.

With the establishment of the principle of fighting fleets in line, which, though by no means then practised for the first time, grew into an elaborate system during the wars of Cromwell and Charles II. with the Dutch, and which James II., as Duke of York, deserves beyond others the credit of promoting, had come also the practice of indecisive battles. But the system must not be disparaged on that account. Not only had this orderly method of fighting become a necessity when fleets were assembled in such vast numbers, but it was the natural product of the age of improved military tactics, and the scientific treatment of the art of war. Louis XIV.'s generals and engineers were bringing their profession to a high state of perfection; how could fleets, which sometimes amounted to a hundred ships on each side, be effectively worked, without adopting military precision as far as in that age it could be made applicable at sea? The process of scientific improvement was natural enough under the circumstances; so also, unfortunately, was the process by which this improved naval science came to be wrongly applied.

The British navy, as we now know it,—for all modern changes count for nothing in comparison with those by which it emerged out of its mediæval condition,—was formed under that tremendous series of conflicts in which it found the Dutch foemen truly worthy of its steel; men of the same race, and, further, with a peculiarity in their naval service, which caused it to approximate far more nearly to the British than that of any other nation with which the latter has ever come into conflict. Having just, in the middle of the seventeenth century, succeeded in elbowing Spain and Portugal out of their old commercial position, the Dutch seamen swarmed all over the world, and, like the English, made the sea their home. The

English could thus alone compare with the Dutch in the possession of an extensive and experienced marine from which a fighting navy could be supplied. This was only a part of the circumstances which caused them to be so well matched. It happened that both nations had also been engaged in violent military conflicts, one in its splendid struggle for independence, and the other in the war of the Great Rebellion; and both had developed a high type of fighting officers on shore.

The advantage, however, lay with England on this point. Her experience was more recent; and the authorities of the Commonwealth made no scruple of placing over the heads of naval men the tried officers of Cromwell's invincible army. In times of peace the mere nautical experience and aptitude for seamanship possessed by the officers of a navy, by no means insures a supply of men who combine first-rate ability in war with the heroic courage which turns the scale when fleets are evenly matched, and, what is still more uncommon, with the coolness, patience, and discretion which are almost as necessary in the varied services of naval warfare. Such officers may come to the head of affairs after years of conflict; sometimes they are carried off before they can rise to a sufficient height to attract notice; sometimes an accident prevents their being discovered. Blake, Monk, and Montagu were exactly the men required at that crisis of the English naval service, when fleets were suddenly called into action after a long peace, when supremacy must be obtained at any cost over an unflinching foe, and when seamanship was only useful so far as it could be turned to account by military experience of war, and by a calculated recklessness of life or of any kind of odds.

It was not—if the reader will pardon the digression—the first time that soldiers had commanded fleets; for, as everybody knows, the sailors who worked the English ships were not, originally, the fighting men at all. It was the sagacity of the Tudor sovereigns, Henry VIII. and Elizabeth, which devised a separate class of fighting sea-officers, trained to the sea, not often perhaps, as afterwards, from childhood, but still specially trained. Until, however, the supremacy of the English over the Dutch navy was at last secured, soldier-officers and sailors were still much intermixed. The struggle once over, the system of entire separation between the military and naval services prevailed, and took root. It was perhaps, partly, besides the natural tendency of things, the rise of such first-rate sailors as Sir John Narborough and Sir Cloudesley Shovel which prevented the recurrence of the old irregularity in this matter. Making their way up from the rank of common seamen, these gallant and accomplished men, trained in the Royal Navy from their earliest days, proved themselves so perfectly competent for the service in all the requirements of the period, that fashion insensibly changed; and if a soldier now and then crept in from the Court, or from some great family, he found he must relinquish all his former ideas, and become a sailor out and out. Such instances have occurred in modern times.

But it must be noticed that there was to be found at this time among the chief officers of the navy, along with their great experience and seamanship, a certain unsophisticated roughness natural to the profession, and especially likely to characterise those who had not inherited the high cultivation of an age which produced, with all their faults, a Charles the Second and a Louis Quatorze, the brilliant Courts and the sparkling literature of Paris and London. The unpolished, homely, honest naval officer mixed very imperfectly with the young scions of good families, who continued to press into a service always popular, and in which family interest has always held a paramount influence. These men often enough turned out anything but sailors. Such men of family as Herbert and Russell, William III.'s admirals, were sailors indeed, but only able to hold their own by adopting the boisterous manners of the hardy "tarpaulin."

Perhaps we may date more especially from this time, though it was always naturally inherent in the race of seamen, a dislike of soldiers as such. It was too well reciprocated. It is only quite in modern times that the contempt mutually felt by each profession for the other has died out. It lay at the bottom of much of the discord which wrecked so many joint expeditions; and the recriminations consequent on such failures kept up the rivalry, not to say antagonism, between the forces. Great men rose above these absurdities; but the feeling which found expression in the lower ranks by such terms as "landlubber" on one side, and "drunken swab" on the other, was by no means confined to those ranks. Walpole, whose friends were army men, often reports their prejudices; as, for example, where he gives General Mostyn's saying that "he was not amphibious enough to like seamen,—there is as much difference between a sailor and a landsman as between a sea-horse and a land-horse." Common dangers, common services, gave a temporary check to such antipathies; but they have only died out under the march of civilisation, and the gradual elevation of the tone of both services.

The mingling, however, of the two elements, the high-born courtier and the rough sailor, did gradually produce a peculiar result of its own. In the wars which we are now to deal with, that product was conspicuous in the officers who rose to chief command. Anson, Hawke, Boscawen, and Pocock, may be taken as representatives of the thoroughbred seamen and gentlemen who have set the peculiar tone of the British navy from that time down to our own.

It was not a mere accident that, amongst all the officers who came to the head of the profession, from the conclusion of the Dutch wars down to the time of these last-named, excellent as many of them were, there was not one who, as a commander of fleets, could be said to rise above mediocrity; and to break through the abuse of the system of fighting in line, it was requisite that some such man should arise. The fact is that the whole mind of the profession was cramped and confined by the prevalence of this abuse.

There was, indeed, a fine officer, who might at first sight be considered an exception to this remark, George Byng (Lord Torrington); but though he held quite the highest rank in the period under review, he was not—perhaps he had not the opportunity to become—a real exception. His peerage was well merited by successful and distinguished services as a subordinate officer, as second in command, as ambassador, and as the admiral who annihilated the Spanish fleet in 1718; but the last-named action, fought off Cape Passaro, which was the only one of his services to place him in a high rank, has never, as a matter of fact, ranked high. It was a victory over a fleet inferior in strength, and which made a poor resistance. It was politically justifiable, as the Spaniards had full warning, and it was useful to England inasmuch as it crippled Spain for future wars ; but the ease with which it was won has somewhat detracted from Byng's merit. His method of fighting must, however, be presently noticed; for it introduces us to the place occupied by the subject of this memoir.

It has been already said that the scientific system of naval tactics, established in the seventeenth century, was open to abuse. It was abused by being pressed too far. Having been justly felt to be a system so necessary as to require a place in the printed instructions, by which all officers were strictly bound, it was, by a not unnatural exaggeration, held to apply to all cases where fleets or squadrons ever came into conflict. No body of men are more tenacious of anything established than seamen. This is, indeed, a general characteristic of Englishmen; but when the life at sea is passed from early youth to old age in regular gradations of service, during which the precept and example of old and respected officers have stamped on the naval mind a particular mode of performing an operation, this tenacity becomes a part of the life and character to a degree which, to be fully understood, must be experienced. It is enough that it is "the service." "Such and such a great officer would never have it done any other way." How much stronger was such a predisposition when fighting in line was inculcated by authority which it might cost a man his life, by sentence of Courtmartial, to despise!

The main reasons for fighting in line, broadside to broadside, each division sailing opposite to its counterpart in the enemy's line, were these. The admiral's motions might in this way, and this alone, be accurately followed, and his signals attended to, and thus the disasters proceeding from isolation and independent action on the part of captains of ships, often at first imperfectly trained, and likely enough to make mistakes of all kinds, were minimised. The fleet was, theoretically at least, one vast machine. Still more advantageous was the system when fleets could be long kept together. The constant practice of sailing in close order, exercising as it did all the skill and vigilance of the officers, and teaching those of each ship to regard themselves as a factor in the whole body, caused them to acquire a habit of comprehending whatever was required of them, and performing it as if by instinct. We hear very little indeed of ships fouling one another on sea-cruises; and the seamanship which could keep together old rotten vessels, with rotten spars, up to the very last moment, for fear of the enemy taking advantage of their absence, was never so signally triumphant as in these wars. In presence of the enemy the fleet tacked, or more usually wore, with unerring judgment, according to the manœuvres of the enemy, or the shifts of wind, ready, at the signal, to take advantage of any errors he might commit. How proud must an admiral have felt of the exact order which he had taken such pains to ensure! How distressing to his mind the contemplation of his disciplined force throwing away in the battle all the advantages it had gained beforehand!

But long custom had prevented naval officers in general from perceiving that the system was, after all, only a rudimentary stage of tactics, and that, however useful, it was by no means so important for the smaller kind of squadrons, with which battles were fought when colonies had to be protected and fleets of merchant vessels convoyed, as for large fleets; as also that it was wholly unfitted for dealing with an enemy which was desirous of avoiding an engagement, and which sailed well enough to be able to escape.

What was worse, it inevitably led to indecisive combats.

Some of the most gallant officers came to be gradually imbued with the idea that if the battle was fought according to rule, it was a secondary question whether it was decisive or not. Scores of such cases might be quoted. While the system lasted in undiminished traditional force even the very best admirals were most seriously hampered by it. In short, its effects were not altogether unlike those exemplified in the later *condottieri* of the Middle Ages, who hired their troops out to the Italian republics at handsome prices, the men being covered with such thick plates of armour that the worst which could befal them was to be unhorsed, and who were thought to have earned their pay if two or three on each side were killed or wounded at the end of a fierce battle. They have been the standing joke of history; but it must be confessed that it was a method which at the time suited all parties, and it is a pity that all wars could not be carried on in this harmless way. But, as we know, the French ferociously broke in upon luxurious Italy, and commenced a sanguinary struggle, waged unceasingly for thirty years, between the chief nations of Europe, who were all eager to prey upon these comfortable people; and we know that the sad result has been a miserable Italian servitude of 350 years, only broken at last, most happily, in our own day. Much later, the principles of military tactics on the Continent betrayed symptoms of abuse not unlike those of the naval services, until Napoleon arose and delivered his lessons to Europe in a voice of thunder.

Now it is usually taken for granted that to the great Lord Rodney belongs the sole credit for putting an end to this state of things by "breaking the enemy's line," an operation which he put in practice, with distinguished results, in his famous battle off Dominica, and which, after 1782, became the tactics of the British navy. This is in a sense perfectly true, and not a word should be said to diminish Rodney's well-earned fame. But we have to consider what the full strength of the old practice was, in order to give due praise to those who broke through it, and led the way to the entire change which Rodney introduced. Such advances always pass through some previous stages. There is an entire omission of these previous stages in a book once famous—Clerk's "Naval Tactics." In that book Hawke's share in the education of his followers is simply ignored. His victories were gained over fleets which ran away, and nothing more need be said. The reader will see that a great deal more must be said, in this book at least.

There were three officers who set Hawke an example in this respect; but he was the first to discard on an intelligible system the old method, wherever it did not strictly apply. All contemporaries agree that he invariably taught his officers beforehand, and uniformly exemplified the teaching by his practice, that fighting in line must never for a moment be adhered to if anything better could be done; and that hostile fleets were thus not merely to be injured, as they had been under the system of Instructions by which he, like his predecessors, was nevertheless bound, but to be destroyed out of hand. Rodney and Howe were Hawke's chief captains. It should never be forgotten that they must have learnt from him the general principles which they as commanders-in-chief splendidly put in practice. At the very least his famous battles of 1747 and 1759 could not but have taught them the lesson of disregarding the old system; for serving under him, one on each of those occasions, they were thus led to victory. It was natural that the method of fighting in line having once lost its hold on the imagination through the successes of Hawke, the pupil should hail with eagerness the idea which was certainly afloat towards the end of his master's career, if Rodney did not, as seems probable, originate it, of carrying the advance a step further. That next step was to cut through the enemy's line, and double the force on each ship so cut off. After the time of Nelson, who had, or made, so many opportunities of practising the operation, any other method of action began to appear inconceivable.

Of the three predecessors of Hawke, Sir George Byng was the first to lead the way. The circumstances of the two fleets being as above described,* and the Spaniards declining battle, Byng, of course, pursued. In his despatch occur the following words:— "Finding we lost time in forming the line, I made the signal for the whole squadron to chase." He could hardly have done anything else; but it was a pregnant innovation.

The unfortunate Admiral Mathews, who had com-

---

* P. 66.

manded a ship in Byng's action, afforded the second instance. His conduct in the too-celebrated battle off Toulon will presently come under review in connection with Hawke, who was one of his captains. His case was not the same as Byng's; for the combined French and Spanish squadrons were of equal force with the English, and had by no means made up their minds to run away. But they were shy, as the naval phrase goes; and Mathews, relying too confidently on the co-operation of his ill-compacted fleet, took the exceedingly bold step, as it was at this period, of bearing down out of the line to prevent their escape, and so breaking the line of the Spanish squadron. If he had succeeded, the fame of no admiral would have stood higher, for he had chosen what, with a fleet well in hand, was the right moment of attack; but he had not gone the way to succeed. He had given no intimation of his intentions to his officers, and there was no bond of good feeling running through the fleet such as might supply the want of complete instruction. He himself fought like a brave man, as he was, but that is all that can be said. In point of fact, taking the whole action as one, he, during three days, committed a series of blunders which prevented anything more than a very slight success. The enemy got off, and he was broke by Courtmartial; but he was much more sinned against by his chief subordinate than sinning.

The third example was given by Anson in 1747. It was more like Byng's case than that of Mathews. Anson's squadron came up with one of the French, not half its size. It was taken by surprise, and, naturally, made off as fast as ever it could. Anson, instigated by Warren, very properly " made a signal for the whole fleet to pursue the enemy, and attack them without having any regard to the line of battle." They were soon caught and captured, though not without a very creditable resistance, Warren and the captains of Anson's fleet having, as it happened from their position, taken a far greater share in the process than the admiral himself. The peerage conferred on him was understood to express not only the joy of the king and people at having at last done something at sea (for the depression caused by Mathews' unfortunate battle was still profoundly felt), but also to show the national appreciation of his wonderful voyage round the world in the "Centurion." By that expedition he had amassed such wealth as to make a peerage less inappropriate than it might otherwise have seemed. The Acapulco ship captured by the "Centurion" was alone valued at half a million of money. He had, too, already infused new vigour into the Board of Admiralty, and the country gratefully felt that it had discovered the right sort of administrator to repair the damaged credit of its favourite service.

Just so far had the old routine been broken down. In the course of the following narrative it will be seen that Hawke's share in changing naval opinion on this vital point was of a very different character. He began to give a sort of private lesson of his own in Mathews' battle by bearing down out of the line and capturing the Spanish ship "Poder," which had already shown herself so formidable as to cause her opposites in the line to fight shy of her. He followed it up in his action of October 14th, 1747, when his own ship bore the chief brunt of the battle; and he gave the finishing blow to the old traditions by his magnificent conquest of the French fleet at Quiberon, fought amidst rocks and shallows, on a lee-shore, during a heavy gale of wind which was driving in full force before it the waves of the Bay of Biscay. He thus, by the destruction of the expedition, prevented the invasion of England or of Scotland which was about to take place.

These were, however, only the luminous and conspicuous points in a career which, during the wars now before us, was one long round of arduous service. They were the rewards of tedious years of most anxious cruising in the British Channel and the Bay of Biscay, winter and summer, amidst furious gales; often with ships ill-fitted for such work, and with crews whose hard fare was made ten times worse by the abuses which even an Anson could not eradicate from the victualling offices. The paternal care our admiral bestowed upon those crews, and by means of which he kept them ever ready and willing for their work, as well as the judicious relations in which he stood with his officers, can only now be gathered and inferred out of a mass of details which it would be useless to inflict upon the reader, but some indications of which will be presented as we go on. So, also, we shall have opportunities of observing not only the patriotism, courage, and endurance of the man, but his modesty, patience, subordination to superiors, his dignity and good sense. His just rights and those of his officers he exacted, but he never asked a favour for himself, and scarcely ever for others. It was thus, by conduct, temper, and character, as well as by his great military qualities, that he was selected out of the whole navy as the sword and shield of England; and it was thus that, though they now and then forgot their obligations, he obtained the confidence of its people. Thus whoever might be the officers entrusted with distant expeditions, the country never felt safe unless Hawke was kept at hand to command the Channel or Bay of Biscay fleets. Then people felt, as about Nelson in later times, that they could sleep in their beds.

But having mentioned the great hero of modern days, it is right to say here that Hawke's nature was far more akin to that of Blake than to that of Nelson. A man of few words, but with a fund of controlled energy which now and then broke out with volcanic force; strict, accurate, impartial; there was none of Nelson's romantic genius in his composition, nothing to make people weep or go mad for him. Nothing could be farther removed from his nature than to flatter the mob, or show any care for its praise or censure. He was to do his duty, and praise must follow him. "A peerage or Westminster Abbey,"— if, indeed, Nelson ever used the expression,—was so far from representing his idea, that he always, to the last, "disdained to ask"* for that dignity—which was, indeed, only conferred on him a little before his death, and seventeen years after his last great battle, the crowning victory of the Imperial war.

How marked was the significance of such conduct in the early years of George III., let those testify who have made a study of that base, intriguing period, the outcome of the Walpole and Pelham administrations. We shall observe some reasons, as we proceed, why his merits so long failed to be recognised, as also why he was not summoned to the headship of the Admiralty immediately on the death of the experienced Anson. The five years he passed in the position of First Lord, it being a time of peace, could hardly afford distinction. At the end of them we shall find him suffering, like his predecessors, for the sins of the Government; but we shall also observe some remarkable evidences of the sound principles on which his administration was conducted. The last glimpse we obtain of the veteran is in a land-storm, in which he was probably less able to " find his bearings " than in a winter hurricane at sea. It was when the whole country went nautically mad over Admiral Keppel's Courtmartial. Keppel was the old man's pupil and friend, and, right or wrong, it was more than he could bear, that he should, under the circumstances, be brought to trial by his subordinate officer. At the head of the list of admirals who publicly protested against Palliser's conduct was the name of Lord Hawke; but this is a complicated

---

* Inscription on his monument.

question which must be reserved for its proper place. Shortly after that affair he died.

It has no doubt had something to do with the neglect with which this remarkable man's memory has been treated, that he died at a moment when party spirit ran at an unexampled height. He had been a Whig all his life. His uncle and early patron, Colonel Martin Bladen, from whom he probably took his politics, was Whig member of Parliament for Portsmouth; and Hawke followed him, within a short interval, as member for that place from 1747 to the date of his peerage in 1776. The First Lord of the Admiralty held the patronage of the naval boroughs, and he first sat as the Duke of Bedford's nominee; but as this occurred at the moment when his first victory had just been rewarded by his being made a Knight of the Bath, it probably did not require much interest either to obtain or keep the representation of a town which has so often shown its appreciation of naval merit.

Unlike Anson, who never spoke in Parliament, Hawke took his part in debates ; but probably he was no orator. Few naval men possess that accomplishment, for they do not receive the necessary training, and their profession is one of deeds, not words. The second Lord Mulgrave was an exception, and he obtained for his pains the title of "the marine lawyer." Horace Walpole has a characteristic sneer at both Hawke and Saunders on the occasion of their having to discuss, in Parliament, a question that bore on naval affairs. He has, indeed, more than one fling at Hawke;

but no one who knows the writings of that effeminate critic—to whom, however, we are indebted for so much light on his times—attaches any importance to his sneers. If a man's career was in any way opposed to that of one of Walpole's public or private friends, it was enough to ensure his disparagement; and Hawke found himself at Rochefort opposed to Conway, the relative and idol of the witty letter-writer, who has not, indeed, many good words to say for any nautical man. They came "betwixt the wind and his nobility." He did not understand them; and they were, probably, far from appreciating him.

These Whig politics, publicly exhibited in connection with his friendship for Keppel, were injurious to Lord Hawke's subsequent fame. His memory would naturally receive whatever discredit was afterwards attached to his friend's cause, so triumphant at the moment. It is now well understood how the extraordinary degree to which that famous Courtmartial carried the division of the country into two distinct parties on the question, was due not to the merits of the case, but to its political significance. It afforded a grand opportunity for a national demonstration—coming, as it did, just when the country had arrived at the highest pitch of disgust with the American war, and with the Government which had so unfortunately managed it. The share of the Whigs in bringing on the quarrel had been already forgotten; and the King, in struggling to free himself from the overbearing Whig oligarchy to which he had so long been subject, had not only lost all his old popularity, but had been obliged to throw himself on a party which was not, till the younger Pitt appeared on the scene, strong enough to hold its own. As soon, however, as that event took place, —and the King had not long to wait—the tide turned, and, setting one way for half a century, carried with it no small portion of the literature of the times. It was not worth while to rescue from oblivion the name of one whose sun had set in the transient blaze of Keppel's popularity; and this, indeed, is not altogether a poetical phrase, for it seems that the aged Lord's illuminations on the occasion of his friend's acquittal attracted special observation, even in that moment of delirium.

Finally, the very next year after his death the laurels of Rodney, the Tory captor of De Grasse, completely overshadowed those of the Whig conqueror of Conflans; Howe followed Rodney; and soon Nelson and his paladins filled, to the eyes of the nation, the whole firmament of naval glory.

Still, if we look to the feeling shown by the country at the loss of "the father of the British navy," as Keppel called him in the House of Commons, it will not be too much to say that the people felt his loss more than they did that of any public man of the period except Chatham. Burke spoke of him in the House as "the great Lord Hawke"; the newspapers and periodicals of the day indulged in a sort of apotheosis of the hero, about the details of whose career they were, by the by, singularly ill-informed; and Keppel, quoting his authority on a nautical question, two or three months later, declared that "having sat with him at the Board, he knew his conduct both in his civil and military capacity; and that he had left behind him a name unrivalled in the maritime records of his country."* Keppel had every reason to speak as a friend, but no one then living was a better judge of the real place occupied by his old commander. A few months later still, he himself was raised to the rank of Viscount, and became First Lord of the Admiralty.

So much for the general conspectus of the rank held by Hawke in the line of the greater naval worthies of England. Before entering on his career it may be well to muster around us his immediate contemporaries, and so to launch him fairly as their pupil, comrade, and master.

When our admiral first went to sea as a boy, about 1717, there were three great officers at the head of the profession, men who had been admirals or captains in the reigns of William III. and Anne, and to whom the officers of the peaceful period which ensued looked up with respect not unmingled with awe. These were Lord Torrington, Sir John Norris, and Sir Charles Wager. Admiral Herbert, the previous Lord Torrington, was just dead. Admiral Russell, Earl of Orford, was past going to sea. The handsome and gallant Sir George Rooke, whose drawn battle of Malaga, in 1704, was the last that had been fought before Byng's, had died some years previously, nearly at the

---

* "Life of Viscount Keppel," vol. ii. p. 363.

same time with his companion in arms Sir Cloudesley Shovel, who was wrecked in a three-decker, with all his crew, in a Channel fog, upon the Scilly Isles.

Of Byng something has been said. After his death in 1733, Norris and Wager, his juniors, filled the highest places, and fairly enough carried down the old traditions of the navy during Hawke's early years of service. Both were essentially good officers, masters of the routine of their profession, but not much more. Both were much employed by Walpole as commanders of his numerous, and, it must be said, for some years successful, "demonstrations" in the Baltic and at Lisbon. Russia, Sweden, and Portugal were each in turn brought to reason, quite as much by the skill and tact of the admirals as from dread of their armaments. Wager supported Walpole in Parliament with some effect during the conflict of parties already noticed. His reputation would have stood higher if he had not been First Lord of the Admiralty when the war broke out. That has always been a trying moment for "First Lords"; for a peace establishment, however the people may expect it, cannot even now be raised to a war level in a moment; and at that time organization was feeble indeed, and the credit of the minister so low as to make money scarce. Wager resigned in 1742, on hearing, it is said, that he was called an "old woman." *

Norris also would have left a higher reputation if he had not outlived his full powers. He had per-

---

* Walpole's letters to Mann, 1742.

formed many fine services of the minor kind, often commanded fleets, and had been, as ambassador, successful in awing the wilful Czar, Peter the Great. When the Spanish war broke out he was not thought too old to command "the grand fleet," and suffered unpopularity for an inactivity which was part of the Minister's policy. Even in 1744 no one but old Sir John Norris could be trusted to command the squadron which was to protect the country from the invasion of Marshal Saxe under cover of De Roquefeuil's fleet. With that fleet he came up off Dungeness, and anchored for the night. In the morning it was found that the enemy had slipped away. This would never have happened had Norris not been a very old man. He had served for sixty years. But a timely storm dispersed the expedition as effectually as a successful battle. It was by a stroke of poetical justice that the admiral was indebted to a storm at last; for so uniformly unfortunate had he been in this respect, that, like Admiral Byron afterwards, his *soubriquet* was "Foul-weather Jack."

After these two old admirals, the chief officers of the next grade, at the opening of the war, were Nicholas Haddock, Vernon, Ogle, Mathews, Lestock, Rowley, and Anson—not to mention men like Hardy, Balchen, and other good officers who never came prominently before the nation. With the exception of Anson, none of them rose to importance, though more than one of them sank into notoriety. It was the natural consequence of the long peace. There had been scarcely any opportunity for distinction. The

Admiralty did the best they could; and fondly hoped that the experience gained from long service, and the courage these officers had displayed when a chance opportunity had offered, might prove to have been an earnest of the ability which was required for the task they saw before them. That task was not only, when the occasion came, to deal with the fleets and forts of the enemy in the manner best calculated to destroy them; but to train, as it were at a moment's notice, the great mass of officers upon whom the subordinate work would fall: for scarcely any of these had seen service before an enemy, and a great deal of weeding out would be required. A word or two on each of these chiefs will be necessary.

Till France openly joined Spain the channel was tolerably safe, and the Mediterranean was the most important command. For this post Haddock was selected. He was a good officer, already distinguished, and not too old for the work, which he performed successfully, though without brilliancy of any kind. He harassed the Spanish trade, and the Spanish fleet did not dare to come out of port. It is certain that he might have done more had he been better supported from home; and as no one imagined Walpole's heart to be in the war, it was absurdly believed that the admiral was hampered by secret instructions. It was indeed a true instinct which prompted the feeling that the forces of a nation are never properly handled by one who does not sympathise with the cause in which they are engaged; and the nation was making up its mind to get rid altogether of the man whom it could not trust. Haddock fell ill, and soon made way for Mathews, Lestock, and Rowley, who will come before us in their place.

Vernon was still on the list of captains when the war broke out, but was now made vice-admiral at a leap. He was an officer of old standing, kept back by his vehement Tory politics. For years this representative of a great old family had made the House of Commons ring with his patriotic denunciations of the minister of peace, conceived in the roughest nautical style. While Walpole was at the height of his power he could afford to smile at these extravagances; but when sinking under the combined attacks of his opponents, closing round him nearer and nearer amidst the cheers of the nation, it was a different matter. With a stroke of his old dexterity he saw his opportunity, and performed the double operation of getting rid of a tenacious foe, and at the same time satisfying the popular clamour. Both to him and the nation Portobello had been a bugbear. It was believed, chiefly on the absurd ground that Hosier's fine fleet had not taken it, to be a much stronger place than it really was; but that unfortunate admiral had never been allowed to try. Vernon loudly declared that it might be taken with six line-of-battle ships, was taken at his word, sailed off, and with scarcely any loss took the place at once. The frantic joy of the English people when the news arrived, and the popular manifestations of it which filled the country with "Vernon's Heads" as signboards to the public-houses, are matters of common history; as also the turn of fortune which condemned him to joint action with an incompetent general in the subsequent West-Indian operations, and the glaring personal faults which helped to cause the failure of the grand and not ill-conceived expedition.

Vernon had one more trial. In the critical year of the Rebellion, 1745, he was selected to hoist his flag for the protection of the Channel and the North Sea. His duties were well performed; but he fell into a quarrel with the Admiralty, hauled down his flag, and ended by being struck off the list of flag-officers. Nevertheless, the historian of the Seven years' war, writing in 1767, dedicated his volumes to the hero who "entirely suppressed the piracies of the Spanish guarda-costas," and whose "services reduced the pride of Spain, recovered a free trade, and curbed the ambition of France"; while he represents him when dismissed in 1745 as " discharged by the interests of such as were jealous of your superior abilities at home." "It was your conduct and judgment that intimidated the enemy, and totally defeated their resolution to make a descent on England, though you had no more than four ships of the line, and six from fifty to twenty guns," &c.

This is a view of Vernon's merits to be found, perhaps, in no single history of modern times, yet there is no doubt some truth in it. He made so many enemies, and failed so signally, that people forgot that he had, after all deductions, effected much. The mere exhibition of the powerful forces commanded by him and Ogle, fighting the Spanish forts everywhere and at all hazards, even though they often blundered, put a stop to all the complaints and grievances with which England had rung for so many years. And there certainly were two sides to the special quarrel which ended his stormy naval career.

Sir Chaloner Ogle's early reputation had been made, like the later Lord Torrington's, by splendid courage and conduct against pirates. He bore a high character as an officer, and at the opening of the war was appointed to the command of a squadron at Gibraltar. But he was soon sent to the assistance of Vernon; and, like nearly all others who served under that unfortunate man, his fame, through no fault of his own, suffered in these operations. After his West Indian command, in which he succeeded Vernon, we hear no more of him. Like his chief, he had previously served on that station, and it was there that he had been Hawke's patron. Perhaps there was some connection between the families, as the name "Chaloner" occurs among the Hawkes of a later generation. At any rate we shall not be far wrong in supposing that it was to him that our admiral, when a young captain, was indebted for some of his professional excellence.

The great West Indian expedition was only one part of the Government plan for putting a stop to "Spanish depredations." The other part was to send a squadron round Cape Horn to attack the Spanish Pacific settlements, and to cut off their treasure-ships. Anson was selected for the latter command. The whole scheme was well conceived; and if only the force entrusted to Anson had been properly equipped and selected, that part at least, under such a commander, must have succeeded. It was impossible to have selected a better chief; it is impossible at the present day to conceive a more miserable instance of administrative blundering than attended the fitting out of the expedition. But though again, like Vernon's, but from a different cause, the expedition was far from being as successful as it ought to have been, the result of it was to cripple and alarm the Spaniards in no small degree; to bring forward some who turned out the best officers of the war; and, above all, to point out to the nation the one man who, by a happy union of courage, prudence, and fertility of resource, was the most exactly fitted for the task of reorganizing the navy after a long peace. This fine officer will come before us constantly. He deserved the good fortune which attended him after all his sufferings, not the least of which felicities was that his marvellous exploits during the voyage of the "Centurion" round the world found a man of real genius to relate them. His biographer has well shown how much that fascinating book, not even yet forgotten, owed to Major Robins, the father of scientific English artillery. Nelson was scarcely more fortunate in having his life translated out of the dull narrative of his first biographers into the brilliant prose of Southey.

A wider survey than is here possible of the state of the navy during the first few years of the war, would confirm the impression conveyed by the above sketch, and fit in only too well with what we should expect. A few facts must suffice.

The Courtsmartial were numerous, and the sentences often far from satisfactory. It is plain that there was often an abundance of courage without conduct, sometimes a deficiency of the first and most necessary quality; for the exigencies of war bring out what a time of peace may fail to discover. The system of signals was grossly deficient, and the whole body of rules necessary for manœuvring fleets had to be learnt by most officers for the first time. The absence of surveys and charts of the enemy's coasts was a constant source of danger, causing, when attacks had to be made, a dependence on foreign pilots, which was often disastrous; while, for some reason or other, the only compensation for this serious drawback, a good proportion of frigates and small craft, was generally denied to the fleet. It has always been so. Who does not remember Nelson's frantic complaints on the same score?

The crews were of course impressed, and we shall see the system at work. It was not till long afterwards, when the watchword of "Wilkes and Liberty" had been shouted through the ranks of society that an outcry was raised against this rude method of conscription,—a problem which, however evaded by the excellent modern arrangements for training seamen, has never yet been fairly faced by the country. We do not hear so much of the badness of the provisions as might have been expected; but one signal exception must be made. The scurvy was then, and for long before and long after, the scourge of the navy; the long-continued cruises of fleets before the ports of the enemy exposed their crews to its deadly ravages. Where it did not kill it maimed, or enfeebled, or ruined the strongest constitution. There was as yet only one known remedy, where fresh provisions could not be obtained, and this was beer. Ships took to sea nearly as much beer as they did water; and as the latter could never be kept sweet for any length of time in casks, the beer was often the only and always the chief beverage of the men. But what if the beer was bad? In Hawke's later cruises pages on pages of his letter-books are filled with complaints on this score. Beer at best must always have been difficult to keep; but if it was bad to begin with—and so it seems to have been most frequently—it simply meant death and inefficiency. This was, then, very far from a trivial matter, and as it troubled our admiral far more than the enemy, so it probably did other officers. Many years were yet to pass before the "grog," which we have so long learnt to associate with the idea of a sailor that we can hardly imagine him ever to have toasted his sweetheart or "spliced the mainbrace" in anything else, took the place of beer. In this the Dutchman with his "Hollands" had preceded us; and hence the "nip," which was more easily served out to him before a battle than beer, was supposed to give him "Dutch courage." More than another generation was to pass before "Cook's Voyages" and Sir Gilbert Blane's sagacity were to suggest a regular and a palatable antiscorbutic in the lime-juice which has been the blessing of modern times, and a still longer period before iron tanks provided the sailor with water which after several months was almost as sweet as, perhaps more wholesome than, what he would obtain from his native village pump. The badness of cask-water when kept some time obliged Hawke to deprecate the expedient of supplying wine instead of beer, which was sometimes tried, for it could not be drunk without water, and that was "stinking."

To add to these difficulties, with which an officer had to contend perpetually, was another from which modern fleets are happily free. The sanitary arrangements were bad enough; but the rotten state of the ships, which were continued in commission long after they should have been broken up, made matters worse; for diseases of various kinds were due to this cause alone. That officers were learning to mitigate such defects may be seen by the subjoined abstract of a letter in the "Annual Register" for 1760[*];

---

[*] The "Torbay," Captain Keppel, was kept so healthy during a cruise of four months that she did not lose a single man, by the following precautions:—(1) The men and their clothes were mustered twice a week. (2) The hammocks were sent on deck every morning, and the ports hauled up; the lower deck scraped and washed every day in fine weather; the beams dried by burning, in matchtubs partly filled with sand, dry wood sprinkled with powdered resin. (3) Portable ventilators were constantly in use, and water was let into the ship and pumped out again daily. (4) The beams were occasionally washed with warm vinegar.

It is interesting to watch the very beginning of sanitary methods, most of which have seemed, for many generations, so natural in a man-of-war, that no one dreams of inquiring into their origin.

and no doubt the experience of these trying years led to the far superior organization of ship-life under which the later wars with the French were conducted; but the most terrible commentary on the state of things above disclosed is the summary drawn up at the end of the Seven years' war, and which is to be found in the "Annual Register" (1763) and elsewhere. From this statement it appears that in all the naval battles of that war there were but 1,512 sailors and marines killed, while 133,708 had died of disease or were " missing." Many of these last were no doubt cases of desertion; but as the sternest precautions were taken at this time against that offence, the balance of deaths from disease must have been great to an almost incredible extent. Scarce a hundredth part of them could have occurred under modern conditions.

All this was rather worse than better in the other navies of the time; and the Englishman, if he ran a poor chance of escaping the diseases which would prevent him from enjoying his prize-money, had at least a larger share of it than the enemy. But he had something much better. He had more than his full share of the growing patriotism of that day, and was rewarded by the admiration, if not the gratitude, of his fellow-countrymen. He was felt to be their fore-fighter and representative in the mighty conflict with forces which were rising up on all sides against the islanders of the west, and which must be kept at all hazards off their shores. The idea of duty was not for the first time put before fleets by Nelson's celebrated signal; and in its pursuit they learnt to smile at hardships, or at death itself. If at first they exhibited too many of the faults incident to the state of the profession, improvement soon commenced. When nobly led, as they came to be, was the chivalry of the ancient stock, even in the glorious reigns of old English history, ever more signally exhibited?

The treatment of the sailor varied, of course, very much with the officer under whom he was serving; but we may be quite sure that there were but few of the alleviations of his lot which have been gradually progressing ever since the mutinies of the Nore and Spithead, when the overwhelming importance of the man-of-war's man to the country was at last, by the force of stern necessity, recognised. Some idea of the sort dawned on the executive mind even in 1742. It was—much to the credit of the Admiralty—openly admitted that some limit must be put to the improper treatment of seamen which had become, during the long peace, almost customary. In that year no less than three post captains were most severely punished for offences of this kind—Captains Fanshaw, Sir Yelverton Peyton, and the Hon. William Hervey.* We shall find Hawke, like the best of his contemporaries, devoting himself to the welfare of his men, and such an officer as Keppel—in that respect a rival to the mythical Tom Bowline—the "darling of the crew." When the great mutinies broke out at the end of the century, the tone of the service had changed. It was no longer, or

---

* The two former had hired out their men to merchants.

at any rate not at all to the same degree, the tyranny of the officers which was complained of; it was the crass negligence of successive naval administrations, which had taken for granted that the patience so long and so touchingly displayed would last for ever.

On one point the enemy had a decided advantage. Both France and Spain were at this date in advance of England in the art of building fine men-of-war. The "Princesa," taken by a superior force from Spain after a gallant resistance, and the "Magnanime," under the same circumstances, from the French, taught the English a much-needed lesson. The first was just half as large again as the ships of corresponding rate in the British navy. These ships gave ocular demonstration of what was perfectly well known, however slow the building department had been to recognise it,—that instead of leading Europe, as they had once done, the people of this country had been shamefully allowed to fall behind their neighbours. It was not so long previously that the four Stuart kings—in some respects the worst of our dynasties—had paid so much attention to this subject that the case had been exactly reversed. Even James I. exerted the sagacity which he too often allowed to lie dormant, in going out of the beaten track, and employing a mere mathematician, Peter Pett, in whose family the art continued to reside for more than one generation, to construct a superior kind of vessel to that which the yards had hitherto turned out. Even his unfortunate son proceeded in the same direction, and it was with the fine ships he provided with the doomed ship-money that Cromwell and Blake conquered the Dutch. Charles II. and James II. were scientific naval architects and experienced sailors. Princes Rupert and Maurice exemplified the tastes of the family. All the bravest and best-born men of the time, whatever their politics, were truly proud to find themselves on the quarter-deck of a man-of-war, which was the equal, and generally the superior, of any vessel afloat on the ocean.

All this, or most of it, ceased with the Revolution, which brought to the front a sovereign like William III. and a general like Marlborough, men whose whole attention was naturally fixed on the support of the armies by which Europe was to be led to the triumphant overthrow of Louis Quatorze, the common enemy. Not so that magnificent despot himself. He saw his opportunity; and while destroying the resources of his country in the effort to make head against England, Holland, and the Empire, encouraged his able ministers to create a marine which should contest the sovereignty of the seas. The improved construction of his ships extended itself to his vassal, Spain; while no corresponding progress had been made by the English. In the absence of encouragement from the throne the navy stagnated. What had served the old officers might do well enough for the new; but it gave the latter no small disgust to find themselves, when the war commenced, out-sailed and over-matched by the enemy who had stolen a long march in the art of ship-building;

and it was not till towards the end of the Seven years' war that the energy of Anson and his peers, acting on the hints supplied by captured ships, had made up for the loss of half a century. And yet, so hard is it to prevent the excellent principles of order and routine from obtaining too great a hold on the British mind, much the same process has been repeated at intervals since those days. However, the sovereignty of the seas was not to be gained by *matériel*.

In the matter of gunnery, also, this superiority of ships in size carried a great advantage. The heavier ships could carry heavier guns. It was not till after the year 1744, when the fifty-gun ships were ordered out of the line because, inferior as all the rest of his ships were, Mathews saw that these were too ridiculously unfit for the work, that a new and improved scale of proportion of guns to tonnage was made the rule; and, of course, it took long to carry it out. Ships were now, however, loaded with heavier metal than they could bear, and proved crank and bad sea-boats. And it was not till Lord Keppel's administration in 1782 that the true proportion of guns to tonnage, both as to number and calibre, was fixed as it remained, substantially, down to the day when steam and iron superseded wood and sails. The difference between the English and their enemies was, in short, though not so great, yet not unlike that which was discovered when the war with the United States of America broke out in 1812. The English were then expected to capture ships of the same nominal rate, but almost twice their size, with guns throwing almost double their weight of metal, and sides which their feeble shot could not penetrate; and these ships manned with seamen as good as their own—some of them, indeed, being actually British seamen who had deserted from their own ships after having been trained as British seamen alone were at that date trained.

But in the war before us it was precisely the character of the seamen which, in conjunction with that of the officers, made all the difference, and neutralised all other advantages possessed by the enemy. With inferior ships and often weaker metal, the coolness, readiness of resource, and, above all, quickness of firing which distinguished the British sailor, almost always, except when ships were very badly manœuvred, carried the day, and generally with little loss. These qualities, exhibited quite as much in the independent spirit of the seamen themselves as in their officers, were in truth the outcome of the national characteristics, and, at any rate, came very naturally to men of whom a large proportion had been used to the sea from childhood. There were always enough of these to give tone to the rest, while their enemies had a far smaller stock of seamen to draw from; and their inferiority in this respect came, as the war proceeded, to be still more marked; for the English fleets were always at sea blockading the ports, while the enemy did not, indeed, wear out his ships so fast, but his officers and crews gained very little experience.

In the later French wars these causes operated still more favourably for the English, and it required all the French gallantry of character to bear up against such reverses as, almost necessarily, ensued; but the change was gradual. Thus, in the earlier wars both sides were far more evenly matched than in the later. The engagements of single ships were often long and sanguinary, and in more than one battle of fleets or squadrons the enemy made a most determined defence. In the East Indies especially, the skill and courage of a Pocock and a Watson were not unevenly matched by those of D'Aché.

It may be noticed here that the experience gained in this war, under great leaders, developed many improvements in gunnery, such as locks and tubes for firing guns, flannel cartridges, and canister shot. When the war with the American colonies brought France and Spain once more into conflict with their old opponent, the British navy started in a very superior relative condition to that in which it began the war with Spain in 1739. The school of Hawke had faithfully handed down the traditions of the master, and probably the gallant Comte de Grasse, when Rodney received his sword on the quarter-deck of the "Formidable," did not much exaggerate when he said that his conquerors were a hundred years in advance of their enemy in naval matters.* When Howe opened the still later war of the French Revolution, the French navy was, relatively to the English, still further inferior; for that Revolution had cost it the loss of almost all its best officers, who were

---

* Mundy's "Life of Lord Rodney," vol. ii., p. 290.

Royalists to the backbone. The Nelsonic maxim that one Englishman was equal to three Frenchmen, might be true enough in Nelson's time, but it was very different in the middle of the century. Even after the English had asserted their superiority, no fleet of theirs could have ventured to attack a force half as large again as itself, though Hawke, as we shall see, had no objection to his enemy having a ship or two more. As a matter of fact, so excellent was the management of Anson and Hawke, that the British fleet was almost always in superior force. The case of John Byng's fleet was exceptional, but it was large enough, if properly commanded.

It must be added to this rapid survey of the causes of the British success that the system pursued by their officers of engaging fleets or single ships from to windward was just one of those cases where, at that time, practice was better than theory. The opposite system was more scientific. The French perceived that, in waiting to leeward for the attack, they secured a great advantage in crippling and raking the enemy as he bore down; and no doubt it required a cool and resolute crew to bear unflinchingly the handling which the attacking ship sustained in the process, while she was all the time herself unable to fire. But these were just the qualities the English possessed; and in the state of gunnery at that period the attacking force only suffered a certain loss; it was not destroyed, and often even, since the enemy fired at the rigging on principle, not seriously damaged. But when a captain or an admiral like Hawke, or

Boscawen, or Keppel, or Howe, or Rodney, brought his ship at last within pistol or "half-musket" shot of the enemy, chose, with consummate seamanship, his position, and hammered away into his antagonist's hull, it was soon all over with him; and the largely superior number of men carried on board the French and Spanish ships only made matters worse.

Perhaps it has not always been observed how characteristic of our French neighbours was this practice of over-filling their ships with men. It may not be so evident in modern times, since all nations are running a pretty even race in the development of the new navies which, in their future conflict, will once more decide the fate of the world; but the same difference between the two nations may even yet be traced in the deep-sea fishing-boats which frequent the Channel or the German Ocean. A French boat of the same tonnage as an English one will carry twice the number of men and boys; and it is found to pay, for so much more clever and temperate are the French in regard to food, that their crews can live at half the expense of the English.

It was probably this inferiority in the number of men which prevented the English from developing, what became more common in modern times, the practice of boarding the enemy. We read but little of it in this earlier war. The enemy struck after a more or less prolonged cannonade at close quarters. The English ship became, after the officers had acquired some experience, a very handy machine, and it was the part of a seaman so to use it as to make boarding unnecessary. It was an obvious mistake to give the enemy the advantage of his superiority in numbers if he could be taken without running such a risk. The one thing which must not be done was to waste shot by a distant cannonade. One of the few instances of boarding, of which we read in the period before us—for it was not so uncommon in the wars of the seventeenth century—was in Byng's action off Cape Passaro. When Captain Streynsham Master, of the "Superbe," took the Spanish flagship by boarding, his first lieutenant, Thomas Arnold, of Lowestoft, who worthily closed the line of naval heroes sent forth during two centuries from that place, was the officer who suggested the measure, and, gallantly leading the boarders, was dangerously wounded.* The Spanish admiral's flag, which he hauled down, was generally used in after years at weddings, for the public decoration of the town, in which Arnold passed his declining years; and it is interesting to observe that the direct descendant of this officer was Dr. Arnold, of Rugby. In the above case boarding was certainly a proper manœuvre; as it was afterwards in the case of the demoralized crews with which Nelson and his officers had, for the most part, to contend.

The melancholy state of the navy at the opening of the war might, in relation to its working officers, be largely illustrated. It will be sufficient here, as Mathew's battle will itself be extremely suggestive,

---

* "History of Lowestoft."

to mention a curious case which will help us to understand out of what a chaos our admiral and his colleagues had to raise their profession.

Captain Thomas Watson was a contemporary of Hawke's, who greatly distinguished himself under Vernon's command in the West Indies. In 1744, when in command of the "Northumberland," of 70 guns, he fell in with two French ships of 62 and 60 guns respectively, accompanied by a frigate. Having determined to engage them, he gallantly attacked, though in a somewhat blind way, and had almost succeeded in capturing them when he was mortally wounded. In this state the master and the gunner of the ship, who by no means shared the audacity of their chief, persuaded him to strike; and strike he did. The lieutenants seem to have been at their batteries, and to have known nothing about it. The captain soon died of his wound. The master was tried by Courtmartial and imprisoned for life. It turned out that Watson had recently sustained a fracture of the skull by a fall, had drunk more than he could under such circumstances bear, and was by no means in a state to be responsible either for attacking, fighting, or surrendering.*

Another contemporary captain, of good family, was executed for murdering an elder brother whom he had decoyed on board his frigate for that purpose.†

In a different way the career of a third officer, a

---

* Charnock's "*Biog. Nav.*," vol. iv. p. 374.
† *Ibid.*, vol. iv. p. 245.

little senior to Hawke, throws light upon the period. At the trial of Admiral John Byng, in 1756, we come across Admiral Thomas Smith as President of the Courtmartial. This was a natural brother of Sir George, afterwards Lord, Lyttelton. He did not add much to his reputation by his management of that blundering affair, nor had he seen much active service. But he was a very well known character, and a general favourite, as might be gathered from his *soubriquet*, " Tom of Ten Thousand." Great things were expected of him if he ever had an opportunity; but, though he was entrusted with a responsible command in 1745, distinction never came. His whole reputation was founded upon his conduct in 1728, as lieutenant of the " Gosport," when lying in Plymouth Sound, and his captain being on shore.

A French frigate, putting to sea from Plymouth, passed very near him without paying the usually exacted compliment of lowering his topsails. Mr. Smith very spiritedly fired at the French ship and compelled her commander to perform the act of complaisance. As the greatest harmony subsisted at that time between the courts of England and France, a serious complaint was made by the ambassador of what was termed an outrageous act of violence. Mr. Smith was accordingly brought to a Courtmartial; and it being impossible to deny or controvert the fact, was accordingly broke. His conduct was, however, so highly acceptable to the sovereign and the nation, that, although political reasons rendered the above apparent censure indispensably necessary, he was advanced on the following day without ever passing through or occupying the intermediate subordinate station of commander of a sloop of war.*

This characteristic proceeding may justify a few

---

* Charnock's " *Biog. Nav.*," vol. iv. p. 209. This account is not quite accurate. Smith only threatened to fire; was broke by words on the history of the claim thus boldly asserted by a subordinate officer. It was not surprising that other nations did not approve of the English claim; but it would be quite a mistake to suppose that it was really obsolete, or that it had long been thought a matter of little consequence. It still formed, and long continued to form, a part of the "Instructions to all Captains of His Majesty's Ships" in the following words:—

Upon your meeting with any ship or ships within His Majesty's seas,—which, for your better guidance herein you are to take notice, extend to Cape Finisterre,—belonging to any foreign Prince or State, you are to expect that in their passage by you they strike their topsail and take in their flag, in acknowledgment of His Majesty's sovereignty in those seas; and if any shall refuse to do it, or offer to resist, you are to use your utmost endeavours to compel them thereunto, and in no wise to suffer any dishonour to be done to His Majesty.

This claim was quaintly expounded in Sir John Borough's celebrated treatise in the reign of Queen Elizabeth:—

The Sovereignty of our Seas being the most precious jewel of Her Majesty's crown, and next under God, the principal means of our wealth and safety, all true English hearts and hands are bound by all possible means and diligence to preserve and maintain the same, even with the uttermost hazard of their lives, their goods and fortunes.

Both Sully and Richelieu bear witness to the rigorous exaction of the claim in their time, for it was even forcibly exercised upon the ship which carried the former as ambassador to James I.; and

---

order of the Government, not by Courtmartial; was not reinstated for a year; nor, though rapidly promoted, did he skip over the rank of commander.

the latter, in his "Testament Politique" betrays his shame and indignation that even Henri Quatre had to put up with the insult. The wars between the English and Dutch were, indeed, the result of many quarrels, and would have been fought out under any circumstances, for they represented a desperate struggle of rivals for commercial supremacy; but the occasion seized was the contemptuous denial of this very claim by the Dutch, a denial accompanied with every circumstance of bravado, something after the fashion of the followers of Montague and Capulet in Shakspeare's Play. William III., though half a Dutchman, found the ancient claim of his new kingdom exceedingly convenient, and inserted it in his Declaration of War with France:—

> The right of the flag, inherent in the crown of England, hath been disputed by his [the King of France's] orders, in violation of our sovereignty of the narrow seas, which in all ages hath been asserted by our predecessors, and we are resolved to maintain the honour of our crown and of the English nation.

Thus it was impossible to have a more respectable antiquity for any claim; nor was it a mere formality. It had been a leading part of the system under which England had not only grown great, but, in consequence of that greatness, had preserved inviolate the safety of her shores. For it carried a corresponding duty. It involved as a correlative that the English must always have a naval force at hand superior to any which her enemies could bring against her; and it established the principle of "wooden walls." No wonder the claim was held sacred, and the "narrow seas" fondly regarded exactly in the same light as so much land, a territory fought for over and over again, and English by right of conquest. Had not her kings been "kings of France"? If they had been unjustly deprived of their inheritance on the opposite side of the "silver streak," it was still the "British Channel," and the people deeply resented the new policy which deprived them of their rights. But the House of Hanover, yielding to no former dynasty in personal spirit, brought with them many fresh European obligations; and a disputed Succession had rendered it desirable to remove all but absolutely necessary grounds of quarrel. It thus became customary, while leaving the words of the claim in the "Instructions," to consider it rather as a question of good manners than of strict right to be enforced at all costs, except in war-time, when the compliment was still rigidly exacted. Even this gradually disappeared after the close of the Seven years' war, till, like the once equally respectable claim to the crown of France, it came to be a mere name, and was at last, but not till after the Battle of Trafalgar, removed from the code which kept the notion afloat.

For our present purpose this sketch of a series of transactions which lasted down to a later date than is generally supposed, has a special significance, forbidding us to judge of the events, even of the last century, by exclusively modern ideas, and reminding us of the violence which must have been done to the feelings of a people who still claimed the signs of maritime supremacy, though only in the "narrow seas," when the Spanish insults to their flag were reported to them by every trader which arrived from the West Indies. They knew well that the Spaniards had no such rights in the Gulf of Mexico as they were themselves reluctantly resigning in the British Channel, and yet the pretended claims of Spain were being exercised with every circumstance of insult, injury, and barbarity.

The difficult situation in which the first kings of the House of Brunswick found themselves on points of this nature connects those sovereigns with the subject of our memoir. If they could not display their spirit as they evidently desired, they would at least show their appreciation of it in their subjects. Though Hawke, in consequence of the political struggles of George III.'s reign and his Whig politics, was somewhat neglected in the later part of his career, he had been an undoubted favourite with George II., who had carefully watched its commencement. First attracted by the contrast which his conduct displayed to that of too many in Mathews' battle off Toulon, the King never forgot his "own Captain." Sir John Barrow, Anson's biographer, asserts that it was his hero's merit to have discovered that of Hawke. But while the claim may be admitted to some extent, there is no reason for doubting the story that it was the King who, when the list of captains for promotion to the rank of admiral was submitted to him, finding that Boscawen, Hawke's junior, was selected, and not Hawke, personally insisted that the list should include him; and this was the turning point of his fortunes, for he might otherwise have been shelved. Immediately afterwards a second admiral was wanted for the home squadron; at Sir Peter Warren's instance Hawke was allowed to act in his place for one cruise; and within a few weeks he fought the finest action which had yet taken place, only indeed excelled in either war by his own final victory at Quiberon. It was to Hawke, as commander-in-chief, that the aged monarch entrusted the naval training of his grandson, Edward, Duke of York, though Lord Howe was what might be termed his special tutor. Some letters which have escaped the wreck of the Hawke correspondence will afford an insight into the manner in which it was supposed at that day that royal princes could be rendered fit for the naval service of their country.

The mention of the House of Brunswick leads to a question which may here be dismissed without discussion. We know how the Jacobite intrigues penetrated, all through the first half of the last century, into every department of public and private life. How far did they affect the Royal Navy? It may be safely answered:—scarcely at all; at least in the period with which this book is concerned, and probably very little before. With the exception of Captain Alexander Geddes, who lay under some, perhaps unfounded, suspicion, no such questions seem to have received any attention; and the navy went heartwhole with the Government in the critical years 1744 and 1745. Even Vernon's violent partisan Toryism, though, indeed, it subsequently appeared by his own publications that he had allowed his politics to interfere, as no naval officer ought, with his duty, did not prevent him from being placed in high command at the most critical moment. Along with him, Smith, Boscawen, John Byng, Knowles, Martin, and others were entrusted with the naval *cordon* which was skilfully drawn round the island. Hawke, no doubt, would have found his place at the point of danger, had he not been at that time in the Mediterranean.

There were difficulties enough in replacing their country in the position to which she was entitled by the heroism of previous generations; but the above was not one of them. Naval officers were so far from being tortured by the political difficulties which beset their predecessors at the period of the Revolution, that they were, on the contrary, inspirited in their most arduous labours by the reflection that they were performing their duty under the eye of a king in whom, whatever might be his private faults, they recognised a gallant patriotism akin to their own, and who took care to show that he was perfectly acquainted with all that was passing on the ocean. The conduct of George II. at Dettingen, however it might suit his caustic nephew, Frederick the Great, to make a joke of it, was never forgotten either in the British army or navy. Thrones are tolerably safe when princes risk their lives like common men in their country's battles. Towards the end of his reign, as we shall see, this respect developed into affectionate enthusiasm.

CHAPTER IV.

EARLY HISTORY AND SERVICES OF LORD HAWKE.

THERE is very little known about the ancestors in the paternal line of Admiral Lord Hawke. His grandfather, a London merchant, had, like his ancestors for many generations, been settled at Treriven (or Treraven), in the parish of St. Cleather, in Cornwall, about half-way between Launceston and Tintagel Head. Cornwall has thus the honour of having produced the two greatest admirals of the period, Hawke and Boscawen. But our admiral's father, Edward Hawke, was a barrister of Lincoln's Inn, who seems to have kept up no connection with that county, and to have retired to Bocking in Norfolk, where he died in 1718, at the age of fifty.

We know more about the admiral's mother, Elizabeth Bladen. She came of a family of Yorkshire squires, the Bladens of Hemsworth, who had been settled there since the time of Queen Elizabeth. Her father, like Edward Hawke, was a barrister of Lincoln's Inn (whence perhaps the connection), and her mother a daughter of Sir William Fairfax of Steeton, in Yorkshire. Her grandfather was Dr. Thomas Bladen, Dean of Ardfert, and her grandmother Sarah, daughter of the second Lord Blayney. Mr. Hawke was her second husband, she having been previously married to Colonel Ruthven.

What is more important in reference to her son's career is that she had a brother who was a person of considerable distinction, Colonel Martin Bladen, under whose auspices young Hawke was sent to sea, and to whom he owed much.*

Martin Bladen had served under Marlborough, was for a time Controller of the Mint, and held for many years the important office of "Commissioner of Trade and Plantations." To this office he perhaps owed his seat for Portsmouth, which he represented in five successive Parliaments; and as a considerable authority on commercial and colonial questions, he was thus able to afford Sir Robert Walpole efficient support in the debates which preceded the Spanish war of

---

* It may also be worth recording that she had another brother, William, who settled in Maryland, through whom the family name has been perpetuated in the United States. William's son, Colonel Thomas Bladen, became Governor of Maryland as well as an English Member of Parliament, and founded the town of Bladensburg, the scene of a modern battle which gives its name to the family of General Ross, the victor. Bladen County in North Carolina was named after Colonel Martin Bladen. To dismiss Colonel Thomas Bladen,—it may also be mentioned that he married the daughter of Sir Theodore Janssen, and that one of his daughters was married to General St. John, the other to the fourth Earl of Essex.

1739, and became a Privy Councillor. He combined with politics and official life a taste for literature, which he evinced by dedicating to his old chief, Marlborough, a translation of "Cæsar's Commentaries." In consequence of his marriage with the heiress of Aldborough Hatch, in Essex, he settled at that place, and died in 1746. His position gave him facilities for placing his nephew in the Royal Navy, and as the father died just when the boy was old enough to go to sea, he seems to have taken, up to the time of his death, a father's place to the young officer. It was he also who, as already said, bequeathed him, in all probability, the political opinions which the Portsmouth of those days required of her Member.

Young Hawke was now about twelve years old, having been born in 1705, a date which, it is necessary to say,—since the Peerages have agreed to bring him into the world in 1716—is ascertained from the monument at North Stoneham, near Southampton. Many notices of the admiral have been framed on the erroneous supposition of the later date, and which therefore contain references to his early promotion, the youthful age at which he fought his battles, and his want of preparatory service,—the whole of which is entirely gratuitous. On the contrary it is, we may safely say, owing to the fact of his having served a fairly long apprenticeship in the lower grades of his profession, that he was distinguished for his peculiar thoroughness of character and seamanship, as well as higher qualities. It is not going out of the way to observe that the best officers have not generally been those who have got on most quickly at first. Such so-called fortunate men are really unfortunate. They are tempted to ascribe to their own merits what was due to accident, and not knowing the feelings of less-favoured officers, to exhibit a deficiency of sympathy with them which is sure to avenge itself. Discipline has too often in such cases been only imperfectly acquired, while deference is all the more rigidly exacted from inferiors, because experience in the lower ranks has not taught its difficult lesson of the proper way to reconcile that deference with due independence of character. The course of our narrative will bring us into contact with cases of this sort.

The following account of Hawke at his first going to sea is from an Article in the "Westminster Magazine" of November, 1782, just after his death. The Article contains, however, so many errors that it must only be taken as a sort of record of traditions, quaintly enough expressed :—

"His uncle [Colonel Bladen] sent one morning for young Hawke, and said 'Ned, would you like to be a sailor?' 'Certainly, Sir,' replied the little hero. 'Are you willing to go now, or wait till you grow bigger?' 'This instant, Sir,' said young Hawke. In a few days his friends were consulted, but his father, who was, we believe, a merchant in the City [we have seen that he was a barrister] seemed totally averse to the sending an infant to encounter all the dangers and fatigues necessarily attendant upon such a profession. Young Ned was not, however, to be diverted from his purpose; he continually teased his mother; and she who possessed equal spirit and sensibility, was not proof against her son's perpetual entreaties. At length Mr. Hawke was prevailed upon, and the first cruise we believe our little midshipman made was under Sir Charles Wager who was sent to the relief of Gibraltar, at that time besieged by the Spaniards, in the year 1726, or the beginning of 1727. [This is certainly a mistake.] The morning of his departure to go aboard, his mother summoned all her fortitude, and addressed him with great calmness, or rather with a degree of pleasantry;—'Adieu, Ned,' says she, 'I shortly expect to see you a captain.' 'A captain,' replied he,—'Madam, I hope you will soon see me an admiral,' and instantly stepped into a coach which was waiting to convey him to his inn, whence he was to proceed to Portsmouth, where the fleet lay, without the least apparent emotion."

Such an anecdote, which might be told of hundreds of English boys, would not be worth copying if we could find a single other trace of the admiral's early years. But it must be said that this obscurity is shared by every other officer of the times. Until he becomes a captain, any notice even of the name of the ship in which an officer served as midshipman, lieutenant, or "master and commander," may, except in rare instances, be looked for in vain. The long previous peace was the chief cause of this obscurity. In war-time the history of a man who rose to greatness might be traced with perhaps a little more certainty. In the memoir above referred to, the writer skips from the boy's leaving home to his share in the battle of 1744, not long before he became an admiral,—which certainly gives point to his anecdote. Charnock simply observes that he—

passed with the greatest reputation through those inferior and subordinate stations which were necessary to qualify him for the command of a ship of war, in which he acquired a perfect knowledge of every branch and particular of his duty. He was, about the year 1733, made Commander of the "Wolf" sloop of war. On the 20th of March 173¾ he was promoted to the rank of Post-Captain, and appointed to the "Flamborough."

The author then makes an entire mistake about his next appointment (though in a Note he shows that he has come across him as commanding the "Portland" in 1741), and brings him, like the previous writer, as soon as possible to the battle of 1744, where he is at last on sure ground. This difficulty as to Hawke's early history he turns into a moral which illustrates the above remarks :—

Captain Hawke, during these his early years of service, laboured under a misfortune which has not unfrequently attended the bravest and best of men; and as no person ever lived to acquire a more just or honourable title to fame, even to a degree of popular adoration, so may it, to other brave men who pass a considerable part, if not the whole, of their lives, almost in actual obscurity, or at least in a state of inaction and unnoticed service, highly grating to a generous and warlike spirit, afford some consolation when they reflect that a commander so renowned as Hawke, laboured under the same inconvenience for ten years after he attained the rank of captain.*

By the help, however, of the documents preserved at the Record Office in London, and at Deptford, it is possible in some degree to fill up the gap. Though

---

* "*Biog. Nav.*," vol. iv. p. 263.

the earlier services of the future admiral were not distinguished, we at least know where they were performed, and can glean some indications of the coming man. Indeed there is a passage in one of his letters to the Admiralty in 1739, from which it might be inferred that he was engaged in that action with two Spanish ships of the line under Captain Thomas Durell which has already been noticed.* In this letter, written when about to sail for the West Indies, he states that he "had been six years first and last on the New England station," and that he had "four times made passages from the West Indies to Boston with Captain Durell," for the purpose of refitting at that port. It was unlikely he should have been one of Durell's Lieutenants without sharing in the voyage to Sal Tortugas, and sustaining the attack of the Spaniards. It would be quite natural that he should not talk about it, and equally so that he should obtain no promotion for it under Walpole's pacific *régime*, when such conduct as Durell's was a sort of "untoward event." It would be consistent with all this that the gallant Sir Chaloner Ogle, who commanded in the West Indies about that period, should become his patron and give him his first Commission into the "Wolf" in 1733. At any rate he was fortunate in serving at least four years of his West India service under so brave an officer as Durell, who, when the war broke out, was selected to command one of the ships of Vernon's squadron, but was detached by the Admiral

---

* P. 40.

to cruize for a rich Spanish fleet of merchant-ships then expected. A little later, his ship, the "Kent," formed one of the squadron which captured the Spanish "Princesa" before mentioned, in which service her Captain lost a hand: he died at sea in 1741.*

No other names of officers under whom Hawke learnt his profession can be recovered. As he had already spent many years on the New England and West Indian stations, so he was destined to spend there the whole period of his service as Commander and Post-captain, till he received his appointment to the "Berwick," and took his part in the great events of which the Mediterranean was the scene in 1744. In thus being trained for his work in those seas he resembled Nelson, but, unlike him, he never found himself there again. The variety of climates, the absence of dockyards, and the delicate nature of the service in the neighbourhood of the Spanish settlements, made it an excellent station for forming an officer. The violent gales of wind and hurricanes which beset the cruiser in those seas, and the necessity for periodically heaving down the ship, gave lessons in seamanship which could not be learnt so well elsewhere, and the responsibility of an officer was eminently called forth on that station. In the "Journal" of the "Flamborough,"—that of the "Wolf" cannot be found—we might have expected to find more indications of the "Spanish depreda-

---

* Charnock's "*Biog. Nav.*," vol. iv. p. 82.

tions" than we do; but these "Journals" are necessarily of the most brief and prosaic description. In the "Journal" of the "Portland," which commences with the war, the thing which strikes one as most remarkable is that the war seems scarcely to have affected her at all. The Captain's time had not yet come.

Dull and uninteresting as these Journals are, they must not be altogether passed over. We are attempting to understand one of the greatest officers England has produced; and as no one becomes great, any more than he becomes base, all at once, it would be most unphilosophical to neglect the traces which we may be able to discover, even in these details, of the processes which went to form his character. The reader may be assured that only those which are strictly essential for this purpose are placed before him.

The first entry in the "Journal" of the "Flamborough," a small "frigate" of twenty guns, which, like the "Wolf" and other vessels, was kept out for years and years together on the West Indian station, is dated from Port Antonio in Jamaica, and runs:—
"March 20, 1734; this day was appointed Commander of H. M. ship "Flamborough" by Sir Chaloner Ogle, Kt."; the word "commander" being often used as synonymous with "captain." Jamaica is the headquarters of the ship for the whole of the year and a half (March 20, 1733¾ to September 5, 1735,) during which Hawke commanded her. During the first nine months he careened the ship twice at Port Royal, and once lost his bowsprit and foremast in a gale of wind

while at anchor. In 1735 he is sent to Campeachy, and receives the English "Factors" with 11 guns; is cruizing off Matanzas in Cuba, where the Spanish Governor would not allow him to water the ship, in consequence of which he has to put his crew on short allowance; heaves down at Port Royal; proceeds to England, sighting Bermuda on the way, and pays off at Spithead.

Of the next four years there is no record whatever; and as there were no signs of war, and as we know that our Captain married during this period, it is highly probable that he spent it on shore. It is also probable that it was the first time he had so spent since he went to sea,—a period of sixteen years, for the two last of which he had been in responsible command. He was now an experienced officer in his thirtieth year, and had passed through a more prosperous career than most of his brother officers; though fortunate in escaping the rapid promotion to the rank of Post-captain which some others, who were born, as the saying is, "with a silver spoon in their mouth," succeeded in obtaining. Colonel Bladen's interest, and perhaps his own merits, were enough to give him a fair lift out of the mass of unfortunate men who never got farther than lieutenants, if so far. Smollett, in his vilely coarse novel, "Roderick Random," describing the Navy at this period, and exaggerating no doubt every defect of a service for which he was entirely unfitted, declares that a Lieutenant was actually appointed to the command of a small vessel at the age of eighty. But no doubt, all through the century, it was common enough for officers to serve on for life in the junior ranks; and after a while they even got used to it, and expected nothing else. What could be expected of *them?*

The exact date of Captain Hawke's marriage is not known within a year or two, but it was probably in 1738, when he was 33 and his bride 18. It could not have been later, as the Register of Barking in Essex records the burial of two infant daughters of "Captain Edward Hawke," one on September 13th, 1739, and the other on April 3rd, 1740. Of his lady there is nothing more to tell than can be gathered from her pedigree and her monument. She was "the daughter and sole heir of Walter Brooke, Esq. of Burton Hall, Co. York," her father having inherited Gateforth in direct descent from Humphrey Brooke, who, like the Bladens, had settled in Yorkshire in the time of Elizabeth, and bought the manor of Gateforth from Lord Darcy in 1564. Catharine Brooke was also, through her mother, the heiress of the Hammonds of Scarthingwell, Towton, and Saxton in Yorkshire; and these properties she brought with her to her husband. The family had lived at Scarthingwell Hall, as a better house than Towton Hall, but it was the latter property which Lord Hawke selected for his title. It was a very natural marriage, as the lady was connected with the Bladens, her uncle having been married to Catharine Maria Frances, sister of Colonel Bladen and of Mrs. Hawke, her husband's mother.

The pompous inscriptions on monuments are

proverbially untrustworthy as to their laudations of moral excellences and personal gifts; but if we may trust what is stated in the present case as to Lady Hawke with the same confidence as we certainly can the account of the merits of her husband, the pair fairly exemplified the words of the poet—

None but the brave deserve the fair.

It may be as well to give the whole inscription here, as it stands in North Stoneham church, the parish in which Swathling, Lord Hawke's principal residence, was situated.

This monument is sacred to the memory of Edward Hawke, Lord Hawke, Baron of Towton, in the county of York, Knight of the Bath, Admiral and Commander-in-Chief of the Fleet, Vice-Admiral of Great Britain, &c., who died October 17th, 1781, aged 76. The bravery of his soul was equal to the dangers he encountered; the cautious intrepidity of his deliberations superior even to the conquests he obtained. The annals of his life compose a period of naval glory unparalleled in later times: for wherever he sailed victory attended him. A prince unsolicited conferred on him dignities which he disdained to ask.

This Monument is also sacred to the memory of Catharine, Lady Hawke, his wife, the beauty of whose person was excelled only by the accomplished elegance of her mind. She died October 27th, 1756, aged 36. In the conjugal, parental, and social duties of private life, they were equalled by few, excelled by none.

The fact of the two first children of this marriage having been buried as infants in Barking churchyard, suggests, what we might have expected from the manner in which Colonel Martin Bladen fulfilled his duty to his nephew, that the young couple found a residence either with him at Aldborough Hatch, which was in Barking parish, or close by him. In all four of the tattered letters from him to Hawke which have but just escaped destruction, dated in 1739 and 1742, he uses the language of a father, both towards his "dear Ned" and "Kitty" his wife; and we may fairly suppose that he had been the person concerned in bringing about the marriage, which his position as well as family connection would facilitate. The two first of the above-mentioned letters are written when, at the opening of the war, Hawke had just commissioned the "Portland" frigate of 50 guns; the others towards the close of his Commission. The former are chiefly concerned with recommendations of officers in whom he felt an interest. The second of them begs that his nephew, John Bladen, who goes to sea with Hawke,—not apparently on his first voyage,—may be "recommended to the care of the Chaplain and of the Master of the ship," and ends thus:—

And now, my dear child, as this may possibly be the last letter you can receive from me before you sail, let me recommend you in the sincerest manner to the protection of Providence. May God preserve you and prosper you in all your undertakings; and if it may contribute anything to the satisfaction of your mind to know that during your absence all possible care shall be taken of my niece, be assured that, as well for her own sake as for yours, nothing shall be wanting that either my wife or I can do for her, and that we will endeavour to make her abode with us agreeable to her.

This letter is dated "October 2nd, 1739," and was therefore written within a month of the death of the infant daughter of the young couple, which must have added no little to the trial of their parting. As the uncle sends his "service to Kitty and his blessing to

Jack," she was apparently with him at Portsmouth up to the last moment.

By the next letter from the Colonel, dated May 29th, 1742, it would seem that "Kitty" had gone out to join her husband at Barbadoes, and that the Captain's mother was still living. With her, probably, Hawke's only sister, Frances, who married the son of Dr. Henry Maule, Bishop of Dromore, lived till that event took place. He had no brothers. But the letter has some slight interest of its own, as it was written soon after the fall of Walpole's Ministry, and may be given *in extenso*.

DEAR NED, ALBROHATCH, May 29, 1742.

I send this letter at a venture by my friend Ling, who goes in Sir Thomas Robinson's service to Barbadoes, though I am very doubtful whether he will reach the island before you come from thence. If he does he will be able to give you an account of my family, to which I shall only add that by a letter I lately received from your mother, she was then in good health, and that my nephew, Tom Bladen, is made Governor of Maryland, and sails at the same time with Sir Thomas Robinson. You will have seen by some of my former, if they came to your hands, the changes that have lately happened in the Administration. Sir Robert Walpole is no longer in the Treasury, and there is a Committee of Secrecy appointed by the House of Commons to examine into his conduct for the last ten years of his Administration. But the conviction his friends have of his innocence and integrity has procured him very great support, and the King has created him Earl of Orford. Lord Wilmington is at present at the head of the Treasury; Mr. Sandys, Chancellor of the Exchequer; Sir John Rushout, Mr. Gybbon [*sic*] and Major Compton, Lords of the Treasury. There has likewise been a clean sweep at the Admiralty; but I hope I may have some friends amongst the new Lords at that Board that will upon my account afford you their protection. Pray give my blessing to Jack, and excuse me to my niece if I do not write to her on this occasion. Pray

God send you a safe voyage to England, and grant us all a happy meeting at this place. In the meantime I send you and Kitty my best wishes, and am sincerely, dear Ned, your very affectionate uncle and most obedient servant,

M. BLADEN.

The last of the letters, dated from "Hanover Square, 29th January, 174$\frac{3}{4}$, shows that the old politician had not miscalculated:—

DEAR NED,

I was this morning at the Admiralty to inquire what they intend to do with you, and am informed the Lords design to pay-off your ship in a short time, and I believe at Portsmouth. I have likewise been told that they cannot confirm your Commission in favour of Jack Bladen because you are not a Flag, but that he must come to Town and pass another examination, whereupon they will give him a Commission, and order his pay to commence from the time that he has acted as Lieutenant in the "Portland," for which purpose I think it is absolutely necessary for him to set out to London with all convenient speed. I believe he either has or will receive directions from Mr. Corbet [the Secretary to the Admiralty] to that effect. My colleague, Mr. Cavendish, has already laid in his claim for another ship for you. But after so long a voyage I think you should be allowed a little time to spend with your friends on shore. It is some consolation, however, that I have some friends at the new Board; and let me know what you think best for your service upon this occasion, and you may be assured I shall do everything in my power for your advantage. All my family send you and Kitty their best wishes, and I am always, with perfect truth and esteem, dear Ned, your very affectionate uncle and sincere friend,

M. BLADEN.

In these letters we have some dim outlines of a happy family-picture; and may well believe, after reading them, that the domestic character of the future hero was as faultless as the inscription on the monument asserts. From the mention of "Kitty" it seems clear that she came home in her husband's ship.

We shall only hear of her once more, and that incidentally. She certainly did not make any more such voyages. The eldest son, who succeeded to his father's title, was born on April 29th, 1744; the second in December 1746, and the third in 1750. He had also a daughter, Catharine, who appears to have been the comfort of her father's life in declining years.

Swathling became the home of the family. Perhaps it was not till after the death of the good uncle that they moved from Essex, and probably in connection with the seat for Portsmouth which fell to Hawke in 1747. To live on his Yorkshire property was out of the question for one who was tied for the next sixteen years to the south coast of England by the bonds of incessant sea service, as well as for a still longer time by Parliamentary obligations. In his later years the Admiral had a house at Sunbury in Middlesex, where he died. His mother died, amongst her Yorkshire kin, and was buried at Bolton Percy.

We have seen that Lady Hawke died young. It must have added to the trying position in which her husband found himself in the Mediterranean, when sent out to supersede Byng in command of the fleet, to be absent from her side when she was cut off at that early age. He never married again. If we may judge by some indications in letters still extant, his eldest son grew up to take a full share in his father's confidence. To conclude this scanty notice of the early days of Lord Hawke, it may be remarked that subsequent generations of the family have shown their appreciation of the good man to whom they owed so much, by perpetuating both his names, Martin, and Bladen, in their children.

In order to make the domestic history intelligible it has been necessary to pass over the period of Hawke's service in the "Portland," to which we must now return. This ship had been commissioned, and for some time commanded, by the Hon. John Byng; but on July 30th, 1739, by which time the war had really commenced, though not yet declared, Hawke received his Commission to her,—no doubt through the influence of his uncle,—and was ordered to prepare to take out Byng's brother, the Hon. Robert Byng, as Governor of Barbadoes.

Six days before this, Vernon had sailed with his squadron for Portobello. Hawke was perhaps fortunate in not being concerned with his operations, which, as already said, eventually coloured with misfortune and failure the career of nearly all who came within their sphere. Nor was his ship to be one of Anson's immortal band. She was to make Barbadoes her head-quarters, and to protect that and the adjacent islands, convoying fleets of merchant ships to the Tortugas and elsewhere, and taking her chance of whatever might turn up on that part of the West India Station. If the French had followed up the policy they at first adopted, of making a vigorous effort to support Spain in the West Indies, according to their Treaty, the "Portland" would no doubt have supplied her Captain with some earlier experience of active service in war than he actually gained; but a series of storms, and then—in consequence of the death of the Emperor Charles VI.—a change of policy, brought their three West Indian squadrons to a futile end; and the period of nearly four years which elapsed before the "Portland" was paid off will throw but little light on the subject of our memoir. What we obtain is but a glimpse or two of preparatory training before his really public life began.

The earliest letter of Hawke's to the Secretary of the Admiralty is dated from his ship at Spithead, September 18th, 1739; and it is from this that the suggestive notice as to his previous West Indian service has been quoted. It occurs in connection with a request that he might be permitted to refit his ship each year during the hurricane months at Boston, rather than, as was the custom, at the island of Antigua. He points out that when he sailed with Captain Durell he had observed the great benefits of the practice; that the passage only took 17 or 18 days; that the refreshments for the crew to be obtained at Boston were of a far better kind than at Antigua, and the cost of them "less than even in England." "It is generally the fatigue of heaving the ship down that causes a sickness among the people, but at this place we can work the men with safety." To this very sensible request the Admiralty give their assent. The passage between the ports led, however, on one occasion to disaster; and the permission was withdrawn,—not however on that account, but because the West India merchants complained of so long an absence. It has not been till quite modern times that the sanitary considerations which Hawke so well understood have been systematically applied towards our seamen, so that by periodical alternations from bad climates to good, the diseases attendant on prolonged service in the former may, at least to some extent, be evaded.

The Captain's Journal shows that he had not laid an unreasonable stress upon the danger attending the unhealthiness of cruising in those seas. For months together, not a week occurs without the record of the death of some of the crew; and the notices grow so monotonous that the Captain soon drops the formal "departed this life," and merely writes "died." But, though he had passed so much of his life in the West Indies, we never meet with any indication of his own ill-health till much later in life, when the overwhelming fatigues and responsibilities of his commands tell heavily upon his constitution, which could hardly have escaped previous damage had he not been a man of temperate habits. The Peace of Paris probably saved his life for many years.

No doubt a large part of this great unhealthiness of the "Portland's" crew was due to the state of the ship; as indeed it probably was in most cases. She was extremely old, and ought to have been broken up long before. In a letter to the Secretary of the Admiralty, on his arrival in England to pay off, he says his ship is always leaking. "Whenever it rains there is not a man in the ship that has even a dry place to sleep in, she being what the carpenters call 'iron-sick,'" which meant, no doubt, that the wood was too rotten to hold the iron bolts. He goes on to report that he would proceed to the Downs, but is afraid to move farther than Portland without another ship in company. The state of Anson's ships will recur to the memory as a pendant to this picture; which will receive further illustration from the following extract out of the Captain's Journal. To naval men at least it may not be unacceptable.

On November 6th, 1741, the "Portland," her annual refit being completed, was lying at Boston. Having on that day "fired 13 guns, it being Gunpowder Treason," she sailed for Barbadoes on November 8th. On November 14th, being in Lat. 39° 30' N. and Long. 10° 20' E.—*i.e.* East from Boston, for the reckoning of Longitude from Greenwich had not yet become the rule,—she fell in with a hurricane which began from South, changed to W.S.W., and blew, finally, from N.W. On that day Hawke writes :—

Found ship making eight inches of water an hour from two leaks in the larboard wing under the wale. Lay-to under mainsail and mizen.

. Sunday, Nov. 15: Hard gales, with violent squalls of lightning and rain, with a great sea from the S. and S.S.E. Found our mainmast sprung below the partners, lowered the main-yard, unbent the mainsail, and set the mizen staysail. In the meantime the carpenters clapped on two fishes to it, but to no purpose, the spikes being no sooner drove but started with the labour of the ship and badness of the mast. Sent up hands into the top to unbend the maintopsail and send the yard down. Struck the topmast and saved what we could, but to no purpose. The ship rolling, and the mast fetching such way, was obliged to call the men down again; and night coming on I called a consultation of my officers to know whether we had not better cut the mainmast away; and it was their opinions it ought to be done as speedily as possible, lest upon its going away it should tear up the upper deck and endanger the pumps; upon which, stripped the mainyard and launched it overboard, cut away the rigging and mainmast, cleared ourselves of it; then loosed the foresail and swayed the yard two-thirds up, lowered the mizen-yard, and scuttled the lower deck to ease the ship from the great quantity of water that lay between decks. At 9 P.M., it blowing extremely hard, the foremast rolled overboard, giving way in the partners, ripped up part of the forecastle, carried away the larboard cathead and spritsail-yard. Cut away all our rigging, and cleared ourselves of that, but could not save anything. We had scarcely cleared ourselves of this mast before the mizen-mast went away, and carried the yard, awning, and life-rail with it. We cleared ourselves of it as fast as possible, but could not save anything. Got a maintopgallant-sail for a sprit-sail; it blew away. We bent another, and scudded until daylight; then got up topgallant-masts for jury-masts until the weather would permit us to get better, there being a very great sea.

Monday, Nov. 16: The wind being abated, our people employed fitting jury-masts and rigging for them. In the morning raised sheers, and got up a maintopmast for a foremast, a topsail-yard for a fore-yard, a topgallant-mast for a top-mast, and a topgallant-yard for a topsail-yard; bent the sails and set them.

Tuesday, Nov. 17: Got up a spare top-mast for a main-mast, and a lower studding-sail boom for a main-yard. In the morning got up a maintopgallant-mast for a maintop-mast, and a spritsail-topsail-yard for a maintopsail-yard; bent the sails and set them.

For nearly the whole of this time he reports "a large swell and fresh gales"; so that to have jury-rigged his ship in two days was not a bad performance. On December 12th he arrives at Barbadoes, buys new masts, and refits.

In his letter to the Admiralty, describing the disaster in nearly the same language, he reports that the stumps of the old masts when taken out were found to be so rotten that they crumbled to powder, and that a stick was driven a full yard into the foremast. The anxiety he shows to convince their Lordships that every care had been taken to save the spars, suggests that the Board was regarded even in those days with a due amount of awe; and he ends with a characteristic ejaculation;—" Thank God, in all the misfortune I lost not one man." That was certainly no small praise to his seamanship, judgment, and—perhaps we ought to say—humanity.

The question arises—how could the masts have borne the strain of constant heaving-down when in such a state?—but the support afforded them by outriggers and tackles under the exact seamanship of those days did in reality take off nearly all the strain. What a perfect knowledge of everything connected with a ship must such constant practice have given! The multiplication of dockyards has made the practice unnecessary. Probably not a dozen officers now alive have ever belonged to a ship which was hove down, and themselves assisted at the performance.

In Hawke's last letter from the "Portland" before paying off, he presses on the Admiralty the claims of some of his officers with a touch of humour:—" Had they been in England during the time of so many preferments they might have stood some chance of coming in with the rest of mankind."

This brief sketch of Hawke's early career may conclude with the remark that Sir John Barrow, the author of the "Life of Lord Anson," must have taken little advantage of the stores of information open to him as Secretary to the Admiralty, when he could make the following remark:—"Hawke at this time (1747) was an officer not much known, and from the year 1734, when he was made captain, had chiefly remained on shore until, in 1743, he was appointed to the 'Berwick,' of 74 guns, and ordered to join Admiral Mathews."* We shall see that he was extremely well known some years before 1747. As to his "chiefly remaining on shore" it is evident that this writer, like most others, was unaware that Hawke had already commanded both the "Flamborough" and the "Portland." The mistake is possibly attributable to the fact that in the lists of ships given in the books of the last century, the name "Hawes" is placed opposite that of the "Portland," instead of that of our hero; and people have copied from one another without enquiry.

---

* P. 171.

CHAPTER V.

LORD HAWKE'S SHARE, AS CAPTAIN, IN THE BATTLE OF
ADMIRAL MATHEWS OFF TOULON, 1744.

COLONEL Martin Bladen's good-natured desire to have a little of his nephew's company at Aldborough Hatch was very sparingly gratified. Captain Hawke paid off the "Portland" on March 17th, 174$\frac{2}{3}$; and three months afterwards, on June 28th, 1743, his first letter to the Admiralty is dated from H.M.S. "Berwick," a ship of 70 guns. Neither he nor his uncle were likely to let the Admiralty alone at such a moment; for the junction of the French fleet at Brest under De Court with that of the Spaniards in the Mediterranean, which had been previously effected in 1741, and had then obliged Admiral Haddock to decline an engagement with a force double his own, was now again likely to be dangerous. Reinforcements had been sent out under Commodore Lestock, who, on Haddock's resignation, was raised to the rank of Rear-admiral, and, in temporary command of the whole fleet, blockaded the combined fleets in Toulon. But more ships were wanted in order to match the two fleets if they should attempt to come out of harbour; and a battle on a grand scale was expected.

To command this formidable English armament Admiral Mathews had been appointed in 1742; and the "Berwick" was one of the last ships added to his numbers. Fortunately we have now the advantage of being able to refer to her Captain's own official letters preserved in the family, but lost at the Admiralty, or at any rate not to be found now. Later on, we discover letters at the Record Office which are not to be found in the private collection; and, curiously enough, these are some of the most interesting, since they are papers of a more private, and therefore characteristic nature, which the writer did not choose to trust to his own Letter-book. The two collections in fact very conveniently supplement one another.

We are first of all introduced to the subject of Impressment. It may be well to know what it really was in those days, instead of gathering our ideas from fiction.

From the moment of the Captain's appointment we find ourselves in the midst of a whirl and bustle which indicates plainly enough the difficulty of the contest in which the country had embarked. The great fleets in the Mediterranean and West Indies had taken up all the seamen who could be in any manner obtained; and to man the "Berwick" there was nothing for it but a "hot press." The Admiralty are hastening the ship to sea, but where are the men? Hawke has to report that "the Pilot will not take charge of her" down the river, from Deptford, where she is fitting out, "unless she has at least four hundred men on board." He has to send a Tender to cruise off Hull and Yarmouth "upon the trade." When they are obtained, he has infinite difficulty to keep them from deserting. On August 12th he writes:—

> I expect the Tender up the river every hour, and shall be very glad when she comes, as her men will be of great assistance to me in carrying my ship to the Nore, where I long to be, as I am in hopes I shall be able to pick up some men myself when we get there.

On July 11th, having sent off 40 men in the Tender, he writes:—

> I should not have got these men to have gone in her if I had not sent midshipmen all about the town to look after them, and they picked them up by one and two at a time; and as we got them, put them on board the Tender who lay at anchor, to secure them till she was ready to sail.

However, when he had obtained men in sufficient numbers to enable him to drop down the river, his account of their quality is instructive. On August 23rd, he writes from the Nore:—

> I beg their Lordships' permission to acquaint them that among the pressed men sent me down by the Regulating Captains there are several of them very little, puny, weakly fellows that have never been at sea, and I think any officer must allow, can be of little or no service. The reason why I did not complain of them before was because I was willing to get the ship to the Nore as soon as the wind offered fair. This is likewise the case with the men that are come from the "Princess Royal," there being several of them poor little sickly fellows that are of no service, and are more properly to be termed boys than men; and though a few of these lads are serviceable aboard of ship, a great number of them distress a large ship like this greatly, and what is worse, most of these poor creatures are now sick; but I shall

not presume to put them on shore unless their Lordships will be so good as to give me leave, though there are several of them that should they stay on board will breed a sickness in the ship. ... I beg their Lordships' pardon for mentioning this affair, but I thought it my duty to do it, for when a ship is very badly manned she can be but of very little or no service.

Exactly what he foretold came to pass. He was detained for a convoy, and set sail as second in command under Captain Burrish of the "Dorsetshire," who had the charge of it. On October 27th they are in the Mediterranean, and he reports to his senior officer that he had

123 working men ill; out of that number 84 have fever; 6 or 8 of these are dangerously ill; the rest are mostly troubled with scurvy. The greatest part of these fell ill since we left Gibraltar, particularly these two or three nights past, and what is worse, the men falling ill by tens and twenties every day, we have great reason to fear it will go quite through the ship's company. We can no ways account for the men falling ill so fast otherwise than that a great number of them are lately come from the East Indies, and others of them are raw men picked up by the pressgangs in London, and are poor, puny fellows; and the ship being raw and green is consequently damp, notwithstanding all my endeavours to keep her clean and dry, which I have taken care to do ever since we have been out.

I am extremely concerned that I should have to acquaint you with this, but as it may be some time before we get to Port Mahon, having a convoy with us, and my men falling down so fast, I am apprehensive we shall not have men enough to carry the ship thither, if we should be out many days longer. I should be sorry to desire to leave you, as I know you have a troublesome charge with you; but as this is the case, unless Providence puts a stop to this disorder, I wish we may not become troublesome to you likewise. I am therefore to beg you will be pleased to consider whether it will be most for the service for us to make the best of our way to Mahon by ourselves, there to put our people on shore, or to continue with you.

Whichever it is I shall be satisfied, as I am sensible you will do for the best; and I beg you will be persuaded that I am very sincerely, sir,   Your obedient, humble servant,   E. HAWKE.

On November 6th, Captain Burrish having still detained him, he in more pressing language, reiterates his request. No less than 27 of his men are now dangerously ill; his marines are suffering; the surgeon is ill, and his first-mate dead; and only a couple of very young men left to look after the health of the ship's company. At last he reaches Port Mahon, and lands his sick; but many more of his crew are still falling ill. Nevertheless, immediately afterwards, he reports to Commodore Graves, that he is revictualling his ship, and will soon be ready for sea. He probably picked up some men from merchant ships.

Such lengthy extracts would be unjustifiable if they did not both exhibit the real state of the navy at that date, and enhance the merit of Hawke's performances on the day of battle which quickly came. With so little time to make seamen and gunners out of such a miserable crew, and after such a sweeping epidemic, one would hardly have expected that the "Berwick" was to be the only ship to capture one of the enemy, and her Captain to be marked out for future greatness by the manner in which she behaved that day.

Between the date of this correspondence and that of the battle off Toulon we have neither letters nor Journal to guide us. But we know that on December 30th the Commander-in-Chief was, in virtue of his office as Ambassador to the Court of Sardinia, at Turin, that he heard on that day of the departure of the French squadron, under M. De Roquefeuil, from Brest, and, expecting that the combined fleets would now come out of Toulon, despatched orders to his ships at Port Mahon and elsewhere to meet him off that harbour. Among those which joined his fleet on January 11th, 174¾, was the "Berwick"; and on February 8th his whole force was assembled in the Bay of Hiéres, near Toulon. Meanwhile the Spaniards having received, it would seem, orders to fight, and the French orders to assist them, both came out of Toulon unmolested, and the two great fleets, each of 28 line-of-battle ships, were in sight of each other off that port on February 9th.* The English had the advantage in the number of frigates and 50-gun ships (which, for the first time, were not allowed to form in line of battle), and in the total number of guns; the enemy in the size of their ships, their speed,—as they were all clean, while the English were foul,—and the number of men on board.

The battle about to be described is perhaps the most difficult to understand of all those fought by Englishmen. Being an unpleasant subject, it is passed over cursorily by our later historians of every description, and indeed it could not be expected that they should afford the space necessary to deal with so complicated a series, both of engagements and Courts-

---

* It must be remembered that the English had not yet adopted the New Style; so that eleven days must be added to make the dates correspond with those already in use on the Continent.

martial. It would be agreeable to leave it in exactly the same condition; but Hawke's share in the matter makes that course impossible. It was out of the Slough of Despond in which this battle shows the navy to have been sunk, that Anson and Hawke dragged their noble profession. If, on a review of the whole, a conclusion is arrived at not exactly coincident with that which historians copy from one another, it must be remembered that, as the temptation to judge of this purely professional question from a political point of view was certainly too strong for the Courtsmartial concerned, so it proved, in general, too much for the virtue of those who wrote on the subject within a hundred years of the time, whether of one side of politics or the other.

It must be premised, to account for the renewed vigour of the French at this moment, as well as for Mathews' position in the Mediterranean, that a change had lately taken place in the international relations of the European Powers, and that it was brought about by the following circumstances. The first and most important of these was the uncompromising attitude of Maria Theresa, so recently hard pressed by the King of Prussia,—she having found herself encouraged by the leading part which England had taken at Dettingen and elsewhere, but still more taking counsel of her own noble heart.

The second was the death of the great Minister, Fleury, which had brought Cardinal Tencin to the head of French affairs. He had been indebted for his Cardinal's Hat to the English Pretender, and deriving encouragement from the feeble condition of the Pelham Government, enlisted all France in the Jacobite cause. The projected invasion under Marshal Saxe, and Admiral De Roquefeuil failed indeed; but it issued in the Rebellion of 1745.

Lastly, the practical sympathy for the cause of his family in France and Spain evinced by Charles, the Bourbon King of Naples, whom Walpole, under Fleury's fascination, had allowed to succeed peaceably to that throne, had made it necessary to take strong measures with him. Admiral Mathews had accordingly sent Commodore William Martin with a squadron to bring him to reason. This, as is well known, he did in true nautical fashion. Finding that he should otherwise be the dupe of diplomatic evasions, he informed the King's Ministers that he should open fire unless he had a favourable answer in half an hour's time.* As Naples was in no state to resist, the King had to submit; but he never forgot the insult. Fifteen years later he became King of Spain; and his junction with France, at what he supposed to be a critical moment for England, has been considered due to his undying hostility.†

For the moment the effect of these proceedings was to band the whole Bourbon family in a close union around the young Louis XV., who had just come of age, and was anxious to take an active part in affairs. France and Spain signed the Treaty of Fon-

---

* Letter from Commodore Martin: Charnock's "*Biog. Nav.*," vol. iv. p. 74.

† Coxe's "Kings of Spain of the House of Bourbon."

tainebleau, by which both nations were to assist each other with all their forces against Great Britain; and intrigues of every kind, hatched in the petty States of Italy, gave full occupation to Mathews and his successors. Austrian Tuscany and Sardinian Piedmont were surrounded by a circle of enemies or questionable friends; but fortunately for those States these could, as long as the British fleet was supreme in the Mediterranean, be effectually dealt with on the coast of Italy.

Hence the importance of the Admiral's position. He had to coerce Genoa and other petty States; to act as Ambassador at the Court of Turin, and to keep up the closest connection with that of Florence; while at the same time he was to guard the coasts of France and Italy, and to be ready to engage both French and Spaniards should they attempt to come out of Toulon.

Some amusing references to Mathews and his Captains at this time occur in the correspondence of Horace Mann, the Minister at Florence, with his friend Horace Walpole. Mathews evinces much eccentricity, and goes by the name of "Il Furibondo"; but his spirited behaviour had a great effect.

Tencin's obvious policy was to overwhelm the English in the Mediterranean before they could muster sufficient force to resist; and thus to set Italy free. He hoped at the same time to paralyse England, and force her to withdraw from the assistance of Austria, by means of the invasion which Marshal Saxe was to effect under cover of Roquefeuil's fleet. It was well conceived. We have seen what became of the invasion: we are now to witness the fact that even the feeble and disreputable battle of Toulon was decisive enough to dissipate the Cardinal's plans for the emancipation of the Mediterranean.

Thus began, openly and in earnest, the tremendous struggle of Great Britain with France and Spain, which, since Spain by herself could make no real resistance at sea, had hitherto scarcely taken shape. The animosity with which it now commenced was never appeased till the battles of three generations concluded by leaving Europe pretty much in the state in which it at present exists.

Who could believe that the chance of a decisive battle, thus offered at such a critical moment, should have been thrown away by the diabolical hatred of the two chief English commanders towards one another? Yet so it was. How it arose has never been satisfactorily explained; but it was probably in connection with politics. Both Mathews and Lestock were Members of Parliament, the former a Tory, but not a Jacobite; the latter a Whig. Both were men of approved courage and professional reputation. But so far pronounced was this antagonism that Mathews is said to have made it a condition of his accepting the appointment that Lestock should be recalled. Perhaps he only expressed a wish to this effect; but no attention was paid to it. It is not altogether surprising, though most blamable, that the Admiralty should have failed to perceive that it could be a matter of importance; but the following account of the two men will explain the phenomenon. Everything in this battle turned upon their conduct and character.

Mathews had seen much and good service; had commanded a line-of-battle ship with the highest credit in Sir George Byng's action, and shown himself not only a man of decided character, but possessed of some cultivation and general ability. The former quality he displayed much after the same fashion as "Tom of Ten Thousand." * Not long before the engagement about to be described he was at Villafranca with a few ships, when a French man of war passed without paying " the usual and expected compliment" to the English flag. The two countries were not yet at open war. He ordered one of his ships to slip and pursue her; and the French commander continuing obstinate, his vessel was immediately sunk by a broadside from the Englishman.†

His pride also went before his destruction. Let us hear the most favourable account that can be given of it by a writer partial to the admiral:—

> Mr. Mathews is said to have been austere, haughty, and imperious, when in fact he was nothing more than a severe disciplinarian, a rigid observer of forms, and a man who, when in a subordinate station, as he had always paid the utmost obedience to command, so he now justly thought he had every reason to expect and insist on a similar conduct in those who acted in a subordinate station under him. His pride was not that of a vain upstart, ridiculously puffed up by an unexpected exaltation to a high national trust, but of a man who entertained

---

* P. 102.
† Campbell's "Lives of the Admirals," vol. iv. p. 39.

a proper sense of his own dignity and command; most feelingly alive to every slight insult, which he did not consider as merely personal to himself,—for that perhaps he might have forgiven, but as an indignity offered to his station and an injury to the service of his country.*

The manner in which the Admiral received his second in command, when they first met, scarcely bears out this favourable view. It came out at the Court-martial that though Lestock had sent a frigate to meet his chief, which had missed him, the admiral would not listen to any excuse, and reprimanded him severely and publicly, before some officers of the King of Sardinia who happened to be present.

But there is not much to be said for Lestock. He also was a man of violent temper, to whom such treatment suggested a sullen revenge. He had served with credit under both Byng and Wager, but may perhaps have suffered, like others, by his West Indian service under Vernon. It was he who gallantly took the forts of Bocca Chica. It was he, on the other hand, who behaved in as arrogant a manner to the gallant Captain Barnett, as Mathews now behaved to him.

Confiding too much in his abilities, which were very great, and demanding both from his equals and superiors in command a deference which all men are ready gratuitously to offer, but pay most reluctantly on compulsion, he found himself on many occasions in the irksome state of being neither loved nor feared. Success requires true benevolence of heart.†

---

* Charnock's "*Biog. Nav.*"
† *Ibid.*

It seems also that, in addition to his other faults, he was a man of loose moral character.*

The relations between the two chiefs exhibited themselves on the very eve of the engagement. On February 20th, the two fleets having been manœuvring all day without engaging, the English anchored for the night in the Bay of Hiéres.

> As soon as they came to an anchor, Vice Admiral Lestock went on board the "Namur," Mathews' flag-ship, with a design to concert with the Admiral on the proper measures for attacking the combined fleet with advantage. Admiral Mathews did not on this occasion treat Mr. Lestock with the respect due to his rank; for, on the Vice Admiral asking him if he had any particular orders and instructions for him, he said, "No"; observed it was a cold night, and desired him to go on board his own ship again.†

Probably there were faults of manner on both sides; but it was exactly this want of concert that led to disaster. At the Courtmartial it was much pressed by witnesses against Mathews that he held no Councils of War, and the questions of the Court implied that he should have held them; to which he replied that there was no occasion to do so. Now Councils of War have generally done more harm than good; and the Admiral was technically right; but the resolution to take no one into his confidence, and to leave everything to the moment of battle, could never have been adopted by a man of even Mathews' ability unless his judgment had been warped by the deadly feud which existed between him and Lestock.

---

* Stanhope's "History of England," vol. iii. p. 323.
† Beatson's "Naval and Military Memoirs," vol. i. p. 197.

The 10th also passed without an engagement. The winds were light, and though the combined fleet contrived to form a very fair line, partly no doubt owing to more favourable airs, the English were straggling about in all directions, and, when night came on, were four or five miles off the enemy. On the morning of the 11th the distance between the fleets was found to have increased; so also was the distance between the divisions of the two fleets respectively; the English line, if so it could be called, which was to windward, extending over something like nine miles, while the enemy's line, though less extended, covered about six miles. Both were standing to the Southward with light Easterly winds, the combined fleet closing up and making sail, while the Rear Division of the English, which was widely separated from the rest, never got up till the close of the day. It cannot be stated with certainty whether this took place through the Admiral's signals not being wisely made, or through the influence of partial currents affecting, so near the shore, in such light winds, some of the scattered ships more than others, or whether, as Mathews asserted, through wilful negligence on the part of Lestock. Thus, as the day wore on, the question which presented itself to Mathews, was whether he should let the hostile fleet escape, as he believed it certainly would if he shortened sail and waited for the Vice-admiral, or engage him as soon as he could, with whatever ships were at hand. In fact he fell into the trap which the wily De Court, who commanded the enemy's fleet, was setting for him. Observing the disorder of his opponents all through the previous manœuvres, and its culmination on the morning of the 11th, the French Admiral used his advantage by drawing Mathews after him to such a distance that he was in a position to deal with only a portion of the English fleet. If he had not been hampered by the slower sailing of the Spaniards he would probably have succeeded in inflicting a defeat on that portion, led as it was by an admiral with courage, but without conduct. As Lestock proved at his Courtmartial that he made all sail, and did his best to come up, we must give him the benefit of the doubt; but it was unfortunate for his reputation. This was, however, only part of the charge which was laid at his door.

At 11.30 the Admiral, himself leading the centre division of his fleet, having got his van, under Rear-admiral Rowley, up into line ahead of him, crowding a press of sail in pursuit of the enemy, and disregarding the distance which separated his two divisions from the third, made the signal to engage. This was repeated by Rowley, but not by Lestock, who indeed had no enemy to engage anywhere near him. By one o'clock Rowley found himself abreast of the "Terrible," the flag-ship of De Court, who commanded the centre Division; while Mathews was abreast of the "Real" of 114 guns, bearing the flag of Don Juan Josef Navarro, the gallant Spanish Admiral who commanded the rear. This division consisted exclusively of the Spanish ships, twelve in number.

The French van under Commodore Gabaret, consisting of eight ships, now getting well ahead, and out of fire from any of the English, Mathews, at 1.30, made up his mind that he had no chance of bringing the enemy to action unless he bore down at once upon him, and stopped his further progress. The favourable moment had arrived. He argued that as his two Divisions were a match for those they had at last overtaken, he might hope that the remaining one would come up in time to assist him before the French van could be brought into effective operation. In this hope, which would not have been unreasonable with hearty commanders who understood their leader and were zealous for action, he found himself grievously disappointed. Not only did Lestock fail to appear in time to be of use in the earlier part of the battle, or to help him when he did arrive, but not more than half the Captains of his own divisions were of any real service. Fortunately, though the difference of nationality did not turn out so fatal to the enemy as the internal jealousies amongst the English to themselves, there was not much more concord or cordiality between the French and Spaniards. Fortunately also the enemy lost the advantage they might have gained by help of their van, owing to the clever conduct of the three leading English ships, which kept their wind alongside of them, when the rest bore down out of line. Here, in order to understand Hawke's share in the action, we must give a list of the English ships and officers, according to their proper place in line of battle.

VAN: Rear-admiral William Rowley.

Ships.	Guns.		
Stirling Castle	70	Captain	Cooper.
Warwick	60	,,	Temple West.
Nassau	70	,,	James Lloyd.
Cambridge	80	,,	Charles Drummond.
Barfleur (Admiral)	90	,,	Merrick De L'Angle.
Princess Caroline	80	,,	Henry Osborn.
Berwick	70	,,	Edward Hawke.
Chichester	80	,,	William Dilke.
Kingston	60	,,	John Lovett.

CENTRE: Admiral Thomas Mathews.

Dragon	60	Captain	Charles Watson.
Bedford	70	,,	Hon. George Townshend.
Princessa	74	,,	Robert Pett.
Norfolk	80	,,	Hon. John Forbes.
Namur (Admiral)	90	,,	John Russel.
Marlborough	90	,,	James Cornewall.
Dorsetshire	80	,,	George Burrish.
Essex	70	,,	Richard Norris.
Rupert	60	,,	John Ambrose.
Royal Oak	70	,,	Edmund Williams.

REAR: Vice-admiral Richard Lestock.

Dunkirk	60	Captain	Charles Purvis.
Somerset	80	,,	George Sclater.
Torbay	70	,,	John Gascoigne.
Neptune (Admiral)	90	,,	George Stepney.
Russell	80	,,	Robert Long.
Buckingham	70	,,	John Towry.
Boyne	80	,,	Rowland Frogmere.
Elisabeth	70	,,	Joshua Lingen.
Revenge	70	,,	George Berkeley.

The moment of Mathews' attack was selected with judgment. The Spanish line had an immense gap in it; five ships being a long way astern of their Admiral and of his two seconds, the "Constante" and "Santa

Isabel." On these three ships Mathews gallantly bore down till within close fighting distance, supported with equal gallantry by Forbes in the "Norfolk," and Cornewall in the "Marlborough"; while the three leading ships of the Spanish Division left their Admiral to his fate, and held on with the French centre. The "Poder" alone remained; a ship exceptionally well manned and commanded, while the remaining English ships of Mathews' division, and two more which had strayed from the other Divisions, nine in all, were so badly commanded that this one Spaniard held them all at bay. She had no great difficulty, it seems, in driving the "Princesa" and "Somerset" out of the line; and the "Bedford," "Dragon," "Dorsetshire," "Essex," "Rupert," "Kingston," and "Royal Oak" amused themselves with ineffectual shots at her from too great a distance to penetrate, or pursued much the same course, when they thought they saw an opportunity, with the three Spanish ships which were locked in deadly embrace with Mathews, Cornwall, and Forbes, or with the five lagging Spaniards who were out of the reach of shot. It is even said that in this random firing the "Somerset" received several shots from the "Kingston."

Of the three officers mentioned, Forbes had the easiest task, as he soon drove the "Constante" out of the line, though at the cost of great damage to his own masts and rigging, as well as of several men killed and wounded. But the "Namur" and "Marlborough," receiving no assistance worth mention from any other ships, were left at the end of a close engagement, lasting some three hours, in as bad a state as their opponents. Not that they lost nearly so many men : for it is said that the Spanish Admiral, who had nearly 2,000 soldiers and sailors on board, lost 500; but the " Marlborough " lost 171 men, killed and wounded, as well as her main and mizen masts, and the " Namur" was so badly damaged that Mathews shifted his flag towards the evening, into the " Russell." The chief loss however sustained in the battle was that of the gallant Captain Cornewall, of the " Marlborough," the same officer who had been originally proposed as Anson's coadjutor in his expedition to the Pacific. Had he lived he might have become a great man.*

Turning now our attention to the English van :— when the Commander-in-Chief and his seconds bore down on the Spanish Admiral, Rowley, supported by his second, Osborn of the " Princess Caroline," did the same by the French Admiral, De Court, who commanded the centre of the combined fleet. His task was in one respect a more difficult one than his chief's, for the Frenchman appeared to wait for him till he came close up, and then set all sail, drawing off to

---

* The disproportioned grandeur and costliness of Captain Cornewall's monument in Westminster Abbey, erected at the public expense, is, like that of some similar national monuments to mere Captains who fell in command of their ships, historically interesting, inasmuch as they testify to the enthusiasm or special feeling of the nation at the moment. Parliament felt it could not too strongly mark the general approval of the contrast afforded by Cornewall's gallant conduct to that of too many who were engaged in the battle; and he was a member of the Lower House.

leeward, and coming to the wind again; thus, without running away, avoiding with much dexterity the close action which he knew was what he had most to dread. However he could not pursue these tactics very far, or he would have gone too much to leeward of the Spanish rear; and thus Rowley and Osborn came up with him and his two seconds at last. After a close conflict of some two hours the two English ships, not without a considerable loss of men, obliged their three opponents to make off; but they did not succeed in capturing one of them. Those were the only three ships of the French centre which were engaged; as the rest kept their wind with a view of tacking and coming down upon Rowley, and so to place him between two fires. This was prevented by the independent action of the three leading ships of the English van, which, as has been said, disobeyed the signal to bear down and engage, and, keeping their wind, not only paralysed the enemy's van, but also the leading ships of his centre. For this their Captains, Temple West, Cooper, and Lloyd, were tried by Courtmartial, and cashiered; but within a year restored to their former rank. As they saved the fleet by their disobedience, this sentence was only one of the many anomalies of an extraordinary battle, and still more extraordinary series of Courtsmartial. As to the remaining ships of Rowley's division, the "Cambridge," "Chichester," and "Berwick," it is difficult to discover what service was performed by the first, but her Captain was not tried by Courtmartial, and was no doubt reasonably excused: Captain Dilke of the "Chichester" was tried and found guilty of not engaging sufficiently close; the "Berwick" remains.

Captain Hawke's station was towards the rear of the van, and his first opponent the Spanish "Neptuno,"* one of the ships which we have seen leaving the rear Division and pushing forward into the centre. After about an hour's close engagement he drove her out of the line, with heavy loss. It seems she lost that day her Captain, First Lieutenant, four other officers, and 200 men; but she did not strike. This battle produced the effect of bringing the "Berwick" within no great distance of the "Poder," the ship which, we have seen, had driven two English ships out of the line, and kept several more of the centre Division at bay. Hawke at once, with that rapid intuition which was his characteristic, made up his mind to put an end to such a disgraceful spectacle. Bearing down upon her within pistol, or "half-musket," shot, his first broadside killed 27 of her men and dismounted several of her lower-deck guns. In twenty minutes he had dismasted her; and at the end of a two hours' conflict at close quarters, during which the "Poder" lost 200 men killed and wounded,† the brave Spaniard struck his colours. It is said that, on the occurrence of this event, which cost the "Berwick" the loss of only five men wounded, more than one ship was sent to take possession of the "Poder"; but the Captain would deliver his sword to no one but the officer sent

---

* See the evidence of Mr. Cole, Master of the "Berwick," given at the Courtmartial on Mathews.

† Log of the "Berwick."

by the ship to which he had struck, pointing to the "Berwick," and saying at the same time that he held the others in the greatest contempt.* Lieutenant Lloyd was the officer sent by Hawke, with 22 men, to take possession ; he was First Lieutenant of the ship, and was examined on Mathews' Courtmartial. From his evidence we obtain some valuable information. It was about 4 P.M. when the "Poder" struck, and a good deal had happened, which must be noticed before we return to her, since the two Admirals had borne down out of line.

The "Real" (or "Royal Philip") and the "Marlborough" were lying like wrecks on the water, and the "Namur" and "Norfolk" had become almost unmanageable from the damage incurred in their rigging. Mathews, finding he could not make the "Real" strike, and having drifted to some distance from her, now determined to set her on fire by means of the "Ann," fireship. All fleets carried with them two or three of these vessels, though they were but seldom used in the open sea. In this terrible emergency the Spanish Admiral could only with great difficulty bring any guns to bear on the "Ann"; and she was coming down under full sail upon him. He was saved by a series of accidents. Some of his shot struck the vessel, and his launch approached so near as to cause the Captain of the "Ann" to fire his guns at her. These set fire to the explosive material, and the "Ann" blew up, with all who were still on board, before

---

* Hervey's "Naval History," vol. iv. p. 250.

reaching the "Real." It came out at the Courtmartial that the officers of the fireship were "fuddled"; the Admiral's orders to her were delayed till the opportunity was lost; every detail on board the vessel went wrong throughout; and the "Essex," which was particularly ordered to support her, did nothing of the sort.

The French Admiral, if he did not gain the palm of valour, carried off by the brave Navarro, who had received two wounds, now showed the skill of an accomplished admiral. In the midst of the rude assault of Rowley, he perceived the state of the "Real" and her consorts, and fearing that the British rear must by this time have come up, disengaged himself from Rowley and Osborn, made the signal for the fleet to tack,—the log of the "Berwick" says that they wore—and quickly formed his ships into a good line of battle on the starboard tack. Rowley followed his example, and, collecting his own ships, rallied to the side of his own admiral, who, in consequence of the five Spanish ships (which had been so far astern when the action began) having at last come up, was unable to pursue his advantage over the "Real" any farther. Mathews now, therefore, finally collected both divisions round the crippled "Marlborough," standing on the opposite tack from the combined fleet, or as Lestock described the manœuvre, running away from his enemy. Nothing more of importance was done that day. But where was Lestock? If two Divisions of the fleet could, in spite of numerous defections, prove a match for the whole of the enemy, something decisive might certainly have been expected from the three together. But no help came from the Vice-admiral. There had been an error in Mathews' signals; and though Lestock had arrived during the afternoon within fighting distance, he took advantage of the error not to fight at all, but to keep aloof. The signal for "engaging" had been made when that for "the line of battle" was still flying. Nothing but the above-mentioned feud could have so warped the judgment of a man, who had behaved well in previous battles, as to persuade him that he was doing his duty in obeying the literal construction of both signals while disregarding the evident spirit which dictated the last signal, the signal to engage. Nevertheless it was the letter of the law; and a Courtmartial acquitted him!

To return to Hawke and his prize. The operations above described* had the effect of leaving them both well to leeward of the rest of the fleet, and boats were passing between them. Lloyd, on his way from the prize, was hailed by Admiral Rowley, who, with his division, was now standing to windward in order to join Mathews, and went on board. The Admiral told Lloyd on the quarter-deck of the "Barfleur" that "he would do his endeavours to save the prize, and give Captain Hawke the honour of carrying her to Minorca; that he had not been well acquainted with Captain Hawke before, but he should now be very well acquainted with him from his behaviour." Before

---

* In Clerk's "Naval Tactics" there is a plan of the battle which gives, on the whole, a fair general idea of it.

Lloyd could get to the "Berwick," which was also trying to rejoin the fleet, he had to pass near the prize,—the February night was now closing in,—and, to his horror, descried a French ship close to her. He immediately rowed back to Admiral Rowley, to report the fact. Rowley ordered him to go on board the "Berwick" instantly, and take his orders to Hawke to bear down again and drive off the French ship. This the "Berwick" did, and again rejoined the fleet. Lloyd now brought a boat's load of prisoners from the prize, but not being able to overtake his own ship, put them on board the "Royal Oak" for the night, and rejoined the "Berwick" with them next day. When this officer, by that time a Captain, gave his evidence, the Court asked:—"And did a large body of His Majesty's fleet run away from a division of the enemy's fleet, and leave them in possession of the only prize His Majesty's fleet had taken that day, and desert that ship which had distinguished itself by taking her?" Lloyd:—"Our fleet stood from her, which obliged the 'Berwick' to follow them, upon the French fleet's coming down on her."

It was now too late to get the Fourth Lieutenant of the "Berwick" and his 17 men—(the Master deposed to the number being 22)—out of the "Poder," and the French fleet, finding themselves close to her, took possession of Hawke's prize, and made prisoners of the officer and men. Thus the one trophy of the day was gone; and we may imagine the feelings of her captors. Not the least bitter part of the affair was that Mathews had ignored them altogether, and when the "Poder" was afterwards abandoned by the enemy, gave the orders for her destruction, not to Hawke, but to Captain Norris of the "Essex," who had behaved disgracefully from first to last. Again, such was his mismanagement, that when Rowley had ordered the "Diamond" frigate to lie by the prize, Mathews countermanded the order. The evidence showed she might have been saved if the directions of the former had been obeyed. This was far from a trifle. In such a balanced and confused action, one line-of-battle ship captured and retained, would have refuted the claim of the enemy to have gained a victory; though indeed the claim, absurd as it was, may be forgiven, since its effect was to make the noble Navarro the Marquis de la Victoria. National vanity, however, is pardonable: that the excellent historian, Ranke, should speak of this battle as a victory for the combined fleets, is one of the few errors which can be detected in his "History of England."

Mathews having at last collected his fleet, worked to windward all night, the wind being still from the Eastward; and in the morning appears to have been surprised to find the enemy far away, running to leeward, as fast as their shattered state would allow, and already at least a dozen miles off. This was bad management to begin with. The whole of the day was taken up in the pursuit; but the winds were light, and the distance was only lessened by about a half, while the enemy, hampered by the state of the "Real," which was towed by another ship, and still more by the dismasted "Poder," were obliged to relinquish the latter, and tried to set her on fire. This however failed, and Norris of the "Essex," in pursuit of his orders, completed, when his ship came near enough, the combustion. She soon blew up. So passed the 12th.

Again the night was lost; but though the wind had freshened, and the enemy had made the utmost use of it, there was still one last chance. Lestock's division was nearest to the combined fleet, and when the day broke, reported that he had discovered it. He was ordered to chase; the rest followed. They were fast gaining on the enemy, who had still the "Real" in tow; when, to the equal astonishment of all alike, Spaniards, French, and English, Mathews, at 9 A.M. of the 13th, hoisted the signal for recall, and relinquished the pursuit.

This act crowned his series of blunders, and formed the chief charge against him. Lestock now had his revenge. He had done his best to overtake the flying foe, on the last day at least; and it was Mathews who stopped him at the moment when, with his division all fresh—for he had never been engaged, he had every prospect of success and distinction. It was no wonder that this proceeding should have been universally assigned as the direct consequence of the quarrel, and attributed to the Admiral's jealousy of his Vice-admiral; but on his defence, strange to say, the former had more to say for it than he had for his other blunders; and it is probable that, however mistaken, he did really feel his responsibility for the safety of Italy with which he was entrusted, more than anything else. The freshening East wind was driving both fleets fast towards the mouth of the Straits of Gibraltar, and he might not be able to get back to his station for weeks; he had information that the Spaniards were prepared to take advantage of his absence; and as—so little was there of the true English admiral about him—he did not expect, as he said, to effect more by a battle than to take the "Real," he considered that the Italian question ruled the situation.

That we may not have to return to this inefficient officer, it may be remarked here that he certainly was far from having fair play at his Courtmartial, which did not take place till nearly two years afterwards. During a part of this time, having speedily got rid of his obnoxious Vice-admiral by sending him home under arrest, he managed his duties in Italy with considerable success. But Lestock's political friends soon came to the head of affairs ; and, to the astonishment of the world, he got off ;—only however to fail finally at the expedition to L'Orient in 1746, with the naval part of which he was entrusted. When Mathews' turn came to be tried, not only were the witnesses allowed to hear each other's evidence, so that one copied from another, while the Judge Advocate most improperly tampered with the evidence; but, if we may believe Horace Walpole (who gives no proof of such an incredible statement), the members of the Court were changed if they showed any sympathy with the accused. The sentences of the two Courts were indeed surprising. The man who fought as hard as he could, at close quarters with his enemy, was cashiered, and rendered incapable of further employment. The man who kept out of action was acquitted. Campbell, in his "Lives of the Admirals," which, though a standard book, is full of prejudice and inaccuracies, sums up the verdict of the country at the time, and of most historians since, by the remark that "Mathews might want head: Lestock certainly wanted heart. The one might deserve censure; the other ought to have been shot. The sentences of the Court-martial must for ever remain a blot on the annals of the country."*

Nevertheless, after a careful survey of the whole of the evidence in this the most voluminous and tedious series of Courtsmartial in the history of any nation, it may be admissible to demur to the above judgment. Some allowance should be made for both chiefs, obliged to use codes of signals so imperfect as to suggest error; and the greatest blame attaches to the Admiralty for employing in high command men who were decidedly unfitted for it, still more for employing them together when aware of the impossibility of their cordial co-operation. Mathews should have been shelved on the Superannuated List, but he ought not to have been cashiered. Lestock should have been placed in exactly the same position. Neither could command his own temper, and therefore they should never have been suffered again to command fleets.

---

* Vol. iv. p. 50.

Perhaps the mistakes of Mathews were exhibited as much in his conduct towards his Captains as in his general management of the fleet. Venting all his wrath on his personal enemy, he took no steps to bring the Captains who had so shamefully misbehaved, to a Courtmartial. Neither, it must be said, did the Admiralty. This the country, speaking through its representatives in Parliament, did for them both. The House of Commons demanded that the two Admirals, and six of the Captains, should be put on their trial; and the Admiralty, waking up, added five more of the latter to the list. Of these, Captain Frogmere of the "Boyne" died on his passage home; Captain Richard Norris, of the "Essex," accused by his own officers, resigned his command, and deserted; two were acquitted, Captains Pett of the "Princesa," and Sclater of the "Somerset"; three, as we have seen,* were (unjustly) cashiered, but restored; Captain Williams of the "Royal Oak," and Captain Dilke of the "Chichester," were dismissed their ships, but afterwards restored and placed on half-pay; Captain Ambrose of the "Rupert" was cashiered, and mulcted of a year's pay, but eventually restored; and Captain Burrish, Hawke's late senior in command, was cashiered and rendered incapable of further employment.

The reader may enquire why, even though he has been required to follow a detailed account of the battle, he should be expected to take an interest in

---

* P. 151.

these Courtsmartial. Almost any sketch of Hawke's career which he may take up will supply an answer. He will find successive compilers copying from one another the absolute error that Hawke, though he was the only Captain to take a ship, was tried by Courtmartial for breaking the line, broke, and immediately reinstated. In an exceedingly brief notice of the Admiral which appears in the latest and most respectable authority, the new edition of the *Encyclopædia Britannica*, which has only just got as far as the letter H, this statement occupies a large part of the space allotted. It probably first appeared in the "Gentleman's Magazine" for 1760. Here Hawke is said to have been "broke for his bravery and restored by the King"; and later authors may well have supposed that, as he lived, without contradicting it, for twenty years after the statement occurred, no doubt could attach to it. But such matters were quite out of our Admiral's way; and the story may be disposed of henceforward. The officers just mentioned were the only ones accused or tried, and our narrative has shown that no charge of any kind could have arisen out of Hawke's conduct in the battle. Within a few weeks he was placed in command of a squadron of line-of-battle ships on a delicate service in the Mediterranean. Charnock, towards the end of the last century, was, perhaps, the first to throw discredit on the story; but even he was staggered by the absence of any subsequent information about Hawke till, in 1747, he became an admiral. That blank we shall be able to fill up. If truth in these matters is of importance, it certainly was high time that some connected account of this great admiral should be put forth.

A few further words must be said about one of the officers already noticed, Captain Richard Norris, of the " Essex ";—partly because his case enables us to dispose of Admiral Rowley, the last of Hawke's seniors of whom an account has been promised, and partly because Norris's connection with Hawke's prize brings us to the concluding notice of our hero in relation to the Battle off Toulon.

Norris shared with John Byng the disadvantage of being sons of the two great officers of their time. Under the auspices of the fine admiral whose career has been noticed, Norris early arrived at rank; whereas his disgraceful personal conduct in the battle just described, according to the evidence of all his officers (of whom Hugh Palliser, afterwards so well known, was one), showed that he ought never to have been allowed to go to sea at all. Disastrously for himself, Admiral Rowley, out of regard no doubt to the father (who this very year was placed in command of the Channel fleet to protect England from invasion), received the unfortunate man, who had resigned his command, on board his own flagship as a volunteer on half-pay. Norris begged to be tried by Courtmartial, but Rowley declined, on the ground that a half-pay officer could not be tried; and when the Admiralty, incited to vigorous action by pressure from the House of Commons, insisted on a trial, they complained to the Lords Justices that Rowley did not properly instruct the Courtmartial when it was held, but exhibited the strongest marks of partiality, never even confining the accused officer, who was charged with cowardice and disobedience.; and this at a time "when the discipline of the navy is already too much relaxed." The Lords of the Admiralty therefore beg the Lords Justices (the King being in Hanover) to recall the Admiral, who had been in command of the Mediterranean fleet since Mathews had been ordered home for trial. Rowley now at last sent Norris to England. He deserted at Gibraltar on the voyage, changed his name, and was never more heard of; but his friend the Admiral was superseded, and never again employed at sea. Thus ended, though he became a Lord of the Admiralty, and succeeded to honorary posts, the promising career of a good officer, who was one of the few who did his duty in the battle, and who had subsequently commanded the fleet for a year with high reputation.*

The following Letter to Admiral Mathews, from the Letter-book in possession of the Hawke family, will sufficiently explain the later transactions in relation to the "Poder," as far as Norris was concerned:—

SIR,   "BERWICK," at Sea, 24th February 1743.†

I intreat the liberty of intruding a little upon your time to acquaint you that I sent one of my officers to Captain Norris to demand the colours and things which he and his officers have taken out of the "Poder," the Spanish man-of-war we took; and his answer was that he could not deliver them unless it was

---

* See Letters from the Admiralty to the Lords Justices, May 29th, 1745; Record Office.

† Or 13th February 174¼. Hawke is writing in the Mediterranean, where the New Style was already observed.

by your orders. I beg leave to say, sir, that it is not a little hard upon myself and my officers that we should be deprived of these things who had the justest right and title to them. And as I was not conscious to myself that I had done anything to offend you, at least I am sure not designedly, I flattered myself with the hopes that I should have had the honour to have burnt her, as well as to have taken her, but the hurry you was in might very possibly not give you time to think of it. I am therefore to beg that you will do me the justice to order Captain Norris and his officers to restore the things that they have taken, and the colours which he has in his possession, which I am convinced he cannot lay the least claim to. However, Sir, I submit this to your will and pleasure, as I shall be glad to do everything which relates to me while I have the honour to be under your command.

Hawke concludes with an account of the circumstances under which he had been obliged to leave the "Poder," substantially the same as that already given from Lloyd's evidence. Whether he obtained the colours does not appear; but this behaviour on the part of the admiral may either be the cause or effect of the extraordinary fact that the "Poder" is only mentioned in Mathews' despatch as "a ship of Navarre, of 66 guns, which was obliged to surrender; and that of 900 men only the Captain and 200 were saved, when she was ordered to be burnt": then, without noticing who captured her, the "Gazette" goes on to say "Captain Hawke of the 'Berwick' left her, but could not get his Lieutenant and 23 men out of her; his First Lieutenant having done all he could to persuade the men to quit her, but in vain."

No doubt the completeness of Hawke's success contrasted unfavourably with his own; but this gross misrepresentation on the part of Mathews—for its suppression of the truth amounts to that—is unpardonable; and it is connected with an evident desire to procure some credit for Norris, whose misconduct he had not only perceived, but reprimanded during the battle. There cannot be the least doubt that he ought to have punished the man instead of rewarding him. There were in fact six officers who had distinguished themselves in command, Mathews, Rowley, Cornwall, Forbes, Osborne, and Hawke; but the last was the only one of the six who so fought his ship as to cause his opponent to strike; and this was his reward!

Hawke received orders to give evidence at Mathews' Courtmartial, and his letter acknowledging the order, is extant; but he did not appear, and we know not why. His opinion on the whole affair would have been more interesting and more valuable than any that was given. It would be in keeping with the magnanimity which he frequently evinced, if the reason was that he was unwilling to press too hard against a man, who, though he had public and private grounds for condemning him, he yet perceived was likely to get hard measure. Perhaps he thus in some way contrived to evade an appearance which, whatever else happened, must certainly have enhanced his own reputation. However this may be, Hawke's fortune was made from the moment he made up his mind, after his battle with the "Neptuno," that it was his duty to attack the "Poder": his countrymen thereby discovered the admiral of the future; and, above all, the King, as already said, never forgot the act.

From the date of this battle till the close of the

year 1745, Hawke was for the most part employed in command of large squadrons under Admiral Rowley. With seven line-of-battle ships under his command, we find him cruising in the Straits of Gibraltar and on the Coast of Italy. In October 1744, he rejoins the Admiral. In December he is detached with another squadron to watch the French fleet at Cadiz; and, in January of the next year, to act against French and Spanish troops on the Genoese coast. There is nothing worth noting in the mass of correspondence connected with this period, but it may be remarked that Hawke's letters to his captains are uniformly kind, courteous, and thoughtful; and that those to his admiral show an extreme care to avoid giving offence, even when he has to explain that he has had orders which it was impossible to carry into effect. They are generally well expressed, and always the letters of a gentleman. At the end of September he finds himself once more at Plymouth, having brought home Rowley's flagship, the "Neptune," with a convoy, in a state which he describes as "foul and very leaky," and he is soon afterwards paid off.

For about a year Hawke is once more on shore; and as his uncle had just died, it was now, probably, that he settled at Swathling. When, on June 9th, 1746, he acknowledges the summons to attend Mathews' Courtmartial, he dates from Lymington.

By way of contrast to the favourable impression Hawke had now created, it may be noticed that it was in this very year, 1746, that Commodore Peyton and his squadron "disappeared" after his indecisive combat in the East Indies with Labourdonnais; that Lestock made his final failure at L'Orient; and that Commodore Mitchell behaved in the West Indies much as Peyton had behaved in the East. Mitchell was broke: Peyton died just before the Courtmartial ordered to be held upon him. It was tolerably plain that the country had not yet, during the first seven years of the war found the men it wanted for the command of fleets. But the dross was now nearly purged away, and there was plenty of true metal at bottom. Unsatisfactory as the naval service had proved itself in the late battle, some fine single actions had been fought, and it had already inflicted twice the amount of damage on the enemy's commerce that they had on the English. The final discomfiture of the Jacobites had also given a sense of security and hope to the nation of which it did not as yet measure the importance. It was ready for further sacrifices, and had not much longer to wait for results. Seven years had been, however, a long time to wait.

CHAPTER VI.

BATTLE WITH THE FRENCH OFF USHANT, 1747.

The great improvement in naval affairs which commenced from the year 1747 must be attributed, in the first place, to Lord Anson. This excellent officer, though only eight years older than the subject of our memoir, had, in consequence of having been fortunate enough to serve as a Lieutenant in Byng's action, come much earlier into notice. He thus, in addition to his seniority by age, gained three years more upon Hawke in the race for the rank of Post-captain. When the war broke out he was a Captain of considerable standing, and it was creditable to the authorities that they had discovered his merits, and selected him for the expedition to the Pacific which was to make him famous for all time. Like Hawke he came of a family in the position of gentlemen, and something more, since they both inherited brains which had been strengthened by training in the ranks of the bar. When he came home in 1744 his great reputation for ability as well as courage naturally pointed him out as the man most fitted for the reorganization of the naval service. He was of mature age, had gained a vast experience, and the great fortune he had made on his expedition rendered him independent. In less than four years from his becoming a junior Lord of the Admiralty, he had made himself so necessary to the Duke of Bedford, and to Lord Sandwich, the next in rank to the Duke, that he became the virtual head of the Board, over which he soon afterwards came to preside as First Lord, with one short interval, till the time of his death.

Anson's experience suggested the system, which soon grew to be habitual, of collecting the scattered squadrons which had hitherto cruised upon the French trade, and forming them into larger bodies, capable of overpowering the French squadrons sent from Brest and other ports to convoy fleets of merchant ships to their colonies in the East and West Indies. It was just at this period that, finding all attempts at invading England, exciting rebellion, and commanding the Mediterranean, had completely failed, the French were directing their whole attention to the new project of founding, by the help, as far as possible, of Spain, a great Colonial Empire. But the efforts which they steadily pursued from this time forward, till Pitt destroyed all their hopes, had an unfortunate commencement.

Presuming upon the negligence of the British Admiralty, the French Government equipped two small squadrons for the above purpose. These, under the command of M. de la Jonquière, who was to attempt the recapture of Cape Breton (lately taken from the French by the American Colonists, assisted by Captain Peter Warren), and of M. de St. George, who was to assist Dupleix in India, were to keep company till out of reach of British cruisers. Anson had, however, himself embarked in command of a squadron, more than twice as large as both those of the French put together. Nothing could have been better planned. The French were caught, just where they were expected, off Cape Finisterre; and the whole of their ships, though after a resistance which was most honourable for so weak a force, were captured. Almost all the actual fighting fell to the share of the second in command, Peter Warren, lately made an admiral, and to the Captains Boscawen, Denis, Grenville, Brett, Saumarez, Hanway, and Montagu. Temple West, who has been noticed in the last Chapter, was Warren's flag-captain.

Here indeed was a behaviour very different from what was observed in 1744; and here we make our first acquaintance with some of Hawke's most gallant contemporaries. Warren and Boscawen will alone however require any special notice. The others were fine, dashing officers, but took up no great position. Grenville, who seems to have inherited the talents of his family, was killed in this battle. Anson speaks of him as "by much the cleverest officer I ever saw."[*] "Mad Montagu," Lord Sandwich's brother, exhibited on this occasion a timely madness, very near akin to heroism. Peircy Brett, Anson's old First Lieutenant

---

[*] "Bedford Correspondence," vol. i. p. 214.

in the "Centurion," had already destroyed the prospects of the young Pretender by his brave action with the "Elizabeth" in 1745, and lived to be a Lord of the Admiralty. Saumarez, another of Anson's school —for it was one of the marks of that Lord's ability that he distinctly formed a body of fine officers out of those who had shared his voyage round the world— survived this battle but to die on the quarter-deck of his ship, in a few months, under Hawke's command. Denis, another of the school, gallantly fought in command of his chief's old ship, the "Centurion," and of him we shall hear again.

Boscawen is the officer who, of all who rose to fame in this period, ran the hardest race for glory with Hawke. As it will be more convenient to sketch his career when we have made further progress in tracing that of Hawke, it will be sufficient to state that no ship contributed more to Anson's victory than the "Namur," which Boscawen commanded, unless we except the "Devonshire," which carried Warren's flag, and that admits of doubt. The last-named officer had the honour of capturing M. de la Jonquière's own ship, the "Sérieux," and soon aftewards, with the help of Montagu, that of the other Commodore, St. George, which had, however, been already roughly handled by Boscawen. And here, as Warren was soon to have the opportunity of lifting Hawke to fame, he must engage our attention. He received for this battle the Knighthood of the Bath, as a pendant to Anson's peerage, and we may therefore speak of him as "Sir Peter Warren."

Of Irish extraction, this officer, who is now forgotten, except by those who have remarked Roubiliac's fine monument to his memory in Westminster Abbey, seems to have had many qualifications for taking a place in history, but to have lost opportunities enjoyed by others through the ill-health which he had contracted during long service in the West Indies. A little senior to Hawke, he had had the good fortune to be in command of a small squadron off Martinique which took such rich prizes that, having afterwards added to these some other valuable captures on the home station, he was said to be one of the wealthiest naval officers of the day. Horace Walpole* called him "richer than Anson and as absurd as Vernon," referring to his speeches in the House of Commons; but we are not bound to accept all Walpole's *obiter dicta*.

In 1745 Warren commanded the naval forces which, assisted by the Colonists, took Louisbourg, the capital of the island of Cape Breton, and the centre round which the conflict for Western Empire raged till Boscawen retook it in 1758. This also had added to his wealth. Here he showed both courage and conduct, as indeed he did most signally in Anson's battle. The decision taken on that occasion by Anson to disregard the old tactics of waiting to form the line, and to order a general chase of the enemy, was suggested by Warren, who—

suspecting that the enemy's design was only to gain time, and that as soon as the ships they convoyed had got to a considerable distance they would make off and endeavour to escape under

---

* "Letters to Mann," vol. i. p. 283.

favour of the night, bore down to the Vice-Admiral and told him his suspicions, advising him to haul down the signal for the line, and to hoist one for a general chase.*

It was then natural that Anson, who had formed an early friendship with Warren on the American Station, should obtain for him the succession to himself in command of the fleet, which command he had relinquished when he received his peerage and resumed his place at the Admiralty. Sir Peter hoisted his flag in the "Devonshire," taking over the charge of the fleet, on July 20th, 1747.

When Anson on April 9th, 1747, had sailed from Plymouth, with his band of heroes, on the successful cruise just mentioned, he had left behind at that port an officer who fretted not a little at being excluded from the number. It seemed as if none but the admiral's immediate friends were to have a chance of distinction; and indeed this was a fault very commonly found with Lord Anson. How long Hawke had been there, we do not exactly know; but he had been some time employed by the Admiralty, perhaps with a view of occupying a restless mind which could not be otherwise used at the moment, in the tedious task of superintending the repairs of the "Mars," then in dock. The first letter of his which occurs since he acknowledged the summons of the Admiralty to attend Mathews' Courtmartial is dated April 24, 1746, and conveys a request that, as he can be of no use at Plymouth, looking after the "Mars," till she is finished, he may be allowed to go

---

* Beatson's "Naval and Military Memoirs," vol. i. p. 357.

"to his house in Hampshire." This request is refused. But very soon afterwards all such difficulties came to an end, and we find our Captain included in the list of promotions to the rank of Admiral, the first promotions which had been made for three years, and the first occasion on which the modern system of promoting to a Retired List of Admirals was brought into operation. Up to this time the method of selection, necessary in some form for the higher commands, had worked most unjustly. The Captains who had been passed over never moved up to any higher rank; and the greatest inequalities and hardships had consequently prevailed. This, like many other reforms, must be placed to Anson's credit.*

It was probably due to the delay of promotions that had occurred, and to the want of admirals of different grades for immediate employment, that Hawke was made, as it would seem, Rear-admiral of the White at once, without passing through the previous grade. His Commission, like those of Knowles, Forbes, Boscawen,† and the rest, was dated July 15th, 1747; as also was the advancement of Sir Peter Warren to the rank of Vice-Admiral of the White. On July 20th, Warren was appointed to the command of the "Western Squadron"; two days afterwards, Hawke hoisted his flag on board the "Gloucester." On August 8th, Warren informs him that he is to place himself under his command. Next day Hawke sailed from Plymouth;

---
* Barrow's "Life of Anson," p. 143.
† Ekins attributes to the generous advocacy of Boscawen some share in Hawke's promotion.

and on August 20th he writes from the "Windsor" "at sea."

The above dates have been given in order to explain Hawke's position at this time, which has never yet been understood. Anson's plan was to employ both these admirals in the execution of his new plans, one of which had just proved, under himself, so successful. Warren he was sure he could trust, and he had formed a high opinion of Hawke.

The actual form of Hawke's employment was suggested by Warren himself, and grew out of his own state of health. He was suffering from a "scorbutic disorder." In a letter to the Admiralty dated August 3rd, 1747, he writes thus :—

> I should be extremely obliged to their Lordships if the present service at sea does not require the attendance of more than one admiral, they would be pleased to join Admiral Hawke, now here with me, in the command, who, I dare venture to say, will not be displeased with it, and may sail, if their Lordships shall think proper, on the return of the express that carries this, with the "Monmouth," "Windsor," "Eagle," and "Amazon" to join (for this cruise) Captain [Harry] Norris, or the senior officer of the squadron in the Bay, by which time I shall hope to re-establish my health so well as to be able to relieve, or act in conjunction with, Mr. Hawke in the next [cruise], which will probably be of greater consequence than the present by the expected return of the galleons, who make it a general rule to come home late in the fall or winter.

Anson, it would seem, hesitated: for, on August 7th, Warren writes again :—

> I observe what you say about the ships abroad being under so young an officer. I am and have been uneasy about it, though I hope he will do well, and it could not then be avoided. Harrison will soon be there, who is a good man and an elder

officer, if Mr. Hawke should not be put under my command; which from your letter I have so little reason to doubt that I have his instructions all ready; and he is prepared to go at a moment's notice.

On August 20th Hawke ends his letter to Warren, in which he reports proceedings, by saying:—

I flatter myself you will do me the justice to believe that I have nothing so much at heart as the faithful discharge of my duty, and in such manner as will give satisfaction both to the Lords of the Admiralty and yourself. This shall ever be my utmost ambition, and no lucre of profit or other views shall induce me to act otherwise.

These words suggest a hint, which subsequent letters illustrate, that although the junior admiral was bent on satisfying the senior if possible, he intended to act on his own responsibility, and that he did not share his chief's anxiety about the galleons. He was thinking a great deal more about meeting the enemy's men-of-war. There could hardly be a more delicate position, but it did not last long. It may here be observed, as we shall often come across the fact, that the circumstances of victualling, cleaning, and repairing ships in those days necessitated the employment of a much larger number on any cruising service than the most careful and skilful admiral could expect to bring into action on the day of battle. There are no less than 25 line-of-battle ships in this "Western Squadron," and 19 of them were handed over to Hawke; yet he had only 14 with him in his battle of October 14th.

Warren's illness increased so much that he was obliged to ask the Admiralty to relieve him altogether from the command for a time, and substitute Hawke in his place. "I am unable to continue in command of the Western Squadron by a violent flux, in addition to my former disorder." This letter is dated September 5th; and on September 8th, the Admiralty issue orders to Hawke to take the independent command, which Sir Peter Warren had obtained temporary leave to resign. In addition to the 19 large ships now formally placed under his orders, five of which were only of 50 guns, 7 frigates and 2 fire-ships, are attached to his squadron. He is to cruise between Ushant and Cape Finisterre, 20 leagues to the Westward of each Cape; to make the land of Ushant every fortnight; and to station one of his best sailing ships and frigates off each Cape to communicate with the Admiralty.

No intimation to this effect did, however, reach Hawke for nearly a month. He still supposes himself to be acting under Warren, and had not even orders to make separate reports to the Admiralty. He was joined by the rest of Sir Peter's ships under Captain Fox's command on September 26th, and received his orders through him. After studying the despatches he considers it is his first duty to use his utmost endeavours to intercept the French convoy bound out from Rochelle; and therefore, he says, in acknowledging a letter from the Admiralty, dated August 28th (in which he had been ordered to make direct reports to their Secretary, independently of those to Warren), he means to keep all his ships together, "as it is of material consequence to the nation that we should be a full match for the enemy in case of meeting with them." He apologises for not having made these reports previously, and announces that he finds his "cruise must be very much shortened for want of water."

His letter of October 6th to Sir Peter Warren is more distinctly characteristic, and may be given almost in full:—

I am sincerely concerned to find you have still that troublesome disorder, and that your health will not permit you to come out. It would have been a very great pleasure to me to have had the honour of paying my respects to you here, but as I cannot have that satisfaction I shall endeavour to do everything in my power to forward the service, only wishing I may be so fortunate as to have your approbation of my actions, as I can say very truly there is not anything I have more at heart than your good opinion.

I have considered well all the intelligence you have sent me, and by what I can learn from thence I think our only view at present must be to lie in the way of the French convoy outward bound. In order thereto I propose cruising between the latitudes of 45° and 47° 30′ N., in the meridian of Cape Ortegal, and am making the best of my way thither as fast as the winds will permit me. This appears to be the most likely track for them, and everybody else here is of the same opinion. I hope we shall have the good fortune to meet with them, if they should come out while we are in a condition to keep the sea.

With respect to the intelligence you sent me relative to the galleons, as it is uncertain when they will come home, and likewise impossible for me to divide my force in the present necessitous condition of the ships under my command, I must lay aside all thoughts of them during this cruise, which cannot be of long continuance. And indeed, if I may presume to give my opinion, I should think sixty or seventy leagues to the westward of Cales would be the best place to look out for them; in which case a squadron must go out from England directly thither, well watered and victualled. For by the uncertainty of weather and the negligence of the agent-victualler, I find the ships that join me are so far from being in a condition to go on distant or different expeditions that it is with difficulty I can keep them any reasonable time with me. ... You will perceive by the "state and condition" of the ships that I shall not be able to stay out past the month of October. ... I am in great hopes that the station I am going to will throw us in the way of the enemy, either outward or homeward bound. With regard to lying in wait for them, all that any man can do is to put the most reasonable supposition in practice, and that I hope you will think I have done.

I wish with all my heart this may find you perfectly recovered and in a good state of health, and that I may be so happy as to obey all your commands in the way you would have me. I don't know that anything would give me more pleasure. I am always, with the greatest truth and respect, Sir, yours, &c.

EDWARD HAWKE.

These letters are dated from the "Devonshire," Warren's flagship, of 66 guns, of which Captain Moore was now Flag-Captain, she having been sent to join Hawke with the rest of Warren's ships. Few of the letters of this date are without some special allusion to the unwholesome and "stinking" state of the beer with which his ships have been supplied; and as we find it of still more dangerous consequence to the service in the later cruises of the Seven Years' War, it may be presumed to have been a chronic state of things.

Between October 6th and October 12th the Admiralty Despatches of September 8th, conferring the independent command, must have reached him, since the letters to Sir Peter Warren are now only sent as a matter of courtesy, while the first Reports go to the Admiralty direct. On October 12th, he informs the latter that "the situation we are now in seems very well calculated for intercepting both the Eastward and homeward-bound trade of the enemy. I shall do everything in my power to keep the ships out with me as long as possible, and intend staying out myself while I can keep any number of them together."

On October 14th all these anxious considerations came to the end most desired by the Admiral. He was now rewarded for having refused all temptations to cruise for galleons, or to detach portions of his fleet on that service. His Despatch, or rather the greatest part of it, describing the battle of that day, has been printed more than once, on the ground that no other account of it could be half so good. The same reason applies in the present case; but it will here be given in full. And indeed, throughout this book, the same plan, at the risk of a certain necessary stiffness inherent in official correspondence, will be pursued. It is a career worth studying in the hero's own simple words.

Let us premise that the English fleet, on October 14th, consisted of the following fourteen ships:—that of the French, under Admiral L'Etenduère, of the following nine.

English.

Ships.	Guns.		
Devonshire (Admiral)	66	Captain	John Moore.
Kent	64	„	Thomas Fox.
Edinburgh	70	„	Thomas Cotes.
Yarmouth	64	„	Charles Saunders.
Monmouth	70	„	Henry Harrison.
Princess Louisa	60	„	Charles Watson.
Windsor	60	„	Thomas Hanway.
Lion	60	„	Arthur Scott.
Tilbury	60	„	Robert Harland.

Ships	Guns.		
Nottingham	60	Captain	Philip Saumarez.
Defiance	60	,,	John Bentley.
Eagle	60	,,	George Brydges Rodney.
Gloucester	50	,,	Philip Durell.
Portland	50	,,	Charles Stevens.

French.

Le Tonnant (Chef d'Escadre, M. de L'Etenduère).	80	Captain	M. Duchaffault.
L'Intrepide	74	,,	Comte de Vaudreuil.
Le Terrible	74	,,	Comte Duguay.
Le Monarque	74	,,	M. de la Bédoyère.
Le Neptune	70	,,	M. de Fromentière (killed).
Le Trident	64	,,	M. D'Amblimont.
Le Fougueux	64	,,	M. Duvignault.
Le Severn	50	,,	M. Durouret.
Le Content	60		—

"DEVONSHIRE," at Sea,
October 17, 1747.

SIR,

At seven in the morning of the 14th of October, being in the latitude of 37° 49′ N., Longitude from Cape Finisterre 1° 2′ W., the Cape bearing S. by E. 94 leagues, the "Edinburgh" made the signal for seven sail on the South-East quarter. I immediately made the signal for all the fleet to chase. About 8 A.M. saw a great number of ships, but so crowded together that we could not count them. About 10 made the signal for the line of battle ahead. The "Louisa," being the headmost and weathermost ship, made the signal for discovering eleven sail of the enemy's line-of-battle ships. Half an hour after Captain Fox, in the "Kent," hailed us and said they counted twelve very large ships. Soon after I perceived the enemy's convoy to crowd away with all the sail they could set, while their ships of war were endeavouring to form in a line astern of them, and hauled near the wind, under their topsails and foresails, and some with topgallant-sails set. Finding we lost time in forming our line, while the enemy was standing away from us, at 11 made the signal for the whole squadron to chase. Half an hour after, observing our headmost ships to be within a proper distance, I made the signal to engage, which was immediately obeyed. The "Lion" and "Princess Louisa" began the engagement, and were followed by the rest of the squadron as they could come up, and went from rear to van. The enemy having the weather-gage of us, and a smart and constant fire being kept on both sides, the smoke prevented my seeing the number of the enemy, or what happened on either side for some time. In passing on to the first ship we could get near, we received many fires at a distance, till we came close to the "Severn" of 50 guns, which we soon silenced, and left to be taken up by the frigates astern. Then perceiving the "Eagle" and "Edinburgh" (who had lost her foretopmast) engaged, we kept our wind as close as possible in order to assist them. This attempt of ours was frustrated by the "Eagle's" falling twice on board us, having had her wheel shot to pieces, and all the men at it killed, and all her braces and bowlines gone. This drove us to leeward, and prevented our attacking "Le Monarque" of 74, and the "Tonnant" of 80 guns, within any distance to do execution. However, we attempted both, especially the latter. While we were engaged with her the breechings of all our lower-deck guns broke, and the guns flew fore and aft, which obliged us to shoot ahead, for our upper and quarter-deck guns could not reach her. Captain Harland in the "Tilbury," observing that she fired single guns at us in order to dismast us, stood on the other tack, between her and the "Devonshire," and gave her a very smart fire. By the time the new breechings were all seized, I was got almost alongside the "Trident" of 64 guns, whom I engaged as soon as possible, and silenced by as brisk a fire as I could make. Just before I attacked her, observing the "Kent," which seemed to have little or no damage, at some distance astern of the "Tonnant," I flung out Captain Fox's pendant to make sail ahead to engage her, as I saw it was in his power to get close up with her, she being somewhat disabled, having lost her main and mizen topmasts. Seeing some of our ships at that time not so closely engaged as I could have wished, and not being well able to distinguish who they were, I flung out the signal for coming to a closer engagement. Soon after, I got alongside, within musket-shot of the "Terrible," of 74 guns and 700 men. Near 7 at night she called out for quarter.

Thus far I have been particular with regard to the share the "Devonshire" bore in the action of that day. As to the other ships, as far as fell within my notice, their commanders, officers, and companies behaved with the greatest spirit and resolution, in every respect like Englishmen. Only I am sorry to acquaint their Lordships that I must except Captain Fox, whose conduct on that day I beg they would give directions for inquiring into at a Courtmartial.

Having observed that six of the enemy's ships had struck, and it being very dark, and our own ships dispersed, I thought it best to bring-to for that night; and seeing a great firing a long way astern of me, I was in hopes to have seen more of the enemy's ships taken in the morning; but instead of that, I received the melancholy account of Captain Saumarez being killed, and that the "Tonnant" had escaped in the night by the assistance of the "Intrepide," which, by having the wind of our ships, had received no damage that I could perceive. Immediately I called a Council of War, a copy of which I send you enclosed.

As to the French convoys escaping, it was not possible for me to detach any ships after them at first, or during the action, except the frigates, and that I thought would have been imprudent, as I observed several large ships of war among them; and to confirm me in this opinion, I have since learned that they had the "Content," of 64 guns, and many frigates from 36 guns downwards. However, I took a step which seemed to me the most probable to intercept them; for as soon as I could man and victual the "Weazle" sloop, I detached her with an express to Commodore Legge (Leeward Islands).

As the enemy's ships were large, except the "Severn," they took a great deal of drubbing, and lost all their masts, excepting two, who had their foremasts left. This has obliged me to lay-by these two days past, in order to put them into a condition to be brought into port, as well as our own which have suffered greatly.

Their Lordships, I hope, will excuse me for not sending them by this opportunity the State and Condition of our ships, as I have not yet been able to collect them, every ship being so much employed.

I propose sending as many ships into Plymouth as I can spare, exclusive of a sufficient number to carry the prizes into

Portsmouth. We have taken "Le Monarque," 74; "Le Terrible," 74; "Le Neptune," 74; "Le Trident," 64; "Le Fougueux," 64; "Severn," 50. Captain Stanhope sent his boats and took up numbers of pacquets thrown into the sea from the "Severn" and "Fougueux." I could not spare time to get them translated; besides they were too wet to be handled. I hope you will get some important intelligence from them, as I have,—that six ships of war are fitting at Brest for the East Indies.

I have sent this express by Captain Moore, of the "Devonshire," in the "Hector"; and it would be doing great injustice to merit not to say that he signalised himself greatly in the action.

This Despatch was accompanied by a letter more specially recommending Captain, afterwards Sir John, Moore, and by another of the same date to Sir Peter Warren.

If I had not had the misfortune of having my right hand and side of my face burnt with powder, I should not have made use of an amanuensis, but given you a full detail of our action on the 14th. For though your bad state of health has obliged you to resign the command of the squadron, yet the many great obligations I lie under induces me to send you enclosed the most material parts of my letter to the Lords of the Admiralty. Wishing you a speedy recovery, I am, &c.

EDWARD HAWKE.

To this may be appended the letter to Commodore Legge, mentioned in the Despatch, and written the day after the battle.

Yesterday I fell in with a fleet of French ships of war, with a convoy of about three hundred sail bound to Martinico. I have taken the ships named in the margin [as above], and for particulars refer you to Captain Midwinter. While I was engaged, and by favour of the night, the convoy escaped, led off by a 64-gun ship and a few small frigates; and this morning I find all my ships in so shattered a condition that I cannot pursue them. This intelligence I have thought proper to send you express by

Captain Midwinter in order that you may use your endeavours to intercept them. I have likewise intelligence of six sail of French ships of war which are to sail with a convoy for France on the arrival of this at Martinico. Wishing you repeated acquisition of reputation and fortune, I am, with real regard, Sir, yours, &c.

EDWARD HAWKE.

This prompt action with regard to the convoy was rewarded with great success. Midwinter was ordered to "proceed without speaking with anything, or suffering yourself (if possible) to be spoke with on your passage." He was too late to tell Legge, for he was just dead; but he fortunately fell in with Pocock who had taken his place; and a very large number of the ships were captured by his squadron.

Before proceeding to notice the two matters in Hawke's Despatch which require attention, viz., the Council of War, and the affair of Captain Fox, a few more facts regarding the battle should find a place here.

Besides the flagship, those which distinguished themselves were commanded by Captains Scott, Harland, Cotes, Watson, Saunders, Saumarez, Hanway, and Rodney; and of these the highest honour was won by Harland, who was particularly mentioned by Hawke and of whom we hear again in Keppel's action; by Watson, who had been so distinguished in Anson's battle, and who, when Admiral in the East Indies, covered himself with glory; by Saunders, who forced the "Neptune" to strike after a very close action of two hours; by Saumarez, Anson's gallant *protégé*, who was killed in the attack upon the "Tonnant," and whose monument is in Westminster

Abbey; and by the immortal Rodney, who earned his first laurels in this battle, where the "Eagle" attacked ship after ship. But it is especially observable that the Admiral not only omitted nothing which was required to prove him to be a first-rate Commander-in-Chief, but that the personal part he took in the fighting, where all had an equal chance, was by far the greatest. It was like the lion's share of the danger which the ancient leader of chivalry, a Percy or a Talbot, a Douglas or a Bruce, or an Edward the First or Third, or the Black Prince, loved to seize for his own, and of which he would let no one rob him. Out of the six ships captured, Hawke, in the "Devonshire," a heavy ship indeed, but mounting only 66 guns, took the "Severn" of 50, and the "Terrible" of 74 guns; while he silenced the "Trident," of 64 guns, leaving her to be taken by others, and attacked the "Tonnant," of 80 guns, in such a way as would probably have added her to his list, had it not been for the lower deck guns of his ship carrying away their breechings at the critical moment. This of itself was a proof of the work he had already got out of his guns; and, with many other indications, though we have no direct evidence from logs or other books, shows that he must have paid extraordinary attention to the practice of quick firing. Such wonderful results were not gained without constant exercise and remarkable skill; but those qualities would have been of little service had the Admiral not possessed, to a degree beyond any of his contemporaries, the cool judgment, the rapid decision at the critical moment, and the unshrinking resolution, which are the property of few, and which alone ensure brilliant success on the day of trial.

In contrast with the personal share of the day's fighting taken by Hawke, it must strike anyone as remarkable that with so many gallant Captains, so very little more was done than he did himself; and, curiously enough, the unfortunate Captain Fox, who suffered by sentence of a Courtmartial for not taking his proper share, was one of the few to whom a ship of the enemy, the "Fougueux," struck. But though Hawke excepts him alone from the general praise bestowed on his officers, it is clear that they were not all of the calibre of those who have been specially mentioned above; and this it was in all probability which prevented the Admiral's Despatch from giving entire satisfaction in the squadron. He had said all he could say, but omissions would be suggestive. Thus we find Warren writing to Anson, on November 26th, as follows:—"I have set all matters straight with the gentlemen of Sir Edward's squadron, who were a good deal dissatisfied at some expressions in his account of the action."*

But if only a portion of the English squadron behaved consummately well, what must be said of the French? M. L'Etenduère and his Captains have never received their full share of credit for this battle. It was a splendid achievement. They did nothing which was not the best that could be done under the circumstances. When the English squadron, which, making

---

* Anson Correspondence, Addl. MSS., British Museum.

all allowance for their smaller size, and weight of metal in each ship, were a decidedly superior force, was first descried, one large ship was detached to help the frigates to protect the convoy; and so sufficient was that protection that it saved the whole; while the remaining eight ships were skilfully formed into line, with a van, centre, and rear; and though ready to make off if the English would let them, yet they contrived to keep the weather gage, and make an excellent fight of it. Indeed they inflicted on the English a loss of 700 killed and wounded, a loss very nearly equal to their own, which amounted to about 800. Finally the "Intrepide," which, as Hawke reports, had received less damage than her neighbours, goes down at the critical moment to the help of the French admiral, and, dangerously surrounded as the "Tonnant" was, contrives to bring her off, in spite of Rodney, Saunders, and Saumarez—to say nothing of the blundering Captain Fox. So gallant was the front shown by those two ships that the English when morning broke, thought it best, after the rude handling they had received, to decline the pursuit. Thus the French admiral, who was badly wounded, might well be pardoned, for having, with a touch of the vanity sometimes attributed to the nation, magnified the number of English line of battle ships with which he had been engaged to 20, instead of 14. If their navy had distinguished itself in other encounters as they did in this and in Anson's engagements, the history of the times might have been very different.

On a consideration of the whole affair it is clear

that much of the success of the French resistance should be attributed to the comparative size, and thickness of the sides,* of their ships, to the number of their crews, and weight of metal. It has been already mentioned with regard to size that in consequence of the capture of the enemy's ships in the early part of this war, and the discovery that they were so greatly superior to the English vessels of the same nominal rate, an entire change was gradually commenced, by which in the course of time some sort of equality was at last obtained. On the other points also changes were in contemplation.

It was shortly before Anson's and Hawke's battles that Warren wrote thus to the former:—

> I am greatly pleased to hear it has been proposed, with a prospect of success, to augment the number of men and weight of metal in all the different classes of our ships, to put them on a par with those of the French. When that is the case there will be no excuse left for ill-behaviour; and I dare say upon all occasions, when no extraordinary or unforeseen accident shall intervene, our ships and people will give a good account of their enemies of equal force when and wherever they meet. For I cannot help thinking we have this advantage of them, that our officers are better seamen than theirs, and I hope as valiant, and our men in general more robust and stronger; and they never were thought to want courage, though they have very little virtue of any other kind.†

The last remark may go for what it is worth. If these statements required confirmation the testimony of the clever Admiral Knowles, at about the same date,

---

* Out of 134 shot from lower-deck guns which struck the "Tonnant," only one penetrated. See "French Account by Authority," Ekins' "Naval Tactics," p. 18.

† Anson Correspondence.

THE SIZE OF THE FRENCH SHIPS. 191

might be added. He says, in a letter of suggestions to Anson :—

> The unthinking populace are too free to censure without inquiring into the reasons of things, and imagine it strange an English ship of war of 70 guns cannot take a French ship of the same force, whereas it is pretty apparent that our 70-gun ships are little superior to their ships of 52 guns.*

Still further,—the expression used in Hawke's celebrated Despatch, as it probably referred to this superiority, and not only to the number of guns, supplies a commentary both on the need of improvement, and on the phenomena of the battle he describes :—" As the enemy's ships were large, except the 'Severn,' they took a great deal of drubbing." It was this homely English word which puzzled King George II. when Lord Chesterfield, Secretary of State, was reading the Despatch to him. He asked what it meant. At this instant the Duke of Bedford, First Lord of the Admiralty, entering the closet, Lord Chesterfield begged leave to refer the King to his Grace, as he could explain it perfectly. The King who had heard of the story, laughed heartily, and said he now knew very well what "drubbing" meant. The Duke had, a short time before, been assaulted on the Lichfield race-course, and roughly handled.

The respect for the size, force, and conduct of the French ships, impressed on the English fleet, is remarkably evidenced by the Council of War to which Hawke refers in his Despatch. For once we may be sure that such a Council was not summoned to take off

---

* Anson Correspondence.

a responsibility which the Commander-in-Chief ought to have undertaken himself. His letter to Commodore Legge gives his own opinion that "all my ships are in so shattered a condition that I could not pursue," and we may be quite sure that eight Captains, of whom Rodney, Watson, and Saunders were three, would not have signed the minutes if there had been any help for it. The Resolutions to which they came were as follows:—

1. That four ships, the least of them of 60 guns, could only be sufficient to go in quest of the two French ships, the "Tonnant" of 80 guns, and the "Intrepide" of 74, which had escaped from the action in the evening of the 14th.

2. That none of the ships under their command were at present in a condition to be sent on this service.

3. That by the time a sufficient number of them could have been got ready it would be impracticable to come up with the enemy's ships.

Though there could not have been stronger testimony to the superior importance of heavy batteries and large ships, it can hardly be imagined that such men could come to such resolutions if the course of the battle had not left the ships of the best officers in a very bad condition, and suggested a want of confidence in the rest. Hawke, we have seen, was himself wounded, and his own battered ship was no doubt one of those which must have remained. And here it may be remarked that the gallant Frenchmen would probably, even if sought, never have been found; for not only had they the start of a whole October night, but they took care not to steer towards the French coast, but out to sea, until they were about a hundred leagues West of Ushant, in a track not much frequented. There they lay-to, and repaired damages; and, after some time, when the coast was clear, made their way to Brest.

Before however the Council of War would allow itself to be constituted, Captain Watson, supported by the whole of the other seven Captains who had been summoned, made a formal objection to "ranking with Captain Fox till his character should be cleared up with regard to the aspersions cast upon it for his behaviour in action with the enemy on the 14th instant"; and Fox was accordingly excluded from the Court. In order to collect all the facts connected with the battle into one group, and to form a clear idea of Hawke's position, it may be well to refer at once, in a few words, to the Courtmartial held upon this officer soon after the arrival of the squadron in port. It may be premised that Fox had a very fair reputation in the Service and, while under Warren's command, had, only a little before, successfully led a small squadron which had frightened away a French force not much inferior to itself, under M. Dubois de la Mothe, and captured a very large number of merchant ships which were under its convoy.

All the numerous details of the battle which came out in the evidence adduced before the Court, over which Sir Peter Warren presided, exactly corroborate, it need hardly be said, the public account given by Hawke. He himself was necessarily the official prosecutor, but it is evident that though he agreed with his Captains that there should be a Trial, the pique, disgust, and contempt felt for Fox was on their side, not on his. On November 4th he tells the Admiralty that he "could not avoid desiring the attendance of the Captains of his squadron in order that they might give their reasons for refusing to rank with Mr. Fox. It is doing justice both to His Majesty and to Mr. Fox." His own position is dignified. He asks but one question; and there is an entire absence of anything like a desire to crush the prisoner. But the evidence of Fox's fellow-Captains was uniform; it was formed from independent points of view, and it really left the Court no choice. The admirable behaviour of Saunders and Rodney came out strongly in evidence; but it was their sense of being deserted by Fox, and of the two French ships having escaped through his failure of duty, which forms the chief feature of the Courtmartial. Rodney especially describes his being exposed to the fire of four of the enemy's ships when, as he asserted, Fox's ship the "Kent," might well have taken off some of it.

In his defence the prisoner spoke with great respect of the French:—"The members of this Court know how well the French ships of war fight;" and he defended himself from Rodney's charge by declaring that the reason why he did not support the "Eagle" was because he believed that she was moving forward to attack the next ship ahead, and leaving the "Neptune" to him; but finding she did not, he himself went off to the "Fougueux," which, after three quarters of an hour's engagement within pistol shot, he forced to strike. But he was quite unable to get over the fatal charge of leaving the "Tonnant" while the signal for "closer action" was flying from the flagship. The Court decided that his duty was to have stayed by her till he took her; and it rightly detected other errors in judgment which he had made throughout the action. It was unanimous in the conclusion that he had only erred in "conduct," and was only guilty of part of the offences charged.

<blockquote>
His courage has been so fully proved to them as not to leave room for suspecting it, and part of his misconduct seems to them to proceed from his listening to the persuasions of his First Lieutenant and Master, and giving way to them.
</blockquote>

Thus he was only sentenced to be dismissed his ship. He was never employed again, and in 1749 was placed on the list of Rear-admirals for half-pay.

It is thus clear that Hawke had taken exactly the right line on this difficult question of bringing an officer to a Courtmartial. An admiral has to steer between Scylla and Charybdis. He is culpable if he allows misconduct to pass. He has every temptation to be too severe. The failure of a part of the great machine must grievously try the mettle of a man who knows how it could, and ought to, be worked.

Of the two last documents in reference to this battle from which extracts may be made, the first is dated October 28th, and states to the Admiralty what promotions and appointments the Admiral has made into vacancies. It concludes thus:—

<blockquote>
The Count Du Guay, who commanded the "Terrible," and is now prisoner on board the "Devonshire," with the major part of her officers, has desired me to intercede with their Lordships
</blockquote>

for permission to return as soon as possible to France on his parole. He is an old man, and very infirm and weakly, so afflicted with asthma that he can hardly breathe.

The French officers in command were often old men. M. De Court who commanded against Mathews was nearly 80 years of age.

The next extract is from a letter to Sir Henry Penrice, the Judge of the Admiralty Court, and has reference to the prizes, about which some difficulty had arisen from want of the proper papers:—

Sir,

It is impossible to conceive the confusion Prize ships of war are in as soon as they have struck. Their common men rob and plunder their own ships and officers. The latter confusedly throw their own things together. Neither is there any restraining our own people, egged on by their resentment, from plundering, when they first enter them, and destroying papers and everything else which appears useless to them. So that there is seldom a paper to be found.

The French ships taken by the squadron under my command were mere wrecks within-board. Shifting of prisoners, replacing them with our own men, and getting the ship to rights, prevented the taking the care of papers there ought to have been. These reasons, joined to that of there being no Bills of Lading, Cargoes, &c. to occasion a dispute of property, have induced me to beg that, if possible, you will dispense with the want of papers, and condemn the remaining four ships, "Monarque," "Terrible," "Trident," and "Severn," which will greatly oblige yours, &c.

Edward Hawke.

It will not be doing an injustice to those times if we infer from this letter that what we now call "red tape" was not even then entirely unknown.

It was not till October 31st that Hawke arrived at Portsmouth with his squadron and prizes. As four of the latter had been dismasted, and the remaining two only retained their foremasts, it had taken some days to refit them with jury masts, since it had to be done by the crews of ships which themselves stood in need of great repairs. The rejoicings in England were great, and the reward of the K.B. conferred on Hawke, though far below what had been thought proper in Anson's case, was not altogether inadequate. The King at any rate showed his appreciation of the merit he had long before detected, by granting the admiral a "most gracious reception." Perhaps the Government were afraid of showing too great a readiness to award distinctions to a man from whom they had begun to expect a great deal more.

On November 2nd, "Sir Edward Hawke" writes to the Admiralty as follows:—

> I return their Lordships many thanks for honouring me with the command of the Western Squadron since the 8th of September last. As Sir Peter Warren seems in a great measure to have recovered his health, I shall esteem it as a particular favour if their Lordships will permit me to serve under him, an honour of which I am extremely desirous:

and on November 7th:—

> I beg their Lordships will accept my most sincere and grateful acknowledgments for their generous approbation of what was no more than my duty, and which I always shall at all times endeavour to merit.

The letter to which this refers contains the following passage:—

> Their Lordships direct me to congratulate you in their name for the great service you have done your country in defeating so great a force of the enemy, and taking so many of their capital

ships, wherein you have shown a conduct that has very much distinguished your character, and fully answered the expectations of their Lordships who entrusted you with the command of this squadron. You will know from other hands what great satisfaction you have given, not only to the King and his Ministers, but to the Trading Interest in the City, and indeed to all His Majesty's good subjects.

It is at this time that, in a letter to Admiral Chambers, occurs the one only brief mention of Lady Hawke which is to be found in any extant correspondence:—"My wife, who is now here [Portsmouth], joins with me in compliments to you." "Who is now here"—it was a proud moment for her. She had come to meet her victorious husband, had shared in the raptures of the population at the arrival of his French prizes, and this time at any rate found his merits recognized by the title which she was to share. It is to be regretted that nothing should be found beyond this trifling notice concerning one who must have well performed her part in the training of a national hero.

So much for the battle which, from the nearest land to the place where it was fought, is commonly called Hawke's Battle off Ushant. There is not much more to be said about the admiral himself, till the war was over, or rather succeeded by the Truce which goes by the name of the Peace of Aix la Chapelle. He obtained his wish, which was to be continued as second in command under Sir Peter Warren, who had recovered his health; and he practically commands the Western squadron till Warren definitely retires on July 26th, 1748. He was summoned to receive the

Order of the Bath on November 13th, but the Grand Master, the Duke of Montagu, on the 23rd, finding he should not "have the pleasure of waiting on him in Town before he goes to sea, sends His Majesty's Dispensation to wear the Star of the Order, although he has not been installed,"—but at the same time requiring the fees immediately. He was wise in making that cautious proviso, for the new Knight was not installed till December 11th, 1753.

These documents have been preserved; so also has the letter from the Duke of Bedford, "recommending" Sir Edward Hawke as Member of Parliament for Portsmouth. It runs as follows:—

SIR,   ADMIRALTY OFFICE, Dec. 18, 1747.
On occasion of the melancholy news of Commodore Legge's death being confirmed, I have this day wrote to Mr. Mayor of Portsmouth, recommending you to the Gentlemen of the Corporation to be their Representative in Parliament. I most heartily wish you good success, and am, Sir, yours, &c.
BEDFORD.

On December 23rd, Keppel writes to Anson from Portsmouth:—

I hear the town is to have Sir Edward Hawke for its Member, and the bells were very troublesome all yesterday on that account.

Thus, according to the customs of those simple times, the Admiralty showed their appreciation of a distinguished officer. The King should make him a Knight; the First Lord of the Admiralty a Member of Parliament. Whether for better or worse, the navy has never had the place in the Councils of the nation which it had in the "good old days." Who would think of calling back those days? Yet, perhaps, if naval men could not shine in debate, it was not a bad thing to have in the House a few of that class of them who did not owe their seats to the mere accidents of birth or fortune, but who had attained distinction by the display of noble qualities in the face of the enemy. These men presented the visible emblems of one constituent element of British greatness. Nor were they the men to urge their country to unnecessary wars, for they knew what war meant; but they understood also what the safety and honour of Great Britain required.

We may now regard our admiral as fully established in the great position which he held for so many years in the eyes of his countrymen. They well understood the significance of the motto which he selected when, soon after this battle, his arms were granted,— "Strike." It was a compact. He never failed to strike when they gave him fair play.

That there were some who understood the sacrifice he had made in refusing to look for galleons or merchant ships, in order that he might concentrate the national force upon the destruction of the enemy, is evidenced by the following letter from a Mr. Perrie:—

DEAR SIR,
Amidst the universal acclamations of the public for your late services to your king and country accept my private congratulations for your good success, so much owing to your own courage and prudent conduct. I could have wished, indeed, that more of the enemy's merchantmen had fallen into your hands; but when I consider that what you lost in this way in point of

fortune is very amply made up to you in the lustre of an unsullied reputation, I doubt whether I should not be in the wrong to wish the affair otherwise than it has happened.

Before finally quitting Sir Peter Warren, who seems to have assumed a little too much of the position of patron to such a man as Hawke, only two years his junior in rank, we find him placed, before he dies, by a curious touch of poetical justice, in a somewhat comical position. His riches and his fame had not only brought him in as Member for Westminster at the General Election of 1747, but at a later date, inspired the City of London, or rather the Billingsgate Ward, with a very strong desire to make him their Alderman. This the Admiral with all politeness declined. In vain did Billingsgate press him to reconsider his resolution, and adjure him by their unanimity, their sense of his "high abilities and distinguished merit, the greatness of his character and true worth," as well as by "the further assurance you have been pleased to give us of the honour of your friendship," which indicated an eye to the future; the Admiral was obdurate. In vain he sent them £200, "one moiety to be distributed among the poor, and the other to be disposed of at their discretion." This only caused the Deputy and Common Council to wait upon him in person, and renew their suit, which, like Cæsar, he thus "thrice declined." Nevertheless, the importunate citizens proceeded to his election. Did they detect a lurking "Yes" under the stern "No"? If so, they were mistaken. "On the 23rd of June [1752] Sir Peter sent a message to the Court of

Aldermen, desiring to be excused from serving the office to which he had been elected; and paid the fine of £500 for that purpose."* Next month, at the early age of 49, he died.

Of Warren we shall, then, hear no more; and now as the first of the two wars, so closely connected, draws to an end, an end materially hastened by the battles described in this Chapter, it will be proper to bring the history of Boscawen, Hawke's nearest rival in glory, up to the same level.

We may despise and discard Horace Walpole's gossip as to the reason why Anson sent Boscawen out to India in 1747; but it is necessary to notice it, since in the present day his Works pass for history. He attributes Boscawen's employment in the task of besieging Pondicherry (where he was the first admiral to whom a general's Commission had been granted since the reign of Charles II.) to Anson's desire to ruin him. He was sent out, "upon slight intelligence and upon improbable views," to perform a Herculean task, because "when he and Anson came together from the victory off Cape Finisterre, he complained loudly of Anson's behaviour";† and he tells a ridiculous story as to a

sea-piece, which Anson had lately had drawn of the victory for which he was lorded, in which his own ship, in a cloud of cannon, was boarding the French Admiral. This circumstance, which is as true as if Madame Scudery had written his life,—for he was scarce in sight when the Frenchman struck to Boscawen,—has been so ridiculed by the whole tar-hood that the romantic part

---

* Charnock's "*Biog. Nav.*"
† "Letters to Mann," vol. i. p. 338.

has been forced to be cancelled, and one only gun remains firing at Anson's ship.*

Anson was politically and socially hateful to Walpole, and though no doubt his distinction did not rest on the same grounds as those of the greater naval heroes of his time, nothing but malignity could fasten any blame upon his courage or conduct, still less on his motives for employing Boscawen. It was, on the contrary, only another proof of the sagacity which enabled him to select the right man, as we say, for the right place. Boscawen had already displayed, like the far inferior officer, Knowles, talents for military as well as strictly naval command. The son of Lord Falmouth, and great nephew of John Duke of Marlborough, he owed but little to his birth, and almost everything to his own abundant zeal and conspicuous merit. He had served as a volunteer under Vernon, and soon showed his mettle at Portobello: but unlike so many other officers in the subsequent campaigns, he served at Cartagena and elsewhere without any loss of reputation; and we have seen him largely contributing to the success of Anson's battle, though Walpole appears to attribute to him the brilliant performances of Warren. It is not indeed clear that the incongruous union of the military and naval commands in the person of the Admiral was much more successful in India than might have been expected; but everything which gallantry and perseverance could perform, under very trying circumstances, against superior

---

* "Letters to Mann," vol. i. p. 284.

forces, was effected by Boscawen, assisted at a critical moment by young Clive, who here commenced his extraordinary career. When the Peace put a stop to further proceedings, he came home with a character only second to Hawke's. He had preceded him by some years as a Member of Parliament, and in 1751 found a place at the Board of Admiralty. Thus when the smouldering war again burst forth in flame, these were the two men to whom the country had learnt to look. Pocock had scarcely yet begun to earn his high reputation; but he had acquired the necessary experience. Rodney, Saunders and Watson had already commenced a fine career, under Hawke's leadership; and Keppel, who addresses Anson as if he were his son,—and indeed, having been the favourite midshipman of that officer in the "Centurion," he had clearly established some such relationship,—was learning to look upon Hawke as his friend. It so happened that the first duty which awaited Hawke, the very day after his arrival in England with his prizes, was to preside at the Courtmartial held upon Keppel for the loss of his ship. He had lost her on the Coast of France in the too eager chase of an enemy, but was honourably acquitted: and here it was that a mutual esteem, which ripened into friendship, first commenced between the two officers. "Sir Edward," he writes to Anson, on coming under Hawke's command, early in 1748, "is extremely civil to me, and I hope he will do well and please everybody"—a difficult task. Few letters are more entertaining, it may be added, than the familiar, "happy-go-lucky," epistles of this ever-youthful "little Keppel" which we find in the Anson Collection. Howe was as yet but little known. He also was preparing to be one of Hawke's most distinguished pupils.

And now let us ask the question whether history has been wholly true to her vocation in ascribing everything to Chatham in the Seven Years' War. It is too common a practice with our historians to notice only the contrast between the disastrous commencement of that war under Newcastle, and the splendid operations which established the Empire under Chatham. But they forget the immense progress which had been made by the navy in the previous war, and the still greater contrast between the fleet of Mathews and the fleet of Hawke. They fail to observe the work which had been done by Anson, and the noble spirit which had been infused into the service by the gallant men of whom a few short notices have been given in this narrative. These were the men made to Chatham's hand, whom even he at first did not understand how to employ, but who, as soon as he had acquired his lesson, carried his name to the highest pitch of glory.

In these pages it is of course necessary to abstract, and cut short the masses of detail which would expose to the world, if people could stop to read, how much good and first-rate work went to the making of such a character as Hawke's. Suffice it that the impression produced upon one who has necessarily studied the whole series of documents, is that the prudence, fortitude, high-mindedness, and simplicity which they display, are of themselves the indications of a great upward bound in the *morale* of the nation, and that it would have been surprising if they had not borne the fruit they did in the ensuing struggle for national existence. This ought not to detract from Chatham's merit, but it is absurd to worship an idol.

After so high a flight, it is an act of audacity to descend to such a matter as naval uniform; but there is something to be said for linking the higher and lower subjects in one. It is by no means difficult to imagine a connection between the fine spirit with which the Royal Navy emerged out of the first Spanish war, and the order issued by Anson at the close of it, for a uniform dress. The chaos which had marred its opening efforts was well typified by the varieties of naval attire. Smollett's description of the dandy captain's dress in "Roderick Random" reads like an absurd caricature; but if the following anecdote given by Charnock[*] is as true as the author believed it to be, the caricature is little more than another version of the fact. Captain, afterwards Sir William, Burnaby, was the dandy. His ship went out to the West Indies to join the fleet of Vernon, whose slovenly habits were quite as much an affectation as the Captain's.

Burnaby, immediately after his arrival at Jamaica, proceeded, as is customary, to pay a visit of ceremony to the Commander-in-Chief. On this solemn occasion he equipped himself gorgeously in a suit of silk, or, as some say, velvet, very splendidly laced. The Admiral was, as was not uncommon with him,

---

[*] "*Biog. Nav.*," vol. v. p. 131.

coarsely dressed in a very ordinary manner. When Mr. Burnaby was announced, Mr. Vernon rose from his escritoire with much pretended and apparent confusion, and hurrying into an inner apartment, put on a wig of ceremony, which having adjusted with pretended haste and embarrassment, he advanced towards Mr. Burnaby with great gravity, and desired to know his commands; when the latter informed him with much precision and attention to form "that he had the honour to command the bomb-vessel which had just arrived from England." Mr. Vernon, with a ludicrous and grotesque alteration of countenance, replied, "Gad so, Sir, I really took you for a dancing-master." Certainly the coarse rudeness and reprehension of the admiral was, to the full, as ridiculous as the finical attention to dress of the other.

The following order shows, that there was much irregularity, and, below the rank of Lieutenant, that there was no attempt at a uniform at all.

ADMIRALTY, April 19th, 1748.

Whereas we judge it necessary in order the better to distinguish the rank of sea-officers, to establish a military uniform clothing for Admirals, Captains, Commanders, and Lieutenants, and judging it also necessary that persons acting as midshipmen should likewise have a uniform clothing, in order to their conveying the appearance which is necessary to distinguish the class to be in the rank of gentlemen, and give them better credit and figure in executing the commands of their superior officers, you are hereby required and directed to conform yourself to the said establishment by wearing clothing accordingly at all proper times, and to take care that such of the aforesaid officers and midshipmen who may be from time to time under your command do the like . . . patterns of which for Admirals and Vice Admirals, and also for Rear Admirals, may be seen at the Admiralty Office, and patterns for each class of other officers, viz., Captains who have taken post for three years, and by His Majesty's regulations rank as Colonels, all other Post Captains who by the said Regulations rank as Lieutenant Colonels, Commanders not taking Post, and Lieutenants, and likewise for midshipmen, will be lodged at the Navy Office, and with the Storekeepers of His Majesty's yard at Plymouth.

The colours, blue and white, according to the Duke of Bedford, were suggested by the King's admiration for the riding dress worn by " my Duchess."*

On May 5th, 1748, the Proclamation for the cessation of hostilities was made, consequent on the signature of the Preliminaries of Peace; and one of the marks of the cessation was a promotion of Admirals, by which Hawke became Vice-admiral of the Blue. From July 26th, 1748, when he is ordered to succeed Warren in supreme command of the fleet, till November 10th, 1752—a period which, added to that which had passed since he hoisted his flag in July 1747, amounts to nearly five years and a half—he is continuously employed as Commander-in-chief, nearly all the time at Portsmouth, but in 1750 in the Thames and Medway. For the next two years and a half he seems to have been unemployed, until the notes of war are again sounded. On February 12th, 1755, he is ordered to hoist his flag once more. His service is then again continuous till very near the conclusion of the Peace of Paris.†

This Chapter may close with some verses from the " Gentleman's Magazine " (October, 1747), which, though not worth much in themselves, indicate the sense of relief and recovery which the nation had begun to entertain in that year, and the persons to whom it owed its improved position.

---

* Barrow's "Anson."

† It may be mentioned, to prevent mistakes, that though Hawke was appointed in 1749 to command the squadron ordered to convoy the transports to Nova Scotia, he was not actually sent.

> Her lance inverted, head reclined,
>   As late Britannia pensive sate,
> Revolving in her anxious mind
>   The woes of her declining state,
> Fame in her rapid flight drew near,
>   And sounding loud from every tongue,
> "Hawke," "Anson," "Warren," in her ear,
>   The Genius roused, depressed so long.
> "If Anson, Warren, Hawke," she said,
>   Now rising with a sprightly bound,
> "Are known to fame, my laurelled head
>   With pristine glory shall be crowned.
> No more I'll sigh, no more complain,
>   My ancient rights at length restored,
> Restored my empire o'er the main,
>   And dreaded round the globe my sword."

The effect produced by the action of the Royal Navy was, indeed, the sole ground on which the country could claim a Peace. The land forces had never had a fair chance, and nearly 80 millions of debt had been incurred, chiefly in subsidies and the pay of Hanoverian troops. But the Navy of France had been most seriously crippled in battles and single fights, her hostile colonial enterprises effectively checked, and her support of Spain had fallen still more ruinously than ever on that decaying State. The commerce of all three nations had suffered enormously; but the balance of prizes was estimated to be in favour of Great Britain by two millions sterling.

CHAPTER VII.

HAWKE'S POSITION DURING THE PEACE AND AT THE OPENING OF THE SEVEN YEARS' WAR.—CONDITION OF THE GOVERNMENT.

THERE is naturally little worth mention in the history of Sir Edward Hawke during the Peace from 1748 to 1755; but the all-important part he took in the Seven Years' War which succeeded it, demands a few preliminary words on the general course of events which led up to that war, and brought him and his peers once more to the front.

As the too-pacific policy of Sir Robert Walpole, coupled with the weakness inherent, during its earlier days, in the Hanoverian Succession, had been the direct cause of that French aggression and Spanish arrogance which forced England into the first of the two wars under consideration, so the incapacity of the two Pelhams, who succeeded to Walpole's place, aggravated by the political factions which struggled for supremacy over his coffin, encouraged the French to pursue the colonial enterprises which had been checked by the British navy, and to take every advantage of the Peace as a preparation for reopening the war under better auspices.

The Peace of Aix la Chapelle, concluded in October 1748, had been chiefly due to the exertions of Mr. Pelham, the Prime Minister, of Lord Chesterfield, and of Lord Sandwich. It was specially distasteful to the English, who found themselves obliged to relinquish their one acquisition made during the late war, the island of Cape Breton, and to consent to the disgrace of giving hostages for the performance of that condition. Nothing could more clearly show the importance attached by France to her scheme of colonisation than these terms. On the other hand, Hanover had been preserved; Holland was saved;—always, and most wisely, a central point in English foreign policy; and France had to give up by land what had cost her much more than the English had spent at sea. As far as England and France were concerned, it was simply a temporary return to the *status quo ante*, as the best escape from an anomalous and confused political situation, in which the nations of Europe were losing sight of the Balance of Power, and spending vast sums of money they hardly knew why. The English felt their system of subsidies had become, not only ruinous, but ridiculous.

And yet, as far as France and England were concerned, both countries had a very clear instinct that the ground of their particular struggle was not obscure, and could not be really removed by the Peace. It might suit either party to side with Austria, or Prussia, as the case might be, and the position of Hanover necessarily led to such combinations; but behind those alliances lay the mighty contest for supremacy at sea, for ships, colonies, and commerce. The three Bourbon thrones had not been acquired for a mere show of grandeur; the prospects of a French America and a French India had succeeded to the merely European ambition of Louis Quatorze. If the English had preceded them in both directions, the Dutch had preceded the English, and the Portuguese the Dutch; why should not France have its turn? And in truth the French and English were now so intermixed on the St. Lawrence, and on the adjacent shores and islands of North America, that it was no more possible that their petty jealousies and differences could be composed at that period without hostilities, than the West Indian quarrels of Spain and Great Britain in 1739. The rival interests of the two countries in India, though natural enough under the circumstances, were, more distinctly still, the fruit of an aggressive policy on the part of the French.

Thus, whatever might be the comfortable dreams of the British Government, the French never stopped for a moment in their career. All they wanted at the moment was a free passage for their ships and soldiers between France and her colonies, undisturbed by the ubiquitous navy of Great Britain. All their attention was directed to this point. In India Dupleix was encouraged and assisted to follow up the advantages over England already gained. In the West Indies and on the African Coast all neutral territory was claimed for France by the process of setting up posts and proclamations, and, in some cases, by actual occupation. In North America no pains were spared to strengthen the fortifications of Cape Breton, and especially of its capital, Louisbourg; to form extensive alliances with the savage Indian tribes at the back of the English settlements, who were now armed, and to some extent disciplined, for the conflict which would soon begin; and, above all, to establish a chain of forts which should connect their prosperous Canadian Colony with the Mississippi, and so with Louisiana and with the forces of their allies, the Spaniards. They were also bent on obtaining water-access to Canada by lake and river to the south of the St. Lawrence, which is ice-closed in winter.

This was an extremely clever scheme. If the sturdy English colonists, who had already given so much trouble to France and Spain, could only be hemmed in by a military cordon in their rear, and choked by great naval and military stations in front, there would be some real prospect of a French America. Jonquière and Galissonière were, as schemers for the aggrandisement of their country, only second to Dupleix and Lally, but they have dropped out of history. It did not much trouble the national conscience that some of these aggressive forts were built within territories which the English had long considered their own. Why should these people be the only colonists to extend and encroach upon their neighbours? If in the process the French Indians cut off a few straggling settlers, and used the scalping-knife rather freely, bodies of French soldiers had been gradually introduced during the Peace into the new forts; the colonists could make no united, and therefore no effective, resistance; and England was not at all likely to begin over again an expensive war for such a trifle.

The British Government did, indeed, in 1749, at the instance of the President of the Board of Trade, Lord Halifax, take one step which showed they were aware of what was going on. This was the establishment of a military colony, which took the name of its projector, planted at that splendid and commodious harbour in Nova Scotia so well known in modern times as the favourite station of English ships and regiments. But this only led to further French aggression. Though the limits of Nova Scotia, or Acadia, as the French termed it, had been carefully recognised by the Treaty of Utrecht, the French Colonial Governor made no scruple of pursuing the same policy as had been decided upon in the case of the older colonists. He seized upon unoccupied territory; built forts at the back of the Colony; cut off the British fur-trade, and encouraged rebellion among the old French settlers who, having accepted the arrangements of the Peace of Utrecht, had hitherto lived in quiet subordination to the British Government. The Jesuit missionaries were particularly concerned in the latter operation.

Thus a petty border-warfare had commenced between the colonies of the two nations, in which the English were sure to come off the worst, not only on account of the feebleness of the Home Government and of its colonies, but also because of the peculiarly unsatisfactory representation of Great Britain at the Court of France. Lord Albemarle was famous for his exquisite manners; but this was a poor set-off against his incompetence. His remonstrances on the subject of the French aggressions in America passed unheeded, and when the English appeared to show some signs of waking up, the wife of the French ambassador in London, Madame de Mirepoix, dexterously hoodwinked the Court. So far had the Pelham Administration been from comprehending the dangers which lay before them, that, in 1750, there had been a large reduction of the navy, over which Anson sighed, and against which Pitt, from the side of the Opposition, protested in vain. Even the Spaniards renewed their old methods of harassing English trade by their guardacostas in the West Indies, and by their treatment of English merchants in Spain. Yet as late as 1753 Parliament opened with a Speech from the throne in which the King was made to say that " he had the satisfaction to be assured of a good disposition in all the Powers that were his allies to adhere to the same salutary object" [of peace].

Lord Anson was the main link between this feeble Government and the Royal Navy, of which he had been the chief administrator for many years before he became, in 1751, First Lord of the Admiralty. His position was, in reality, an unfortunate one for his reputation; but it was the natural consequence of the marriage which took place at this time between him and the daughter of Lord Hardwicke. That clever lawyer was the political ally of the Pelhams; and Anson, who never became independent of him, was thus mixed up with that particular section of the political world which was more tainted than any other with the intrigue and corruption of faction, and less capable of taking in hand the greater politics which a nation in such a position as Great Britain can never neglect with impunity. The very success of this party was its greatest misfortune. All the various, often inconsistent, elements of the Opposition had gradually melted away. Pulteney, Chesterfield, Bedford, Wyndham, Bolingbroke, had either died or disappeared from the political arena. Carteret had sunk to a mere secondary position. Frederick, Prince of Wales, whose factious Court had at least afforded a standing-point for the gradual formation of a new phase of Party Government, had passed away, unregretted. Pelham himself followed in 1754. Who was left? One man only remained, who had, from long habituation, acquired the practice of holding in his hands all the threads of official life, one man only to whom the King was sufficiently accustomed to be able to act with him; though he freely confessed that in Germany such a man would hardly be reckoned fit for the post of Chamberlain at one of its smallest Courts. This was Pelham's elder brother, the Duke of Newcastle.

It was not the King's fault that he was reduced so low. He had, through a long series of years, been contending against unceasing difficulties in the support of the interests of his hereditary States; for it was necessary that they should be kept in close connection with those of Great Britain. During every one of these years such policy was hateful to the people; yet that people nevertheless felt, with true political instinct, that they could not possibly dispense with the ruler whom they had deliberately chosen. He had long lost the clever consort who had reconciled English men and English women to much they both disliked and disapproved. Thus Walpole and Pelham, in succession, had governed the realm; for they alone —the latter in close connection with Carteret—had contrived to combine the interests of Great Britain with those of Hanover; and the oligarchical form retained as yet by the British Constitution, had enabled them to tide over, by means which were not then thought disgraceful, the difficulties which arose out of the national discontent. Each of them in turn led the House of Commons ; and from his seat in the House as from a throne, showering down places and pensions, could still the wildest tempests, and restrain within bounds, up to a certain point, the most formidable patriots. But Newcastle was far inferior to these men ; and he was not in the House of Commons. No wonder the old King's mind misgave him. It was a real difficulty. How was the Government to be carried on? No wonder the watchful enemy on the other side of the Channel observed the situation, and began to do openly what had hitherto been shrouded under some sort of decent veil. No wonder also that the English people, enraged beyond measure at what they called the "Machiavellian," the "perfidious" policy of France, began to rally round the one man whom the King, because he had hitherto been the chief opponent of the Hanoverian policy, and had resisted every effort which had been made to sap his blunt and courageous independence, would on no account consent to call to his counsels. It was precisely here that the French overreached themselves. This sudden resolution to throw off the mask had the effect of giving a shock to the resistance of the King, and of gradually bringing Pitt, destined to be the worst enemy the French ever had, to the head of affairs. But it cost two years and more, two years of misery and failure, to produce this result.

The person who might seem most to be pitied during the struggle for a good Government which now took place in England, is the Duke of Newcastle; but that would be a species of historical sympathy which it would be an error to waste. The Duke was a bustling, active man of business in his own way, had a very large knowledge of foreign affairs, and was perfectly happy in all the intrigue and chicane of these complicated politics. He delighted in speaking, was by no means a bad debater, and was never fatigued. While corrupting others, he was himself immaculate; and, the possessor of a fine fortune, impoverished himself by spending it in public life and public affairs. Above all he had no sense of the ridiculous, and, as Lord Waldegrave says, had "lost all sensibility."* ' So long as he could carry his point, he felt not the stings of sarcasm.

* Memoirs, p. 70.

The man whom this curious compound of ill-mixed qualities would fain trust to manage the House of Commons was the elder Fox, perhaps as able a man as the elder Pitt, and with many of the great qualities which distinguished his own more famous son; but like that son, his want of character hung like a weight of lead about his neck. Such a man was of course a rotten stick to lean upon. These were the rulers of Great Britain at a moment when she required the highest statesmanship and noblest patriotism.

The only excuse for recapitulating what is so well known is that the course of our narrative leads over the quarterdeck on which Byng was shot to death; the appointment of Byng to the command in the Mediterranean was the outcome of the chaos above described; and it is only in connection with the political situation that the professional blunders of the Courtmartial which brought about that "judicial murder" can be understood. Hawke's position also is inseparably connected with that of the miserable Byng. However different their character and fate, their paths crossed and recrossed each other's. Hawke had succeeded Byng in command of the "Portland," and Byng Hawke in charge of the cruising ships in the Bay of Biscay. When Byng was selected for the post in which he failed, it was because Hawke could not be spared from the Channel. When the unfortunate result of his battle with the French became known, the cry of the whole country was—"It could never have happened if Hawke had been there"; and the first step taken to repair the disaster was to send him out to supersede Byng in the command of the Mediterranean fleet.

If we enquire why an officer who had been entirely undistinguished in active service should have been thus placed on a level with such men as Hawke and Boscawen, and when so able an administrator as Anson was at the helm, there is but one answer, and that unfortunately would apply to too many similar cases. Byng was the son of a great officer; had, like the wretched Norris, been pushed through the lower ranks of the Service with rapidity by the mere force of Lord Torrington's position, and was very high for his age upon the list of admirals; had been made Governor and Commander-in-chief of Newfoundland when still a young man; had performed the ordinary duties of Commodore and Admiral with credit, and if nothing else had been required of him, would never have been heard of any more. Unlike Richard Norris, he was a man of courage, and had more than the average share of education and mental ability; but his career had fostered the growth of qualities which made him nearly as unfit for high command as even Admiral Mathews himself; and he had the misfortune of being brought face to face with the enemy under circumstances which required that he should possess the exact qualities which were not his by nature, and which he had never acquired.

On this point it may be well to quote at once the sensible remarks of Charnock, in his "*Biographia Navalis,*" a work now almost forgotten, and indeed only to be followed with caution, but occasionally, as we have seen in the account of Mathews and Lestock, displaying remarkable insight. It must be premised that the author condemns the execution of the admiral as strongly as anyone, and indeed writes as his advocate :—

> Ministers could not perhaps have made a worse choice than they did in appointing Mr. Byng to his last command. It ended in the destruction of his own fame and life, and tended, at least in the minds of all impartial men, to excite the highest indignation against those who had first appointed, and afterwards despatched him on a service which certainly not his force, nor, it may be, his abilities were competent to the execution of. As a commander he was far from being popular. He was austere, rigid, almost to a degree of undue oppression, and proud even beyond comparison. Destitute by nature of those conciliating qualities which create love and esteem, fortune had on her part denied him the means of acquiring admiration and popularity by withholding from him all opportunities of creating to himself either. Though we cannot by any means acquiesce in what his enemies most indecently, violently, and untimely insisted on, that he was deficient in personal activity of mind, or what in plainer terms is called courage, yet we cannot but fairly confess that we do not imagine him to have possessed that ardent spirit of enterprise which might have enabled him to surmount the several difficulties that unfortunately surrounded him. . . . He was too great an observer of forms, ancient rules of discipline, and naval etiquette; and deserved rather the character of a parade officer than of a great commander. . . . In whatever respect he might be deficient as a commander, the blame certainly attaches, in a much stronger degree, to those who sent him on such a service than to himself, who was, if at all, *naturally* incompetent to the task imposed upon him.[*]

As, then, Lord Anson must share, in a very large degree, with the Ministry, the blame which attaches to Byng's appointment, so, in a much smaller degree,

---

[*] Vol. iv. pp. 177–79.

he was responsible for the series of errors which resulted in supplying him with so poor a force at the critical moment when the fate of Minorca hung in the scales. To understand the Minorca question we must go back to the opening of the war in 1755, the year before the capture of that island by the French, and the affair of Byng.

The steps in the process are these. As early as 1754 the war in India, which, under Lawrence and Clive on one side, and Dupleix on the other, had never ceased, assumed such dimensions that Admiral Watson was sent out with a squadron to the support of the English East India Company. It was then that he performed those remarkable exploits which rendered his imposing monument in Westminster Abbey, erected at the expense of that body, more appropriate than many such sepulchral memorials. In America, the expedition which first brought Washington into notice, was due, not to the spirit of the Home Government, but to that of the Virginian colonists, who could no longer put up with the audacious encroachments of the French at Fort Duquesne; and its failure was succeeded by that of General Braddock, an officer of much the same type as Byng, and whose appointment reflected equal discredit upon the Ministry. They were indeed only shamed by the outcry of the nation into sending him out at all, in order to retrieve the recent failure of the Colonists. This, however, did, as Horace Walpole and many more foresaw, bring matters to a crisis. "We begin to think," says Walpole, on October 6, 1754, "that the world may be roused again, and that an East Indian war and a West Indian war may beget such a thing as an European war. In short the French have taken such cavalier liberties with some of our forts that are of great consequence to Virginia, Carolina, and Georgia, that we are actually dispatching two regiments thither . . . too many if the French mean nothing further; too few if they do." *

The French, no longer satisfied with supporting their governors by the dispatch of bodies of troops in a quiet and unobtrusive way, now prepared a large military force and equipped a powerful fleet in their Western harbours. It was a difficult position for the English Government. Anxious to preserve peace, yet unable to suffer their Colonies to be conquered, the Duke of Newcastle was fairly at the end of such wits as he possessed, and his colleagues could not act without him. Nevertheless it was resolved that the least which could be done was, like their enemy, to equip a fleet, and impress seamen. "The French," says Walpole again, on March 10th, 1755, "have sent demands too haughty to be admitted, and we are preparing a fleet to tell them we think so. In short, the prospect is warlike. The Ministry are so desirous of avoiding it that they make no preparations on land. Will that prevent it? Their partisans d—— the Plantations, and ask if we are to involve ourselves in a war for them. However, the late Rebellion suppressed, is a comfortable ingredient at least in a new war." †

---

* "Letters to Mann," vol. iii. p. 82.
† *Ibid.*, vol. iii. p. 93.

And here it may be mentioned that to Anson is due the credit of, for the first time, enabling a fleet to be started forth on an emergency with a body of permanently organised sea-soldiers, the Marines. Heretofore the country had been obliged to depend on regiments, specially raised indeed for the purpose, but disbanded when not immediately wanted, and never combined in one corps. He had long pressed for this great reform, which had been an old scheme of Lord Sandwich's, but now took the organic form with which we have been familiar ever since that day, and to which no little of the success of the British Navy has been due. Like so many other simple improvements it seems strange that the country could ever have hesitated to adopt it; but less strange when one reflects upon the difficulties which have been so often placed in the way of a hearty and generous recognition of the value of the services of the Royal Marines. No less than fifty Companies were raised at this period; but not with sufficient promptitude to satisfy Hawke's eager wish to substitute them altogether for the regiments of the Line with which some part of his fleet was supplied. He probably had some hand in the establishment of the force, for he writes as if it was a scheme long familiar to himself as well as to the Admiralty. By the year 1759 the numbers of the corps had mounted up to 18,000.[*]

It was to Hawke that the general equipment of the fleet was entrusted; and we find his flag flying from

---

[*] Barrow's "Anson," p. 235.

the " Terrible" at Spithead as early as February 12th, 1755. Boscawen soon joined him, the destination of the latter being to deal with the great French fleet collecting in North America; while Hawke was to superintend the home service at sea. Of course this was all too late. The fleet should have been equipped in the previous autumn, an ultimatum sent to the French the moment the fleet was ready, and the ports then instantly blockaded—just indeed as was done next year. We have seen how alien such measures were to the spirit and capacity of the Government.

One portion of the British policy had indeed been sound, and was destined to bear fruit. This was chiefly due to the King. Impressed before all things with the danger to which his Continental possessions had been, and would soon again be, liable, and forcing himself to forget the insults he had received from his nephew, Frederick of Prussia, he and the Government had of late carefully cultivated the friendship of the one Power which they saw would be likely to assist them effectually when the inevitable European war should break out afresh. The position of Frederick with regard to Austria was much the same as that of England with regard to France. The Peace of 1748 had been quite understood to be a mere temporary expedient. Neither side disarmed. Indeed England was the only power that dreamt of such a thing. Austria had by no means reconciled herself to the permanent loss of Silesia, and Frederick had not the smallest intention of relinquishing it. We have in modern times learnt to believe that there is something more to be said for the morality of this conquest than the world had been accustomed to admit. At any rate Silesia had been won; and the necessity of the acquisition, if Prussia was to take permanent rank as one of the Great Powers of Europe, was part of the creed of every native of that country.

Thus the most unexpected alliances came to pass. While Prussia was reconciled to England, her recent enemy, Austria, became the fast friend of France, with which nation she had been in bitter feud for many generations. It must be confessed that this alliance with Prussia was more natural than the former one with Austria. There had been many reasons for supporting the magnanimous Maria Theresa; but the interests of Great Britain and Hanover were far more concordant with those of Prussia; and the religious questions which had, not so long before, played a chief part in European combinations, were by no means laid asleep. They were indeed more prominent than is sometimes supposed in the struggle which was proceeding between the French and English Colonists in North America.

Hawke's letters and despatches of this date are replete with all the masses of detail natural to the equipment of a great fleet, which had been allowed to dwindle down to nothing during the Peace. The difficulty of obtaining seamen was, however, by far the greatest of those with which he had to deal. All sorts of questions relating to impressment come before him, and every effort is made on his part to alleviate the extreme hardships incident to the system. Desertion however must be stopped, and soldiers are largely employed on this service. When, a little later, the need of seamen to man Holburne's squadron becomes serious, he tells the Admiralty:—

> Last night at 12 I sent boats to Ryde, Cowes, Yarmouth, Lymington, Southampton, and Chichester; and sent the "Savage" sloop to Poole, and the "Arundel" to cruize off Portland for a few days. At the same time I ordered a press ashore and from the merchant ships in this harbour, by which we have got about forty men. I shall use my best endeavours to get the squadron to sea.

Of course with such material the difficulties of fitting out and preparing ships to meet an enemy at a moment's notice are very great. Both he and Boscawen have to reject large numbers of these very men, who had cost so much trouble to impress, as "totally unserviceable"; and even, after this,—just as we have already observed in 1743,—the sickness and mortality among them is tremendous. Boscawen's fleet lost something like 2,000 men on his short North American expedition,—where the climate could not be in fault,—from this cause; and we shall soon see Hawke's own squadron in the same condition. It is during Hawke's superintendence of the equipment of this fleet that he turns his attention to Haslar Hospital, which he finds sadly deficient; but he reports that the whole system of attending to the sick on board ship is still worse. The necessaries for this purpose, supplied from the Government stores, were disgracefully bad in every respect. A reform dates from his report. It is also at this time that he decides upon Porchester Castle as a better place for the reception of

French prisoners than the premises of a certain Mr. Ward at Fortune [Forton] near Gosport.

While on these local matters, it may be observed that Hawke's delicate position as Member for Portsmouth during the years of the Peace, while his flag was at the same time hoisted at the Port, was a test of tact and good sense which his official correspondence thoroughly satisfies. The same may be said as to his treatment of the complaints made by certain officers, and in reference to prizes taken in the recent war, as to which nice questions arose ; and the remark may be extended to his conduct of the numerous Courtsmartial on which he had had to sit either as President or Vice-President during the Peace, and which seem to have been assigned to him as his special province.

In his management of this difficult part of an officer's duty no one seems to have excelled him ; and the remark made in Collins' Peerage fairly summing up the opinion of the service, has been adopted by other writers:—" He always took the greatest care to distribute justice without any regard to rank or connections. The innocent were sure to meet with his protection and the guilty to feel the rod of punishment." It is scarcely possible to overrate the importance of such a service at a time when the mismanagement of the navy, during almost the whole period which had elapsed since it was actively employed in Queen Anne's reign, had left it in the condition described in a former Chapter. A standard of professional duty was thus created and maintained, all the more seasonable after the disgraceful exhibition furnished by the Courtsmartial on Mathews and his officers; and we are the more reminded of the loss sustained by Hawke's absence on that occasion, as well as on the melancholy Trial which issued in Byng's execution. The most important of the Courts-martial at which Hawke presided was that held in December 1750 on Admiral Griffin, the Commander-in-chief in the East Indies, who was suspended from his rank for misconduct before the enemy. But neither on the records of this or the other Courts-martial is there anything worth extracting.

Here then was the man pointed out by every possible sign for the headship of the working and fighting naval forces, just as Anson was for the administrative department. We shall see in the next three Chapters how little the use of an instrument so finely tempered was understood during the early years of the war, and in the subsequent Chapters, how ill, till many years after the great Peace, his surpassing services were requited.

Long after the period at which we have now arrived, in the year 1770, Chatham, denouncing the want of foresight and preparation shown by the Government on the occasion of the dispute with Spain concerning the Falkland Islands, used the following language :—

Oliver Cromwell, who astonished mankind by his intelligence, did not derive it from spies in the Cabinet of every prince in Europe; he drew it from the cabinet of his own sagacious mind: he observed facts, and traced them forward to their consequences:

from what was, he concluded what must be; and he never was deceived.

The Government of the Duke of Newcastle had "intelligence" from neither species of cabinet. They could not but be aware that the French were making great preparations both by land and sea; yet so dexterously were they amused by the Duc de Mirepoix and his wife, that the French fleet stole away from Brest by half a dozen at a time, between January and March, 1755. No less than three squadrons got off in one way or the other to the West Indies and Canada. Even so, the Government were entirely misinformed as to their total number; and when they received certain information that the final expedition under Macnamara and Dubois de la Mothe mustered between them twenty-five sail of the line (some of them only armed *en flute*), while Boscawen had preceded them with no more than eleven, the alarm was excessive. Captain Holburne, a friend of Anson's, and an officer of character and experience, was instantly made an admiral, and despatched with the exceeding haste which the following letter indicates, carrying with him six sail of the line to reinforce Boscawen.

DEAR SIR, ADMIRALTY, May the 8th, 1755.

I have the satisfaction of wishing you joy on your promotion of Rear Admiral; it was the last thing I did with the King, but would not let you know it till I mentioned it to the Lords of the Regency. I must now intreat you, for the sake of your own character as well as to justify me in the opinion I have given of you, that not a moment's time may be lost in your getting out of Channel. You must sail from Spithead on Friday morning, let the wind be how it will. In short your getting to America, and joining Vice Admiral Boscawen before the French get to Louisburg, is of such immense consequence to the kingdom, that I must again intreat you to be very assiduous in making your passage in as little time as possible. I know the French are much longer in their navigation than we are, and as the wind has been Westerly, and the French ships were not more than [this word is wanting in consequence of a hole in the paper] leagues from Ushant on Saturday, they can have made but very little way in the voyage. I know you will find all the facility imaginable from Sir Edward Hawke in so material a service. I heartily wish you success, and be assured I am most sincerely your friend,

ANSON.*

Admiral Holburne did not disappoint his friend. He sailed on May 11th, and succeeded in joining Boscawen on June 21st, but not before that officer had fallen in with the French. The tables were, however, unexpectedly turned; for Macnamara, as soon as he had seen his consorts clear of the coast, had gone back to Brest with nine sail of the line; so that the English, after the arrival of Holburne, had seventeen ships to sixteen. M. Dubois de la Mothe was indeed fortunate enough to get off with the loss of only two ships, which Boscawen caught before they could rejoin the fleet, from which they had been separated by a fog; and after landing his reinforcements he got away again from Louisbourg, next year by favour of a storm which drove off Holburne's blockading squadron. But this act of Boscawen's was war; and that admiral had acted upon the orders he had received to fight: .still there had been no Declaration of War, and the French Government

---

* MS. letter in the Library of the United Service Institution, Holburne Collection.

affected to be surprised and indignant. They had indeed received due notice; to which their ambassador had pompously replied that the first gun fired would be the signal for his departure; but the only question in reality was how long the patience of the British could be expected to last without taking action. As soon as the news of Boscawen's proceedings arrived, Mirepoix, literally true to his word, left England; but there was a great deal more to be done before his country was ready. No Declaration of War took place on either side. England equipped a fleet and hoped for the best.

CHAPTER VIII.

HAWKE'S POSITION IN RELATION TO ADMIRAL BYNG.—
COURTMARTIAL ON BYNG.

In order that we may be able to form an opinion as to the morality of the next step taken by the English Government, and in which Sir Edward Hawke was deeply concerned, it is important to bear in mind and to realise the relations of the two countries as described in the last Chapter. For it was now determined to send our admiral to sea instantly, with a large fleet, and with Secret Instructions, which, having been preserved in the family, are here for the first time, it is believed, published;—and not before it was necessary; for they have been generally misrepresented. It so happens, also, that from sources already public, we are in a position to understand some of the more private circumstances under which they were issued. The question before us is this:— Were the French in the right when they declaimed against the English, in consequence of the action now taken, as "pirates"? This, however, is a matter of far inferior importance to the questions discussed in Chapter II. as to the morality of the Spanish War of 1739. In the present case the general obligation of the English to protect their Colonies governed the situation. That there was a *casus belli*, has never been challenged by impartial judges, and Boscawen's orders need no justification. It is only a question of time and method, a question of justice and right with respect to a special portion of a whole line of policy, with which we have now to deal. Nevertheless, as the most opposite opinions have been expressed by historians, the subject requires investigation.

The Instructions which follow would naturally have been signed by the King, but he had departed for Hanover some time previously, leaving the Government in the hands of the Lords Justices. No one but himself could prepare his hereditary Dominions for the storm which was about to burst, or gather up the threads of the Continental alliances which alone could save them.

By the Lords Justices.

Secret Instructions for Sir Edward Hawke, Knight of the Bath, Vice Admiral of the White Squadron of His Majesty's Fleet. Given at Whitehall, the twenty-second day of July 1755, in the twenty-ninth year of His Majesty's reign.

Whereas divers encroachments have been made by France upon His Majesty's rights and possessions in North America, by building forts and making settlements upon lands undoubtedly belonging by Treaty or otherwise to the Crown of Great Britain; and whereas actual hostilities were committed by the French in the month of April, 1754, by their summoning a fort which was building on the Ohio, under the command of an officer bearing His Majesty's Commission, and the said officer was compelled to surrender the same; in consequence whereof His Majesty found himself obliged, in order to maintain the honour of his Crown and to defend his possessions in North America, to give the necessary orders to repel force by force, and to prevent the French from landing additional troops in North America, for which purpose they had sent a large squadron of men of war and transports into those seas, which could only be intended to make other encroachments, or to support those already made; and whereas it is the King's determined resolution not only to continue the most effectual methods for the protection and defence of his rights and possessions and the trade of his subjects in North America, but likewise to provide for the defence of his dominions and the security and protection of the navigation and commerce of his subjects in all parts, which is now become more immediately necessary, as all the means of negotiation have hitherto proved so ineffectual that there is reason to apprehend it is the intention of France to pursue the hostilities they have already committed by an open rupture; and whereas Monsieur de Mirepoix, Ambassador of the Most Christian King, in consequence of orders he has received from his Court, has actually left this kingdom without taking leave; We have therefore thought proper, in the present circumstances, to give you the following Orders, and we do, in His Majesty's name, order and direct you to take under your command Rear Admiral West and sixteen of His Majesty's Ships of the Line, with such frigates as shall be directed by the Lords Commissioners of the Admiralty, and proceed immediately to sea, and cruise between Ushant and Cape Finisterre, in order to put in execution the following Instructions; taking care not to go to the Southward of Cape Finisterre unless from some intelligence you may receive, you shall, without leaving however the Home Service too much exposed, find it necessary to go beyond the same Cape Finisterre.

1st. You are to protect the trade and ships of His Majesty's subjects; and in case you should meet with the French squadron under the command of Monsieur de Guay, or any other French squadron, or French men of war of the Line of Battle, you are to intercept them, making use of the means in your power for that purpose, and to send them under a proper convoy directly to Plymouth or Portsmouth, taking care that every person belonging to all ships so intercepted be well treated, and that no plunder or embezzlement be made of any effects on board. But if you shall have certain intelligence that the French have committed hostilities by their men of war, or in consequence of any Commissions granted to Privateers, or of any Letters of Marque, or Reprisals against any of His Majesty's subjects, or their ships, or effects, you are then to commit all acts of hostility against the French, and endeavour to seize and take by every means their ships and vessels, as well those of war as merchants, that you shall meet, sending them into some convenient port in His Majesty's dominions, to be there kept till His Majesty's pleasure shall be known concerning them.

2nd. You are to fix upon some proper place where the ships under your command shall rendezvous in case of separation, notice whereof you are to send, sealed up, to the Secretary of the Admiralty; and you are constantly to keep a ship or vessel passing between the fleet and the Rendezvous, that you may the more readily receive such orders as it shall be necessary to send you.

3rd. You are to continue on this service till further order, or so long as the ships' provisions and water will admit, and then you are to return with them to such ports as the Lords Commissioners of the Admiralty may direct.

4th. You are to transmit to one of His Majesty's Secretaries of State and to the Lords Commissioners of the Admiralty every ten days (or oftener if anything material occurs) a particular account of your proceedings, the frigates and other vessels being appointed to attend you for that purpose, and to proceed with your despatches to Plymouth, from whence they are to be forwarded by express.

5th. You are to observe and follow such orders and instructions as you shall receive from His Majesty, under His Royal Sign Manual, or from the Lords Justices during His Majesty's absence, or from one of His Majesty's principal Secretaries of State, or from the Lords Commissioners for executing the office of Lord High Admiral of Great Britain for the time being.

WILLIAM.	HOLLIS NEWCASTLE.
THO. CANTUAR.	DORSET.
HARDWICKE C.	ROCHFORD.
GRANVILLE P.	ANSON.
MARLBOROUGH C. P. S.	T. ROBINSON.
RUTLAND.	H. FOX.
ARGYLL.	

These Instructions it will be perceived, relate to men-of-war. A few days afterwards they were extended, on grounds explained in the following letter, so as to include a wider cruising ground, and the seizure of merchant ships as well as men-of-war.

On August 3rd the King sent word from Hanover that the French were—

endeavouring to persuade the Danes to fit out a squadron under pretence of covering their trade from the insults of the English, but in reality to protect French effects under Danish colours; whatever may be the reason of it, it is certain the Danes have augmented the ordinary number of their seamen. France has likewise been tempting the Swedes to enter into their maritime views; and besides a proposal of the same sort with that made to Denmark, they are contracting for vast quantities of timber and other materials for building ships, as also for guns of all sizes and sorts, both iron and brass.

Hence the Additional Secret Instructions which were issued on August 6th, but which did not reach Hawke till August 30th, too late to carry into effect his first, and to perform fully what was required in his second, orders.

By the Lords Justices.

Additional Secret Instructions for Sir Edward Hawke, Knight of the Bath, Vice Admiral of the White Squadron of His Majesty's Fleet; given at Whitehall, the sixth day of August 1755, in the twenty-ninth year of His Majesty's reign.

Whereas since our signing of the Secret Instructions for you on the twenty-second of last month certain advices have been received of the farther hostile preparations of the French, particularly against these kingdoms, we have thought proper in His Majesty's name to give you the following additional Instructions.

You are to take under your command such an additional number of ships of war as the Lords Commissioners of the Admiralty shall direct, some of which being now under orders for particular services (whereof you will receive information from their Lordships) you will take care that the said services are duly performed by those ships so appointed, or by such others as you may think proper; the intention of this reinforcement being to enable you to employ part of the squadron under your command in such stations between Cape Ortugal and Cape Clear as may be most proper for their intercepting all the French merchant ships bound into the British Channel, as well as those bound into the Bay of Biscay, and for their protecting the ships of His Majesty's subjects from being annoyed by the ships of war or privateers of France in their going from, or on their return to, any part of these kingdoms.

You are to endeavour to seize and take, by every means in your power, all French ships and vessels, as well men-of-war and privateers as merchantmen, that you shall meet, sending them into some convenient port in His Majesty's dominions, together with their effects, to be there kept till His Majesty's pleasure shall be known concerning them, in like manner and according to the directions given you by our said former Secret Instructions relating to French ships of war.

WILLIAM.	HOLLIS NEWCASTLE.
THO. CANTUAR.	DORSET.
HARDWICKE C.	ROCHFORD.
GRANVILLE P.	ANSON.
MARLBOROUGH C. P. S.	T. ROBINSON.
RUTLAND.	H. FOX.
ARGYLL.	

In the "Memoirs of James Earl Waldegrave, K.G., Privy Councillor and Governor to the Prince of Wales" [afterwards George III.], there is an account of the differences of opinion which prevailed among these Lords Justices; but as it has been more than once printed, only such extracts will be selected from this well-informed writer's journal as are necessary for the present chapter.

The Lords Justices, I mean the leaders only, who in their private meetings determined all affairs of consequence, were the Duke [of Cumberland], Lord Granville, the Duke of Newcastle,

Lord Anson, Sir Thomas Robinson, and Mr. Fox. . . . The preparations for war and all military operations were chiefly conducted by the Duke, Fox, and Lord Anson. An affair just now came under their consideration of the greatest importance. A powerful fleet was ready to sail under the command of Sir Edward Hawke, and the King trusted to his Regency to prepare proper instructions. Was Hawke to have hostile orders? If hostile orders were given must they be unlimited? Ought war to be declared when the fleet sailed, or were we to commence hostilities without any declaration? The Duke of Cumberland, naturally inclined to vigorous measures, seeing the nation impatient for war, it being also the general opinion that the enemy was yet unprepared, thought it advisable to strike the blow while our fury was at its greatest height: at the same time he was very sensible that, notwithstanding our very formidable fleet, we were not ourselves in such perfect readiness as many people imagined. On the other hand the Duke of Newcastle, who was not fond of danger at a distance, and seldom grew bolder on its nearer approach, was for keeping off the storm as long as possible, and gave his opinion that Hawke should take a turn in the Channel, to exercise the fleet, without having any instructions whatsoever. The Chancellor had more courage than the Duke of Newcastle; but agreeable to the common practice of the law, was against bringing the cause to an immediate decision. Lord Anson, as usual, said little; but as an admiral, and First Lord of the Admiralty, thought it became him to seem rather inclined to the spirited side of the question. After mature deliberation it was resolved that Hawke should sail with hostile orders, but war was not to be declared.

Lord Waldegrave then pronounces against this half-and-half decision in words which have been quoted and adopted by modern writers; but there is something to be said, irrespective of the question whether England ought not to have been ready long before with her alliances to protect Hanover, and her fleeets to blockade the French harbours. That not being so, from causes already noticed, and the question of

repelling force by force having been already settled by Boscawen's Instructions, the points left to the judgment of the Lords Justices were three in number.

First: Was England to play into the hands of France by declaring war when she was not prepared, and when it was evident that her enemy was himself only playing a waiting game till he was prepared? The answer might well be in the negative.

Secondly: Ought England to refrain from any other than purely military action? If so, what punishment were the enemy receiving for stopping the American fur-trade, and committing injuries of many kinds, personal and pecuniary, on British subjects in those parts? The answer might again well be that she ought not to refrain from action of some retaliatory kind.

Thirdly: Was this a case for the "reprisals" which were the usual weapon of those times when operations short of declared war were contemplated? Of course the enemy would denounce the seizure of merchant ships without a Declaration of war as "piracy"; it was to be expected; but what was the proper name for his own conduct during recent years when no suspicion of war was even afloat. The decision arrived at was that reprisals were to be taken. Was it just?

It must of course be earnestly desired that the policy of Great Britain could always be regarded as of such a character as to need no defence. Complaints like those of France on this occasion ought to be impossible: but it does not follow that they were strictly just. There was not much to choose between the two parties in the matter of political straightforwardness. The question is—which began? And that has been explained. Perhaps the best proof that the English policy was justifiable is that the French contented themselves for nearly a whole year with remonstrances. They were well assured that they had so much the best of the bargain, both in what they had already effected, and in the scheme they were preparing for the surprise of Minorca, that a certain amount of affront and loss might well be pocketed. It will of course be observed that Hawke's orders were confined to the seizure of vessels, and sending them into English ports for detention; they were not to be confiscated. This was strictly attended to. The captured vessels were faithfully retained as a kind of deposit against the claims made by the English: nor were they sold till every attempt at an accommodation had proved hopeless.

Scarcely anything need be added to Lord Waldegrave's skilful sketch of the members of the Government who were chiefly responsible in this matter. We may be sure he is not far wrong in his account of Newcastle's ludicrous proposal; and "the Duke," as he is invariably called in the Memoirs of the age, only advised in accordance with his usual straightforward, patriotic common sense. Few characters have had so little justice done them in history as "Butcher Cumberland." Weighted with that terrible epithet, and no doubt reprehensible on many points, he was yet a thoroughly brave, and often showed himself a noble-minded, man. At more than one crisis of English history, before and after the death of his father, he was a tower of strength to the nation; and if he was but a third-rate general, he displayed a lofty standard, both in civil and military affairs, which was better understood when he was removed by death from the councils of the realm than it had been in his life-time. The construction of the orders bears the plainest evidence of Lord Hardwicke's hand. Supported as he always was by Anson, and perhaps the only one of the number, besides Fox, capable of taking in the full aspect of the situation, it was he in all probability who contrived the dexterous compromise which obtained unanimous signature within the Council, and has ever since afforded so much room for controversy outside that body. Granville's tremulous signature suggests the wreck which self-indulgence had rendered premature.

Those who wish to study the principles of these Instructions more fully are recommended to read the spirited Addresses of both Houses of Parliament at the subsequent Session of Parliament, the angry Memorial of the French Government at the close of the year, and the reply to that document penned by Fox, which last, being short, may here, as the concluding paper on the subject, be transcribed:—

SIR,   WHITEHALL, January 13, 1756.

I received on the 3rd instant the letter of the 21st prox. with which your Excellency honoured me, together with the memorial sub-joined to it. I immediately laid them before the King my master; and by his command I have the honour to inform your Excellency that His Majesty continues desirous of preserving the public tranquillity. But though the King will consent to an equitable and solid accommodation, His Majesty cannot grant the demand that is made of immediate and full restitution of all the French vessels, and whatever belongs to them, as the preliminary conditions of any negotiation, His Majesty having taken no step but what the hostilities begun by France in a time of profound peace (of which he has the most authentic proofs), and what His Majesty owes to his own honour, to the defence of the rights and possessions of his Crown, and the security of his kingdoms, rendered just and indispensable.

To return to Hawke and his cruise for M. Duguay, the very officer, it would seem, whom he had taken prisoner in 1747, and begged might be dismissed on parole on account of his age and infirmities. If indeed he were the same, he proved himself on this occasion to possess at least the wariness which age and experience are supposed to imply. Suspecting that he should be waylaid on his return from the westward, whither he had been sent to convoy some merchant ships to France, he wisely put into Cadiz, and there obtained information as to the cruising-ground of Hawke's fleet. The orders which the first set of Instructions conveyed were unfortunate on this point. The extent of cruising ground was not sufficiently wide; and Duguay contrived to elude his enemy by steering to the westward from Cadiz, making a circuit of Hawke's fleet, and getting back to Brest in the rear of it. A large number of captures of merchant ships were however made, after the receipt of the second set of Secret Instructions; and before the end of the year, Hawke and Byng (who succeeded Hawke on the cruising-station for a short time), brought in as many as three hundred, many of them with rich cargoes from Martinique and St. Domingo. What was of more importance, some 8,000 sailors were thus detained, a very serious addition to the difficulties experienced by the French in equipping further fleets.

Among the letters from Hawke which require notice at this period as showing character, is one written from Spithead on June 23rd, in which he begs that his First Lieutenant, James Hobbs, may be made Commander into a small vessel—"a very diligent officer, who has served with me long. It is the first favour of the kind that I have ever asked." On September 15th, "at sea," he reports as follows:—

> While the beer was taking out of the tenders, I sent the "Ambuscade" out to chase. She brought in a French brig from Louisburg, with a missionary on board, who, you will perceive by the accompanying letters, was very active in the disturbances in America, on which account a price was put upon his head by the English. I have directed Captain Steevens to see him strictly guarded till their Lordships' pleasure shall be known with regard to him. From these letters likewise their Lordships will learn the state of the French in those parts. All the papers were thrown overboard, but the weight to which they were fastened parting from them, they were taken out of the water by an officer of the "Ambuscade."

Several letters contain the inevitable complaints about the beer, such as the following:—

> The beer which came off in the two tenders from Plymouth was very bad: so that I was obliged to direct it to be expended immediately; and if what is now coming should prove to be the same, the squadron will be greatly distressed, as good beer is the best preservative of health among new-raised men.

There is terrible sickness amongst his crews. On

September 14th he tells the Admiralty:—"I find the ships' companies falling down so fast with fever that I am afraid I shall not be able to keep out long." His ships have to be sent in to be cleaned in pretty regular rotation. One of his Captains took a sort of "French leave,"—Lord Harry Powlett, in the "Barfleur," who had been sent in chase of some ships, and never came back. When Hawke, on his return, found him quietly lying at anchor at Spithead, he had no course but to try him by Courtmartial. He received however very tender treatment, being only "admonished." The unfortunate carpenter of the ship who had reported defects in the rudder, was found a convenient scapegoat for the young nobleman, who was not indeed much to blame. He afterwards succeeded to the title of the Duke of Bolton.

We have now to watch Hawke's first quarrel with the Admiralty. Finding that Duguay had escaped him, and his own crews being in such a wretched condition, the admiral left a portion of his fleet to lie in wait for merchant ships, and reported his arrival at Spithead on September 29th. This was displeasing to the Admiralty, as no doubt had also been his complaints of the beer; and they could not but have felt that the failure to intercept Duguay was their own fault. Hence the Secretary's remark, which may be seen on the back of the Admiral's Report of his arrival, and no doubt transmitted in the shape of a formal letter, to the effect that "their Lordships regretted that he was obliged to return, as the French fleet were daily expected."

On September 30th, Hawke replies:—

I can assure their Lordships that had I staid out a week longer there would not have been men enough to have worked the large ships; they fell down so fast.

And on October 3rd:—

I am extremely sorry to find that their Lordships think any of the ships of my squadron could have staid out longer; I hope they will be of another opinion when they reflect that most of the men have been pressed after long voyages, cooped up in tenders and ships at Spithead for many months, and the water in general long kept in new casks, which occasioned great sickness, besides the number of French prisoners and the men spared to navigate them into port. For my own part I should not have come in had it been possible for me to continue longer out.

After entering into some further details, he concludes:—

Upon the whole I am conscious of having used my utmost endeavours to answer the end of my being sent out, and of having never once lost sight of the principal object of my cruise. If their Lordships should be of another opinion I am ready and willing to resign my command to anyone else in whose abilities they have more confidence.

Not having received any reply to this letter, he writes again on October 6th, in the following terms:—

It has been sufficient mortification to me that my utmost endeavours did not meet with success, or answer the expectations either of others or of myself. How then can I be easy under the superadded neglect and tacit disapproval of their Lordships in not thinking me worthy of an answer to mine of the 1st of October? I can assure them, in my own breast I find no upbraidings, or any reason either to be ashamed or afraid of my conduct. As I underwent great fatigue for six months before I sailed, and have had ten weeks' uneasy cruize, I hope their Lordships will indulge me with leave to go to my family for eight or ten days.

None of the letters from the Admiralty of this date are to be found; but Hawke's next letter shows that they must have acted with propriety, and soothed the feelings of the injured chief. On October 9th, he writes :—

> I have received your letters of the 7th inst., and beg leave to return my hearty thanks to their Lordships for the trouble they have taken to explain themselves. . . . On Saturday morning I shall strike my flag; and I thank their Lordships for the leave of absence with which they have indulged me. I did not ask it before I wanted it, and I am confident the Captains of His Majesty's ships under my command have the refitting their ships as much at heart as I have; and none can have it more.

On October 30th, 1755, he returns from leave, hoists his flag again, and is in command at Portsmouth or Spithead through the autumn and winter; while Byng is sent to take his place at sea. He appears to have been subject to severe colds, and it was often necessary that he should be bled.

One cannot but feel respect for the manly tone of this remonstrance. It carries the stamp of a man who knows his duty, and fears nothing while he does it. It was indeed natural that the Admiralty, finding it extremely difficult to satisfy the expectations of the country without taking measures which the Government were not prepared to sanction, should insist on impossibilities. It was fortunate that they had in Hawke an officer whose position enabled him to speak plainly. It is true that the country would not have allowed them to dispense with his services; but this does not make it the less creditable to them that they were not above correcting their error.

Byng was not more fortunate in falling in with French squadrons than his predecessor had been; and perhaps it was as well that the catastrophe of the next year did not occur nearer home. He returned in the early spring, and was relieved in his turn by Hawke, whom we find in March, 1756, again at sea, in command of the Channel squadron, and, having been joined by Keppel's ships, employed in watching the French fleet at Rochefort. On May 8th he is once more at Spithead.

And this brings us to the concluding manœuvre of the French Government, by which, when fully prepared, after years spent in amusing the English, they opened the war in earnest.

We left the French and English Ministers at Christmas, 1755, hurling official documents at each other's heads. These were accompanied on the part of the former with the most truculent threats of invading England by land and sea forces, and Hanover by 200,000 troops. Great numbers of flat-bottomed boats were constructed in several French ports. Infantry and artillery were marched into the maritime provinces. Marshal Belleisle was a sort of mouthpiece by which the feint was kept before the British people, who remembered only too well how imminent the prospect had been in the previous war, when Marshal Saxe's veterans had been actually embarked. The people might be deceived by these threats: it was unpardonable that the Government should not have known better; for Mann was sending word from Florence that a large fleet and army were preparing at Toulon to attack Minorca, and other advices to the same purpose had come thick on one another even from as early a date as September, 1755. In February 1756, there remained no doubt about it; for Blakeney himself, the acting Governor of Minorca, gave full intelligence. Yet Newcastle's Government neglected every warning, and Anson distributed the fleet, under Hawke, Keppel, Osborn, and other officers, in the Channel and the Bay of Biscay. With the exception of two or three ships at Gibraltar and Port Mahon, the Mediterranean had been left to take care of itself. Who could believe that with these two fortresses exposed to attack at a moment's notice, there was no such thing as a Mediterranean fleet? It required yet another war to teach the nation, what even the loss of Minorca failed to teach, that it must always, and under all circumstances, keep an overwhelming naval force in that sea.

It was not till February 3rd, 1756, that the numerous officers on leave of absence from Minorca were ordered back to their posts; nor was any means even then provided for their return to duty. So entirely occupied were the Government with the panic of an invasion that, on the very day above-named, they issued a Proclamation that all horses, oxen, and cattle "should be driven and removed at least twenty miles" from the place where an invasion should be made," —not a very encouraging order, in the absence of every sort of land-preparation to resist it. Nor was it till March 8th that Byng was ordered to equip a squadron of ten line-of-battle ships to reinforce the garrison of Port Mahon, and protect Minorca from invasion.

So unimportant did the service appear, that no frigate was sent with Byng; nor was he allowed to complete his deficient complements of men from Keppel's large force, which was only cruising in search of some stray frigates. His unpopularity had not been favourable to speed in manning his ships; and when he got off at last on April 7th, so ill-equipped and ill-manned a squadron had seldom been sent forth from a British port. The blame fell upon Anson; and it is not easy to understand, though we shall see that Hawke exculpated him, how he can escape a large share of the responsibility. No doubt, however, he must divide it with others.

So far, at least, Byng was not in fault. He had done his best; nor could he control the winds, which made his passage to Gibraltar unusually long, though this was afterwards one of the popular accusations. But what could have been expected? The French had obtained a start of more than six weeks. Sailing from Toulon on April 10th, their fleet was unopposed by Byng till May 20th!

The incompetence of the general in command at Gibraltar was perhaps the last incident over which Byng had no control. All the rest was due to himself, and to no one else. The small reinforcements which might have been landed at a moment when the little garrison was pressed beyond measure, were not landed; there was no spirit or dash in any portion of the operations; the squadron on the day of battle was handled nearly as ill as possible, and the battle was not renewed when it should have been. Like Mathews, Byng made the mistake of supposing there was some other service required of him more important than the straightforward one of destroying the enemy; and little as Galissonière—the officer already noticed in America—deserved to carry off the fruits of victory,—for a better admiral would have taken better advantage of such an opportunity,—he certainly did. Perhaps Byng's own ill-advised letters and unfortunate Despatch may be added to the general summary of his incapacity.

But from this point the page of history, in epitomizing the remaining portion of Byng's career, must in all fairness take his side. So desperately bad was the treatment of him by the people, the Government, and the Admiralty, nay—by almost every person concerned,—that the final decision of the King may be excused, and the judgment of those who have turned the incompetent martinet into a hero and a martyr must not be dismissed as absolutely absurd. If heroism is proved by dying nobly when death is certain and imminent, Byng was a hero; if to suffer death as a scapegoat for others is to be a martyr, Byng deserved the title. Perhaps, however, no one should despise too much those who quail under a lengthened and universal popular fury,—at any rate not till he is put to the test. Such a scene as England presented when the news of the capture of Minorca, following on Byng's action, arrived, has rarely been witnessed in this country. The long-pent-up disgust with a Government which the nation despised, and yet could not overturn, and the ill-humour which the aggressions of the French had been gradually fanning into hatred, alternating with panic fear, suddenly expressed themselves in a way which made Newcastle tremble for his head. The ridiculous and impossible story told by Horace Walpole of his replying to the deputation from the City: " Oh, indeed, he shall be tried immediately; he shall be hanged directly," was only too exactly typical of the whole of the proceedings : the tragical death of Colonel Byng from the shock he sustained at witnessing the conduct of the Portsmouth mob when his brother was taken ashore as a prisoner, was only too typical of the extent to which English feeling was at the time, and has been ever since, excited by the sad story.

"Those," says Richard Glover, the author of " Leonidas," " who did not live at this period cannot by any description conceive the excess of national resentment and rage against that commander, which was artfully and industriously fomented by a corrupt administration, [in order] that to his cowardice singly the disgrace of our armament might be charged, together with the loss of Minorca, which, after a very indifferent defence, surrendered to Richelieu on June 29th. Unheard and untried, Byng was immediately devoted to destruction by King, Ministry, and people.*

Pursuing the plan, already sketched out, of illustrating the condition of the British navy and the British Government as they reciprocally bear upon

---

* " Memoirs of a celebrated Literary and Political Character," p. 59. (1813.)

one another, and as they both affected the foundation of the Empire at the commencement of the Seven Years' War, and taking it for granted that the main outline of Byng's Courtmartial is sufficiently well known, it will be best to gather up at once the processes which led to its deplorable decision. We can then return to Hawke's proceedings when sent out to relieve him.

The most prominent figure is, under this aspect, not the timid Newcastle, not the miserable Byng, but the usually undaunted Anson. As First Lord of the Admiralty, he represented the Government in all these transactions, was held responsible at the time, and, with the leave of Sir John Barrow, his biographer, who passes very lightly over these matters, must be held responsible, within certain limits, now. To what has already been said as to his share in producing the catastrophe, which was, like Byng's own share in it, due to the error in judgment of an honest man, must in all fairness be added that Pitt himself, at two different periods of his career, gave two exactly opposite opinions on the subject of Anson's liability to censure. In the debates on the conduct of the Ministry, which followed the execution of Byng, "Pitt spoke with vehemence, and directed his invective against Lord Anson, the late First Commissioner of the Admiralty."* But in 1770, looking back at this period, and anxious to depreciate Hawke's adminis-

---

* "Memoirs of a celebrated Literary and Political Character," p. 94.

tration of the navy in comparison with that of Anson, "the greatest and most respectable naval authority that ever existed in this country," Lord Chatham said :—

> The merits of that great man are not so universally known, nor his memory so warmly respected as he deserved. To his wisdom, to his experience and care (and I speak it with pleasure) the nation owes the glorious naval successes of the last war. The state of facts laid before Parliament in the year 1756 so entirely convinced me of the injustice done to his character that in spite of the popular clamours raised against him, in direct opposition to the complaints of the merchants, and of the whole city (whose favour I am supposed to court on all occasions), I replaced him at the head of the Admiralty, and I thank God I had resolution enough to do so.*

When Lord Chatham made this speech he had forgotten that the appointment of Anson had really been the work of Lord Hardwicke and the King,† but he might fairly claim to have cordially co-operated with them. At any rate it is the judgment of knowledge and reflection, correcting the impressions formed under excitement; and therefore, making all allowance for the necessities of rhetoric, it deserves weight. Also the greatest allowance should be made for officials under trying circumstances; but the facts of the fatal absence of a Mediterranean fleet when it should have been there long previously, and of the tardy equipment of Byng's squadron, cannot by any process of rhetoric be got rid of; and it would be well if we could not trace too plainly in the subsequent

---

* "Parliamentary Debates," and "Chatham Correspondence," vol. iv. p. 10.

† See the "Anson Correspondence," June 18, 1757.

proceedings the effect of the conviction that the blame did indeed remain not only at the door of the Government, but of the Admiralty. For something much worse follows.

Byng's ill-judged, but too true complaint of the insufficiency of his force, written in a tone of despondency which shadowed forth the subsequent failure, was no doubt provoking enough to the Admiralty; but it was no excuse for the shocking act of garbling the despatch which conveyed the Admiral's public account of the battle and defence of his proceedings. At a moment when his friends, and the few sober people who demanded fair play, required every support which could be derived from the words of the absent man, the public impression was formed from what was given out to be his Despatch to the Admiralty, but which had been pruned of words and sentences which would have told either directly in his favour, or indirectly as fixing some portion of the blame upon the Government. In one case an important phrase had been actually altered.*

Nor was this all; for the publication of what was left of the Despatch was delayed for ten days, during which time the worst possible reports of the battle,

---

* For a detailed account of the importance to Byng's case of the omitted passages see Entick's "History of the War," vol. i. pp. 328–30, and Beatson's "Naval and Military Memoirs," vol. i. p. 483. It is, however, but fair to say that some good judges have not felt the importance of this proceeding to be so great as that which has been assigned to it in the text. No doubt it was common enough to publish certain portions only of Despatches; but in this case all the omitted parts tell one way.

and especially the French Admiral's false and insulting account of it, were allowed uncontradicted circulation. The excesses of the unthinking populace are therefore to be considered as entirely merged in the guilt of those at the head of affairs. It requires no proof that it was the overwhelming and sustained fury of the people, thus excited, and afterwards kept alive by petty arts, which coloured every portion of the Second Act of the tragedy, and enabled the King to say at last that in refusing to commute the sentence of death he was only acting as head of the nation. Although we may fix others besides Anson with the blame attaching to the cruel indignities heaped on Byng, upon and after his arrival, the First Lord of the Admiralty cannot be excused in his own person for allowing the famous Despatch to be tampered with: yet Barrow, admitting the fact, sees no cause for censure; but merely remarks:—"The Admiral's account of the action is very long, and one of his complaints was that it had been garbled, and a great part omitted in the 'Gazette'"!* This seems to suggest that not only was this method of proceeding a matter of no consequence, but that the poor admiral richly deserved such treatment for having been guilty of writing too "long" a Despatch. If Byng's death was thought to have had some effect in improving the resolution of naval officers, this writer has certainly done his best to improve the occasion by suggesting to them the advantages of laconic brevity. But in

---

* "Life of Lord Anson," pp. 252, 254.

saying nothing more, the late Secretary of the Admiralty made himself *particeps criminis*.

Before noticing the second and final act of this drama, the reader must be reminded of two or three facts which accompanied and ensued upon the success of the French *ruse de guerre*.

The long-expected Declaration of War could now no longer be delayed; and to the vast satisfaction of the English people, and somewhat contemptuous indifference of the French, it issued from London on May 18th, 1756. Byng's battle was fought two days afterwards. In August Frederick of Prussia began to earn his title of "the Great" by forestalling his foes; and, splendidly commencing the war which was to raise Prussia to an equality with the four other great Powers of Europe, burst into the territories of allied enemies whose population amounted to eighteen times that of his own little realm. In September the Prime Minister began to discover that however the nation might desire to make a victim of Byng, it was equally resolved to get rid of himself. In vain he attempted to lay the loss of Minorca on the shoulders of Anson,* who was indeed already sufficiently, and perhaps deservedly, unpopular. In vain he besought Fox to support him against the wrath of Pitt, which was impending with the opening of Parliament. Fox knew better, and resigned. Murray "scampered out of the House of Commons,"† and fled

---

* Bubb Doddington's "Memoirs," p. 381.
† "Memoirs of a celebrated Literary and Political Character," p. 60.

for refuge to the House of Lords. At length, in November, driven to bay, the guilty Minister, with all his Cabinet, was himself forced to resign. Byng was so far avenged. Anson's occupation was gone; till Pitt, as we have seen, recalled him once more, next year, to office.

And this will be the place, as it has been necessary to trace Anson's part in these affairs, to record the impression left on the mind of a sensible man like Lord Waldegrave by his first administration of the Admiralty, which now came to an end. It is more valuable than Walpole's witty slanders, or Chatham's posthumous eulogy.

> Lord Anson was also dismissed from the Admiralty; a violent clamour having been raised against him of which he was no more deserving than of the high reputation which preceded it. He was in reality a good sea-officer, and had gained a considerable victory over the French in the last war: but nature had not endowed him with those extraordinary abilities which had been so liberally granted him by the whole nation. Now on the contrary he is to be allowed no merit whatsoever; the loss of Minorca is to be imputed to his misconduct, though many were equally, some infinitely more blamable: his slowness in business is to be called negligence; and his silence and reserve, which formerly passed for wisdom, takes the name of dulness and of want of capacity.*

This judgment has been confirmed by the great modern authority of Lord Stanhope.† The reader can compare it with the facts as stated in these pages. If somewhat too favourable in reference to the Minorca question, it is nearer the mark than the

---

* Memoirs, p. 85.
† "History of England," vol. iv. p. 34.

undiscriminating praise of which he has sometimes in our own day been the subject. It is the absurdity of these later writers which has perhaps led an historian of the Navy (Professor Yonge) to go too far into the opposite extreme. "The general estimation," says he, "of Anson, even in the present day, leads to a comparison of him, not with Blake or Hawke, but with Cavendish or Cooke,"—a highly honourable place, but this he might claim by his voyage round the world. Anson added to that class of merit the distinction of being by far the best administrator of naval affairs who had yet appeared, or perhaps has appeared since. We have not yet done with him, and shall find the affair of Byng and Minorca an exceptional stain on a career which was both useful and honourable. Perhaps we shall not be far wrong in attributing even the conduct he showed on this occasion to a distrust of his own judgment, under the influence of Newcastle and Hardwicke.

For a short period after Anson's fall it looked as if he was to be the public victim instead of, or perhaps in company with, Byng. Walpole is probably correct —for he is substantially confirmed by Lord Waldegrave[*] and others—in saying that the new Government, of which the Duke of Devonshire was nominal chief, but Pitt the head, had at once "employed a lawyer to draw up articles of impeachment against Lord Anson;"[†] and that—

they show great tenderness to Byng, who has certainly been most inhumanly and spitefully treated by Anson.

---

[*] Memoirs, p. 135.   [†] "Letters to Mann," pp. 171, 195, 196.

And again, when the Courtmartial on Byng had begun:—

<blockquote>
The Court and the late Ministry have been most bitter against him; the new Admiralty most good-natured. . . . Their bitterness will always be recorded against themselves: it will be difficult to persuade posterity that all the shame of last summer was the fault of Byng. Exact evidence of whose fault it was, I believe posterity will never have.
</blockquote>

Perhaps it is not so difficult to understand it now as Walpole supposed it would be.

The danger of Anson was not, however, real; Byng's peril was mortal; and the Courtmartial which sat upon him in December, 1756, and lasted on into January 1757, soon occupied the attention of every man and woman in the whole country. Admiral Smith presided, but was not of any great assistance to the Court, or subsequently to Parliament. "Tom of Ten Thousand" might be a very "good fellow," but neither he, nor any other member of the Court, were men who had given proofs of the ability, combined with courageous independence, which was required in such an emergency. They may have been, and probably were, right in condemning Byng's misconduct on the points specified; their blunder was in not piercing their way through the apparent difficulties presented by the Articles of War; and it is scarcely conceivable that they would have failed so signally, had it not been for the popular voice which penetrated, as it never should, within the sacred, but invisible cordon which separates a Courtmartial from the public. It might be thought that Keppel's subsequent celebrity and well-proved gallantry should except him from this general remark; but his conduct, though honourable, and creditable to his conscientiousness, proved him to be intellectually, if not morally, weak. Much the same characteristics may be traced in the circumstances which led to his own famous Courtmartial at the end of his distinguished career.

Summing up the seven charges on which the Court found Admiral Byng guilty, they may be reduced to four. (1.) His not sending his small contingent of officers and men ashore when he arrived off Port Mahon. This may be dismissed, as an act which, though perhaps of consequence as to the fate of Minorca, might be explained and excused. (2.) The second, third, fourth, and fifth clauses refer to mere mistakes in conducting the engagement, on which differences of opinion might well exist, though Byng was probably wrong throughout. Characteristically, the Court did not blame him for keeping the signal for line of battle flying during the whole combat, which was indeed in accordance with the Printed Instructions, but no doubt was one cause of the failure. It would have been, as already observed, discarded at the proper moment by Hawke. (3.) The Admiral allowing his own ship to "continue" firing at the enemy when she was too far off. This was a damaging charge, and, though repelled, left its mark. It told fatally with the country, because, as a matter of fact, there was not a single man killed or wounded on board the "Ramilies"; and people, putting this along with the rest, drew their own conclusions. Still it was but one incident in a confused affair, and could not of itself be possibly made a capital charge. (4.) Byng's failure to return to Port Mahon and follow the enemy, after refitting his damaged ships. This was no doubt a terrible error of judgment; but it certainly was not "wilful negligence."

On these four counts the Court brought the prisoner under the general charge that—

he did not do his utmost to take or destroy every ship which it shall be his duty to engage, and assist and relieve all and every of His Majesty's ships which it shall be his duty to assist and relieve.

The Court therefore held themselves bound to condemn him to death under the Twelfth Article of War, which assigns the punishment of death to everyone who shall "through cowardice, negligence, or disaffection" be guilty of the above conduct. They accompanied the sentence with a handsome acquittal from any charge of "cowardice or disaffection," thus tacitly leaving the word "negligence,"—for they abstained from stating that they found the prisoner guilty of negligence,—to cover the charges which had been proved. They at the same time forwarded a letter to the Admiralty, recommending the prisoner to mercy—

since we find ourselves under a necessity of condemning a man to death, from the great severity of the 12th Article of War, part of which he falls under, and which admits of no mitigation, even if the crime should be committed by an error in judgment.

Here briefly is the whole case. The Court made a gross mistake in the interpretation of words, and hoped that a recommendation to mercy would cover it. "Negligence" and "wilful negligence" are two entirely different things. "Negligence" of itself may mean simple error in judgment, by which a man may do one thing and "neglect" another, may do the wrong thing and neglect the right,—and this, as their words most plainly show, was all the Court meant by their finding. And yet "wilful negligence," and that alone, though the word "wilful" is not used, could be intended by the Article, as shown by the word being placed between two other words, "cowardice" and "disaffection," both of which involve distinct motive. The mere failure to destroy the enemy was not to be punished by death; but only if the failure occurred "through" any of these three causes, which, separately or collectively, were absolutely inconsistent with loyalty, courage, and goodwill —and Byng was credited by the Court with these motives. Even if any reasonable doubt could still be entertained as to the meaning of the Article, the Court should, on its own showing, have fearlessly faced the difficulty, and given the prisoner the benefit of the doubt, instead of slavishly submitting to a too literal interpretation, on the chance of something happening which was beyond its power to control. Nor did it make the slightest difference that the alternative of some other punishment than death, which had been permitted when the Articles were drawn up in the 13th year of the reign of Charles the Second, had been withdrawn a few years previously (22 Geo. II.). The conditions remained the same. However, for fear of future similar blunders, the

Article was restored to its old form a few years later (29 Geo. III.).

The warrant for the execution required the signatures of the Lords of the Admiralty, with Lord Temple at their head, and of whom Boscawen was one. They all demurred, but after a futile appeal to the Judges on the legality of the sentence, all, with one exception, eventually signed. The one name nobly absent from the signatures was that of the Honourable John Forbes. This admiral, already distinguished, and for his conduct on the present occasion, ever memorable, not only remonstrated, but resigned. His manly letter, exposing the error of the Court, and that of Admiral Temple West, equally honourable to the writer, were the only two attempts of any importance to place the matter on a basis of common sense; but they were powerless to stem the tide. These were both remarkable men. Both of them had done their duty in Mathews' action when so many failed. West had also fought nobly, as second in command, under Byng, on the late occasion. He now threw up his command, as well as the post of Lord of the Admiralty, to which he had just been appointed:—

"I can only be answerable," said he, "for my loyalty and fidelity to my king, and resolution of doing what appears to me for his service, which it seems an officer may not want, and yet be capitally convicted for his misconduct or inability of judging right. I am not so presumptuous as to imagine that my actions can always be so rightly governed, nor am I altogether certain that the judgment of others is infallible."*

West, who seems to have known how to write as

---

* Charnock's "*Biog. Nav.*"

well as to fight, died a few months afterwards of the distress caused by Byng's execution. He and Admiral Rowley are the only officers of the fleet in 1742, excepted by Horace Mann in his sweeping expressions of dislike to the class. "West," he says, "is a man of admired good sense, quiet and easy; and who rails with me at the lowness and horrid meanness of his companions."* Forbes' letter is perhaps even more able; but it is better known than West's. He lived to an honoured old age, showing to the last conspicuous proofs of the same upright, independent spirit which animated him on the present occasion.

It would take us beyond due limits to describe the humiliating events which intervened between the sentence of the Court on February 28th, and the execution on March 4th. Of course the Judges declared there was no illegality in the sentence. If technically correct, nothing further was required from them. In vain Keppel and some others of the Court who were in Parliament, attempted to stay proceedings; and with the help of Pitt carried the Commons with them. When examined before the House of Lords, they had nothing to say,—at least to any purpose; and Lords Mansfield and Hardwicke, in league, as Walpole declares †—and it can hardly be doubtful —with Anson, succeeded not only in reversing the decision of the other House, but in obtaining from the reluctant Lords of the Admiralty a withdrawal of their support of Byng. The unfortunate Admiral

---

* Letter to Walpole, Nov. 13, 1742.
† "Letters to Mann," vol. iii. p. 200.

was now left to his fate. "His enemies," says Walpole, "triumph, but who can envy the triumph of murder?"*

The attitude of Pitt, Temple, and the Admiralty had in fact become most unpopular; and the great Minister had no holding-ground but the support of the people. Yet, as the King, observing the popular feeling, dismissed him from office only a few days after Byng's execution, it must ever be a matter for regret that he did not add one more title to the gratitude of his country by standing out to the last on the question, and leaving events to right themselves. His momentary unpopularity would soon have been turned into love and respect, and he would have been borne back to power even sooner than he actually was, and with a higher claim to supremacy.

The King, supported, if not forced, as he thought, by the nation, and by the opinion of numerous officers of great weight, and never himself apparently having doubted that Byng deserved death, refused to interfere with the sentence of the Court, confirmed by the Admiralty. He has been savagely blamed for refusing to pardon the admiral; but in all fairness he must share the blame with very many other persons whom authors have found it convenient to screen. He privately took the most severe view of the case; he adopted for his public guidance, as he almost always did, the expressed will and desire of the people. That came before him in every form known to the

---

* "Letters to Mann," vol. iii. p. 200.

Constitution, and it fell in with his instinct, which was to encourage true military conduct wherever he could find it, and to punish, as far as the law would permit, every deviation from it. One could not expect from an old man of his habits and capacity the breadth and magnanimity of view which would detect the right course amidst such an ocean of difficulties as at that moment surrounded his throne.

After all, this "judicial murder" was not without some useful effect if it taught officers of both services that the country would no longer stand half-and-half battles, and that if a man felt he did not possess the qualities necessary for great situations he had better not press for them.*

---

* The details of Byng's execution, chiefly supplied by Horace Walpole, are to be found in every history : a contemporary account, from one who was on the spot, may not be familiar.

"On Monday, March 14th, 1757, all the men-of-war at Spithead were ordered to send their boats with the captains and all the officers of each ship, accompanied with a party of marines under arms, to attend the execution of Mr. Byng. Accordingly they rowed from Spithead, and made the harbour a little after 11 o'clock, with the utmost difficulty and danger, it blowing prodigiously hard at N.W. by N., and the tide of ebb against them. It was still more difficult to get up so high as the 'Monarque' lay, on board which ship the admiral suffered. Notwithstanding it blew so hard, and the sea ran very high, there was a prodigious number of other boats round the ship, on the outside of the ship's boats, which last kept all others off. Not a soul was suffered to be aboard the 'Monarque,' except those belonging to the ship. Mr. Byng, accompanied by a clergyman who attended him during his confinement, and two gentlemen of his relations, about 12 came on the quarterdeck, when he threw his hat on the deck, kneeled on a cushion, tied a handkerchief over his eyes, and dropping another which he held in his hand as

Hawke was fortunately clear of every connection with these proceedings. He had returned to port, as we have seen, on May 8th, 1755, from his cruise in the Channel. The instant the news of Byng's action arrived in England, although only from the reports of the enemy, he was ordered to sail in the 50-gun ship "Antelope," with sealed Instructions. Rear-admiral Saunders was sent with him, as second in command, to supersede Temple West; and Lord Tyrawley, who had been on a too long leave of absence from his command at Port Mahon, was now, having lost his island, sent to supersede General Fowke in the government of Gibraltar. The wags called it "a little cargo of courage." Hawke's Instructions requiring him to repair to Portsmouth, were dated June 8th: on June 9th he reported that he was ready to sail; and on June 16th he was on his way. The haste with which all this was done has been much blamed; but the main facts of the battle were certainly known, and it was wise to leave nothing more in Byng's hands. It was still hoped that Blakeney might hold out.

The Instructions require the admiral, after superseding Byng, to—

make an immediate and expeditious enquiry into the conduct and behaviour of the Captains of the ships hereby put under your command; and if you find any reason to believe any of them to have been tardy, and not to have acted with due spirit and vigour for

---

a signal, a volley from six marines was fired, five of whose bullets went through him, and he was no more. He died with great resolution and composure, not showing the least sign of timidity in the awful moment."—"The Naval History of Great Britain." Rivington and Fletcher, publishers, 1758, vol. iv. p. 342.

the honour and service of the King and nation, you are forthwith to suspend such Captains, and appoint others in their stead in whom you can confide for properly executing their duty. You are to order the Captain of the "Antelope" to receive Admiral Byng and Rear-admiral West on board, and return with them to Spithead; and if you shall suspend any of the Captains, you are to send them also home in her.

Having done this, if you shall not be well assured that Fort Philip upon the island of Minorca is in possession of the enemy, you are to use the utmost despatch in repairing thither with your squadron, and to exert yourself in doing everything that is possible to be done by you for its relief; and to attack and use your utmost endeavours to take, sink, burn, or otherwise destroy any squadron of the enemy's ships that may be employed to favour and assist in the attack upon that fort.

If you shall find the enemy have succeeded, and are in full possession of Minorca, you are, however, to endeavour by all means to destroy the French fleet in the Mediterranean, and for that purpose to employ the ships under your command in the most effectual manner you shall be able, and constantly to keep sufficient cruizers round the Island of Minorca, and take care they exert all possible diligence to prevent the enemy landing any troops, ammunition, stores or provisions, upon that island, and to annoy and distress them there as much as possible.

He is to protect Gibraltar, secure British trade in the Mediterranean, destroy the enemy's Privateers, and to keep his ships clean by sending them into Gibraltar, or some of the King of Sardinia's ports.

Under these orders, which Hawke opened on his arrival on July 4th, the Commissioned officers of both flagships were sent home along with the two admirals; and the new Commander-in-chief now hoists his flag on board the "Ramilies," from which ship that of Byng had been hauled down. He reports to the Admiralty that Byng made no complaint of any of the Captains who served under him in the late battle.

The following letters are the only ones now extant which relate to this distressing subject, and though merely official, have a certain melancholy interest.

Sir, "Ramilies," in Gibraltar Bay; July 4.

Upon looking over my Orders this morning I find myself obliged, in obedience to their Lordships' directions, to send home all the Commissioned Officers that were aboard the "Ramilies" and "Buckingham" during the late action. I have therefore by this morning's post acquainted their Lordships that I have complied with it, and I shall this afternoon order them on board the "Antelope." I hope you will believe that nothing but a peremptory order could have induced me to do this, as you were desirous of the contrary, and as I should always be exceedingly glad to have it in my power to oblige you, being sincerely, Sir, your most obedient and most humble servant,

EDWARD HAWKE.

To this Byng replied the same day :—

Sir,

I have received your letter of this day's date, and can have no objection to your putting their Lordships' orders in execution; for after their treatment of me I cannot be surprised at anything. I am obliged to you for the excuse you make about it, and shall always be ready to believe your attention and friendliness for me, and hope you will be assured of my being most sincerely, Sir, your most obedient humble servant,

Hon. Sir Edwd. Hawke. J. BYNG.*

An interesting notice of Hawke's own sentiments in relation to Byng's miscarriage is supplied among the "Political Anecdotes" to be found in the "Gentleman's Magazine" (1766). It is written in a spirit of intense hostility to Pitt, who had then just entered upon his second Administration; but may be true enough as to the facts. After describing the

---

* Hawke Papers.

great Minister's patronage of Byng's cause, and his attempt, after he had driven Newcastle from power, to bring the disaster home to that Minister and his Government (partly on the ground of Byng's ships being unfit to cope with those of the French, which carried 50-pounders on their lower decks), the writer tells us that—

a day was appointed by the House to enquire into these allegations, and the necessary papers were ordered to be laid before it, with the opinion of the present President of the Council, preparatory to their judgment. The old Administration were so much alarmed that in several meetings at Lord Royston's, they absolutely despaired of their cause. In the interim Sir Edward Hawke returned from the Mediterranean; and being invited to Lord Royston's, set them all right by a bare recital of facts.

When the day of arraignment [in the House] came, the now President of the Council delivered in the papers at the table, with his opinion "that the late Administration had done their duty." The patriot [Pitt] played all his artillery over again till Admiral Hawke assured the House that the thundering member was mistaken in every point; "that the French ships carried no 50-pounders; if they had, they would have been a great disadvantage to themselves, as being by their weight rendered incapable of being worked; that Byng's ships were so far from being in want of stores and provisions, that, in the condition he received them from Mr. Byng, he proceeded with the squadron to sea, and cruised ninety odd days, without complaint of the want of either." And being asked, if he had commanded in the room of Byng, whether he thought he had force sufficient to beat the enemy, answered:—"By the grace of God, he would have given a good account of them." Every then member of the House may remember how the patriotic abettor of cowardice stood abashed, as well as the author of his information, when facts overthrew him. Sir Edward Hawke was never forgiven by the Secretary.

On July 10th Hawke sailed from Gibraltar; and on July 15th, being "at sea," he reports to the Admiralty that he has just heard of the surrender of the fortress of St. Philip's at Port Mahon, and that consequently the troops sent out are of no use. The French fleet, he finds, had returned to Toulon as soon as the fortress had surrendered, and he shall now make all his dispositions for fighting it if it ventures out to sea. Next month he reports that he hears from all sides that the French fleet means to come out. This is his one hope. It was quite a match for the English, as is proved by a list found among the Hawke Papers; but contented with its late exploit, it never ventured out to meet them.

The Admiral's difficulties now begin; and as the Italian States, on which the English had relied when Maria Theresa was their ally in the former war, were now all ranged on the side of the enemy, the situation is entirely changed. The King of Sardinia's dominions, indeed, were not of much use before, nor are they now. On the coasts of Sardinia itself there is no good port. Gibraltar is not safe for large ships; and cruising off Toulon in the blockade of the French fleet meant, like cruising off Brest or Rochefort, constant and periodical cleaning and refitting of the fleet. The dominions of Spain remained; but though that country, taught by recent disaster, had deliberately refused to join the French at the opening of the war, in spite of the most pressing solicitations to fulfil the old Family Compacts, her king and people were to a man—not unnaturally—hostile to the English, and delighted in every opportunity of evincing their feeling. A part of the fleet is sent to "Poyance Bay," in Majorca, for refreshments. Trumpery complaints are made; and Hawke writes a spirited and yet temperate letter of remonstrance to the Governor of the island.

In the ports on the coast of Spain itself matters are worse; and the spirit shown on these occasions had to be summarily dealt with. A French privateer had taken an English vessel loaded with provisions for the fleet at Gibraltar, and carried her into Algesiraz, under the very eyes of the Admiral. This was too much; especially when the Governor refused to surrender her. Hawke instantly sent his boats, and cut her out; but a hundred men were killed or wounded in the service by the Spanish fort and the French privateer. The Spanish Court justified their governor, and had the impudence to complain of Hawke. The fact was that they were eager to join in the war, but were not yet prepared; nor was the English Government yet in hands strong enough to resent insults. In the West Indies the old claims had again been revived; but this was nothing to the Spanish treatment of Captain Foster, who, in command of the privateer "Antigallican," had captured a French East Indiaman, and put into Cadiz. He was forced to give up his prize and to strike his colours; was fired at for two hours, with the loss of some men killed and wounded, though he did not return a shot; robbed and abused by Spanish soldiers, and thrown into a loathsome dungeon. This was outside of Hawke's jurisdiction; and the English Government bore it, like the rest, with equanimity; but it did not increase the respect for the British flag.*

---

* Campbell's "Admirals," vol. iv. p. 90.

What the consequences of the failure at Minorca had already been, may be judged by the following extracts from a letter addressed to Hawke, on July 27th, by the Consul General at Naples :—

> SIR,
>
> Give me leave most heartily to congratulate you on your arrival in these seas, in the neighbourhood of which a public station was growing, from the reproaches of our friends and the insolence of our enemy, not a little irksome. . . . Our eyes are all turned towards you for the recovery of our credit in these parts ; and though fatal mistakes have lowered it so unhappily, and events are not absolutely within the highest human providence, we have such confidence in the ability which succeeded on the ocean, that we do not despair of finishing the season in the Mediterranean with honour, though we cannot, surely, say we have begun it so. The French ambassador here would however remove one of our hopes ; having said—somewhat meanly—yesterday before the King, upon mention made that you set out from Gibraltar on the 10th to seek the enemy, that he would answer for it they would not be found; and indeed we fear from all accounts that their return with their transports to Toulon will have been, too happily for them, effected before your arrival at Minorca.

Hawke had an opportunity of setting matters right with the Austrian Italians, who in their zeal for France had so far reckoned on impunity as to imprison at Leghorn the gallant Fortunatus Wright, a most successful privateer commander, for whose capture the French had offered a reward. Hawke demanded his release within twenty-four hours ; and the Austrians were forced to comply. This had a salutary effect all over the Mediterranean, and put a stop to the contempt for England which was setting in.

The few salient facts here given must be taken as

the epitome of a very trying command, the details of which comprise a large correspondence. In these letters, it must be remarked as of a former collection, it is difficult to decide whether the patience and forbearance which they display under the delicate circumstances which Hawke is frankly told from England that he must respect, are more noteworthy than the spirit and decision which he shows when he feels that he must, whether the Government like it or not, act on his own responsibility. It is the one bright spot on the whole dark line of the British horizon; and the people, as all the histories of the period testify, felt profoundly the contrast which it presented to the rest. He is ordered home at the end of the year, and arrives in England on January 14th, 1757. In the letters which occur about the time of his arrival, the strain upon his health which the command had caused, again comes before us:—" I will wait upon their Lordships to-morrow if my health will permit." In the "Gentleman's Magazine" occurs the statement, following on the notice of his arrival:—" the Admiral much indisposed." He had also had to bear the domestic trial of the loss of his wife, who had died on October 28th, and the support he had hitherto received from her during his arduous service was now withdrawn. Into that private grief we cannot penetrate if we would. The correspondence also shows that the new Admiralty had questioned his right to appoint certain officers; he defends himself with spirit and success. Amongst other officers who seem to have been brought forward by him at this time are Christopher Cod-

18 *

rington and Captain Collingwood, names subsequently honoured throughout the navy in members of their respective families.

The writer quoted above (p. 271) gives the following account of Hawke's reception by Pitt. After describing the proceedings just mentioned in relation to the overbearing conduct of the Spanish authorities, he goes on to say :—

> On the Admiral's return home, Mr. Pitt sent for him, and said: —"Sir, had I been in your situation in Gibraltar Bay, 'tis probable I should have acted as you did, even though I should have made a concession afterwards." The drift of this speech plainly appearing, he was interrupted with :—" Sir, entrusted with the command of a squadron of the King's ships, I did my duty to my master and my country, for which I never will make any concession: you as Minister may do as you please." This is the hero who terrifies France, Spain, and all the world, from pole to pole. Could he make a Boscawen or a Hawke? Or did they make him? They fought, they conquered, before he had any character; and one of them may live to do so again when he shall have no character left.*

Reading Hawke's career in the light of these anecdotes, which fit in perfectly with all we know besides, we may safely infer that whatever he may have thought of the Newcastle Administration for its blunder in delaying Byng's expedition, he was not disposed to blame Anson, under the circumstances, for its bad equipment. It does not follow that it was not badly equipped; only that he had himself made use of equally bad materials, and could have efficiently used these.

As to his own position, it is plain that he was not only fortunate in his absence from England when Byng

---

* "Gentleman's Magazine," 1766, p. 423.

was fitting out for Minorca, but also that he was out of the way when the struggle between Newcastle's Government and the nation was taking place. But he was none the less opposed to the champion of the nation, Pitt, Anson's detractor; and perhaps it is the strongest proof of his merit that when such a difference had been discovered, Pitt found himself yet able to employ him in the expedition to Rochefort. The explanation may partly be that when Pitt came back to full power in June, 1757, and had become convinced—probably by means of Hawke's blunt remarks —that Anson had been ill-treated by himself and his friends, and when, in consequence, he had replaced Anson at the head of his own Admiralty, the reinstated First Lord was in a position to draw the Minister and the Admiral together; but he was evidently not firm enough in his place to pull Hawke into the Board along with himself. That this was contemplated, is clear from Lord Hardwicke's letter to Anson of June 1757,* in which he tells his son-in-law that he hopes there will be room at the Admiralty for "Sir Edward Hawke, or any other man we shall like." "Room" was not found for Hawke.

All this throws light upon the subsequent relations between the great statesman and the great admiral. There was always a want of cordiality in these relations. It was exhibited in 1757, 1758, and 1759. It partly explains why no distinction was made between Hawke and other admirals by the grant of a peerage

---

* Anson Correspondence.

for the Victory of Quiberon. It accounts for the preference shown by Pitt for a junior to Hawke when, in 1766, he placed Saunders in the post of First Lord of the Admiralty, and for his final treatment of the veteran, at the close of Hawke's official career in 1770. May it not also be suspected that the vast reputation of Lord Chatham, increasing as it has, year after year, down to our own times, has itself tended to carry with it the disparagement of one whose independence of character and title to glory stood somewhat in the way of a solitary supremacy?

The problem remains—why do we hear nothing of Hawke's opinion or action in reference to the finding of Byng's Courtmartial, and the struggle which ended in his execution? Two months elapsed between his arrival from the Mediterranean and that final event. It may be enough to say that it was no business of his. He arrived too late to preside at the Courtmartial, and he was now in a private capacity. Yet at Keppel's Trial he was in the same position, and interfered with effect. We must remember that he was ill; he had just lost his wife; along with Anson he was in opposition; it was not for him to help Pitt out of his difficulty. Perhaps this was all. It is indeed perfectly possible that he thought it right the law should take its course. But we have no evidence one way or the other.

The contemporary historian of the War sums up the whole of the performances of the first two years of it in the following words:—

An inactive campaign in North America which deprived us of

the most important forts we had to cover our Plantations and stem the power of France on that Continent; a squadron on that coast not able to prevent succours from old France to Louisburg and Canada; a total neglect of Newfoundland; squadrons too weak to resist any attempt on our sugar islands and on our settlements on the Coast of Africa; a supine neglect of the East Indies; a fleet in the Mediterranean that could undertake no affair, nor find a more important object for its employ than hunting a few Tartans loaded with provisions for Minorca; and a still more inactive fleet beaten to pieces in the Bay of Biscay; a few cruisers to guard the Channel and watch the French ports, without any success except the surprise of a small island [Chaussée, near St. Maloes] ; . . . and the capture of a great number of [merchant] ships, but with such a neglect of our own trade that our loss in merchant ships fell very little short of the captures made from the French: our fleets had fled before our enemies, and we had lost Minorca. On which side soever we turned, our affairs carried a most disagreeable and ruinous aspect.*

This is scarcely too gloomy a picture. It requires to be studied in order that the national impulse which in its fury first destroyed Byng, then turned out the Newcastle Government in favour of Pitt, and finally, on the King's dismissal of their favourite, forced him once more and permanently to the front, may, with all its mighty effects, be properly understood.

---

* Entick's "History of the War," vol. ii. p. 29.

CHAPTER IX.

THE ROCHEFORT EXPEDITION.

The few words in which Pitt's position at the opening of the war has been described will have been sufficient to explain why, during the early part of 1757, he was unable to make any effectual change in the direction of military and naval movements. Dismissed on April 9th, 1757, by the King, who took advantage of his unpopular defence of Byng, and the country having been nearly three months without a Government, he was reinstated at the demand of the nation, on June 29th, and we are now to trace the combinations of that master-mind.

But though he had been unable during his first short tenure of office to produce results, Pitt had laid foundations. The Highlanders were enlisted in regiments, and thus Scotland was taken up into the strength of the country; the Militia had been modelled, nearly on its present footing, and thus the shameful necessity for defending these islands by foreign troops came at last to an end; and the resources of the country were now for the first time definitely pledged for the defence of Hanover. His change of policy in the last matter was justified by himself, and accepted by the country, on the ground that Hanover was now to suffer for the English interests in India and America, while previously England had been dragged into Continental quarrels for the sake of Hanover. This was by no means the whole case; but the argument served its purpose; and when Pitt finally took the helm the country was prepared to make any sacrifices to help Frederick to defend Hanover, while he kept the resources of France from being employed in forwarding the Colonial policy which lay at the bottom of the conflict between herself and Great Britain. This it was which Pitt had really in view, and Frederick was but his instrument. Very naturally, it was not what the other patriotic leader of the nation, "the Duke," had in view. In his mind, like his father's, the safety of Hanover was the first object, and the operations elsewhere, only second. Hence the jars which occurred between these two patriots—destined, however, only to last till the failure of the Duke removed him from the path of the Great Commoner.

No sooner had Pitt grasped firmly the reins of office than he addressed himself to his task. The safety of the country from invasion being now more assured than it had ever previously been, he determined to execute the military manœuvre which can only succeed when the front is secure, and all other circumstances favourable, viz., to operate upon both flanks of the enemy at once. To divert the French resources from their Eastern frontier he organised an entirely new policy of surprises and descents on her northern and western coasts, and as soon as by this means all attempts of the mother country to act beyond the limits of France were rendered impossible, she was to be dislodged from all the threatening positions in America and India which she had stealthily occupied, during the weakness of English Governments, since the time of Queen Anne. Under the inspiration of the genius of Wolfe and Clive this rough outline was filled up till it came to include not only conquest but expulsion, and the virtual extinction of France as a colonising Power in the world.

For the first time since the days of Queen Elizabeth the Sovereign, the Court, the Government, and the people of Great Britain were in union. The anomalous and unwholesome divisions of party had at last worked themselves out, or rather were for a time powerless in the presence of the uproused and determined patriotism of the people. The travail-pangs of England had been long and distressing; but, as Frederick wittily said, recognising the kindred spirit of Pitt, she had at length been delivered of a man. There was no backwardness in applying the resources which the country was now willing to supply. The need of drawing upon the future was recognised as urgent; for one generation could not repair the losses caused by the failure of a preceding one to do a duty, which, indeed, was hardly within its power. It was useless to play with the crisis. Money must be spent on all sides. Frederick must be largely subsidised, as well as assisted by a diversion on the French coasts; the Duke of Cumberland placed at the head of an efficient army; fleet upon fleet must be added to the navy; and above all a spirit must be infused into both services which should make it impossible that the catastrophes of Mathews and Byng, Wentworth, or Braddock should ever occur again. Perhaps there is no greater proof of the tremendous difficulty of the task which Pitt saw before him in planning the schemes which were destined to end so gloriously, than his offer to Spain to cede Gibraltar if she would form an alliance against France, and help England to recover Minorca. Who could believe such an offer possible after all that had taken place in the reign of George the First? Most fortunately "the Court of Madrid resolved to maintain its neutrality, and turned a deaf ear to his suggestion." *

The events of the year 1757 were by no means commensurate with the lofty ideas with which Pitt commenced his administration: and yet, on the principle that everything is directed for the best, we may perhaps trace a useful process in the distressing failure of his first attempt to realise them. These failures and defeats checked the too sanguine impulses of the nation, without extinguishing its spirit, and by teaching it to suffer and to wait, strengthened its persevering resolution, and instructed it how to deserve success. Nothing really great has ever been achieved in any other way.

---

* Stanhope's "History of England," vol. iv. p. 112.

Pitt was under two disadvantages in the commencement of his proceedings; and to these the Hanoverian and Rochefort failures may be traced. He was not responsible in any degree for the American failures, which had been planned independently of him; but in the two other cases he had to use the instruments ready to his hands, without much power of choice; and the summer was already in the full blaze of July before he could even sketch a plan of operations. The Duke of Cumberland, and no other, must command in Hanover; and Sir John Mordaunt was the best military officer of rank who could be thought of for the secret expedition to Rochefort, which was to inaugurate the new policy on the coast of France. For the naval officer in command Hawke was of course the selection of the nation, quite as much as of Pitt himself; nor was Anson, Pitt's First Lord of the Admiralty, now restored, likely to recommend anyone else in preference. Under Pitt this great naval administrator, finding at last a chief who could understand and appreciate the naval service, proved his title to the praises which that chief, in his old age, so abundantly bestowed. It would have been well for Hawke's reputation if he had not been so universally pointed out for this command; but to him also failure may have been useful. It was the first and only occasion.

We shall see that Hawke was acquitted of all blame, not only technically, and by the absence of any charge against him, but by the universal voice, which speedily discovered where the blame of the Rochefort failure really attached. But this is not to say that, prudent, and perhaps even necessary, as his conduct was under the circumstances, it is quite conceivable that a man of a genius superior to Hawke's for complicated operations on shore, might not have controlled those circumstances, and carved a different result out of the materials at his command. Hawke was essentially a sea-officer, and certainly in his own time, as such, unrivalled. There was no other of his contemporaries who would have been likely to succeed in this particular case. It is absurd to imagine, for example, that Howe would have done better, merely on the ground that he performed one small operation in the campaign with proper spirit. There is nothing in his subsequent career to justify the imagination. Nelson alone might possibly have grappled with the difficulties presented by want of all knowledge and experience of the place, by the wretched selection of military commanders, the lateness of the season, and the numerous accidental circumstances which seemed, by some special misfortune, to cluster round this bootless expedition. That it only cost the nation a million of money without defeat and loss of life, a Courtmartial, a general storm of indignation, and a cloud of pamphlets, that it was not a disastrous rout like the failure of Bligh and Howe at St. Cas the next year, or a *fiasco* like Lestock's at L'Orient, still less like Vernon's and Wentworth's at Cartagena, are only negative results, and a very poor set-off against the failure to do anything that had been intended; but, with such men as Mordaunt, Conway, and Cornwallis, blocking the way, it was something in Hawke's favour that it was no worse.

Pitt had in fact not yet learnt his own lesson. The failure may be attributed to many causes; but besides those which have been mentioned as beyond his control, he himself had ensured that failure by the stress he had laid, in his own "Secret Instructions," on the necessity of holding Councils of War. He meant by so doing to ensure harmony; he was yet to learn that harmony can only exist in mixed expeditions by placing proved and consummate commanders of both services in conjunction. In other circumstances, Councils of War are mere traps and delusions.

The Rochefort Expedition of 1757, like Mathews' battle, is not an agreeable subject to dwell upon, but the duty of describing it cannot, in a Life of Lord Hawke, be evaded; nor can it be dismissed in a few passing words. In placing the outline of it before the reader, the aim of this Chapter will be to abstain from repeating the mere unsupported opinions to be found in English Histories, which cannot possibly afford the space required for such an extremely complicated series of documents, and on the other hand to avoid the confusion in which more prolix accounts have left the subject. From some of Hawke's letters we obtain a little more light than former writers possessed, and the attack and defence of those concerned was at the time so vigorous and various that no excuse derived from want of full materials ought now to be of any avail.

Nor is it a matter so entirely belonging to the past

as it might seem. The inventions of modern times have indeed been of such a nature that many things which interfered with the success of these operations could not well occur again in war; but difficulties of another kind might easily be conceived to counterbalance modern improvements; and it will be seen that the lessons to be learnt from the failure are abiding, and likely to be quite as useful for the future now stretching before us, as they were when applied in the years immediately subsequent to the Rochefort failure.

The first paper here printed will show that Pitt lost no time after his acceptance of office on June 29th. On July 11th Lord Anson writes to Hawke from the Admiralty as follows:—

> DEAR SIR,
> I was very sorry you were gone out of Town, as I should have wished to have had an hour's conversation with you this evening; and indeed it appears to me so material that, though I am very sorry to give you the trouble, yet I must beg the favour to see you in Town, and I should be very glad [if] you would make Portsmouth in your way hither, without raising curiosity and alarm; but it is absolutely necessary that all the ships ordered to clean this spring should without a moment's time [? delay] be got to Spithead, as there may be immediate service for them. I am, &c.
> ANSON.*

What was the exact position occupied by Hawke when he received this letter, is not clear. He had received no Commission to hoist his flag, and he was not a Lord of the Admiralty. It is the first notice we have of him since he hauled down his flag in

---

* Hawke Papers.

January; though it seems he had been intended for the service for which Admiral Holburne had been reinforced in the spring, viz. the recapture of Louisbourg. There had been notes of failure all along the line. The Home service, in the spring and summer of 1757, had been performed by Boscawen, Temple West (till he resigned), and Brodrick; but, in spite of their vigilance, M. Dubois de la Mothe had contrived to evade the fleet once more, and had carried a squadron, along with several transports containing troops, to Louisbourg. Nor was this all. Holburne, though, when reinforced, in command of a large fleet, never found the opportunity to strike a single stroke, and—to anticipate a little—concluded his professional career under a misfortune over which, whatever might be the case previously, he certainly had no control. A tremendous hurricane which swept the American coast on September 20th, dispersed, and almost destroyed his fleet; of which the said M. Dubois de la Mothe, taking prompt advantage, again escaped the blockade. Still more fortunately, he eluded Hawke and Boscawen who, on the arrival of the news, were sent out in hot haste immediately after the return of the Rochefort Expedition, to intercept him. The French indeed lost several of their convoy, and suffered severely from the storm which, like the American hurricane, drove the English squadrons from their post, and enabled their enemy to slip into Brest; but this signified little. Fortune favours the brave, and if the French Admiral evinced his audacity rather in escaping than giving battle, he was certainly obeying the orders of his Government, wise enough under the circumstances; and he deserved the extraordinary good fortune which brought him safe home. The end of such freaks as Duguay and Dubois de la Mothe had hitherto succeeded in playing, was however close at hand. Without a fleet which could hold its own at sea, it was impossible, however reinforced, and however well defended, to save the French Colonies. In the next year Boscawen and Amherst expelled the French from Cape Breton; the year after, Wolfe and Saunders drove them from Canada.

Hawke, it is evident, must have been already named for the secret expedition which the Minister had in view; and already, we may suppose, had Anson hinted his doubts whether the exigencies of time and space could be chained to the axletrees of Pitt's fiery car. It is of this time that Thackeray speaks in his "Life of Lord Chatham," when he reports that Lord Anson informed the Minister that

the ships could not be prepared within the time specified; he moreover desired to know their destination, that they might be victualled accordingly. Mr. Pitt replied that if the ships were not ready at the time required he would lay the matter before the King, and impeach his Lordship in the House of Commons. This spirited menace produced its effect, and the men-of-war were all equipped and prepared according to the time and manner appointed.*

This story is not irreconcilable with Lord Chatham's posthumous eulogy of Anson, but one should not have expected such a scene so soon after the appointment of the new First Lord of the Admiralty with Pitt's

---

* Vol. i. p. 302.

eager concurrence. Possibly it is the original ground for the still less probable story of the great Minister forcing Anson to sign despatches, the contents of which he was not allowed to see. The extraordinary secrecy preserved in relation to the Rochefort Expedition, not only during the whole time of its equipment, but after it had actually sailed, may well have appeared to demand some mythical anecdotes to account for it.

The direction in which Pitt was led to carry out his design of a descent on France must have been due to a conversation, soon after taking office, with Sir John Ligonier, the Commander-in-Chief; for we find Colonel Clarke, on July 15th, writing to the general a full account of the observations he had made upon Rochefort three years previously, and doing so in consequence of a verbal report he had recently made, and which the general desired to have in writing. This engineer-officer deserves none of the blame which was afterwards cast upon him. He showed zeal and ability in making and reporting his observations; the responsibility of founding so costly an expedition upon them rests with Pitt. It is true that the officers he selected for command, Hawke, Mordaunt, Conway, and Knowles were present, along with himself, Anson, Lord Holderness, and Ligonier, when the matter was considered and the French pilot, Thierri, examined; but who could resist Pitt's eloquence when he had made up his mind to do "something" in response to the King of Prussia's urgent solicitations, and when this enterprise had presented itself at the critical moment? It was no doubt late in the year to prepare and send forth such an armament; and everything would depend on its being a surprise; but who would make difficulties?

The question innocently asked by Sir John Mordaunt, at a later date, illustrates the position. If the fleet should be sighted, and an alarm be given some days before the wind allowed it to get into Basque Roads, how was he to act? Pitt indignantly replies:—

> I am commanded by the King to signify to you His Majesty's pleasure that you do in conformity to the latitude given by His Majesty's Instructions, judge of the practicability of the service on the spot according as contingent events and particular circumstances may require,—the King judging it highly prejudicial to the good of his service to give particular orders and directions with regard to possible contingent cases that may arise.*

It was on the actual occurrence of this very contingency that everything ultimately turned.

Hawke, with his flag hoisted on August 15th on board the "Ramilies" at Spithead, receives his "Secret Instructions" from Pitt dated on that day, and Mordaunt similar orders *mutatis mutandis*; the two Generals, Conway and Cornwallis, and the two Admirals, Knowles and Brodrick, next in command, receive copies of the same, sealed, and to be opened only in case the command should devolve on any one of them. To the General of course the direction of the force which is to make a "descent on the French coast at or near Rochefort, and to burn, &c. all docks, magazines, &c. is assigned; to the Admiral, the duty of "co-operation."

---

* Paper No. IV. appended to the Report of the Court of Inquiry.

You are, as far as you shall be able with the fleet under your command, to be aiding and assisting to Sir John Mordaunt in the performance of the several services aforesaid. . . . After this attempt on Rochefort shall have either succeeded or failed, and in case the circumstances of our fleet and forces shall, with prospect of success, still admit of further operations, Port L'Orient and Bourdeaux are to be considered next as the most important objects of our arms on the coast of France.

No arsenals, ships, &c. are to be retained, but all demolished, and the expedition is " to be in England at or about, as near as may be, the end of September." The clause (in Hawke's Orders) on Councils of War runs as follows :—

Whereas it is necessary that upon certain occasions Councils of War should be held, we have thought fit to appoint, and do hereby appoint such a Council, which shall consist of four of our principal sea-commanders, and of an equal number of our principal land-officers [thus adding Rodney and General Howard to those already named], including the Commanders-in-Chief. . . . And all such sea and land officers are hereby respectively directed from time to time to be aiding and assisting with their advice as often as they shall be called together by you, or the officer commanding our land forces, for that purpose.

The fleet comprised 16 line-of-battle ships, six of which were commanded by such men as Denis, Howe, Keppel, Rodney, Byron, and Barrington, 7 frigates, 2 bomb ketches, two fire ships, 2 busses, 1 horse-ship, and 55 transports. On board this fleet were 10 regiments of foot, 2 of marines, 60 light-horse, and a train of field artillery. There were no siege guns, nor was there any idea of a regular siege. It was to be a surprise and an escalade. Scaling ladders were supplied so constructed that 30 men could mount abreast, and a quantity of fascines ; and each transport was to be provided with ten boats carrying 30 men each, so that the entire force might be landed at once. This however was not done. The horses and baggage were to be shipped at Southampton; the troops were encamped in the Isle of Wight. It was the unfortunate mistake about the carriage of these troops which caused the delay that proved, next to the premature alarm given by the appearance of the fleet, the most fatal cause of the failure.

Pitt and Anson had hoped that the expedition would have started by the middle, or at least the third week of August. The fleet was ready, so also were the soldiers; but the tonnage of the transports had been calculated on too small a scale; and it was not till the 17th that Mr. Thames, the agent of transports, represented the fact to Sir John Mordaunt, who reports that he was much "puzzled" by his conversation. Hawke, however, was not puzzled, but writes to the Admiralty as follows:—

In transporting troops to and from Holland with a fortnight's water and provisions, and a short passage, one ton per man might be shifted with. But where troops are to be many weeks at sea men must have room to sit and lie under cover. In this case can it be imagined that a ship of four hundred tons burden could be capable of receiving four hundred men? Let there be deducted from her tonnage the room necessary for her proper crew, ballast, cables, and other stores, room for several months' provisions and water for the soldiers, for their arms, tent-poles, and other baggage;—what remains can, only, be allowed for the reception of men. It was my duty to direct Mr. Thames to remonstrate on this subject to the Navy Board. Notwithstanding I was from the first determined, and am so still, to embark the troops in the best manner possible on board whatever number of transports shall be ordered.

A short letter from Pitt to Hawke of August 23rd, in which the Admiral is ordered to take the soldiers whom the transports cannot accommodate, on board his men-of-war, crossed this letter. It had been preceded by an angry letter from the Admiralty, complaining of the meddlesome agent, "one Mr. Thames, a person sent to Portsmouth by the Navy Board to assist the agent for transports in the embarkation of the troops," who has "raised unnecessary difficulties and uneasiness"; but it was accompanied by another letter from the same quarter announcing that the Admiralty had given way, and had ordered the required addition of transport-tonnage. The letter betrayed dissatisfaction, and Hawke replies to the Secretary on August 24th, in the following language:—

An expression at the end of your letter, I own, greatly astonishes me—"Their Lordships hope everything relating to the transports will be done to *your* satisfaction." I never was dissatisfied with any number appointed, and only thought it my duty for the public credit, as well as the private reputation of the Boards concerned, to give my opinion in a matter wherein some difficulty might have arisen when too late to be remedied. I meant it well; and as conviction is the best argument, I hope that discharge of my duty will not be construed to my disadvantage, since the Comptroller has thought fit to make so great an addition to the first tonnage. If such addition had not been, upon mature deliberation, thought absolutely necessary by his superiors, or even himself alone, I cannot think it would have been done in complaisance to any private person's opinion. Besides, I beg it to be considered that the difficulty arose from a quarter where I had no immediate concern of my own; for upon my honour had the first transports arrived in time, the troops should have been embarked on board them in the best manner they could without the least objection being made by me.

Next day he writes to Pitt that—

> as a number of transports have been taken up at this port by the Comptroller of the Navy, and the "Jason" ship of war is fitted for the reception of soldiers, I hope there will be no occasion to put any on board the ships of war, which are already sufficiently weakened by having two battalions of raw, undisciplined men in their complements; but in case the transports should not be sufficient for the number of troops, I shall, in obedience to His Majesty's commands, accommodate the remainder on board the men-of-war.

Delays still occurred; not only from the transports originally ordered being behind time, but the equipment of the new ones could not take place in a moment; and this sadly tried the patience of all concerned. It is evident that the double organization of the Admiralty and the Navy Board worked ill, as it always did, down to the time of its abolition in the present century. What fate befell the too honest Mr. Thames we know not; but we may be sure that Hawke's resolution that the truth should reach head-quarters, sunk deep. And here a letter of his to the Admiralty of September 1st may be inserted, simply because it is of this date and as it shows the humanity of his character:—

> By this post you will receive the sentence passed yesterday by a Courtmartial on Robert Read. As it is reported to me that this unfortunate man has a wife and family about Plymouth, for the better maintenance of whom he was tempted to desert His Majesty's service, give me leave earnestly to request that their Lordships will intercede with the King for his pardon.

By Monday September 5th the patience of the fiery Minister was exhausted, and the following letter to the two Commanders-in-Chief records the explosion :—

Sir,

The wind having been fair for the transports going to Spithead ever since Friday morning, I am to acquaint you that His Majesty expects with impatience to hear that the troops are embarked; but if by any delay the embarkation should not be completed when this letter reaches you, I am to signify to you the King's pleasure that the most particular diligence be employed in getting the troops on board, and proceeding without the loss of a moment to the execution of your Orders and Instructions with regard to the Expedition under your care. His Majesty having been informed that ten battalions under the orders of Sir John Ligonier, were all completely embarked at Williamstadt within the course of twenty-four hours, in which they arrived at that place, the King expects to hear, by the return of this messenger that the fleet under your command, with the troops on board, have proceeded to sea, in case the wind permits, agreeable to your Orders and Instructions. I am, Sir, with great truth and regard, your most obedient humble servant,

W. PITT.

P.S.—The messenger that carries this has my orders to stay to bring an account of the fleet's sailing.

This was dated at 4 P.M. Next day Hawke replies :—

At half-past five this morning I received by express your letter of the 5th inst., signifying His Majesty's directions to use the utmost diligence in embarking the troops and getting to sea. As I could not doubt of my letter to the Secretary of the Admiralty, by express on Sunday morning, being immediately communicated to you, I should have expected that before yours was sent His Majesty would have been fully satisfied that I needed no spur in the execution of his orders. As the wind was fair here on Saturday I ordered an officer [Lieutenant McKinley], with six cutters, out to cruize for the transports, with positive directions not to come-to at Spithead, but proceed directly to Cowes. Soon after they appeared in sight on Sunday morning I dispatched an officer to acquaint Sir John Mordaunt with their arrival, that everything might be ready. As there was but little wind all day on Sunday but few of them reached Cowes that night, and proving but little wind on Monday morning, I sent boats to tow the "Jason" down with two boats from each ship at Spithead, together with all the boats from the Dock, to assist in the embarkation. One brigade was embarked yesterday, as the other will be by noon to-day, so that the whole time taken up in the embarkation from the arrival of the transports to this day at noon will not exceed twenty-four hours, though we have not the advantage of jetty-heads [as at Williamstadt] from whence the troops could step into the transports. Besides, Sir, as they were detained so long in their passage round, they were in want of considerable quantities of provisions, which, to save time, I sent to Cowes after them, while I watered and victualled the Horse-ships here; the Horse are embarked this morning. . . . Give me leave to add that the mortar was to be shipped on board the "Infernal" bomb-vessel: she will be ready to-night. The men-of-war which came round with them were also in want of stores and some provisions. The squadron is now unmooring, and I only wait the return of the transports to Spithead when I shall take the first wind that offers to go to St. Helens', and if it should prove favourable shall go to sea immediately after. Be so kind, Sir, as to take the trouble to assure His Majesty that as I ever have, so more particularly on this occasion, I shall show the greatest regard to his orders.*

It was not however till September 10th that the expedition got fairly away. On September 8th Hawke reports from St. Helens' that—

a calm obliged me to anchor the squadron again. Yesterday at 4 in the morning I began to unmoor again, and sent an officer [Lieutenant McKinley] to Cowes to see none of the transports were left behind. About 3 in the afternoon I got to this place, and was obliged to come-to, as they could not get out, dispatching officers who were all night employed in ordering them to join me without loss of time. Last night arrived from the Downs a Company of Lord Effingham's regiments, which had been

---

* Paper XXVI., appended to Report of Court of Inquiry.

embarked on board the "Norwich" at Chatham. The transports are all come down, and I am now under way with a moderate breeze at E.N.E.

On September 10th:—

On Thursday last, after I wrote to you, the wind died away which obliged me to come-to again till half an hour past five; then a moderate breeze from W.N.W. springing up, I made the signal to weigh, and at 7 made sail with all the transports. On Friday we had contrary winds till evening, and this morning I was joined by H.M.S. "Essex," by whom I send this. We have now a fresh gale, with the wind at N.N.E.

Here ends the first part of the proceedings. The expedition had not left England till a fortnight before the equinox, and its destination was a roadstead in the Bay of Biscay. It has been necessary to account for the delay at some length, in order to show that no blame could possibly be attached to Hawke. The particular season of the year when the equipment was proceeding is always subject to uncertain weather, and to the weather, as well as the delay in the transport department, must be attributed the disappointment of Pitt's eager hopes. All the elements of action, human and superhuman, were to conform to those eager hopes; but they refused to conform. In calculating the work of the machine the necessary allowance for friction had not been made. It was too great an affair to be conceived in July, and executed in August. The tenth of September, under the circumstances of those times, was too late.

Some sense of this difficulty dawned upon the sanguine mind of the Minister soon after the squadron had sailed. On September 15th he hurries off a

Despatch to catch the two commanders, modifying the order they had received as to their return by the end of September, and saying that they are—

> not to desist from the execution of their orders, or break up the same, merely and solely on account of the time limited for your return by the Instructions above mentioned, but that, notwithstanding the same, you do continue with the fleet, during such a farther number of days as may afford a competent time for the completion of any operation under the above circumstances.

This Order was received in good time, but was interpreted to require a return if nothing of importance was to be undertaken, as near after the end of the month as possible, and no fault could be found with the final decision of the officers, taken under it, as so interpreted.

Before sailing Hawke drew up a rough memorandum for his own private guidance in the conduct of the expedition, and it forms one of the papers preserved in the family. Not being a complete plan it is not worth printing; but two or three extracts will show that there was no mistake on his part as to the nature of the fundamental conditions of success. Thus for example:—

> To consider with the flag and general officers which will be the properest place to attempt: to settle this in going along; and to fix upon the ships and troops that are to make the attack, which, if done at all, must absolutely be done upon the first going in, or otherwise they will be prepared to make head against you: no time must be lost upon these occasions.
>
> Not to undertake anything without good pilots.
>
> To endeavour to cover the landing of the men by sending in two, three, or more small frigates inshore, to fire grape and partridge, to scour the country while the men are disembarking to be particularly careful to do this upon their embarking.

To see thorough discipline and exact order in every respect, kept up strictly on board.

To enquire of Phill. Durell at Portsmouth how Mr. Vernon regulated the transports.

When the troops are landed to send out ships and vessels to cruize between the main squadron and the Isle of Oleron or Bordeaux, and between the do. and the Isle of Ushant or the Penmarks.

To consider well what force is, or may be, at Brest before parting with any of my ships.

To divide the whole number of Tenders [transports] into three Divisions, and to appoint a man of war of the line and a frigate to each of the Divisions to see, in tacking, that they are careful in obeying the signals made by the admiral, and to follow them and make them keep up with the fleet. To keep a couple of men of war in the rear of the fleet; to keep two or three out ahead, and one upon each bow: to spread the ships whenever the weather will permit of it.

In case of going in with a design to anchor upon the enemy's shore, to give positive orders for the Divisions of the fleet to lead it in order of the Line of Battle, and for each Division to follow at such a distance as to give time for each to come to an anchor before the other can be upon them. The transports to follow the men of war in their Divisions. In case of going in upon the enemy's shore, to be careful that you go in with the beginning of the flood, lest any of your ships should happen to touch.

To order the Lieutenant Colonels on board six of the men of war: General Mordaunt, "Ramilies"; General Conway, "Neptune"; General Cornwallis, "Royal William."

Wolfe, the Quartermaster General, found his place on board the "Ramilies" with the two Commanders-in-Chief, and writes home that "Sir Edward Hawke seems determined to do everything that can be done upon this occasion consistent with his orders and instructions, and the safety of the fleet." *

---

* Wright's "Life of Wolfe," p. 381.

It must be remembered that everything in relation to Rochefort had to be learnt for the first time; that there was nothing deserving the name of a chart of the narrow waters into which this great fleet was to penetrate, that no English pilots, or English seamen knew anything whatever about the navigation, and that the French pilots of the country were only to be trusted on the supposition that their Protestantism was a stronger guarantee for their good faith than their nationality. It was a sanguine supposition, but the principal one, Thierri, though ignorant enough, did certainly perform the duty he undertook; and received Hawke's encomium for the courage he displayed. These memoranda are also suggestive as to the Admiral's responsibility for the whole of the French coast as well as for the immediate operations at Rochefort; and it was impossible to be easy under that responsibility when the equinoctial gales were expected.

The delays which were beyond the Admiral's control hampered the expedition to the last. Those of the voyage are best described in his letter to the Admiralty of September 29th. He was ordered to communicate both with that office, and with Pitt himself. The Despatch hitherto printed has been that of September 30th to the Minister, but though the two are identical from a certain point, the portion of the earlier one which here follows, occurs in the first Despatch alone.

"RAMILIES," Basque Roads,
SIR, 29th September, 1757.
From the time I wrote you last on the 13th inst. [which letter is neither in the Hawke Letter-books or Record Office] we

had light breezes, for the most part contrary, with fogs and calms, which prevented our getting sight of the Isles of Rhé and Oleron till about noon of the 20th. I attempted to get into Basque Roads, and made the dispositions for attacking the Island of Aix with the Red Division, composed of the "Magnamine," "Barfleur," "Neptune," "Torbay," and "Royal William," with frigates, bomb-vessels, fire-ships, and cutters. Between 4 and 5 o'clock, and no probability of getting in that night, I made the "Magnamine's" signal [Capt. the Hon. Richard Howe], being the nearest ship, to chase a French ship of war of two decks in the South-east quarter. She was followed by the "Torbay" [Keppel], "Royal William," "Escort" [a sloop], "Coventry," and a cutter. Night coming on, they chased her as far as they could with safety into Bordeaux River, where it is reported she is aground. As these ships could not join the squadron that night, not to lose sight of my principal object, I supplied their rooms in the Red Division with the "Dublin," "Burford," and "Achilles"; and at 7 in the morning of the 21st, made the signal for the Vice Admiral [Knowles] to stand in, in order to attack the Isle of Aix. As he approached the entrance between the islands, the weather being a little hazy, his pilot refused to carry the ship in, as did all the rest of the pilots of his division, which obliged him to tack and join me. About 11 the "Torbay," "Magnamine," "Royal William," and "Escort" joined company. At 3 P.M. the Vice Admiral made sail with his Division in a line ahead. But the wind blowing right out with a tide of ebb, we were obliged to come to anchor at 6. At 7 in the morning of the 22d we weighed, but having little wind, came-to again at 12. At quarter after 3 weighed again, and spreading in a line ahead, got into Basque Roads at half after 9. About an hour before, I was joined by the "Viper" sloop with His Majesty's orders signified by Mr. Pitt, one of His Majesty's Principal Secretaries of State, to finish any operations which might have been begun, after the principal object of his Instructions. With the tide of flood at 10 in the morning of the 23d the Vice Admiral weighed with his Division in pursuance of my former order, and stood towards the Island of Aix, it being the general opinion that the troops could not be landed with safety till it should be first reduced.

Here the two Despatches begin to correspond; and

the rest may come in another place. When Wolfe, some months afterwards, wrote a caustic criticism of the conduct of the expedition to his friend, he remarked :—

I have found out that an admiral should endeavour to run into an enemy's port immediately after he appears before it; that he should anchor the transports and frigates as close as he can to the land, that he should reconnoitre and observe it as quick as possible, and lose no time in getting the troops on shore; that previous directions should be given in respect to landing the troops, and a proper disposition made for the boats of all sorts, appointing leaders and fit persons for conducting the different Divisions.

He then goes on to criticise the conduct of the Generals with still more bitterness, but much more reason.* Elsewhere he says :—

We lost three days without, and three within. We were in sight of the Isle of Rhé September 20th, and it was the 23rd before we fired a gun. That afternoon and night slipped through our hands, the lucky moment of surprise and consternation among our enemies.†

The reader has now for the first time the opportunity of judging from Hawke's own pen how much value should be attached to the opinions of the young officer,—afterwards to become so celebrated,—seasick, as he confesses, on the voyage, ignorant of the true state of the case, and wise after the event. It was this sort of criticism that spread among the vulgar. Wolfe never meant it to be published. His evidence before the Courtmartial, which was not however very lucid, may be fairly held of itself to

---

* Wright's "Wolfe," p. 397.
† *Ibid.*, p. 395.

exculpate Hawke; and it is noticeable that he made no sort of objection, as Quartermaster General of the force, to the final relinquishment of the expedition. What he did was indeed characteristic. Disgusted with his military superiors, he offered at an early stage of the proceedings, to attack Rochefort with three ships and 500 men. The extraordinary genius, then scarcely suspected, which he soon afterwards evinced, has led the world to conclude that he would have succeeded. Such a supposition, though of course possible, is entirely gratuitous. It could only have succeeded as a surprise, and though authorities differ as to the possibilities of a surprise, we must always remember that during the next year, an English spy was discovered, a physician, who had given intelligence to the French of the design upon Rochefort before the resolution of the Privy Council to attack it had been made known either to Hawke or Mordaunt.*

The incident of the chase of a French two-decker, mentioned above by Hawke, formed the subject of many a bitter joke at the expense of Admiral Knowles, in the midst of whose Division of the fleet the ship had found herself, when she suddenly discovered it was not a French squadron, as she had supposed, and made the best of her way back. This Admiral who had formerly been reprimanded by a Courtmartial for not having given the Spaniards as sound a beating as it was thought he might have inflicted—(he and Sir Robert Calder are the only two Admirals who

---

* Entick's "History of the War," vol. iii. p. 82.

have been tried by Courtmartial after a victory)—was the favourite scapegoat of the public for the failure of the Rochefort expedition; and it was not surprising. He was a clever and brave officer, but one of those talkative, turbulent, men that the navy as well as the army occasionally breeds, and was always coming before the public in some form or other. Eventually he was knighted, and took service with Russia. Knowles on the present occasion was so intent on showing General Conway the orderly appearance of the crew of his ship at quarters between decks, that he not only did not detect the Frenchman, but took no notice of her for some time after she was reported; and to the delay of orders for a chase was attributed her escape, and the consequent alarm of the coast. As a matter of fact, however, the expedition was expected; no delay was caused by whatever happened on this occasion; and Hawke attributes no blame to the Vice-admiral. In the general exasperation a great deal was evidently made out of a little. The public were perhaps nearer the mark when Knowles' subsequent conduct of the reconnoissance on Fort Fouras was made the subject of adverse criticism; but as one of the numerous pamphlets of the time said :—

Did Sir Edward Hawke complain of Mr. Knowles?—and if he did not, who can, without beginning at Sir Edward, whom even malice itself, never, that I could yet learn, charged with being either coward or fool.*

---

* "Considerations on the proceedings of a General Courtmartial," &c., 1757.

We may now resume Hawke's Despatch :—

The "Magnanime" led. About 12 the fire began from the Fort with shells and great guns, and continued while our ships approached, till about 10 minutes after 1; when the "Magnanime" brought up within less than 40 yards of the fort, where she kept an incessant fire for about 35 minutes; as did the "Barfleur" [Graves] which brought up, about 5 minutes after her, abreast the fort. About three quarters after One the firing ceased, the garrison having struck their colours and surrendered. They had in the fort 8 mortars of about 14 inches diameter, and 30 guns, 16 of which were 18, and the remainder about 14 pounders. The "Magnanime," though damaged in her rigging, yards and masts, yet had only 2 soldiers killed and 11 men wounded.

On the morning of the 23rd I observed a French man of war, over the land, to the S.E. of the Isle of Aix. Being desirous of destroying her I directed Captain Byron of the "America" to take with him the "Achilles" and "Pluto" fire-ships, and as soon as the Red Division should begin to batter, go and destroy her. But the French flung their guns overboard, cut their cables, and otherwise lightening her, ran up the Charente. It is said she was the "Prudent" of 74 guns, bound for Louisburg.

It having been thought necessary, in order to secure a safe landing for the troops, to sound and reconnoitre the shore of the main, as soon as the fort had surrendered, I directed Rear Admiral Brodrick, with Captains Denis, Douglas, and Buckle, to perform that service and make their report to me. It was the afternoon of the 24th before they returned. A copy of that Report accompanies this. After maturely considering it I was of opinion they might land; on which Sir John Mordaunt desired a Council of War might be assembled to consider of it. There it was granted by everybody that the landing could be effected. In confidence of their judgment and knowledge of their own profession we assented to their reasons for not proceeding to attempt taking Rochefort by escalade. A copy of the result of that Council of War is here enclosed. He desired a second, which was assembled early on the morning of the 28th. Herewith I send you the result of it. Immediately the disposition was made for the landing, under the direction of Rear Admiral Brodrick and all the Captains of the squadron. Part of the troops were actually in the boats, when I received a letter from Mr. Brodrick, a copy whereof I herewith transmit.

Last night I applied to him [Sir John Mordaunt] to know whether the General officers of the land forces had any further military operations to propose, that I might not unnecessarily detain the squadron here. This morning I received Sir John's answer, a copy of which is here enclosed. It was the daily expectation of their undertaking something which induced me to stay here so long. As I have now got their final resolution I shall sail for England to-morrow morning.

Though, before I came here, this place was represented as very difficult of access, and so narrow that ships could not lie in safety from the forts,—nay, the pilots made many baulks before we came in,—yet I find it a safe, spacious road, in which all the navy of England, merchant ships included, may ride without the least annoyance; and that a squadron may at any time by lying here prevent any armament from Rochefort, and ruin all the French trade to Rhé, Oleron, or the Continent, within these islands.

I have ordered the "Burford," "Alcide," "America," "Dunkirk," "Coventry," "Postillion," "Béarn," "Pelican," "Cormorant," "Escort," and "Hawke" cutter to Plymouth to await their Lordships' orders. The rest I shall bring to Spithead with me.

[The above clause is absent in the Despatch to Mr. Pitt.]

Their Lordships may be assured I have discharged my duty to my King and country with truth, diligence, and integrity; and wish more could have been done for the good of the service.

The Pilot of the "Magnanime" has behaved like a man of bravery and skill, and as such I beg leave to recommend him to their Lordships.

Yours, &c.
E. HAWKE.

Before quoting the documents referred to in this Despatch, Hawke's private letter to Lord Anson of the same date, September 30th, must find its place here:—

"RAMILIES," in Basque Roads, off Rochelle,
MY LORD, Sept. 30th, 1757.

The "Viper" sloop joined me within the entrance of this place just before we came to an anchor, Mr. Knowles' Division having brought-to some little time before. I have kept her all this time flattering myself with the daily hopes that the land officers would come to a determination to land the troops, to try what was possible to be done for their country, notwithstanding they were of opinion it was impracticable to take the town of Rochefort by escalade. If there is faith in man, my Lord, you may believe that I have urged this to them continually, painting the absolute necessity of it in the strongest terms that I could possibly think of. But I am infinitely concerned to tell your Lordship that you will see by the result that all this has availed nothing. I made no hesitation in attempting to remove every obstacle out of the way that was in my power, in which I happily succeeded, and wanted no Council of War, nor never would have had any if they had not been demanded to confirm me in opinion that it was right I should use my utmost endeavours for my King and country.

I have wrote the Admiralty as full an account of our proceedings as I can, but it is impossible to give your Lordship a thorough detail of the whole unless I had the honour of seeing you in person, and therefore shall be glad you will please to order me to have leave to go to Town when I shall arrive at Spithead.

This is a much finer Road than what the Chart describes it to be, being much larger and more spacious, and where the whole fleet of England might lie upon occasion with great safety; and now that we are acquainted with it, it is in our power, with a superior force, to prevent the enemy from making up their fleets here, which will lay them under infinite difficulties, and subject them to great hazard, it being always in our power, now that we know the place, to prevent any squadron, fitted at this port, to join [from joining] that of Brest.*

Reading this private letter, written evidently in a hurry, and in the anguish of his heart, along with the letter of May 10th, 1758, which will come in its place, we may form some idea of what the Admiral's feelings were in finding himself compelled to return home with

---

* Anson Correspondence.

such a miserable story to tell. It is needless to say that the thorough sifting to which the whole of the proceedings were subjected at the hands of two public Courts (at one of which his own evidence was taken), as well as the war of excited literature which accompanied and followed those enquiries, failed to shake a particle of the plain, straightforward statement conveyed in the above Despatch. It remains to fill in the blanks, and analyse the whole.

It may not be unnecessary to remark, before going farther, that Rochefort lies in an excellent position for defence, about nine miles up the River Charente, the mouth of which was fortified on the right bank by Fort de l'Aiguille, Fort Fouras, and Fort La Pointe; and on the left by the Fort on Isle Madame. The best defence of these forts is the intricacy of the navigation amongst the shoals caused by the deposits of the river; and nine miles away from the forts stands the Island of Aix, which commands the entrance to these shoals, as well as the anchorage near the island, which is large enough for several ships. The Bay of Chatellaillon forms the coast line running to the Northward from Fouras. Further away to the North, along the Coast, is the Basque Road, a fine sheltered anchorage between the mainland and the Islands of Rhé, Oleron, and Aix. The great distance from this, which is the only safe anchorage for a fleet, to Aix and the intricate passage to the mouth of the river, and still further, to the forts which guard the river's entrance, must be borne in mind by the reader. Rochefort Arsenal, like that of Toulon, was the creation of Louis XIV., inspired by the genius of Colbert.

The first point which demands attention is the capture of the Fort on the Isle of Aix. One of the common charges of the critics was that it had been unnecessary to detain the fleet and troops even for the few hours occupied by Howe and Graves in the attack. This was, however, open to great doubt. Such charts of the place as there were represented the fort as dominating the anchorage; it was known to have been planned by Vauban, and supposed to be much stronger than it was; and it is the first principle of war not to leave an enemy in the rear. As it happened, it had never been completed; only six guns could be brought to bear on the ships; and though Howe's approach to it was as gallant as everything done by that fine officer always was, the capture was a mere bagatelle. Unfortunately the expedition was seriously discredited by the bad conduct of the crews of the ships which took the fort. They not only got furiously drunk, but ill-treated the priest and the chapel of the place. On the other hand a good end was served by the capture, since it enabled the enterprising Wolfe, eagerly looking out for an opportunity, to get on shore and obtain a view of the forts higher up the estuary. What he saw he immediately reported, and thereupon proposed a plan of operations which must now be described. It is not mentioned in Hawke's Despatch, since though at first approved by him, he soon saw that it must be abandoned. It may form a first stage in the consideration of the details before us.

Wolfe's plan was to make an immediate attack on Fort Fouras, along with a diversion to be effected by the bomb-ketches, which would open fire on Rochelle and the Isle of Rhé; thus drawing off the attention of the enemy to places several miles from the real point of attack. Both Hawke and Mordaunt approved of the proposal, at least as to Fouras; so also Conway, with the exception of the part relating to Rochelle, which he thought impracticable, and of which, as Hawke agreed with him, nothing more was heard. It is quite possible that Wolfe may have been right on this latter point, and the rest wrong; but we have no means of judging.

As to the attack projected against Fouras, it was Hawke's business to ascertain instantly if ships could get in near enough to make the attack; and Thierri, the pilot, who in the excitement of the moment of Howe's success, had offered to take the "Magnanime" up to Fouras, was examined by the admiral and vice admiral on the morning of the 24th. Hawke described at the Courtmartial how he gave him time to allow his "gasconade to subside"; and then, on the statement of his belief that the "Barfleur," which drew less water than other line-of-battle ships, might, after being lightened, get near enough, Knowles was sent off to get her ready. Her Captain, however, told Knowles that it would not be of much use, for she was aground already, at five miles distance from the fort; and, indeed, no sooner had Knowles gone, than the pilot altered his mind, and declared it impracticable to bring any ship within battering distance. This was afterwards proved to be true; it not being found possible to bring "even a bomb-ketch within random shot of the fort." On the whole Hawke pronounced him to be "very ignorant of the place." He had observed that even when he piloted the "Magnanime" up to the fort at Aix, "she sewed in the mud." It was clearly impossible to order a landing at Fouras under such circumstances; and his only course was to have the whole shore examined by responsible officers. Here was a day lost; but who could be blamed? To Admiral Brodrick and three Captains the task was that afternoon entrusted: but anyone can see by a glance at a common map that to take soundings, and ascertain the practicability of landing, along so many miles of coast, could not, even by the most zealous officers, be accomplished very rapidly. It took the night and next morning. It was not till the afternoon of the 24th that Hawke received the Rear Admiral's Report that the Bay of Chatellaillon was the only proper landing-place, and that though it had been impossible for them to land on account of the surf, yet in fine weather it would do perfectly well.

Hawke, we have seen, was now satisfied that his part of the work was done. A landing-place had been found; and he would see them all on shore next day without, as it was reported he told the generals, their having to wet their shoes. Mordaunt, however, having heard from Conway, who had examined several French prisoners at Aix, that Rochefort was not likely to be so easily taken as had been thought, considered this to be the occasion provided for in Pitt's Instructions,

A LANDING-PLACE FOUND. 313

and now demanded a Council of War. Here opens the second stage of the proceedings.

Perhaps no English Council of War was ever brought before the public so often as this of September 25th. It will be unnecessary therefore to give more than its results. Hawke, in mentioning these results, reports that "it was granted by everybody that the landing could be effected." This was his point. He would have risked the dangers of re-embarkation, and attempted at least a reconnoissance in force of the place they were sent to attack. To the generals the following arguments told in the opposite sense. They did not dispute that a landing might be effected; but they observed the danger of the coast (which was exposed to the whole force of westerly winds), if bad weather should come on after landing, and that the re-embarkation could not be assisted by the ships on account of the distance they must lie off shore. The evidence of Colonel Clarke seemed also to them, from the length of time which had elapsed since he visited the place, to be almost valueless. Some prisoners (much glorified by French historians for deceiving the English) declared that men had been working on the fortifications of Rochefort for several days past; some neutral vessels had reported that the enemy had been for some time in expectation of a descent; and the ditch which they had been told was not a wet ditch, appeared from evidence to be capable of being made so. On the whole, considering

the long detention of the troops in the Isle of Wight, and our meeting with contrary winds, fogs, and calms upon our passage, the several informations received of troops assembled in the neighbourhood, and the great improbability of finding the place unprovided, or of surprising it, or consequently succeeding in an enterprise founded on the plan of an assault or escalade merely; and the uncertainty of a secure retreat for the troops if landed, the Council are unanimously of opinion that such an attempt is neither advisable nor practicable.

This is signed by all the eight officers ordered by the "Instructions" to form the Council of War; and of these eight, Hawke himself, the President, was one. It is remarkable that while this proceeding might naturally suggest a charge of inconsistency on his part, no remark seems to have been made upon it at the time. The next sentences of his Despatch give his own explanation, which seems to have been always considered satisfactory:—

In confidence of their judgment and knowledge of their own profession we assented to their reasons for not proceeding to take Rochefort by escalade;

or as he more fully expressed it in his evidence:—

Whether they should land or not land, he constantly thought it was the part of the generals to determine that question by themselves. He looked upon them as good and gallant officers, and officers of service; and therefore could not but suppose they were infinitely better judges of their own business than he could be. In confidence of their abilities he acquiesced in their opinion of the impracticability of taking Rochefort by an escalade or storm; however, though he assented to the not landing upon that footing, he did not give it as his opinion that the troops should not land at all for any other attempt which the General officers should find proper and expedient for the service: on the contrary he then urged the necessity of doing something agreeable to the King's Instructions.

If Wolfe had been a member of the Court he might have turned the scale the other way. In the letter above-mentioned he remarks that—

nothing is to be reckoned an obstacle to an undertaking of this nature which is not found to be so upon trial; that in war something must be allowed to chance and fortune; seeing it is in its nature hazardous, and an option of difficulties; that the greatness of an object should come under consideration [as] opposed to the impediments that lie in the way; that the honour of one's country is to have some weight; and that in particular circumstances and times the loss of a thousand men is rather an advantage to a nation than otherwise, seeing that gallant attempts raise its reputation and make it respectable; whereas the contrary appearances sink the credit of a country, ruin the troops, and create infinite uneasiness and discontent at home.

And again:—

This famous Council sat from morning till late at night [it sat till midnight, and its proceedings were not signed till next morning]; and the result of the debates was unanimously not to attack the place they were ordered to attack, and for reasons that no soldier will allow to be sufficient.*

Like the criticism quoted above on the conduct of the Admiral, this savours of extraordinary presumption; but here the future hero knows much more of what he is talking about; and the principles he lays down are not only sound as regards that, but for all such enterprises. However,—to obtain success in a blind enterprise, a genius must appear on the scene. The success of an escalade depends, as Mordaunt said, on a surprise, and the French were now, as was abundantly proved, perfectly aware of the English movements. It must also be remembered that the application of the principle of ignorant impulse produced next year the catastrophe of St. Cas; and the expeditions against Louisbourg, in 1758, as well as of

---

* Life, p. 397.

Quebec, in 1759, would probably have had the same result if a tolerably thorough knowledge of both places had not been in the possession of the conquerors, and—we may say still further—if Wolfe himself had not in both cases been on the spot.

We have now advanced to a third stage in the proceedings. The feelings of the officers and men, soldiers and sailors, in this great fleet of men-of-war and transports, when it got about that nothing was to be done, may be imagined without difficulty; and the general murmur could not fail to reach headquarters. Could not something be done? The uneasiness betrays itself in various ways. "It was my daily expectation of their undertaking something which induced me to stay here so long"—says the Admiral. The French prisoners were examined again, and some fresh information, thought to be more favourable to a landing at Chatellaillon, with a view to an attack on Fort Fouras, was obtained. Vice-admiral Knowles was ordered to see whether the bomb-ketches could not get in near enough to be of use; Hawke sent Rodney to reconnoitre Oleron as a landing place,—on which he reported unfavourably; and various personal observations were made by the generals, including the ever-active Wolfe. The result of all this effervescence was that Mordaunt, on the 27th, was himself induced to reconsider the question of landing, though not with any further idea of attacking Rochefort itself; and a second Council of War was, at his request, summoned for the 28th. It should be noticed that during this period of gestation the engineers had been fully employed in destroying the fort at Aix; but this could have been effected under the protection of half a dozen ships.

The second Council was a less tedious affair than the first, and, for some reason not explained, it seems to have been agreed that there should be no regular Minutes taken of the proceedings. Nevertheless Hawke, as President, had minutes taken by his Secretary for his own guidance, and forwarded a copy of them with his Despatch. Unfortunately, not having been signed by the other members, they are unauthentic; but their substantial accuracy was not impugned, nor was the following passage disputed:—

Sir Edward Hawke, appealing to every member of the Council for the truth of what he said, declared that he was now of the same opinion which he had given both before and at the Council of War of the 25th, that the landing could be effected; that the troops ought to be landed for some further attempt, which was alone matter of consideration with the General officers of the troops, he not taking upon him to be a judge of land operations, but would, from his confidence in their abilities and skill in their own profession, readily assent to any Resolution they should come to, and assist them to the utmost of his power.

The naval members then withdrew; and on their afterwards joining the military members, it was unanimously agreed to land the troops "at Chatellaillon Bay that very night, and make a sudden attack with the land forces upon Fouras and the other forts leading to, and upon the mouth of, the River Charente."

"Immediately," says Hawke, "the disposition was made for the landing under the direction of Rear Admiral Brodrick and all the Captains of the squadron. Part of the troops were actually in the boats when I received a letter from Mr. Brodrick, a copy of which I herewith transmit."

The letter is as follows :—

Sir,

I have prepared all the boats with proper officers to land the troops, agreeable to your order; but am to acquaint you that the Generals are come to the resolution not to land to-night, and to wait till daylight, when they can have a full view of the ground where they are to land.

I am, Sir, yours, &c.

"Achilles," Tuesday morning; Thomas Brodrick.
1 o'clock.

On the other hand Sir John Mordaunt describes the affair thus :—

The necessary orders were immediately given; and about one o'clock the Grenadiers and great part of the troops who were to land with me in the first embarkation were on board [the boats]; when a strong wind blowing from the shore, the officers of the navy appointed to conduct the landing represented that it was with difficulty the long-boats could make way, that it would be day before the first embarkation could get to shore; and that it would be 5 or 6 hours more before the troops first landed could be supported by a second embarkation. Add to this that the boats belonging to the transports would scarce be able to get on shore at all. For these reasons the Generals found the Forces could not be landed that night.*

The discrepancy between these two accounts was much commented upon. The army and navy seemed to throw the blame upon one another; and it was unfortunate that Brodrick did not say that he concurred with the Generals,—for there was no blame to be attached to anyone. The wind, as the evidence before the Court showed, was much too high to land;

---

* Evidence at the Court of Inquiry.

and of this we may be sure, for no one was more strongly of that opinion than the intrepid Howe. The fact evidently is that admirals, generals, and captains were agreed, and were all quite right. If the generals were responsible for the final resolution, it was because the naval officers recommended it. It was an exposed coast, with a heavy surf line; no one could command the winds, which combined with many other causes in producing the failure of the expedition.

It may be added to this summary of the final effort "to do something" that Hawke in his evidence before the Courtmartial on Mordaunt, stated that his own plan of sending in the transports on the afternoon of the day on which the Council was held, "as close to the shore as they could possibly go, and the frigates within them, at the place where the troops were to land, that they might get on shore with the greater expedition," though seconded by all the sea-officers, was objected to by the military members, and especially by Conway, as "it would point out to the French the place at which they intended to land." Thus the public rightly judged that the plans of the naval officers never having been tried, it was not they who could be accused of failure. The military objection was unsound: for there was now no chance of any surprise, and the distance at which the transports lay was too great for boat-work, as it turned out. Hawke, when he found the attack in the early morning was preferred, gave personally some excellent orders to the transports for facilitating the landing of the second detachment of troops. To do this, they were, "at the instant the first body of troops was gone from the ships, to get under sail immediately, and run close into the shore where the troops were to land." However, none of these things came to pass, and are only interesting as they throw light on a complicated series of events.

The fourth and final stage comprises the several steps which led to the departure of the fleet for England on the 30th. On the 29th, instead of making any further arrangements for landing the troops—which had returned to their transports full of indignation at having been kept four hours in the boats, during a windy night, without the chance of striking a blow—General Conway was employed with Colonels Wolfe and Clarke in a further reconnoissance of the coast from Fouras to Chatellaillon. The generals had received information, or rather "it had been reported," that "some camps and entrenchments had been seen on the shore, particularly near the place where the landing was to have been made." Conway reported to Mordaunt and the two other head-officers of the Council that he was still in favour of attempting a landing; but here he was unable to carry his three colleagues with him. Cornwallis had been steadily all through against any landing at all, and admitted that he only signed the Resolution of the 28th against his own judgment. Colonel Howard had been much of the same opinion. Sir John Mordaunt had been hitherto more guided by Conway than by anyone else, and even now offered to go on, if Conway thought he ought to give way. He had been summoned by Hawke to make up his mind on the morning of the 29th in the following terms :—

"RAMILIES," Basque Road,
SIR,   29th Sept. 1757.
    Should the General officers of the troops have no farther military operation to propose, considerable enough to authorize my detaining the squadron under my command longer here, I beg leave to acquaint you that I intend to proceed with it for England without loss of time.

I am, Sir, &c.
ED. HAWKE.

With this letter and Conway's Report before them, all four agreed to give up the whole expedition. Conway, though he had expressed his opinion in favour of further action, declining to press it, joined the rest; and the following letter was the result :—

SIR,
    Upon receipt of your letter I talked it over with the other Land-officers who were of our Councils of War, and we all agree in returning directly to England.

I am, Sir, &c.
J. MORDAUNT.

There is a suggestive abruptness in this final correspondence. Though there is no want of proper politeness, the relations between the army and navy had evidently become much strained. Mordaunt stated to the Court that he applied to Sir Edward for a Council of War to consider the first of the above letters; but—

he declined it, and said that seamen were no judges of land operations, which were to be performed by the troops on shore. In consequence of this conversation I summoned all the land officers who had been of the Council of War and laid Sir Edward Hawke's letter before them. We considered the uncertainty of landing, if the wind should blow as it had done the night before, and the account we had that day received from the Captain of the "Viper" sloop, who had informed Colonel Howard that he had seen a considerable body of troops near the landing-place, whose numbers he did not exactly know, but he had observed five pair of colours; that he saw them in camp; that the next morning the view of the camp was interrupted, so that he could not see them again, which he attributed to their having thrown up some ground on the beach; and that he saw the sandhills on the beach considerably higher than they were on Sunday when we came there. Colonel Howard, in his return from reconnoitring, reported this to me.

It further appeared to us that the attempt upon those forts at this time, could not justify the ill consequences of detaining the fleet in that bay at a time when, from what we had learnt from the conversation of the sea-officers, two great French fleets were expected home; that at this season of the year, so near the Equinox, such Westerly winds were to be apprehended as might' detain the fleet there many weeks; that the foundation upon which the Resolution of the Council of War upon the 28th was taken, was that it might be done during the necessary detention of the fleet in the demolition of the Fort of Aix, and thereupon was directed to be done with all possible despatch; that the demolition of the works of the Isle of Aix was completed that very day, and that the wind was then fair for the fleet to return; add to this that the time limited by His Majesty's Instructions was now expired, and that the time was not prolonged by Mr. Pitt's letter, which allowed us only to complete such operations as we had already begun.

On the receipt of the laconic reply sent by the Generals, the fleet at once set sail for England; and moored at Spithead on October 7th. It was a most inglorious return. It is said that the arrival of the fleet was greeted by "a dumb peal" from the church bells of Portsmouth. This must have been far from agreeable to the Member for that place. But all were alike. The whole country was in a blaze. Were they never to obtain a return for the money they lavished upon sailors and soldiers? It was ardently hoped that this grand expedition would have wiped out the dreadful memory of the loss of Minorca. It had made matters worse. Entick, the historian of the war, reports that—

> the greater part of the nation vented resentment on the commanders . . . another far less numerous part, did justice to their good intentions, but questioned whether the projectors had sufficient ground of knowledge or information to warrant the undertaking. Some, merely guided by private attachment . . . extolled it to the skies; others, envious of Pitt, affected to treat the whole plan as chimerical, crude, and undigested, both in the projection and appointment of the execution . . . some over-refined politicians pretended to discover a connection with the Convention of Stade.*

Of the numerous effusions in which the popular feeling found expression, perhaps the most just and least scurrilous was the following, from the "Gentleman's Magazine":—

> We went, we saw, were seen, like valiant men,
> Sailed up the bay, and then,—sailed back again.

It cannot be said that Hawke suffered seriously in public estimation even on the first blush of the affair, but his feelings were none the less wounded. The generals were the real sufferers, and the King, who had never approved of the expedition, but had allowed Pitt to have his way, represented the national feeling when, the Admiral and General having been sent for to Court, he gave Hawke a reception as gracious as that of Mordaunt was as markedly the contrary.

---

* Vol. ii. p. 346.

This was, however, to settle the question a little too summarily. Mordaunt's character stood high, and the feeling of the army at least was that he ought to be allowed to clear himself and his colleagues. The remainder of the year was taken up by the Court of Enquiry which was opened on November 1st, and by the subsequent Courtmartial on Mordaunt to which it led. Hawke was, happily for himself, out of the way of the general hubbub, for he was sent off with the fleet to watch for the return of M. Dubois de la Mothe, and did not come back till the evidence before the Courtmartial was closed. However the Court was reopened on December 20th in order to hear his evidence, the substance of which has been given above. It will be sufficient here to state the conclusions at which both Courts arrived, and then to sum up the whole.

The Court of Enquiry consisted of the Duke of Marlborough, Lord George Sackville, and General Waldegrave. Their Report has been blamed for its vague and unsatisfactory character; but somewhat unjustly. It is sufficiently clear on the point that Rochefort ought to have been attacked, and that the Council of War which decided against that operation on September 25th was the cause of the whole failure. Nothing else, they thought, was of any real consequence. Being generals, they naturally reflected by implication on the sea-officers for not having joined in the final Council demanded by Mordaunt, and declined by Hawke; but they laid no stress on it. The Court evidently considered the whole matter

COURT OF ENQUIRY. 325

one which ought to go further; and in the agitated state of the nation, with so many uncertainties attaching to the proceedings, and so many suspicions that political intrigue had affected them, it was quite right that the whole matter should be thoroughly sifted, with all the advantages that a Courtmartial has over the Court which precedes it. The only point in the evidence requiring remark in reference to Hawke, who was not there to explain, is the production of his private minutes of the Council of War of the 28th. This was angrily referred to by the other members of the Council of War; but as it turned out that Mordaunt had been asked to produce his minutes, and not having taken any, had applied to Hawke for a copy of his, which the general had sent up without remark, and as no fault of the slightest importance was found with them, the incident is not worth further notice. What came out both before this Court, and more fully before the Courtmartial, was that Hawke, previously to September 25th, at the Council held on that day, and on that of the 28th, when he at last brought the Council to agree with him, had always, throughout, given his opinion that "the landing could be effected," and that he had urged it all along.

But it did not follow that Mordaunt could be found guilty by a Courtmartial. On the contrary when the evidence had all been retaken, with much additional matter, after Pitt and, at the last moment, Hawke, had been examined, and every Instruction and order had been thoroughly weighed, the Court had evidently no choice but to acquit the General; and he was accordingly "honourably acquitted." Campbell in his "Lives of the Admirals" * here remarks:—

> The Minister and the Admiral were also acquitted by the general voice of the people; so that this grand expedition miscarried without a cause.

The historian's bitter verdict is only too near the mark. Mordaunt had no difficulty in proving that he had acted in strict conformity with his Instructions, and where he had been left to his own responsibility, had acted to the best of his judgment. Nor was there any sufficiently strong ground for disputing the conclusions to which he had come. It was perfectly open for a brave and prudent man to take either view. Nothing but success could have proved a movement such as Hawke and Wolfe would have made to be a wise one. There were reasons enough, of a certain kind, against it.

> "The surprise," as Mordaunt's defenders said, "on which depended the only chance of making a vigorous impression, or a *coup de main*, was evidently over; and as to sitting down before it, we had no artillery: our plan admitted of none. Sir Edward Hawke, who was so far from giving his opinion that the troops should not land at all, that he urged the necessity of it, was however satisfied that Fort Fouras was become of no consequence to troops landing in Chatellaillon Bay; and as no other object appeared worth landing for, either to Sir Edward Hawke, who wished it so much, or to the other commanders, what could they do but come away? — for as to Rochefort, all of them had concurred in the opinion of its being not to be thought of more. . . . Surely the little or nothing that obviously remained to be done against Fouras was not an object for keeping the fleet longer upon that coast. It could not be worse to set it at liberty to proceed on

---

* Vol. iv. p. 104.

important and real services than to detain it in fruitless attendance on an imaginary one.*

It is not easy to dispute this reasoning, nor was it satisfactorily met in a single pamphlet of the day. The country was at least saved from the disgrace of another "judicial murder"; and Pitt was too great a favourite with the people to be saddled with the failure as Newcastle and Anson had been in the case of Byng. Nevertheless the Courtmartial had treated the original plan of the expedition with contempt; a very large body of opinion was formed against the Minister; and the preceding remarks have shown that, however natural it was for his political enemies to lay the blame on his shoulders, the impartial voice of history cannot by any means acquit him.

There were many "ifs" in the matter. If Mordaunt had been an able and energetic man, if Conway's good qualities had not been eclipsed by a fatal and very characteristic indecision, if even Cornwallis and Howard had been anything but commonplace men, if Wolfe had been one of the Council of War, instead of merely Quartermaster General; still more, if he had been in command, the matter would have been placed beyond doubt in one way or the other. As the French were prepared, there would doubtless have been heavy losses; and changes of wind and weather might have caused a catastrophe like that of St. Cas, while nothing of any importance might have been achieved; but on the other hand it is quite possible that audacity

---

* "Considerations on the Proceedings of a General Courtmartial," &c., p. 73.

might have prevailed; something might have been gained in the way of information from a powerful reconnoissance, prisoners might have been taken, forts destroyed, and an alarm raised all over France.

This is the risk Pitt meant to be incurred; it is what Hawke earnestly advocated. But it was an immense risk.* While some held that the Minister ought to be very grateful to the generals for not having, in the absence of any certain information of any sort, "sacrificed so many valuable lives to an opinion of his, perhaps too lightly taken up," and warned him against becoming intoxicated with power like Alberoni, and falling under condemnation as a hare-brained plotter of silly enterprises like that charlatan, others attributed the failure to the want of zeal of the naval, as well as the incapacity of the military, chiefs.

The sea-officers had been tempted with wealth instead of reputation, and we have substituted avarice for honour. We have at this hour many who would make brave and excellent corsairs, and I hope that in the long list we have two or three good admirals.†

---

* In Bubb Doddington's "Memoirs" that clever politician declares that it had become known from indisputable evidence that the enemy "had 7 or 8,000 men at Rochefort at the least, that there were 3,500 men behind the sand-banks, and there was a masked battery at each end. That if we had landed when we first appeared we should have embarrassed them; but they thought themselves betrayed when they found we did not land at the time we attempted it" (p. 401). This seems also to be the view of the matter taken by the best French historians, such as M. Martin.

† "The Expedition against Rochefort fully stated, &c.: by a Country Gentleman": 1758.

This reflection on the Royal Navy was certainly undeserved. Hawke's whole career was a protest against it; and neither Knowles, Brodrick, or Rodney could be thought to lie under such an odious charge; but the popular indignation must vent itself somewhere. Pitt was its representative; and he was too angry to perceive that he was lowering himself by condescending to speak, at the opening of Parliament, as follows :—

> He declared solemnly that his belief was that there was a determined resolution, both in the naval and military commanders, against any vigorous exertion of the national power. He affirmed that though His Majesty appeared ready to embrace every measure proposed by his Ministers for the honour and interest of his British dominions, yet scarce a man could be found with whom the execution of any one plan in which there was the least appearance of danger, could with confidence be trusted. . . . Nor was it among the officers alone that indolence and neglect appeared; those who filled the other departments of military service seemed to be affected with the same indifference. The victuallers, contractors, purveyors, were never to be found but upon occasions of their own personal advantage. In conversation they appeared totally ignorant of their own business. The extent of their knowledge went only to the making of false accounts; in that science they were adepts.*

Yet, shamefully exaggerated and unjust as this language was, it is beyond doubt that it had a useful effect. The whole country felt the whip and spur of this imperious rider, and whatever may be our opinion on the spirit with which the navy at least might have acted, whether lashed by the whip or not,

---

* MS. Report of speech in "Anecdotes of the Life of the Rt. Hon. W. Pitt, Earl of Chatham, &c., with Speeches in Parliament, &c., 1792": vol. i. p. 168.

when it had a fair chance, there is no doubt that it did soon begin to perform wonders, and that the army, led by the new men whom Pitt selected from the junior ranks, was not a whit behindhand.

Perhaps the best illustration of the bewildered confusion produced in men's minds by the return of the Rochefort Expedition without effecting anything, is the conviction which so largely prevailed that it was an act of treachery, either on the part of Pitt himself, or of some other members of the Government. Newcastle of course was grievously suspected; some even hinted that the King had a hand in it. Two disasters had come very close on each other's heels. The Duke of Cumberland, overweighted and outgeneralled by the French under Marshal Richelieu, had been all but driven into the sea, and forced (on September 8th) to sign the Convention of Stade or Closter-seven. There was in fact just time for the news to have reached Basque Roads at the critical moment when the decision to do nothing was arrived at; and people not knowing what to believe, insisted that Mordaunt had received secret orders to this effect, with a view to obtaining better terms from the French for Hanover. In the "Chatham Correspondence" are several such letters. Mr. Potter, M.P., reports to Pitt that the people of Bristol and the west country are unanimous in this belief. Horace Walpole tells General Conway that the City of London is equally convinced. Lord Chesterfield, on November 4th, tells his son:—

In all these complicated machines there are so many wheels within wheels that it is always difficult, and sometimes impossible, to guess which of them gives direction to the whole. Mr. Pitt is convinced that the principal wheel, or, if you will, spoke in the wheel, came from Stade.*

Thus while Pitt is himself suspected, he suspects others. Men were absurdly suspicious all round, as they often are when anything strange or unaccountable happens. But by the light of such a simple narrative of events as has been here presented, we can see our way without recourse to a magic lantern.

That, in the opinion of the King, Hawke came well out of the affair, whatever Pitt might think, not only on his arrival, but after the Courtmartial was over, is proved both by his continuous employment, and by the following letter :—

THURSDAY, Dec. 22nd, 1757.

Lord Anson sends his compliments to Sir Edward Hawke, and the King having asked yesterday whether Sir Edward was in Town, his Lordship is of opinion he should go to Court this morning and be presented to the King at his Levee.†

The nation had also made up its mind. Its confidence in Hawke was unshaken. He was still at the head of the active forces of the navy; he had acted with his usual self-command in keeping silence while the storm was raging; and though shattered in health by all he had gone through, and about to be still more tried than ever, was really now on the point of completing his fine career with glory.

Pitt himself was also about to emerge out of the sea of difficulties in which he found himself in the autumn of the year 1757. The brightest day suc-

---

* Chatham Correspondence, vol. i. p. 279.
† Hawke Papers.

ceeds the darkest night. Light dawned from Prussia. The victory of Rossbach on November 5th—a Protestant victory on a Protestant day—turned the tide; and the King, at last discovering the merits of his Minister, Pitt was now able to throw over the opposition in the Cabinet which had hampered him for the first few months of his Administration. Taking every department of the State into his own hands, he was in a position to apply without let or hindrance the whole resources of the country as he thought best. Frederick's consummate generalship crowned his fortunes. The splendid battle of Lissa (or Leuthen) on December 5th, completed the work of Rossbach; the French, the Russians, and the Swedes, were simultaneously expelled from their previous conquests before Christmas; and the Hanoverian army which had capitulated at Closter-seven was set free by the action of the French themselves, who, in the pride of their success, broke the conditions they had imposed. All was now prepared for the onward movements which characterised the years 1758 and 1759, and decided the issue of the war.

It was not the failure at Rochefort alone that had cast such a gloom over the nation, and at the same time steadied its resolution to insist on Pitt's being entrusted with a full Dictatorship. Affairs in America had gone from bad to worse during this miserable year—perhaps the most distressing of the whole war. Montcalm's success in the capture of Fort William Henry was accompanied by details of shocking barbarity. Lord Loudoun and Admiral Holburne had performed as little with their fleet and army towards the capture of Louisbourg, for which they had been sent out in the summer, as the generals had done at Rochefort. Like the expedition against the latter place, theirs had been despatched too late in the year, and without sufficient information as to the strength of the enemy; and Holburne, as has been said, had sustained the additional misfortune of encountering a hurricane which disabled the English ships, and allowed the French to slip back to Brest. The admiral could hardly be accused of raising the gale, but the people, persuaded that he ought to have done more beforehand, visited the disaster on his reputation. In India the terrible catastrophe of the Black Hole of Calcutta left a mark which the brilliant success of Clive had by no means been sufficient to erase. The Spaniards continued to insult the British flag. The fortunes of Frederick had fallen so low that he was on the point of committing suicide.

Who could have believed that after six pitched battles in one year, this wonderful man, with his diminutive force, would before the year was ended, rise superior to the most crushing defeats, and hurl back the united forces of the whole Continent? His spirit infused itself into the English mind. A vista of triumph revealed itself through the clouds; with British troops and British gold to support the gallant Frederick, it was seen that he might be trusted to keep the whole strength of France at bay; while with Pitt supreme, and the herd of Newcastles and placemen of every hue at his feet, some methods might be found by which the failures and disgraces of the past might be retrieved, and the real superiority of the English at sea be asserted without dispute. The Royal Navy was but a weapon. It could not handle itself. Let it be directed for once by the hand of a master. The army had fallen low, even in its own estimation. Let it learn its work under Frederick and his generals. It would soon win back its old fame.

Nor must the effect of the loyalty which now at last gathered round the old King, be forgotten in marshalling the moral forces which placed Great Britain on the lofty heights attained in the next two years. His Hanoverian proclivities were now discovered to have had some good English policy at bottom. He had emptied his own purse to save his hereditary dominions. He had conquered himself to secure the ally round whom the English were now to rally. With all his faults, it was now found out that his great civic virtues of justice and courage were kingly qualities. Never had he failed to elicit the merits of British officers by encouraging the brave, and frowning on the inefficient; and he had earned a personal right in this matter, which made his smiles and his frowns significant. Never had he infringed, though sorely tempted, the conditions of the British Constitution under which his family were seated on the throne. It was no small feat to perform, that he should discover how to work that Constitution in the interests of the people themselves, as distinct from Parliament, and under the pressure of their will, without breaking through the established methods of Government, or displaying the least symptom of a desire to assume despotic power. The ancient Monarchy of England was now at last witnessed in its ideal form, combined with effective national self-government. The nation felt that it ought to burst its trammels, and rise to Empire. It was permitted to reap the reward of sufferings nobly borne.

CHAPTER X.

THE DESCENTS ON FRANCE IN 1758.

THE year in which the gloom of despondency was to change into the bright glow of hope and confidence cannot be introduced better than by the Royal Speech composed by Pitt, and pronounced at the opening of the autumn session on December 1st, 1757. That session had been delayed several days in consequence of the Battle of Rossbach. Pitt felt that so great a victory offered an occasion for a new departure, and the old speech, drawn up on the lines suggested by the former state of affairs, was flung into the fire. The recent failures were to be passed over as mere "disappointments," and a spirit of buoyant hope and determined resolution might now, without exciting opposition or ridicule, connect itself with "the magnanimity and active zeal of my good brother and ally the King of Prussia."

MY LORDS AND GENTLEMEN,

It would have given me the greatest pleasure to have acquainted you, at the opening of this session, that our success in carrying on the war had been equal to the justice of our cause and the extent and vigour of the measures formed for that purpose.

I have the firmest confidence that the spirit and bravery of this nation, so renowned in all times, and which have formerly surmounted so many difficulties, are not to be abated by some disappointments. These, I trust, by the blessing of God, and your zeal and ardour for my honour and the welfare of your country, may be retrieved. It is my fixed resolution to apply my utmost efforts for the security of my kingdoms, and for the recovery and protection of the possessions and rights of my crown and subjects in America and elsewhere, as well by the strongest exertion of our naval force as by all other methods. Another great object which I have at heart is the preservation of the Protestant religion and the liberties of Europe; and in that view to adhere to and encourage my allies.

For this cause I shall decline no inconveniences; and in this cause I earnestly desire your hearty concurrence and vigorous assistance. The late signal success in Germany has given a happy turn to affairs which it is incumbent upon us to improve; and in this critical conjuncture the eyes of all Europe are upon you. In particular I must recommend it to you that my good brother and ally, the King of Prussia, may be supported in such a manner as his magnanimity and active zeal for the common cause deserve.

Both Houses reciprocated these sentiments with the greatest enthusiasm; and supplies, gigantic for those times, were no sooner asked for than obtained. Money in fact the nation could well afford, in spite of its losses: for in proportion as the trade of France had suffered more by the war than that of England, the latter trade had increased. Thus the sources from which the immense expenses of the French for war and subsidies to their allies were drawn, rapidly diminished, and loans could only be obtained at an exceedingly high rate of interest; while the English could borrow at a very low rate, and were making profits which lightened the incidence of taxation. It was neither money, nor men, nor material that were lacking, only the skill to use them.

Pitt's first and immediate care was to prevent the French from transmitting reinforcements to America, whither he was about to send a large force. Admiral Osborn was charged with the blockade of the French fleet at Toulon which was assembling for the above purpose; and though no general action was fought, some actions of the single ships under his command were completely successful in putting an end to any movement from that quarter. That especially of Captain Gardiner, of the "Monmouth," who was killed in the capture of the "Foudroyant," a ship of about double his own force, deserves mention. On February 19th the squadron destined to retrieve the previous failure at Louisbourg started, under the command of Boscawen, with whom Amherst was immediately afterwards associated, and with Wolfe as one of the Brigadiers-General under him. The choice of these officers was excellent in all respects. Boscawen had last been employed under Hawke in the Channel fleet which had been sent out, immediately on its return from the Basque Roads, to look for M. Dubois de la Mothe, and had been driven into port by the gale which brought the French into Brest. If Walpole is to be believed he had declined to serve under him on the previous expedition;* and though he thus escaped the unpopularity attending its failure, was, or fancied himself, in disgrace at headquarters on that and some

---

* "Letters to Mann," vol. iii. p. 24.

other accounts.* But this could not have been serious, as he was still a Lord of the Admiralty; and Pitt knew what he was about in entrusting him with the command of an expedition of such importance at a critical moment. It was suited to his talents for combined warfare, and Pitt used to say of him that "Boscawen never made difficulties." Jeffery Amherst had been but slightly known as yet, and was below the rank from which the selection would naturally have been made, but Pitt had marked his man.

To Wolfe also, from having observed the contrast between him and the other generals before Rochefort, he now gave the very first opportunity in his power to distinguish himself. The highest concord prevailed amongst the chiefs; and though great risk was incurred in landing the troops,

---

* Among the family papers is the following letter from Anson to Hawke, soon after his return from Basque Roads.

DEAR SIR, ADMIRALTY, the 19th of October 1757.

Vice Admiral Boscawen's great uneasiness at not being employed at this time when there is an object in view, has determined the sending him out under your command. I know the delay this must occasion, which must be disagreeable to you, but he determines to be down with you at Portsmouth soon enough for you to sail on Friday morning. I could say to you much if I had you here *tête à tête*, but Knowles' imprudence always hurts him, and he has enemies enough to seize every occasion that offers. I have always wished him well with all his indiscretion. His busy spirit constantly draws him into difficulties. I think Admiral Boscawen comes to you with a disposition to be agreeable to you, and I can only say for my own part that no man can wish you more success, nor is more your friend than, your obliged and affectionate humble servant,

ANSON.

amidst difficulties which were only overcome by Wolfe's gallant personal conduct, the operations of the English arms moved steadily on to the brilliant success which was achieved on July 26th. This success was the more encouraging to the Minister and people because Cape Breton had been so long a cause of grievous distress to the Anglo-American Colonists, and because the capture of a place which had, since the beginning of this later war, baffled every effort of the Government, was justly accepted as an earnest of a turn of fortune in reference to the other plans of the campaign.

So entirely has the importance of this place now receded into the background that it requires an effort to understand why the success of Boscawen and Amherst should have been thought worthy of the solemn thanks of Parliament, and why the captured colours of the enemy should have been paraded through the streets of London, as if the occasion had been comparable with the great victories on which such demonstrations have seemed appropriate. But our sketch has already embraced the conquest of the Island by Warren and the American Colonists, the surrender of it, with hostages, as the shameful price of the Peace of Aix la Chapelle, the vast pains and treasure subsequently spent by the French on the fortifications of Louisbourg, and their resolution to make it more than ever the key to French America; as also the failures of the years 1755, 1756, and 1757 either to prevent reinforcements from being poured into it, or even to attempt its siege. It was in this sense that the Speaker, in addressing Boscawen, declared himself unable to "enumerate and set forth the great and extensive advantages accruing to this nation from the conquest of Louisburg with the islands of Cape Breton and St. John." The place had been not only the sole harbour for the large ships of the French, but the nest of the whole of their privateering system which had broken up the Colonial trade; nor were their lucrative fisheries of any value without it.* It was but an accidental addition to the importance of the capture on these grounds, that six line-of-battle ships and four frigates had been taken along with the place. Both sides of the entrance to the St. Lawrence being now permanently in British hands, the French colony of Canada became perilously insecure, and Wolfe lost no time in putting his plans for the capture of Quebec before the Minister.

With the third part of Pitt's scheme, Hawke, who on February 28th had hoisted his flag on board the "Ramilies," in command of the Channel squadron, was entrusted. The French ships captured by Osborn's squadron, or still blockaded at Cartagena, were intended to have joined the squadron fitting

---

* For a very interesting, and on the whole just, view of this subject see a Pamphlet by "Massachusettensis," entitled "The importance of Cape Breton considered in a Letter to a Member of Parliament, from an Inhabitant of New England: London: Dodsley: 1746." This is in the All Souls' and probably other Libraries. Few papers convey a more accurate description of contemporary opinion on the colonial questions disputed between Great Britain and France in the last century.

out at Rochefort, and together they were to have sailed for the relief of Louisbourg before Boscawen could have taken it. Pitt destined Hawke for the service of dealing with this latter force, and obtained information at the end of February that although it could no longer expect the reinforcements from the Mediterranean, it was all but ready to start unsupported—so urgent was the peril of Louisbourg. It may well be imagined that the admiral was not displeased at being ordered on special service to a place where he had suffered so much distress; and this time without the encumbrance of land-officers and Councils of War. It would not be his fault if the expedition failed. Nor, as far as was known at that time or since, did it in any degree fail. The destruction of the French armament against which Hawke was sent, seemed to the public complete; or if not, no one ever hinted that he could have made it more complete. There was a sort of regret that the enemy would not stay to be beaten; but that was all. No squadron, no troops ever left Rochefort for America. Nevertheless the incidents of this affair were painful to our admiral in the greatest degree; and his correspondence with the Admiralty throws a light upon his character and services with which we cannot afford to dispense.

Some letters of Hawke's, written shortly before starting on this expedition should be previously noticed, since they illustrate his constant desire to improve the condition of the seamen. When men were discharged from ships as unserviceable, from disease or wounds, there were no existing forms under which they could receive their pay up to the date of discharge. "They have consequently nothing to subsist them on their way home. Numbers have been, and still are in the same situation, whose case I hope their Lordships will take into consideration. Their being reduced to beg through all parts of the kingdom deters men from entering into the Service, and has induced me seriously to consider of a remedy. I therefore beg leave to submit what follows to their Lordships' consideration." The plan which he proposes is simple enough, and seems to have been adopted: but observing the date of this interference and that of the quarrel with the Admiralty which now commences, one may suspect some connection. We may remember that the remonstrances about the pressed men and the bad beer were closely connected with the painful correspondence of 1755.

On March 12th the Admiral sails to blockade the Rochefort armament, with 7 ships of the line and 3 frigates, but with no smaller vessels, such as were necessary for operations in shoal water. This was the grievance. The terms of the letter, which will follow presently, show how deeply he felt it. "Last cruise," referring to this one, "I went out on a particular service, almost without the least means of performing it." There is indeed no letter to show that he had asked for these vessels, and been refused; but it could hardly have been otherwise; many letters are missing; and the expression in his Despatch of April 11th:—"I could not help regretting the want of fire-ships and bomb-vessels," is decisive. On April 5th, having received information from England that the French squadron was on the point of starting, he suddenly dashes into the midst of it, and reports the result on April 11th, by which day he had returned to Plymouth. Premising that he found lying off the Isle of Aix 5 line-of-battle ships, 6 or 7 frigates, and 40 merchant ships, which, he reports in a second Despatch, had 3,000 troops on board, he goes on to say :—

At half-past 4, made signal for a general chase to S.E., but took care to preserve the line by verbal orders to the ships astern of me. At 5 the enemy began to cut or slip, and soon to run in great confusion. At 6 their Commodore, who remained last, made off, when we were within about gunshot and a half. Many of those who fled first were by this time aground on the mud. ... It was now too dark to do anything but take up an anchorage. ... At 5 next morning I saw them all aground, almost dry, about 5 or 6 miles distant from us ... many of the merchant and several of the ships of war, were on their broadsides; and then I could not help regretting the want of fire-ships and bomb-vessels.

He then explains how it was that he could not bring his ships nearer in to the enemy.

By this time all the boats and launches from Rochefort and the adjacent places were employed in carrying out warps to drag them through the soft mud as soon as they should be waterborne. In the meantime they threw overboard their guns, stores, and ballast, and were even heaving water out of their ports, all which we could plainly discern. By this means some of them got that day as far up as the mouth of the Charente; but the "Florissante" was not got above Fouras on Thursday afternoon, and the greatest part of their merchant ships were left aground in towards Isle Madame, when we fell down to Basque Road. The frigates' [the "Medway" and "Chichester," which were sent up the channel as far as they could go] boats cut away about 80 buoys laid on their anchors and on what they had thrown overboard.

He concludes by describing the steps he took to destroy the new works which had been commenced on the Isle of Aix since the demolition of the Fort in the previous year's expedition.

From the Admiral's log-book one or two additional facts may be gleaned. It seems the French ships were so eager to make off, and understood their soft muddy shoals so well, that they kept all sail set while on the mud, the wind being fair. It also appears that on the 6th two French Galleys, large vessels, with a light draft of water, propelled by oars, and carrying heavy guns, came out from Fort Fouras and attacked the "Chichester," which had got aground. These were beaten off from a distance by the guns of the other frigates; but there were no craft of their own light draft of water to deal with them; and the ships' boats, at such a distance from the ships, were not fit to cope with such an enemy. This was the addition of insult to injury which rankled in the Admiral's mind.

The account of what was done and what was left undone on this occasion cannot fail to remind the reader of the affair of the Basque Roads in 1809, when Lord Gambier and Lord Cochrane were called upon to perform on the same spot an operation of very nearly the same kind as the foregoing. In the latter case the French squadron, instead of being surprised, was admirably prepared for the attack of the

English; but the arrangements for that attack were of a very far superior description to those at Hawke's command. The result was much the same in both cases. The French were seized with a panic in 1809, just as they had been half a century before, and at both times exhibited the same spectacle of stranded ships, and frantic efforts to carry them over or through the mud to a place of safety. In both cases the shallowness of these intricate waters proved to be an insuperable difficulty to the victors. In both cases the French ships were irreparably damaged; but if in Hawke's case he had had a squadron of light vessels at his disposal, and if, in Cochrane's, there had been no commanding officer to check him in full pursuit, the damage to the enemy would have been far greater. Finally, the conduct of Lord Gambier on the point of his omission to silence the batteries on the Isle of Aix, comes out in unfavourable contrast with that of Hawke in 1757. Hawke's plan of making this the first point in his proceedings was censured at the time as the cause of unnecessary delay; but Gambier's failure to do more than he did was caused in great part by dread of these very batteries, against which he made no attack; and this is the more remarkable, since it could not have been yet forgotten that there was a channel by which Howe in the "Magnanime" and Graves in the "Barfleur" had sailed close up to the Fort in 1757.

The acknowledgment of Hawke's Despatch by the Admiralty displays a coldness and reserve which indicates some previous misunderstanding. There is

COOLNESS OF THE ADMIRALTY. 347

not a word of thanks for the service he has performed. The Secretary on his own account "heartily congratulates" him "on his safe return."

On April 30th the Admiral begs for "three or four days' leave to settle some private affairs, if their Lordships think I can be spared." The reply is not in Hawke's Letter-book; but its tenor is plain from the rough note of the Secretary, endorsed on the back of the above letter :—

> The Lords would be very glad to indulge him on every occasion, but at this time they wish him to be on the spot, as not only the ships at Spithead but those cruising, are under his command.

On May 7th the Admiral makes another untimely suggestion; but if he did not, who was to do it? Who was so fit to bring it before the Admiralty as the man who had suffered from this cause for the greater part of the previous ten years? It seems that there had never been a residence for the Commander-in-chief at Portsmouth; and Hawke speaks of it thus :—

> The great inconvenience Commanding officers at this port labour under for want of a proper house or lodgings, induces me to take the liberty of laying before their Lordships a proposal of Mr. Joseph Smith, which, if approved of, will remedy it at a very moderate expense, it appearing to me to be very just and fair.

His letters are often dated, both before and after this suggestion was made, from George Street. Perhaps the Admiralty, as they do not seem to have made any change in his time, thought the Member for Portsmouth was a little too much interested in the matter to be a fair judge. In the present day it would seem inconceivable that the business of the Service could be carried on without a residence for the Commander-in-chief. No doubt the worry and annoyance of a post so responsible as it was in Hawke's case, must have been largely increased by this circumstance; and we are now to witness the effect of worry, and, no doubt, illness on a sensitive nature.

Pitt having provided for the success of his plans in America, was by no means satisfied with the old routine of blockading and breaking up French expeditions. Undaunted by the Rochefort failure, he had resolved upon a series of descents on the North Coast of France, of a magnitude which should divert her military forces, and relieve Frederick; and he had learnt the lesson taught him in the previous year. He had now made up his mind that these descents should no longer be hampered by large ships which could not approach the shore, nor fail for want of an abundance of small vessels, the want of which had just been so severely felt. A covering fleet there should be, in order to deal with squadrons which might issue from the eastern ports to attack his flotilla. That fleet Hawke should command as of old; but the actual work of landing and co-operating with the troops should be performed by the young Captain who had found an opportunity of distinguishing himself wherever he had had a chance, the Hon. Richard Howe, under whom the French pilot, Thierri, had in the previous year particularly begged to be sent, "*parce que le Capitaine Howe est jeune et brave.*"

It has been universally supposed that Lord Anson was from the first intended to take command of the covering fleet, and that Hawke was only to be, as he came in fact to be, the second in command. The following letter will show that this was not the case. Hawke had been ordered to collect and equip the fleet, and was preparing for the receipt of final orders, when Howe one day waited on him with a message, the effect of which was like that of a thunder-clap. He must describe it in his own words:—

Sir,   Portsmouth, 7 o'clock p.m., 10th May, 1758.

About 4 o'clock arrived here Captain Howe, and delivered me their Lordships' order of the 9th. In last September I was sent out to command an expedition under all the disadvantages one could possibly labour under, arising chiefly from my being under the influence of land-officers in Councils of War at Sea. Last cruise I went out on a particular service almost without the least means of performing it. Now, every means to ensure success is provided; another is to reap the credit; while it is probable I, with the capital ships, might be ordered to cruise in such manner as to prevent his failing in this attempt. To fit out his ships for this service I have been kept here, and even now have their Lordships' directions, at least in terms, to obey him. He is to judge of what he wants for his expedition; he is to make his demands, and I am to comply with them. I have therefore directed my flag immediately to be struck, and left their Lordships' orders with Vice Admiral Holburne. For no consequence that can attend my striking it without orders shall ever outbalance with me [the] wearing it one moment with discredit.

                              I am, &c.
                              E. Hawke.

Before making any remarks on this letter (which, of course, is in his own hand-writing), it will be well to print the rough notes of the Secretary to the Admiralty which appear on the back, since they are a trustworthy record of what took place in consequence of it. They show that explanations had already passed, and that the indignant Admiral had been assured that there was no ground for his chief grievance, the supposed appointment of Howe to attack the French once more at Rochefort, to the disparagement of his superior officer, who had twice already been employed on that particular service, and under whom Howe had himself acted a subordinate part. Time and reflection had convinced Hawke that whatever else remained, it was his business to make the best of it.

May 12, 1758: Sir Edward Hawke being called in, was acquainted that the Lords having received his letter of the 10th, —which being of so extraordinary a nature—sent for him to know what he had to say for taking such a step. His reason for it was he apprehended Mr. Howe was going upon a service where he had the honour to command upon two expeditions, which he thought a slur upon his reputation, and that he might have been represented to the King as an unfit person for such command— which affecting his credit, he hastily determined to strike his flag; but being since informed that he was mistaken, and that his character and honour were not so much touched as he apprehended when the suspicion he had of Mr. Howe's going to Basque Roads arose—from the Lords asking him some days since for a draft of the Roads. Did not strike his flag out of resentment to any particular person, but merely because he thought his honour was affected.

As the official letters begin again on May 17th, from the "Ramilies" at Portsmouth, these rough Minutes no doubt represent the facts. We are unable to pass a full judgment on the causes of quarrel which had preceded this outburst, but that both parties should be willing to make it up is creditable to both. Hawke was too important an officer to be dealt with summarily at that stage of the national affairs, though he had lost his temper, and placed himself in the power of the Lords Commissioners. Such a letter would have drawn down vengeance on a less necessary commander-in-chief. It was written without waiting to ascertain the chief fact on which it was based, and it is the single letter which betrays a want of the courtesy and prudence which are invariably present in the whole course of his official correspondence. On the other hand, every officer must guard his own honour and credit, and there are limits beyond which he cannot be expected to go. Resignation might be better for the service than remaining in a position where the sense of having been disgraced would be sure to interfere with the proper relations between the superior and his inferiors. And we have seen that preceding passages between him and the Admiralty were present to his mind. He could no longer be useful if the conditions of success were denied—and as he thought, systematically denied, to him as Commander-in-Chief. Let some one else, to whom the Admiralty would listen, try his hand.

"Their Lordships," conscious, no doubt, that there was a good deal in all this, must have acted with the greatest promptitude in soothing the feelings of the Admiral, or the explanation could hardly have taken place in London at an interval of only one full day since the letter was written. Nothing could have damaged them or the service more than a public exposure of all these matters; and their dignity was saved by the Admiral's acknowledgment that he had acted "hastily." He was willing to resume command, and to swallow the bitter pill of Howe's independent position, rather than that the affair should go any farther. It was now to be buried in oblivion; nor would it ever have been known, had not the desire to do honour to a great man brought to light, after an interval of 124 years, an incident which there is no reason for concealing, but rather every reason to publish as a contribution to a sketch of character. So little did the public guess the true nature of Hawke's visit to London that, under date of May 15th, 1758, the "Gentleman's Magazine" reports :—

Admiral Hawke arrived at Portsmouth from London where he had been to wait at the Admiralty on extraordinary affairs. He is to command in the intended enterprise of Lord Anson.

This storm cleared the air. Hawke had in an unguarded moment broken through the reticence which on all other occasions seems to have been a part of his nature, and told the Admiralty "a bit of his mind," which it was highly desirable they should in some way or other know. His subsequent relations with the Board show marked signs of improvement. On the other hand, Lord Anson, perceiving that in his desire to carry out the whole of Pitt's scheme, he had put an unusual and somewhat too severe a strain upon one who did not deserve ill treatment, determined to solve the existing difficulty by taking command of the fleet in his own person, with Hawke as second in command, and with Howe at the head of his special flotilla in the independent position for which Pitt designed him. This distinct independence no doubt shaped itself out in connection with Hawke's remonstrance. What the admiral had felt was a very natural repugnance to being responsible and yet not responsible, to having a body of troops and a squadron of ships nominally under his command, while the weapon was being wielded by a far junior and wholly independent officer. If his destination as commander of a mere covering force cruising in the Bay of Biscay had been explained to him, nothing more would have been heard of it.

There have been many difficulties in the Naval Service arising from the want of a clear perception of these simple positions. Men like Nelson, Sidney Smith, Lord Cochrane or Sir Charles Napier were felt to be men who should be used for special services; but their rank was supposed to make it impossible that they should have independent command upon those services. Hence an anomalous relation between these officers and the Commander-in-Chief of the Station, which has generally done far more harm than the attempt to pursue the usual routine has done good. The cases will always be extremely rare where an officer has given proof of such unmistakable genius as to make it a duty to employ him on a large command at an age when he could not, in the natural order of things, be appointed Commander-in-Chief. Where it is so, let him be singled out and trusted, whatever anyone may say, as Wolfe was by Pitt, and as, indeed, Howe was in this case,—though the proper way of doing it was not at first discovered. Not that a Civil

First Lord of the Admiralty can settle the question as Anson did by taking the command himself, and thus procuring that all the Despatches of the officer specially employed should come to him in his double capacity; but there cannot be two masters, and if a junior officer is to be employed with special powers, and to communicate independently with the Government, the senior should be ordered out of the way, and the Government must run the risk of his resignation.

Another, and equally direct, result of this difference with the Admiralty was the illness which, in the course of a very few weeks, entirely prostrated Hawke. There had been several previous indications of failing health; and we may fairly suppose that the above letter would scarcely have been sent off in such a hurry if he had been able to exercise his ordinary power of self-control. The exertions necessary for expediting such an immense fleet must have tried him severely. By the 27th of the month it was ready to sail, and Anson on that day made the signal to unmoor. On that day also Howe's squadron completed the embarkation of the troops from the Isle of Wight (and sailed on June 1st), and on that day the twenty-two ships of the Line which Anson and Hawke commanded proceeded to cruise off Brest and the adjacent coast. On June 18th Hawke wrote to Anson as follows:—

My Lord, "Ramilies," at Sea.
  It is with great regret I am obliged to acquaint your Lordship that the ill state of my health will not admit of my

continuing at sea; and as I am at present in too bad a condition to be moved out of her into any other, I should esteem it a very great favour if you will be so kind as to order the "Ramilies" to Spithead with me. She may return to you immediately.

Anson complies with the request, and on June 22nd Hawke writes from the "Ramilies" at Spithead:—

Sir,

After struggling hard with a severe fever and cold, with which I was seized soon after sailing from St. Helen's I was obliged on the 18th instant to apply to Lord Anson to send the "Ramilies" to Spithead with me, as the bad state of my health would not admit of my being moved into any other ship. The increase of my disorder renders me altogether incapable of duty, and therefore I hope their Lordships will indulge me with leave to go into the country for the re-establishment of my health, which I would fain hope will not take up a great while.

I am, &c.

E. Hawke.

The Secretary to the Admiralty has noted on the back of this letter:—"Own receipt,—acquainting him the Lords are much concerned for his indisposition, and give him leave to come ashore, hoping he will meet with a speedy recovery."

On August 26th Hawke replies from Swathling to some petty question from the Admiralty, concluding with:—

I came on shore so very ill that I neither brought books nor papers with me, so that I can say nothing more to this affair at present.

The Secretary notes once more on the back of the letter:—

Return Sir Edward thanks, and acquaint him I hope his health is established.

Their Lordships, it would seem, had at last found out that the man on whom for so many years had devolved arduous and multifarious duties which would now-a-days be shared amongst several admirals, was only made of flesh and blood like other people, and if anything more was to be got out of him, must have a rest. The tone of the Secretary reflects a change at the Board. For eleven months the admiral is allowed to enjoy the repose of his own home, and we hear no more of him till he hoists his flag once more on board the "Ramilies" on May 13th, 1759.

Meanwhile a very few words will bring us up to the end of the year now before us.

Lord Anson kept the sea all the summer, handing the squadron over to Admiral Saunders in September: but the cruise was perfectly uneventful. Howe's operations were of a mixed character. Some portions of it were decidedly successful; but, as so often happens, the disaster of the last portion caused the public to forget what had preceded it. The three general officers who had pronounced on Mordaunt's conduct at Rochefort were placed in command of the 19,000 troops (including 6,000 marines), which formed the invading force; for it was but fair that they might see if they could do better. The greatest secrecy was observed, and it is not unworthy of notice that great pains were taken not even to whisper the word "expedition," for that was a name of ill omen, having been used to designate the descent on Rochefort. This was an "enterprise." The Duke of Marlborough, however, showed no spark of the genius of his great relative; and it was universally thought that much more ought to have been done with so large and well selected a force than was accomplished; but yet Pitt's purpose was on the whole served. A large quantity of shipping and stores was burnt at St. Malo's, which, since it was a famous nest of privateers, was satisfactory to English merchants; and the alarm was sufficient to relieve the allies of England from pressure on the Eastern frontiers of France.*

The old general Bligh, who succeeded to the command which Marlborough and his colleagues now gave up in disgust as "buccaneering," preferring the command of the troops sent to serve against France in Germany, was at first more successful than they had been; for the destruction of the forts and basin of Cherbourg was a severe blow to the French marine; but the subsequent abortive proceedings at St. Malo, resulting in the disaster at St. Cas, threw the gloom of failure over the whole expedition. It was now discovered that what with the chances of bad weather, the want of information, and the difficulties of re-embarkation, which, even if well performed, has the moral effect of a retreat, this species of warfare was by no means worth the expense it cost, except indeed when weighed in the balance of its indirect effects—a

---

* Walpole bitterly remarks concerning the small results of these enterprises:—"Mr. Pitt maintains that he never intended to take St. Maloes, which I believe, because when he did intend to have Rochefort taken last year, he sent no cannon. This year when he never meant to take St. Maloes he sent a vast train of artillery." No doubt the nation, reflecting on the result of all the money spent this year upon descents on the French Coast, felt it had not in the previous one fully considered both sides of the question in reference to the Rochefort expedition.

method of calculation involving many difficulties. Indeed it could not possibly succeed except in the hands of officers of a higher type than a nation can reasonably expect to have always at command; for almost everything is naturally against success. Even Howe, who showed, if possible, more than his usual intrepidity at the crisis, and wonderful professional skill throughout, was justly held respónsible for allowing the disembarkation of the army

in unsettled weather on a beach from whence, except the wind blew directly from shore, and that but slightly, it was impossible to reimbark them in time of necessity, and where they could not even effect the landing of artillery, nor communicate with the fleet but under the most hazardous circumstances,

and still more for errors which proved to be disastrous in the details of the re-embarkation;[*] while the commission of almost every fault which a general could commit, appears to have led up to the destruction of Bligh's rearguard. The memory of the brave officer slain in command of that rearguard, General Alexander Dury of the Guards, though he did little to mend matters, has been more fortunate than could have been expected, since he has been almost everywhere misnamed "Drury." Against the advantages Pitt believed he had gained by what historians have called the "piratical" work of this summer, must be placed the occasion given to the French to exult over the catastrophe of St. Cas, as if it had been a victory grand enough to wipe out the defeats they had hitherto received, and the correspond-

---

[*] Entick's "History of the War," vol. iii. pp. 210-213.

ing depression experienced in England, of which too many half-hearted politicians were ready enough to take advantage. On the other hand, the moral effect produced by a country's being able to prove itself strong enough to invade another, even though at the loss of a thousand men, must be taken into account, and this effect was undoubtedly great in France, where the threat of invading England had hitherto been a weapon constantly brandished over English heads, and projects for which had formed a part of every plan of a campaign. The tables were now turned. Pitt's admirers summed up on his side ; his enemies on the other.

The effect of the news of the capture of Louisbourg was, however, great enough to turn the popular feeling in favour of the Minister ; and though again depressed by the failure of Abercrombie at Crown Point, it was again raised by the capture of Frontenac and Duquesne—two of the obnoxious French forts which occasioned the war—by Bradstreet and Forbes ; and finally settled in the sanguine belief, justified by the event, that the enemy was on the point of being beaten all along the American lines. Keppel's gallant capture of Goree closed the successes of the year and gave as high a pre-eminence to the British in Africa as they had gained in America. In India the atrocities of the Black Hole had been amply avenged at the battle of Plassey, in the preceding year ; and if Pocock in this year had been unable to obtain a decisive victory over D'Aché, he had carried off the fruits of victory. Frederick's campaigns had not this year been much less chequered than usual, but his star was still in the ascendant; and, what specially affected England, he had found a general in Prince Ferdinand of Brunswick, equal to the post of second in command; and this excellent Prince, at the head of the British and Hanoverian forces, was evidently capable of leading them against the French in a way which would justify the much-criticised alliance. Thus the year ended with a buoyant hopefulness which contrasted brilliantly with the gloom of 1757, and offered the best augury for 1759.

No great naval action had been fought. Hawke in his retirement might fairly feel that he had done his part in the year's work, and that it was not much behind that of any of his brother officers. Osborn, Howe, and Keppel had been more before the public, but their services had not been of the highest class. A new rival in reputation had appeared in the gallant Pocock; but the indecisive character of his two battles with D'Aché, due partly to the old adherence to the line of battle, and partly to misconduct on the part of some of his Captains, barred his way to fame. Boscawen had carried off the chief naval honours of the year. Still it was the result of brave and able assistance given to Amherst and Wolfe, and not of any conflict between fleets. Hawke was not the man to grudge the honours his rival deserved.

CHAPTER XI.

THE BLOCKADE OF BREST.

THE success of Pitt's war policy during the wonderful year 1759 at which we have now arrived, was certainly not the result of accident, but, humanly speaking, the reward of well-laid plans. Those plans would have come to nothing if it had not been for the support of the nation, exhibited in unlimited supplies, his own judicious selection of officers, and the spirit he had infused into the services. And yet, as if to show how easily all such advantages might have been rendered useless, one cannot but reflect that the unforeseen delays incurred by the expeditions of Amherst and Prideaux, so extensive and so delicate were the combinations of his American strategy, all but ruined Wolfe's attack upon Quebec. It may safely be said that nothing but the superlative merits of that officer conferred success upon an enterprise of which the hero himself had more than begun to despair.* And in Hawke's Battle of Quiberon, the other great event of

---

* See Wolfe's Despatch, September 5.

the year, so tremendous were the difficulties of keeping a large fleet watching one of equal force in the Bay of Biscay during the fierce gales of November, that it would seem but a bare possibility that they should meet at sea, much more that the French invading expedition should be utterly broken up.

In both cases,—the crowning victories of the Seven Years' War,—it was the personal character of the commanders that told with decisive effect at the critical moment. Pitt must receive the whole of the credit for selecting Wolfe, for it was he who raised him from the junior ranks for this express purpose.

We have seen enough of Hawke's career to place him in a different position with reference to Pitt. He had long ago made his place. The public quite understood how it was that he had not done more as yet during the new war. From the moment of his victory in 1747, unbounded confidence had been reposed in him by the nation, and no Minister could dare to place the command of a fleet which was to protect England from a threatened invasion in other hands. Thus when the French Minister, believing that England had spent her whole strength upon distant expeditions, conceived that a favourable opportunity had arisen for concentrating all the naval forces of France for one great effort, and launching them against England with a military force double the size of that which Pitt had recently sent against his country, Hawke was at once called to the front, and put in command of the 25 line-of-battle ships which had been got ready for his flag.

Pitt was singularly fortunate in being matched against a Government which was at this time deficient in the ordinary powers of a war-executive. It had in M. Bompart a good officer commanding a serviceable squadron in the American seas. A very little activity on his part, if it had been properly directed from home, would have seriously damaged Pitt's American combinations ; and if an invasion of England was thought possible, the necessary arrangements for the junction of squadrons should have been made at a season of the year when there might have been a chance of success. If not made then, to expose the last fleet on which France could reckon, to the violence of winter gales and English fleets, instead of keeping it safe in port till the next spring, was a desperate and ill-judged act of temerity. After all, England was but enjoying her fair turn in the possession of a superior administration. France had been well served during the rule of the English drivellers.

It was not till May that the equipment of the fleet in Brest harbour gave any serious alarm. On May 13th Hawke hoisted his flag: on May 20th he reports to the Admiralty that he has sailed from Torbay. On the back of the letter the Secretary writes :—" The Lords are pleased with the expedition he has made." This good beginning of civility is followed up in the subsequent correspondence. We hear no more of any differences, except perhaps when in an agony of alarm for fear the French should get out when Hawke is necessarily absent from the blockade, the nervous expression of feeling can hardly be restrained. This year, for the first time, complaints are attended to and abuses remedied; and the Admiral feels strong in his support from home. It is obvious that some petty jealousies and backstairs whispers had been previously at work, and these are now for the most part hushed in the presence of imminent danger, and under the eye of the Minister who by this time understood small things as well as great, a man who would not be slow to single out an offender. Many an abuse had been brought to light by Hawke, and the process had made him many enemies. Their stings had been felt: their day was now over, for this year at least.

It was well that the Admiral had already learnt by experience what it was to keep a large fleet together in the Channel and the Bay of Biscay, but he had never been tried as he was on this occasion. It was exactly six months before he found the opportunity of which he was in search; and the reader will perhaps desire to have something more of the detail of this sort of work than has been hitherto given, with a view to a comprehension not only of the character of the hero, but of the state of the naval service in that day. Nothing more of the sort will be necessary after the narration of this cruise. It is the typical example of the seamanship of the whole century. The names of the ships and officers will come up in the course of the story without any special list in this place; but it must be mentioned here that Sir Charles Hardy, an excellent officer who had seen much service, was the Vice-admiral, and Francis Geary the Rear-admiral, of the Fleet. Of the Captains, Howe, who had succeeded to the peerage in the previous year, commanded his favourite ship, the "Magnanime," and was always to the front. No less than six more were sons of noblemen, Augustus Hervey (the husband of the too-celebrated Duchess of Kingston, and afterwards to be the third Earl of Bristol), Keppel, Barrington, Byron, Digby, and Edgcumbe. Every one of these were, or became, officers of high distinction. Hervey and Keppel were the eyes and hands of the fleet. With them should be named Captain Duff of the "Rochester," who commanded the frigates, and brought on the action at Quiberon. With the exception of Peter Denis, who has already come before us, and James Young, who was sent by Hawke in command of a squadron to cruise for the missing ships after the battle, none of the rest were men of any special mark; but comparing the above list with that of any other in those times, it will be seen that everyone who could make interest to sail with Hawke on this occasion used his opportunity. To these may be added a young officer who had in the previous year seen service under Howe, and who was now to complete what was then thought sufficient education for a prince, under Hawke's flag,—Prince Edward, Duke of York, the next brother to the future King.

Some notices of this young prince will be found in Horace Walpole's letters; and Barrow, in his "Life of Howe," has given one of that officer's letters describing the difficulties under which he laboured in fitting him out and preparing him for sea. All the anecdotes of him in relation to Howe's descents on the French coast go to show that he possessed the hereditary courage of his family, and that he evinced an ardent desire to confront danger and to become a worthy member of his chosen profession. The eyes of the country were turned fondly towards him. In a MS. Journal of 1758, in possession of the author of this Life, the writer, being at Portland, where Howe's squadron was anchored, remarks that Prince Edward

gives great satisfaction to everybody. Besides he has been at church, which in people of his quality is looked upon as a great condescension.

It was not his fault that he did not undergo the training which alone can fit an officer for his work, and at the same time discipline his character so that it might acquire the strength and consistency of which a prince stands more in need than any other person. It was the fashion of the times to ease a scion of royalty of every detail of his profession which might be irksome,—at the same time giving him just a taste of active service, to surround him with a staff, as if he was taking the place of a prince and a superior, while professing to be, like others of his own age, an inferior; and thus to launch him as soon as possible into a position of real command for which he was in the nature of things entirely unfit. It was much to the Duke's credit that he did scrape through the responsibilities both of Captain and Admiral without any catastrophe; but the very brief and superficial nature of his services were a disappointment to the nation, and the dissipated character which he developed might well seem to be one consequence of a mistaken system of education. On his death-bed, cut off by fever at an early age, while travelling in Italy, he seems to have recurred to the teaching of the mother whose pains with her children bore little apparent fruit except in the case of her eldest son.

The Prince's request to be allowed to go to Quebec with Wolfe had been refused, but the old King decided that he should join Hawke's flagship, and bear his share in the expected battle. The Admiral felt himself in something of the same difficulty as Howe had experienced, and writes to the Secretary of the Admiralty as follows :—

SIR, "RAMILIES," in Torbay, June 15th, 1757.

I am much obliged to you for your letter of the 5th. . . . Lord Anson is extremely kind in thinking of the situation I am in with regard to my providing for Prince Edward; for I came away in so great a hurry that I had scarce time to get even common necessaries on board, and therefore only gave directions for sending me the plainest things I had, with the utmost dispatch. Though this is the case I hope I shall do pretty well, with Lord Anson's assistance. I shall take particular care that his Highness wants for nothing that lies in my power to provide for him. To be sure he will not be so happy with me as if he was with his Lordship [Howe]; but I shall do my best to make everything as agreeable as possible to him, from a just sense of the duty and gratitude I owe the King. . . . I never saw so much bad weather in the summer since I have been at sea. We got in here very luckily, for it now blows extremely hard without, and had we laid-to some hours longer we should have drove past this bay.

The list of articles provided by the Admiralty for the prince's convenience does not err on the side of defect. He has amongst other things, a "large case with instruments," a guitar, and what would hardly be necessary at the prince's age—a "mahogany shaving stand with glasses, &c." A "large Turkey carpet" and several "Crimson damask elbow chairs" must have made the Admiral's cabin gorgeous with a splendour ill accordant with fighting trim. The Prince would seem to have already borne the title of Post Captain; but Hawke nowhere mentions his rank.

As Prince Edward's service on board the "Ramilies," only lasted about two months, what notices occur of him may be stated here. The Admiral, having been told, towards the end of July, that the Prince is to come out in the "Hero" (Captain Edgcumbe), "with his retinue," the Admiral says:—

> I am left to myself as to the manner of receiving him. As this is the case I shall pay him all the honour, in the best of my judgment, due to the grandson of my Royal Master.

The Prince is at any rate a good letter-writer, for the Admiral absolves himself from the duty of making reports about him, as "his Royal Highness writes by every opportunity himself." When driven by a gale into Plymouth on October 13th, the Prince, with all his servants and baggage, leaves the "Ramilies." On his arrival he had been "in so great a hurry to send his express away" that the Admiral "had no time to collect the weekly accounts." Thus the Royal youth loses the great battle in which he had hoped to share. We shall come across him again as Hawke's Rear-admiral in 1762.

The latter part of the letter of June 15th refers to

what became the rule of the whole blockade. When a westerly gale came on, it was impossible for the enemy to get out to sea from Brest, or any of the smaller ports on the coast; but there was a very great chance of some of the blockading force being driven on shore; and the question was how to get the fleet into a place of safety like Plymouth or Torbay, and out again before the wind changed and allowed the French to sail. It was like a cat watching a mouse. The vigilance necessary on the part of the blockading force was almost as much a matter of instinct and sagacity as in the case of the inferior animal.

The gales, the victualling, and the cleaning difficulties really govern the situation. We have seen something of this before, and now witness it on a large scale. On this very visit to Torbay the Admiral reports the arrival of five victuallers with 260 tons of beer on board: "otherwise ten of my ships must have gone in within the next week." Another proof of his desire to prevent the usual injustice of passing over senior officers because they are useful, occurs in this letter. He applies for the promotion of his First Lieutenant, Robert Taylor, "the oldest lieutenant now employed, and a sober, diligent, good officer." His ships have suffered severely in the gale which drove him into Torbay, but on June 21st he is off Ushant, and hears from Captain Duff that he counted 17 sail in Brest, and that he is "of opinion they might all be there. I am very happy, after all the bad weather, in having got safe on my station again before they should stir." He is soon able to send home a correct list of 19 sail of the line at Brest, and one in the basin ready to come into the Road, under M. Beaufremont, flag, and M. du Verger St. André, Commodore; and, shortly after, of 20 sail of the line. M. de Conflans arrives early in July to take over the command.

Intelligence now pours in that the invasion is to be made from Havre, and that the French Government are obliged to resort to pressing all the fishermen, and even the ploughmen of the coast districts, to man their ships. As he finds the French are far from ready, the Admiral arranges to send in two ships at a time to Plymouth, at each spring tide, to be cleaned, and he transmits his warm thanks to Captain Hervey for the "diligence and address" he has shown in ascertaining the state of the French fleet. It will "quiet the minds in England which have lately been greatly alarmed." Hervey writes a grateful letter in reply.

Shortly afterwards Hervey wins the Admiral's further approbation :—

> Your behaviour yesterday gave me the greatest satisfaction and merits the highest approbation. I had an additional pleasure too, that of there being so many witnesses of it. I sincerely thank you, Sir, for your conduct and bravery, and beg farther that you will in a public manner, in my name, thank your officers and company for their gallantly seconding your endeavours to destroy the enemy. I have too just an opinion of your discretion, conduct, and resolution, to doubt of the utmost being performed in every service on which you shall be employed; but I cannot think of running the risk of disabling three ships of the line for an object so inconsiderable as a privateer and four or five empty transports, for such they are. You will therefore send back to

me the "Montagu," "Juno" and "Pluto," and continue with the "Achilles" and "Colchester" to watch the motions of the enemy in Brest Road.

Such timely notice of good service was, it is plain, the right way to keep up the zeal and buoyancy of spirit which were put to a heavy strain under the terrible tediousness of a prolonged blockade. What a contrast to the reserve of a Mathews and a Byng! It was of a piece with the enthusiastic encomium he passed on two of his Captains at the battle of Quiberon:—"You behaved like angels"—not that we have much notion how angels would behave on the quarterdeck. Hawke was far from being a man of words or sentiment; but he was essentially just and upright. If a man deserved praise he should have it. And it was the same in his relations to all ranks. It is in this very week that he writes to the Admiralty in favour of the Carpenter of his ship:—

Their Lordships will give me leave to send them the enclosed letter from a person sober, diligent, and in every respect capable of his duty, struggling with the difficulty of supporting a numerous family.

The performance for which Hervey received such praise was his manœuvre off Brest, by which, with one other ship, he maintained his blockade of Conquet Bay, in spite of double the force of the enemy who were sent out to cut him off. After receiving notice of this movement from Hervey, Hawke reports:—

I made all the sail I could with the squadron, and soon discovered the "Monmouth" [Hervey's ship] and "Montagu" chasing three 74's and a 64-gun ship of the enemy. Never did officer show greater conduct and resolution than did Captain

Hervey, and he was bravely seconded by Captain Lendrick; but the distance rendered all their efforts ineffectual. The whole squadron of the enemy had loosed their topsails at daybreak. At about 11 A.M. they made a show of coming out; I had, full in their view, and close to the entrance of the Road, the squadron formed, and lying-to, for their reception.

The French had however no idea as yet of a general engagement. Not long before, the Master of a merchant ship had brought, or pretended to bring, a message from Conflans to Hawke, to the effect that if he would wait fifteen days he would be glad to drink a glass of wine with him, but this was bravado. The English ships were to be worn out with the blockade, and driven off by some storm; and then the time would have arrived.

The Admiral had now to deal with the question of neutrals. The Swedish and Dutch flags were being used for the conveyance of stores to the French fleet which, in consequence of the strict blockade, they could obtain in no other way. On July 16th he informs the Admiralty that he

had given Captain Hervey orders not to suffer a neutral vessel of any nation whatever to enter Brest, but direct them to stand off the coast. The four Swedes he has now sent to me [they had been cut out from under French batteries] are furnished with cargoes which, according to their own account, appear to be be only too necessary to the enemy in their present equipment. Besides, from their manner of stowage and some other circumstances, there is some ground to suspect they have guns and other contraband goods underneath all.

He begs he may have more small vessels to keep up the blockade. Later on he explains to Captain Reynolds:—

My orders were not to suffer any neutral vessels to enter these ports. I did not mean that they should be seized unless found with contraband effects, only that they should be sent off that coast.

The Admiralty cordially approve of his proceedings in the matter: but it appears they forgot this important circumstance; for the Admiral is put to great straits by the subsequent claims of the neutral nations upon him personally.

About this time, the enemy beginning to show a little more life, he has to alter his plans for relieving ships.

The " Hercules' " company being very sickly I sent her in to heel [for cleaning] and refresh her men ten days in port. For the disappointment I met with by the two first I sent in not saving the spring, has induced me to alter my plan, and give orders for no more line-of-battle ships to clean. If the enemy should slip out and run, we must follow as fast as we can. I have not yet received the supplies of butter and cheese, beef, pork, &c., insomuch that I cannot help regretting the want of a commanding officer at Plymouth to see all orders executed with the expedition and punctuality necessary. As I shall not now have it in my power to relieve the whole squadron, and it must in all probability remain here a considerable time, will their Lordships give me leave to recommend to their consideration the sending out live cattle now and then, under such regulations as shall be thought proper.

The beer again!

July 24: The beer brewed at Plymouth is in reality so little relief to the squadron that I have sent in orders to send me no more of it. Our daily employment is condemning of it, which embarrasses us many ways. I have therefore sent this express to intreat their Lordships will send us beer from the Eastward as far as possible, and directly to the rendezvous without touching at Plymouth.

To the responsible officer at Plymouth he writes with more asperity:—

The beer brewed at your port is so excessively bad that it

employs the whole time of the squadron in surveying it and throwing it overboard. . . . A quantity of bread from the "Ramilies" will be returned to you by the "Elizabeth," though not altogether unfit for use, yet so full of weavils and maggots that it would have infected all the bread come on board this day.

Soon afterwards to the Admiralty :—

I am extremely glad to find their Lordships have ordered bullocks and sheep for the preservation of the sick. I hope such numbers will be sent as that the ships' companies may have a share, to prevent their falling down in scorbutic disorders.

In this same letter of July 24th he makes the following interesting remark on the force he thinks necessary to fight the French :—

In my former letter I sent their Lordships the disposition I had made of the squadron. I never desired or intended to keep more line-of-battle ships than equalled the number of the enemy, which is now augmented to twenty-two. I have at present twenty-three, and seldom have had more than twenty-four; and that only during a day. If ships take up a month by cleaning, from the time they leave me to their return, it will be impossible for me to keep up the squadron. The only practicable way is to heel, &c., and confine them to ten days in port, for the refreshment of their companies, in case they should miss the spring.

Hervey now reports to him that he has received information that "the French soldiers and people are much dispirited, and cry out great shame on their fleet for being drove in again," but he says he does not believe they can sail yet. He would destroy the vessels in Conquet Bay if he only had more frigates. Hawke begs for more; and finding Captain Edgcumbe of the "Hero," who had lost his masts in the gale, longer refitting than he expected (being really detained for Prince Edward), he hurried him back, saying,

"I am in the utmost distress for want of frigates." In one of Hervey's letters of this date he says:—

> I don't despair yet of giving the enemy a stroke that you won't dislike, when wind, &c., combine. I thank you, Sir, for the obliging message you sent me by Mr. Lugger. I can never but feel pleasure when employed under you, where you think me of any use; and I own I prefer this to the most lucrative station, as I think we shall yet be of service to you.

The Admiral now explains himself more fully to the Admiralty, who had sent an order that five ships should be sent in at a time for cleaning and refreshment:—

> Their Lordships will give me leave to observe that the relief of the squadron depends more on the refreshment of the Ships' Companies than on cleaning the ships. By the hurry the latter must be performed in (unless the ship continues a month or five weeks in port, which the present exigency will by no means admit of) the men would be so harassed and fatigued that they would return to me in a worse condition than when they left me. This made me prefer ordering some of them to heel and boot-hose-top only, remaining at rest for ten days in port, and at their departure bringing such a quantity of fresh meat as would keep sweet at this season, two or three live bullocks and twenty live sheep. The present bottoms of the new ships in particular are better and will last longer than if they were, by cleaning, to be burnt off, and get a pease-porridge one in their stead. However I shall endeavour to comply with all their Lordships' directions in such manner as, to the best of my judgment, will answer their intentions of employing me here. For as to myself it is a matter of indifference whether I fight the enemy, if they should come out, with an equal number, one ship more, or one less. 'Tis true, in obedience to my instructions, I send their Lordships from time to time such intelligence as I can procure, which has in general been from men intercepted in French boats. But I depend not on it. What I see I believe, and regulate my conduct accordingly. . . . Our daily employment is condemning the beer from Plymouth, insomuch as that article is becoming very scarce in

the squadron. Give me leave therefore to repeat my entreaties for beer being sent with the utmost expedition from the Eastward.

The meaning of the word "boot-hose-top," which is of frequent occurrence in letters of those times, is to heel over the ship as far as possible, to scrape or burn off the grass, slime, shells, barnacles, &c., which adhere to the bottom of a wooden vessel long out at sea, and to daub it over with a mixture of tallow, sulphur, and resin, as a temporary protection. This is the "pease-porridge" bottom of the above letter.

The Secretary replies, on August 13th, that every-one of his requests is complied with. A Commanding officer of proper rank shall be appointed for Plymouth, a "Commissioner of the Victualling" is sent down to enquire about the Plymouth beer; beer from several other places is sent out, as well as wine from Guernsey; and

four transports are to be constantly employed in carrying out to you live stock and refreshments for the use of the sick; and the surplus to be distributed amongst the well of your squadron.

But in a later letter he says:—

Their Lordships being concerned to find such quantities of beer condemned which has been brewed in the King's own Brew-house,

they desire that a Flag officer and some Captains may make a special survey.

It may be noticed, by the way, that this resolute determination to expose the neglect of the victualling offices involves the Admiral in a large amount of disagreeable correspondence with various "Commissioners"; but his reasoning is indisputable, and the new survey entirely bears him out. On August 28th he writes triumphantly:—

> As the Portsmouth, Dover, and London beer held good to the last, I look on it as a demonstration that the badness of the Plymouth beer was owing entirely to a want of the due proportion of malt and hops. . . . The little fresh meat we have has already shown itself in very salutary effects.

The Secretary also says:—

> I am to acquaint you the call for ships is so great off Havre, Dunkirk, and the Northward that their Lordships have it not in their power to spare any 50-gun ship.

The reference here made to Havre and Dunkirk will remind the reader that the French project of invasion embraced, like that of Tencin in 1744, and of Napoleon in 1804, the preparation of a flotilla of flat-bottomed boats which were to cross the Channel with troops, while the fleet from Brest, having disposed of that of England, was to support the landing. A diversion was also to be made from Dunkirk, upon the coast of Ireland, under the celebrated Thurot. Commodore Boys was set to watch Thurot; and he was finally disposed of by Captain Elliot in February of the next year. Rodney, now a Rear-admiral, was selected for the bombardment of Havre, and the destruction of the boats. This he effected in July without loss, but at the painful cost of the destruction of the town itself, a measure which has been much blamed, but was unavoidable. Havre had to be blockaded during the remainder of the year. The other drain upon the resources of the Admiralty was for the squadron of Sir Peircy Brett, who was ordered to leave his command at the Downs, and proceed to Yarmouth Roads for the purpose of intercepting the dreaded Thurot if he should escape from Boys.

Boscawen also had been sent with a large squadron to deal with the French ships under M. de la Clue at Toulon. These were fondly destined to join Conflans, and the united fleet to destroy Hawke; after which was to be the invasion. As usual Boscawen did his duty; and Hawke never for a moment expected that the threatened junction would take place. The tactics of the former were however not a little rash. After failing in the attack upon some French frigates sheltered by batteries at the extremity of Toulon harbour, the ships employed were so much damaged that the whole squadron had to proceed to Gibraltar; and the French taking advantage of its absence, all but succeeded in stealing out of the Mediterranean. Some of them did indeed get into Cadiz, but the rest were caught by Boscawen with a far superior force, and driven on shore at Lagos, with the loss of five line-of-battle ships, as well as of the Commander-in-Chief, and scarcely any loss on the part of the English. The timely nature of this service made it particularly acceptable in England, where Boscawen was deservedly a favourite. He took the first opportunity of giving Hawke the necessary information:—

"NAMUR," off Cape St. Vincent,
SIR, 20th August, 1759.

On the 18th inst. I engaged a squadron of French men-of-war, in number seven, commanded by Mons. de la Clue, they sailed from Toulon the 5th, but parted company with five of the line and three frigates the 18th, in the night, coming through the Streights. The seven I engaged were as followeth:—

Ocean	80	Mons. de la Clue }	burnt.
Redoubtable	74		
Centaur	74 ⎫		
Temeraire	74 ⎬	taken.	
Modeste	64 ⎭		
Souverain	74	escaped but shattered.	
Guerriere	74	escaped, little hurt.	
Fantasque	⎫		
Lion	⎬ 64	lost company coming through the Streights.	
Triton	⎭		
Fier	⎫ 50	do.	
L' Oriflamme	⎭		
Chimere	26 ⎫		
Minerve	24 ⎬	do.	
Gratieuse	24 ⎭		

I heartily wish you may meet with them. I hope to make sail this evening, and as I am bound home, will endeavour to fall in with you. If I do, I will hoist a Dutch ensign at the ensign staff, and a Spanish Jack at the Foretopmast head.

I am, Sir, &c.
E. BOSCAWEN.*

When Boscawen wrote this, he did not know that the above ships which had "lost company" had made their way to Cadiz. Admiral Brodrick soon heard of it, and blockaded them there: but their escape was possible, and added to the anxieties of Hawke's position. He is also pressed from home on the subject of the transports fitting for bodies of troops at Port Louis, Vannes, Nantes, and other places on the coast of Brittany. The failure of the Havre boats had caused increased activity in these western parts, and the cruising squadrons detached from the fleet

---

* Hawke Papers.

are kept continually on the alert, one of them extending its vigilance down as far as Rochefort. Affairs however look more serious when news arrives of M. Bompart's squadron having sailed from America. On August 28th the Admiral writes :—

> If M. Bompart's destination should be Brest I shall do my utmost to interrupt him. But should he be bound to Rochefort I must not think of him for the above reason,

viz. that he must not, as he had previously explained, be left with a number of ships inferior to that of the enemy. His men are also just now "falling down with the scurvy."

It was at this time that he performed the order sent him from the Admiralty to celebrate the "glorious victory" of Minden "before Brest, with the ships under your command; and their Lordships recommend it to you to take all opportunities to make the French acquainted with the occasion of the Feu de joye."

Two points affecting the general progress of the service engage our attention at this point. We have seen that gun-locks and tubes for firing had been favourably reported upon by a Commission which sat after Hawke's action in 1747, and whose appointment had probably been occasioned by the accident from a powder-horn in the action, which nearly incapacitated the Admiral himself. The upper deck guns of ships had accordingly been supplied with this useful invention; but objections, based on the danger of tubes flying about between decks, had prevented their further adoption. The Admiralty now send orders for a further report as to the extension of the system to all the guns of a ship. This is presented to Hawke by Admiral Geary, Lord Howe, and other Captains. Of these the most intelligent evidence is that by Captain Denis, who is strongly in favour of extending both locks and tubes to all guns, as removing the danger of powder-horns, the obstruction by smoke, and the obstacle to quick firing. He had provided them for his ship at his own expense. Howe is only in favour of locks if smaller than as yet adopted. Hawke sums up the seven opinions by remarking that "in my opinion both of them [locks and tubes] will be very useful." It would thus appear that this, which is perhaps the greatest advance in naval gunnery made before our own times, was only very slowly introduced. Indeed, it was not adopted generally till almost the close of the century. Improved construction was even yet required, as Hawke reports unfavourably of those supplied to his ship and used at Quiberon.

The second point is in reference to the grievance strongly felt by the Masters of the service:—

We can spare no pilots from the squadron, in which there are very few; which renders the duty of masters, considering where the squadron cruises, very hard, more particularly [in the case of] such as conduct squadrons; and I cannot help thinking it reasonable that they should have pilotage allowed them.

So little was it yet understood that this valuable class of men ought to be encouraged to make themselves masters of a most important branch of their profession.

In spite of all that had passed the Admiral has to write on October 1st :—

> The supplies of beer and water arrive so slow, and the continual disappointments I meet with from the Plymouth beer, with which the clean ships are supplied, not lasting in a condition to be drunk above a week, I am afraid may occasion the breaking up of the squadron.

In the early part of this month the French began to prepare with vigour for the embarkation of their troops, under the protection of 18 armed vessels and frigates, at Morbihan. The General Quarters were in the Jesuits' College, and the Duc d'Aiguillon had arrived to take the command. Captain Duff is entrusted with the task of watching that they do not come out to join the fleet at Brest. Admiral Geary is now detached by Hawke to cruise for Bompart's squadron, but recalled by the desire of the Admiralty, who had heard from Admiral Cotes in the West Indies that it was not likely to sail for Europe at present. This seems to have been a mistake, since it enabled the French ships, which did sail, as Hawke expected, in October, to elude the English blockade; and their junction with Conflans determined that officer, as it was his last chance, to come out; but it was of no consequence in the end. The letters from the Admiralty now betray a nervous state of alarm; and the Admiral further explains the situation on October 10th :—

> On the intelligence sent me in your letter of September 21st relating to M. Bompart, I thought the intercepting him a very material object. For if the alarm is great now, it must be much greater should he get into Rochefort, and therefore in obedience

to what I thought was their Lordships' intention, I sent a squadron able to perform that service. But since their Lordships rely on the opinion of Vice Admiral Cotes, I have sent orders this morning by a cutter to Rear Admiral Geary to return to me with the "Sandwich," "Hercules," and "Anson," and to send the "Fame," "Chichester," "Windsor," "Belliqueux," and "Vengeance" to Captain Duff.

The Ships' Companies, except the "Foudroyant," are in very good health, and as to myself I shall give their Lordships timely notice to supply my place should my return into port be necessary, which, thank God, there is not the least appearance of at present. . . . Their Lordships will pardon me for observing that from the present disposition of the squadron I think there is little room for alarm while the weather continues tolerable. As to Brest, I may safely affirm that, except the few ships that took shelter in Conquet, hardly a vessel of any kind has been able to enter or come out of that port these four months. We are as vigilant as ever, though we have not so much daylight. And if you can give credit to their own people, they have suffered greatly, having been obliged to unload near 40 victuallers at Quimperley, and carry their cargoes by land to Brest. It must be the fault of the weather, not ours, if any of them escape.

It is a good proof that the English alarm was not unreasonable, that the very day after this letter was written it came on to blow so hard from the Westward that Hawke had to run for Plymouth, from whence, on October 13th, he reports to the Admiralty:—

Yesterday and this day the gale rather increasing, I thought it better to bear up for Plymouth than run the risk of being scattered and driven farther to the Eastward. While this wind shall continue it is impossible for the enemy to stir. I shall keep the ships employed night and day in completing their water and provisions to three months; for at this season there can be no dependence on victuallers coming to sea. The instant it shall be moderate I shall sail again.

Further, on October 14th:—

I shall not stir out of the "Ramilies" myself, and hope to be at sea again in a few days in a condition to keep there without depending on victuallers. . . . Their Lordships may rest assured there is little foundation for the present alarms. While the wind is fair for the enemy's coming out, it is also favourable for our keeping them in; and while we are obliged to keep off, they cannot stir. I own it was with regret I called off Rear-admiral Geary. But as there are many ships now in England I hope their Lordships will soon put it in my power to block up Rochefort, which will effectually distress the enemy everywhere. . . . It blows so very fresh at W.N.W. that we can get neither water nor provisions off.

And once more, on October 17th :—

If their Lordships will consider how necessary it is not to alter any rendezvous, on which I must always keep the Channel open, and that consequently in strong Westerly gales I cannot keep the sea, they will readily lay their account with my putting often into this port. At the same time they may depend upon my keeping the strictest guard over the motions of the enemy that the weather will permit.

The hard service now begins to tell on Hawke's Captains,—Hervey and Tyrrell being both laid up, and the latter obliged to quit his ship. The Admiral sails on October 18th, comforted by the approval of the Admiralty, freely given to all his proceedings and plans. The struggle which is to decide the fate of the war —perhaps of the world—now commences in earnest. November is close at hand, and the position of such a fleet, with all its attendant in-shore squadrons, is hazardous in the extreme. Hervey and Duff are warned that there must not be a moment of relaxation on their dangerous posts. The former had thought it necessary to "send in" some of his squadron to refit without consulting the Admiral, who writes, on October 23rd :—

As I have but 17 sail of the line I desire you will not send any ships in without giving their Captains positive orders to join me first, as I must be left to judge of the necessity of their going in, and often have resources which you can have no knowledge of. What is done cannot be helped. I congratulate you on the recovery of your health, and hope you may be able to stay out as long as I do.

This wish was not realised. The "Monmouth" and "Nottingham" were worn out with their in-shore work off Brest, and these ships had to come home; thus causing both Hervey and Lendrick to miss the battle which they had so good a right to expect to share. On parting with the former the Admiral says:—

Captain Hervey has suffered much in his constitution by the fatigues and watchings of the critical station he has been on since the 1st of July. Through the whole he has given such proofs of diligence, activity, intrepidity, and judgment that it would be doing injustice to his merit as an officer not to acknowledge that I part with him with the greatest regret. He has also been during that time well seconded by Captains Barrington, Digby, Lendrick, and Balfour.

The "Foudroyant" and "Anson," commanded by Tyrrell and Whitwell, are also sent home on account of the "sickly state of their companies," and also Captain Parry of the "Kingston."

It would seem that the Plymouth authorities and those of the Navy Board had not been much conciliated during the five-days' stay of the fleet in October. The Admiral had no sooner returned to his station than he finds his action with reference to a Mr. Wright, the surgeon of the "Nottingham," called in question by the latter body:—

"I have received," says Hawke, "your letter of the 17th inst., in answer to which I am to acquaint you that there was no mistake in Mr. Wright's being ordered by me to be discharged, and the reason marked on the pay list. The "Nottingham" was wanted at a moment's notice to cruise in the Goulette at Brest, a station which required every man in her to be ready at a call. [There was] No probability of being able to try Wright by a Court-martial for his disobedience of orders and other dirty crimes: nor could I, in the circumstances the ship was then in, hourly, in the face of the enemy, admit of sentries being kept on so worthless a fellow. As the least inconvenience, or rather for the real good of the service, I ordered him to be discharged, and his crime noted on his list of pay, for your information. I shall not enter into a dispute with you about my authority as a Commanding officer, neither do I ever think of inconveniences or prejudice to myself, as a party, according to your insinuations, where the good of the service is concerned. Enclosed I send you a letter from Captain Lendrick relating to Wright. By the "Melampe" this day I have sent in Mr. Joseph Cock, whom you appointed surgeon of the "Duke." His infirmities rendering him incapable of his duty, he has applied to be sent home: the surgeon he was to supersede, though very old, still continues in the ship."

The medical service of the navy was certainly in a bad way; and however high-handed the Admiral's conduct towards Mr. Wright would be thought under ordinary circumstances, his chief offence was rank mutiny, publicly committed, and witnessed under the hands of several officers, so that he ought to have been grateful for escaping a Courtmartial, by the sentence of which he would infallibly have been shot.

Soon afterwards the Admiral has to write in an equally indignant strain to the commanding officer at Plymouth, whose impertinent letter is in the Letter-book. The moment of action is close at hand, and the "ifs" and "ands" of the officials who neglect their duty are absolutely intolerable :—

"May I ask," says Hawke, "what is become of the 'Magnanime,' 'Revenge,' 'Defiance,' 'Coventry,' and 'Actæon'? It would have been greatly for the benefit of the service if they could have been ready to have joined me while the Easterly wind lasted. . . . I earnestly desire that immediately on the receipt of this, you will, with any wind, dispatch all the line-of-battle ships that are ready, the frigates, and without fail, two of the best cutters.

Quickly following one another, the Admiral now receives despatches informing him that Conflans has had positive orders to put to sea, and engage the English fleet at once; and then, on November 13th, that Admiral Cotes, writing on September 9th, two months previously, had reported that Bompart's squadron was just then about to sail, so that it must already be somewhere off the coast. It actually sailed on October 1st. Where was Admiral Geary's squadron now?

But before the Admiral could receive this last intelligence he had written (on November 5th):—

I hope their Lordships will not conclude from that remark on my rendezvous in my letter of the 17th, that I should come into port while there should be a possibility of keeping the sea. Single ships may struggle with a hard gale of wind when a squadron cannot. It must always, by wearing, lose ground in working against a strong Westerly wind in the Channel, where it cannot make very long stretches, but more especially if it should blow so as to put it past carrying sail. If for the future this should happen I shall put in Torbay, as I cannot be induced to think there is sufficient room for so large a squadron, or water, for the three-decked ships in Plymouth Sound at this season of the year."

Just as before, Hawke had hardly written this letter when a tremendous gale came on from the Westward, and after struggling against it for three days, he reports from Torbay, on November 10th, that he "was obliged and lucky enough to get in here last night" with most of the ships. He now recommends the withdrawal of the two line-of-battle ships stationed at Quiberon, thus leaving Duff with his smaller ships as "a more manageable squadron" "to preserve itself till my arrival." "It blows a mere frett of wind from the N.W. Bompart, if near, may get in, but no ship can stir from any port of the enemy in the Bay. The instant the weather will admit of it, I shall get to sea again. As boats cannot easily pass I cannot collect the state of the ships." He gets off to sea again on the 12th; is driven into Torbay again on the 13th by the violence of the gale, which is now from S.W.; but once more gets to his station on the 14th. While at Torbay he shifted his flag to the "Royal George" of 100 guns, with John Campbell for his flag-captain, and leaves behind his favourite old ship the "Ramilies," which became "water logged whenever it blowed hard." How nearly Hawke's plans, which were supported by Pitt, were frustrated, and thus how nearly the plans of the French had a chance of success, may be gathered from the following anecdote given in Thackeray's "Life of Chatham,"* from the "*Mémoires d'un Voyageur qui se répose.*" It must, indeed, be only taken for what it is worth, as it rests solely upon anonymous, though contemporary, authority.

"There was a question about sending Hawke to sea to keep watch over M. de Conflans; it was November; the weather was stormy and dangerous for a fleet.

---

* Vol. i. p. 448.

SCENE BETWEEN PITT AND NEWCASTLE.

Mr. Pitt, in bed with the gout, was obliged to receive those who had business with him in a room where there were two beds, and where there was no fire, for he could not bear one. The Duke of Newcastle [the Prime Minister in name] who was a very chilly person, came to see him on the subject of this fleet, which he was most unwilling to send to sea. He had scarcely entered the room when he cried out, shivering all over with cold :—' How is this? no fire?' 'No,' said Mr. Pitt, 'when I have the gout, I cannot bear one.' The Duke, finding himself obliged to put up with it, took a seat by the bedside of the invalid, wrapped up in his cloak, and began the conversation. But unable to stand the cold for any length of time, he said, ' Pray allow me to protect myself from the cold in that bed you have by your side'; and without taking off his cloak, he buried himself in Lady Esther Pitt's bed, and continued the conversation. The Duke was strongly opposed to risking the fleet in the November gales; Mr. Pitt was absolutely resolved that it should put to sea; and both argued the matter with much warmth. 'I am positively determined the fleet shall sail,' said Pitt, accompanying his words with the most lively gesticulations. 'It is impossible, it will perish,' replied the Duke, making a thousand contortions. Sir Charles Frederick, of the 'Ordnance,' coming in at the moment, found them in this ridiculous position; and had infinite trouble in keeping his countenance when he discovered the two Ministers deliberating on a matter of such great importance in a situation so novel and extraordinary. The fleet nevertheless put to sea: and Mr. Pitt was right; for Admiral Hawke defeated M. de Conflans; and it was the most decisive victory the English gained over France during that war."

But the end was at hand. On the 17th, Hawke reports to the Admiralty that he had heard the previous evening from one of the victuallers that the French had been seen at sea, working to the Eastward, having taken advantage of the change of wind which had enabled him to get to his station :—

> I have carried a press of sail all night, with a hard gale at S.S.E., in pursuit of the enemy, and make no doubt of coming up with them either at sea or in Quiberon Bay.

Thus the long-looked-for event had taken place at last. Bompart had sailed into Brest on the wings of the gale which had driven Hawke off his station, and by so doing had proclaimed to Conflans the absence of his watchful enemy. The French admiral acted with praiseworthy promptitude, put Bompart's experienced seamen on board his own ships, and reckoning on the dispersion of the English fleet, and the unlikelihood of their reassembling for some time in sufficient numbers to meet his fleet of 21 line-of-battle ships, craftily set forth on the 14th, on his way to Quiberon. There he would make short work of Duff's squadron, take up the land forces in their transports at Morbihan, and make a descent on the British coast before Hawke should know where he was. It was an almost desperate plan at this time of the year; but it might have answered had there not been a commander opposed to Conflans whose patience, judgment, and resolution were proof against the wildest elements at sea, and the frauds, neglects and stupidity of officials on shore. Much to the surprise of the French, Hawke and his whole fleet of 23 line-of-battle ships, having arrived on the station off Ushant on the very day when Conflans left Brest, were hard at their heels before they could even get in sight of their first destination.

A Letter of November 14th, from the young Duke of York, which does him credit, referring to the labours of the blockade, may conclude this Chapter :—

SIR EDWARD HAWKE,

It is with the greatest satisfaction I observe the gracious manner [in which] the King has taken notice in his Speech of the important service the fleet under your command has performed; closing up the particulars of all the successful military transactions of this year with his testimony of your having discharged your difficult task in the most effectual manner. And it gives me the greatest pleasure, interested as I feel myself in whatever regards the service and reputation of the fleet.

I take this opportunity of enquiring after your health, and of desiring my compliments to Sir Charles Hardy, Admiral Geary, Lord Howe, and the rest of your Captains. Remaining with great esteem and regard your assured friend,

EDWARD.

I desire my compliments particularly to Captain Taylor. I enclose the Speech.*

Captain Taylor was Hawke's Flag-captain all through the period treated in this Chapter, but, remaining in the "Ramilies" when Hawke shifted over to the "Royal George," was lost with nearly all the crew of his ship on the Rame Head in February, 1760. Falconer, the author of the "Shipwreck," a midshipman, was the only officer saved, along with 25 men.

---

* Hawke Papers.

Let it be remarked, by way of comment on the King's Speech, that if the whole circumstances of Hawke's blockade of Brest are compared with those of any other similar blockade, whether by Howe, Jervis, Collingwood, or even Nelson, it may be considered to have been the most noteworthy of all. This of course can only be a matter of opinion; but in weighing their respective merits, it is not only a question of length of time, but of season, climate, weather, co-operation from the Admiralty, the existing methods as to cleaning ships—for they were not yet coppered,—of sanitary arrangements, and the state of naval progress in signals, navigation, and discipline.

CHAPTER XII.

THE BATTLE OF QUIBERON.

To print the business-like details of a Despatch is far from being a sensational method of giving an account of a great and decisive battle; but in the present case, as in 1747, it is done deliberately. Hawke shall tell his own story. If it is correct to say that, of all our naval and military heroes he exhibits the nearest approach to the style and character of the Duke of Wellington, the reader will probably prefer to hear him speak for himself. Though of course in the magnitude of their services there is no comparison, it will not be difficult to trace in their moral qualities the same just sense of duty, the same lofty carelessness as to personal gains, the same fairness and absence of exaggeration, the same simplicity and modesty in the valuation of his own services, and the same sense of the responsibility attaching to the representative of his country, in both cases. In their military qualities may be observed the same combination of patience and decision, the same contempt for public opinion when balanced against a conviction of duty, the same careful adaptation of means to ends, the same swift resolution to strike home, regardless of risk, when the proper time had come, the same stern determination that everyone who served under him should have his due, whether of praise or blame.

The Despatch here follows:—

"ROYAL GEORGE, off Penris Point,
November 24th, 1759.

SIR,

In my letter of the 17th by express, I desired you would acquaint their Lordships with my having received intelligence of 18 sail of the line, and three frigates of the Brest squadron being discovered about 24 leagues to the north-west of Belleisle, steering to the eastward. All the prisoners, however, agree that on the day we chased them, their squadron consisted, according to the accompanying list, of four ships of 80, six of 74, three of 70, eight of 64, one frigate of 36, one of 34, and one of 16 guns, with a small vessel to look out. They sailed from Brest the 14th instant, the same day I sailed from Torbay. Concluding that their first rendezvous would be Quiberon, the instant I received the intelligence I directed my course thither with a pressed sail. At first the wind blowing hard at S. b. E. & S. drove us considerably to the Westward. But on the 18th and 19th, though variable, it proved more favourable. In the meantime having been joined by the "Maidstone" and "Coventry" frigates, I directed their commanders to keep ahead of the squadron, one on the starboard and the other on the larboard bow.

At ½ past 8 o'clock on the morning of the 20th, Belleisle, by our reckoning, bearing E. b. N. ¼ N. about 13 leagues, the "Maidstone" made the signal for seeing a fleet. I immediately spread abroad the signal for the line abreast, in order to draw all the ships of the squadron up with me. I had before sent the "Magnanime" ahead to make the land. At ¾ past 9 she made the signal for seeing an enemy. Observing, on my discovering them, that they made off, I threw out the signal for the seven ships nearest them to chase, and draw into a line of battle ahead of me, and endeavour to stop them till the rest of the squadron should come up, who were also to form as they chased, that no time might be lost in the pursuit. That morning they were in chase of the "Rochester," "Chatham," "Portland," "Falkland," "Minerva," "Vengeance," and "Venus," all which joined me about 11 o'clock, and in the evening the "Sapphire" from Quiberon Bay. All the day we had very fresh gales at N. W. and W. N. W., with heavy squalls. Monsieur Conflans kept going off under such sail as all his squadron could carry, and at the same time keep together; while we crowded after him with every sail our ships could bear. At ½ past 2 P.M. the fire beginning ahead, I made the signal for engaging. We were then to the southward of Belleisle, and the French Admiral headmost, soon after led round the Cardinals, while his rear was in action. About 4 o'clock the "Formidable" struck, and a little after, the "Thésée" and "Superbe" were sunk. About 5, the "Héros" struck, and came to an anchor, but it blowing hard, no boat could be sent on board her. Night was now come, and being on a part of the coast, among islands and shoals, of which we were totally ignorant, without a pilot, as was the greatest part of the squadron, and blowing hard on a lee shore, I made the signal to anchor, and came-to in 15 fathom water, the Island of Dumet bearing E. b. N. between 2 and 3 miles, the Cardinals W. ¼ S., and the steeples of Crozie S. E., as we found next morning.

In the night we heard many guns of distress fired, but, blowing hard, want of knowledge of the coast, and whether they were fired by a friend or an enemy, prevented all means of relief.

By daybreak of the 21st we discovered one of our ships [the "Resolution"] dismasted, ashore on the Four. The French "Héros" also, and the "Soleil Royal," which under cover of the night had anchored among us, cut and run ashore to the westward of Crozie. On the latter's moving I made the "Essex's" signal to slip and pursue her; but she unfortunately got upon the Four, and both she and the "Resolution" are irrecoverably lost, notwithstanding that we sent them all the assistance that the weather would permit. About fourscore of the "Resolution's" company, in spite of the strongest remonstrances of their Captain, made rafts, and with several French prisoners belonging to the "Formidable," put off, and I am afraid drove out to sea. All the "Essex's" are safe, with as many of the stores as possible, except one Lieutenant and a boat's crew, who were drove on the French shore, and have not since been heard of. The remains of both ships are set on fire. We found the "Dorsetshire," "Revenge, and "Defiance," in the night of the 20th, put out to sea, as I hope the "Swiftsure" did, for she is still missing. The "Dorsetshire" and "Defiance" returned the next day, and the latter saw the "Revenge" without. Thus what loss we have sustained has been owing to the weather, not the enemy, seven or eight of whose line of battle ships got to sea, I believe, the night of the action.

As soon as it was broad daylight, in the morning of the 21st, I discovered seven or eight of the enemy's line of battle ships at anchor between Point Penris and the river Vilaine, on which I made the signal to weigh in order to work up and attack them. But it blowed so hard from the N. W. that instead of daring to cast the squadron loose, I was obliged to strike topgallant masts. Most of those ships appeared to be aground at low water. But on the flood, by lightening them, and the advantage of the wind under the land, all, except two, got that night into the river Vilaine.

The weather being moderate on the 22nd, I sent the "Portland," "Chatham," and "Vengeance," to destroy the "Soleil Royal" and "Héros." The French, on the approach of our ships, set the first on fire; and soon after, the latter met the same fate from our people. In the meantime I got under way, and worked up within Penris Point, as well for the sake of its being a safer road as to destroy, if possible, the two ships of the enemy which still lay without the river Vilaine. But before the ships I sent ahead for that purpose could get near them, being quite light, and with the tide of flood, they got in.

All the 23rd we were occupied in reconnoitring the entrance of that river, which is very narrow, and only 12 foot water on the bar at low water. We discovered 7 if not 8 line of battle ships, about half a mile within, quite light, and two large frigates moored across to defend the mouth of the river. Only the frigates appeared to have guns in. By evening I had twelve long boats fitted as fireships ready to attempt burning them under cover of the "Sapphire" and "Coventry." But the weather being bad, and the wind contrary, obliged me to defer it till at least the latter should be favourable. If they can by any means be destroyed it shall be done.

In attacking a flying enemy, it was impossible in the space of a short winter's day that all our ships should be able to get into action, or all those of the enemy brought to it. The Commanders and companies of such as did come up with the rear of the French on the 20th behaved with the greatest intrepidity, and gave the strongest proofs of a true British spirit. In the same manner I am satisfied would those who have acquitted themselves, whom bad-going ships, or the distance they were at in the morning, prevented from getting up.

Our loss by the enemy is not considerable. For in the ships which are now with me, I find only one Lieutenant and fifty seamen and marines killed, and about two hundred and twenty wounded.

When I consider the season of the year, the hard gales on the day of action, a flying enemy, the shortness of the day, and the coast they were on, I can boldly affirm that all that could possibly be done has been done. As to the loss we have sustained, let it be placed to the account of the necessity I was under of running all risks to break this strong force of the enemy. Had we had but two hours more daylight, the whole had been totally destroyed or taken; for we were almost up with their van when night overtook us.

Yesterday came in here the "Pallas," "Fortune" sloop, and the "Proserpine" fireship. On the 16th I had dispatched the "Fortune" to Quiberon with directions to Captain Duff to keep strictly on his guard. In her way thither she fell in with the "Hebe," a French frigate of 40 guns, under jury masts, and fought her several hours. During the engagement Lieutenant Stuart, 2nd of the "Ramilies," whom I had appointed to command her was unfortunately killed. The surviving officers, on consulting together, resolved to leave her, as she proved too strong for them. I have detached Captain Young to Quiberon Bay, with five ships, and am making up a flying squadron to scour the coast to the southward, as far as the Isle of Aix; and if practicable, to attempt any of the enemy's ships that may be there.

I am, etc.,

EDWARD HAWKE.

A Supplementary Despatch, on December 1st, adds:—

The manœuvres of the enemy crowding away on the 20th, prevented our being able to reckon their number exactly. Now I can with certainty assure their Lordships that their squadron consisted of 21 sail of the line, with more seamen and soldiers than I gave in the list which accompanied my last. To the number destroyed I can also add the "Juste" of 70 guns [wrecked on the Charpentier]; and I am in hopes too to find the "Magnifique" run ashore or lost, for she was terribly shattered. The "Dorsetshire," "Swiftsure," "Revenge," and "Magnanime" want great repairs. . . . Inclosed is a list of officers I have appointed to act in vacancies. I must only add that I should be greatly obliged to their Lordships to remember Lieutenant Thomas Neilson, first of the "Ramilies," now commanding the "Success." He has been upwards of 19 years a Lieutenant, upwards of three of which he has been an officer with me.

It is not wonderful that the circumstances of the battle thus modestly, and even apologetically, described by the chief actor in it, should have beguiled contemporary writers into flights of rhetoric which display the character of poetry rather than prose. The historian of the War describes the

"billows, mountains high," before which Hawke's fleet "sailed upon the wings of the wind, till he descried the enemy fluttering at his appearance like a bird at the sight of a Hawke," and then how "descending from the summits of watery mountains, they pounced the enemy, and never parted with them till this mighty fleet was totally destroyed, and in its ruins was buried the maritime power of France. . . . Admiral Hawke, who had long been the darling of the people of England for his abilities and courage at sea, . . . amidst all the horrors of two enraged elements, began a furious engagement.*

And other writers are not far behind.

Horace Walpole is for once betrayed into admiration of Hawke:—

It was the 20th of November: the shortness of the day prevented the total demolition of the enemy; but neither darkness nor a dreadful tempest that ensued could call off Sir Edward from

---

* Entick's "History of the War."

pursuing his blow. The roaring of the elements was redoubled by the thunder from our ships; and both concurred, in that scene of horror, to put a period to the navy and the hopes of France.*

And Smollett describes it as

one of the most perilous and important actions that ever happened in any war between the two nations; for it not only defeated the projected invasion, which had hung menacing so long over the apprehensions of Great Britain, but it gave the finishing blow to the naval power of France.†

It was no doubt a scene calculated in itself to excite the imagination in the highest degree; and when contemplated in connection with the previous dread which the French invading force had inspired, with the incidence of the very gales for which it was known that the enemy was anxiously waiting, with the fact of the British fleet having been driven off its station three separate times in a few weeks, and, latterly, with the information which had reached England that the French had actually put to sea, while it was for days unknown whether Hawke had caught them, it is easy to see that the responsibility which had rested on his shoulders greatly added to the effect produced by the glorious news. The writer of the History of the War is certainly correct in saying that "to such a pitch were the people of England incensed by the opportunity given to M. Conflans on the retreat of Admiral Hawke from the bay, that they would have allowed no excuse, nor considered the irresistible power of the winds and the seas that drove him home, but made

---

* "Memoirs of George II.
† "History of England."

him responsible for his misfortunes." He might have added that the alarm and terror of the populace were such that, on the very day of the victory, a mob was burning him in effigy as a traitor and coward for letting the French get out of Brest.

The burden of this responsibility every officer entrusted with the decision of great issues expects to bear; but in the present case it is not easy to decide which to admire most, the successful struggle for six months with the almost infinite difficulties of the situation, or the grand decisiveness of the final resolution when the moment for action arrived. The least weakness in giving way to the traditions of bureaucracy on the questions of victualling, cleaning, and dispatching back again his ships, would have left Hawke powerless on the day of battle, with sick crews, ships that would not sail, and officers worn out with the endless fatigues of cruising in gales of wind and on a lee shore. The least failure of self-reliance, the least attention to the officious suggestions that beset an admiral in such a time of excitement, the least relaxation of the steady discipline and even-tempered rule which, neglecting no detail, impresses every man in a fleet, from highest to lowest, with a desire to do his duty, and yet spreads around the cheerful spirit produced by human sympathy on the part of the chief, would in all probability have told fatally in such a prolonged conflict.

And it may here be remarked that there is not a single case of a great naval officer, however passionately favoured by the people, having escaped at some perilous moment of his career the violent and often brutal denunciations of its lower ranks. Rodney and Howe suffered in this way, much as Hawke had suffered, and even Nelson's popularity fell to zero when for many months he had failed to find the French fleet which carried Napoleon to Egypt. Nor should the conduct which is the effect of impulsive ignorance and terror be too much condemned. In the last resort a people's instinct tells them they must make themselves felt; a free country cannot afford to choke such impulses; a really great administrator or warrior does not do his duty the worse for the feeling that he has a rope round his neck.

But what of the venture on which Hawke made up his mind to stake the fortunes of Great Britain, and to "stand the hazard of the die"? How many of even the greatest officers would have thought it right to follow up a flying enemy, at the close of a brief November day, into a dangerous bay, the navigation of which, though familiar enough to the enemy, was wholly unknown to himself and every one of his officers? A thousand reasons might be given for hauling off, and waiting for a better opportunity. Doubts were entertained by many at that time whether anything but success could justify such temerity. But this was exactly the stroke of genius which might be expected from a Blake, a Nelson, or a Cochrane, and from these alone. It was a profoundly calculated venture. The peculiar peril of the moment must be balanced against the end to be obtained, and viewed in connection with the difficulty there would be in getting at the enemy if he were not summarily dealt with there and then. Just as Nelson said at Aboukir :—" Where there is room for the enemy to swing, there is room for me to anchor,"—so, long before him, argued Hawke :—" Where there is a passage for the enemy, there is a passage for me. We are so close up to them that their pilots shall be ours. If they go to pieces on the shoals they will serve as beacons. If they have the advantage of knowing the way, we have that of superior seamanship and gunnery when we overtake them. The perils of a lee shore are theirs as well as ours." In short, he considered, as he says in his Despatch, that he was " under the necessity of running all risks to break this strong force of the enemy "; he had fairly calculated those risks; and though he lost two line-of-battle ships in the process, it cannot be said that the price was to be grudged in the achievement of such a magnificent result. It was in this spirit that he made the well-known reply to the master of his ship, who, believing it would wreck the " Royal George " upon a shoal, had remonstrated with him upon his order to lay the ship alongside of the French admiral :—" You have done your duty, Sir, in showing the danger: you are now to comply with my order, and lay me alongside the 'Soleil Royal.'" It was in this spirit that, just as in the battle of 1747, he made it a point of honour to fight his ship like any of his private captains, and to expose them to no danger which he was not to share with them. It was with a view to this very contingency that he had previously instructed his officers that " he was for the old way [his own old way] of fighting, to make downright work with them."

It will at once be seen that the place of this battle in history must not be measured by the number of ships captured in actual battle, but by the ultimate fate of the enemy's ships, by the unparalleled circumstances of the engagement, and the effect it had upon the maritime power of France. With the little daylight left when the ten ships that were near enough the enemy to engage entered the Bay, Hawke could not reckon on more than a partial victory at the moment; what he did reckon upon, and with justice, was that the Frenchmen would act as they did in the previous year, and destroy themselves in their frantic efforts to fly to a place of safety. Besides the six line-of-battle ships taken, burnt, or run on shore in the battle, seven got beyond his reach by throwing overboard guns and stores, and being hauled up through the mud; but only three of these were saved, the remainder having broken their backs by taking the ground at every tide. As for the remainder of the fleet, which succeeded, during the pitchy darkness of the wild November night, in escaping to Rochefort, Keppel, who was immediately sent with a squadron to look after them, soon returned with the Report that they had taken refuge, as in 1758, high up the Charente:—

> The situation and distance of the nearest of the enemy's ships was such as rendered it impracticable to offer an attempt upon them, they being further up by miles than any ship can go without warping through the mud and being dismantled.

Ships in this state were as good as destroyed,—at least for many months to come.

Thus the whole fleet, with all the 18,000 troops, and all the elaborate preparations for invasion, was completely crushed and disposed of at a blow. The victory of Trafalgar was not in reality more decisive, nor were the means adopted by Nelson for that splendid result a whit more to be admired than the tactics pursued by Hawke for the purpose in hand. There was scarcely wind enough to fill the sails when Nelson made his celebrated signal, and Collingwood excited his admiration by the way he led in towards the enemy: it was blowing a heavy gale on a lee shore—the situation of all others most dreaded by seamen—when Hawke swooped upon his prey in the midst of an unknown network of intricate shoals, terrible enough at all times, but involving certain destruction, as the event showed, to ships which ran ashore upon them in a raging sea.

The reader may now like to observe the impression made upon the mind of a gallant and intelligent non-combatant present at the battle. In the "Gentleman's Magazine" for 1759 appeared the following letter from "a Chaplain of one of His Majesty's ships."

QUIBERON BAY, November 25, 1759.

I most heartily congratulate you upon the great event of our defeating Marshal Conflans on the 20th instant. As the express is on the point of setting out, my relation of the victory cannot be particular. On the 14th November, Sir Edward Hawke hoisted his flag on board the "Royal George" in Torbay, where the fleet had put in a few days before, through stress of weather. The same evening we stood out to sea, with 28 ships of the line and 2 frigates; and on the 16th were within eight or nine leagues of the isle of Ushant. In the afternoon we fell in with some English transports returning from Quiberon, who gave the Admiral information that they saw the French fleet the day before, consisting of 24 sail, standing to the S. E., and were at that time 24 leagues west of Belleisle. The intelligence was received with universal acclamations, and every ship prepared for action. The Admiral lost not a minute of time, but pursued with the utmost alertness. In the evening of the 18th the wind came on fresh from the westward, and we spread all our canvas to court the prosperous gale. On the 20th, about half an hour after eight in the morning, the " Maidstone " frigate let fly her topgallant-sails [? topgallant sheets] which was a signal for discovering a fleet; at nine, not a doubt was left of the happy hour being arrived which we had six months been impatiently expecting. We ascertained them to be the French squadron of 21 sail of the line, and three smaller ships; and that they were then chasing Captain Duff's frigates and bombs, the destruction of which was one object of their destination. Upon their having a distincter view of our ships, they gave over the chase, and appeared to be forming a line to receive us.

From the equality of combatants, we concluded the action would be very great and general; but I may venture to assert, there was not an Englishman from high to low, who did not assure himself of victory. Upon our advancing, Marshal Conflans changed his plans, and put right before the wind towards the shore, seeking safety in his flight. At this critical time Sir Edward paid no regard to lines of battle; but every ship was directed to make the best of her way towards the enemy; the Admiral told his officers he was for the old way of fighting, to make downright work with them. At noon our headmost ships were pretty near them, and between one and two the " Warspite " [Sir John Bentley] and the " Dorsetshire " [Denis] began to fire, and were then abreast of the Cardinal rocks. Presently after, the " Revenge " [Storr], " Resolution " [Speke], " Torbay " [Keppel], " Magnanime " [Lord Howe], " Swiftsure " [Sir Thomas Stanhope], " Montagu " [Rowley], and " Defiance " [Baird], came into action.

The firing now became very alert on both sides, and there was no distinguishing any longer English colours from French. M. Du Verger, the French rear admiral, in the " Formidable " bore a very fierce cannonade from the " Resolution "; but upon the

"Royal George's" coming up, they hauled down their flag, and struck to Sir Edward Hawke. This was only a point of honour, the "Resolution" having the merit of subduing them. The "Royal George" continued advancing, and Sir Edward gave orders to his Master to carry him close alongside of M. Conflans in the "Soleil Royal." The French admiral seemed to have the same ambition on his part, and it was a glorious sight to behold the blue and white flags, both at the maintopmast-head, bearing down to each other. The "Royal George" passed the "Torbay," which was closely engaged with the "Thésée" of 74 guns, and soon after sent that unfortunate ship to the bottom. On the other side was the "Magnanime," who kept an incessant fire on one of the largest of the French ships ["l'Héros"], and in the end obliged her to strike. She afterwards ran ashore and was burnt.

The two commanders-in-chief were now very near, and M. Conflans gave the English admiral his broadside; the "Royal George" returned the uncivil salutation; but after two or three exchanges of this kind, the Marshal of France declined the combat, and steered off. The French Vice-admiral [De Beaufremont in "Le Tonnant"] likewise gave Sir Edward his broadside, and soon followed the example of his superior. Another and another acted the same part; the fifth ship ["Le Superbe"] escaped not so well. Sir Edward poured his whole fire into her at once, and repeating the same, down she went along side of him. The "Royal George's" people gave a cheer, but it was a faint one; the honest sailors were touched at the miserable state of so many hundreds of poor creatures. The blue flag was now encountered with seven ships at the same time, and appeared to be in the very centre of the French rear. Every observer pitied the "Royal George," to see her singly engaged against so many of the enemy. It seems indeed a kind of degradation to so noble a ship to be pitied; but really her situation would have been lamentable if the enemy had preserved any degree of composure, or fired with any sort of direction; but their confusion was so great, that of many hundreds of shot, I do not believe that more than 30 or 40 struck the ship.

Sir Charles Hardy, in the "Union," with the "Mars," "Hero," and several other ships, were crowding to the Admiral's assistance, when the retreat of the French, covered by the obscurity of the evening, put an end to the engagement. Happy circumstance for the enemy, as an hour's daylight more would have brought on their total ruin!

The battle was fought so near the coast of Brittany, that ten thousand persons on the shore were sad witnesses of the white flag's disgrace.

When I sat down to write, I intended to have given you only a general account, but upon such an animating occasion as this, there is no possibility of leaving off whilst a margin remains unoccupied. We have burnt the "Soleil Royal" of 84 brass guns, M. Conflans' ship, together with the "Héros" of 74 guns, both which ran ashore near Crozie. We have sunk the "Thésée" of 74, and the "Superbe" of 70; we have driven the "Juste" of 70 guns upon the rocks, where she overset; and have taken the "Formidable" of 80, the French rear-admiral, 62 of whose guns are brass. Ten or eleven other ships were aground, but got off again by throwing their guns and stores overboard. They are now crept into the entrance of the little river Vilaine, where we do not despair of setting them on fire. Whether we succeed in this or not, we have room to believe they have undergone so much damage that few of them will be able to put to sea any more. The rest made their escape the night after the engagement, under the command of Mons. Beaufremont, their vice-admiral, and stretched away for Rochefort.

We have had the misfortune to lose the victorious "Resolution" of 74 guns, and the "Essex" of 64; the former struck upon a sand called Le Four the night after the battle, and next morning, the "Essex," going down to her relief, unhappily ran upon the same shoal. Our endeavours to get them off were unsuccessful, but we have this consolation, that almost all their people are saved, and are embarked on board the "Formidable."

I should be esteemed a very unjust historian if I omitted to make known to you that Captain Denis of the "Dorsetshire," and Captain Speke of the "Resolution," have acquired immortal honour: the Admiral told them in the warmth of his gratitude, they had behaved like angels. I would in this place attempt the most honourable mention of Sir Edward Hawke; nor would I by any means omit my Lord Howe, and Captain Keppel; neither should Captain Campbell pass unnoticed, but that there was a certain greatness in their behaviour which exceeds the ability of my pen to celebrate. I have particularized only a few names, as some of the ships were more immediately under my observation. There were many others had a considerable share in the action, and will doubtless be honoured by those who were more connected with them. It gives me a most sensible pleasure to assure you that Sir Edward has been very liberal of his praises, without a single imputation to cast a shade upon the triumph of the day. The glory of the British flag has been nobly supported, while that of the enemy is vanished into empty air.

The remarkable accuracy of this letter in all main particulars gives it a special value, and suggests a few remarks.

As a pendant to the picture presented by the writer of the marks of joy displayed at the prospect of at last bringing the French to action, may be mentioned the ecstatic proceeding of the crew of the "Rochester" frigate, Captain Duff's ship, one of the slower sailers in whose squadron was just within the very jaws of a French 74 when Hawke's fleet was descried from the mast head. They nót only gave the accustomed three cheers, but there was "scarce a man but threw his hat overboard as a sort of defiance to the enemy. The other ships of this little fleet followed the example set them by the Commodore's ship."* It may next be remarked that the Chaplain's statement, confirmed by all other good authorities, disposes of that generally copied from Horace Walpole, viz., that only eight ships were engaged in the battle. This is as inaccurate as a great deal of that writer's gossip turns out, when sifted, to be; for there were certainly ten in the action, and it is of a piece with his statement that Hawke, when driven off his station to

---

* Beatson, vol. ii. p. 333.

Torbay, had "retired to Gibraltar to refit." But in the case of the "Magnamine" the "Chaplain" hardly does justice to Howe, who led the fleet to battle, who after a fine attempt on the "Formidable," frustrated by two English ships in succession falling foul of him, attacked the "Thésée" (the ship which afterwards, with 800 men, sunk under Keppel's broadsides), and finally engaged the "Héros" till she struck. Also in assigning the merit of the capture of the "Formidable" to Denis in the "Resolution," he omits to notice the share which Keppel, in the "Torbay," had taken in "silencing" her, as Keppel himself claims in his log to have done.* But these are trifling omissions in an account which it is wonderful that any one could have written from his own observations on such an awful day, and sent off before he could well have consulted any but the officers of his own ship.

It has been supposed that the French Vice-admiral went off with his squadron to Rochefort, at the time he did, with a design to draw the English ships into the dangers of the narrow passage by which he escaped, and that Hawke's fleet was exposed to the danger of being crushed in detail by these ships if they had doubled back into the Bay.† But that is to suppose a skill and spirit on the part of the French which are quite beyond human nature. The gale was still in its full fury. The Vice-admiral's

---

* Keppel's "Life of Lord Keppel," vol. i. p. 284.

† Beatson, vol. ii. p. 331; Thackeray's "Life of Chatham," vol. i. p. 451.

squadron, flying from its enemy, could not by any possibility know, on the morning of the next day, how the English fleet was situated; and no ships in the world would venture to throw themselves into the midst of a force of twice their number, and already victorious, even though a good deal scattered by the darkness of the night, and by the state of the weather which made it impossible that the Admiral's signal to anchor should be understood. That night was indeed terrible both to the victors and the vanquished. It has been well described in the following words:—

<small>The dangers of the coast, the darkness of the night, the fury of the tempest, all united to perplex the scattered fleets both of England and France. Although minute guns were heard on every side, yet none could afford relief to either friend or foe. To the bellowing of the waves from below, and the thunders of heaven from above, was added the constant roar of cannon from the ships.*</small>

The Captain Campbell who is quaintly classed with Hawke, Howe, Keppel, Denis, and Speke, as men whose "greatness in their behaviour exceeds the ability of the writer's pen to celebrate," was a very remarkable Scotchman who had risen from the ranks, and about whom many good stories were told. He was a thorough seaman as well as scientific astronomer; and no doubt his cool head and experienced eye were of great service to the Admiral in the supreme hour of trial. He carried home the Despatches. Many years afterwards, though then an admiral, he volunteered to serve under his old friend

---

<small>* Thackeray's "Chatham," vol. i. p. 451.</small>

Keppel as "First Captain," on the celebrated occasion of that officer's command in 1778, and his spirited offer was thankfully accepted.

One more incident, or rather accompaniment of this famous battle, which was much talked about, must be mentioned. The gallant Admiral Saunders happened to arrive in the Channel from his distinguished service at Quebec, just after Hawke had sailed from Torbay; and on hearing of it, without waiting for orders, altered his course and made all sail, along with the rest of his squadron, to join his old friend and fight by his side at Quiberon. He was too late; but the circumstance was remembered.

The remark with which the Chaplain concludes his letter is important and suggestive. When had a great naval battle been fought without a single Captain being even suspected of misbehaviour, neglect, or cowardice? We have seen such things in later times, but by no means always. Here is the common mark of identity between the management of fleets by a Hawke and a Nelson. The whole body was animated by one spirit; and the process by which such a result was attained is obviously traceable. It was felt in the light hand of the skilful rider, the grasp of whose reins was never for a moment relaxed, the perfect example of devotion to duty, the pains bestowed upon little things as well as great, and the resolution that previous counsels, as well as dangers on the day of battle, should be shared by all alike.

The necessary Courtsmartial which were held at Quiberon in January 1760, on Captain Lucius O'Brien, of the "Essex" and Captain Henry Speke of the "Resolution," for the loss of their ships, issued in their honourable acquittal. They had no pilot, no "Neptune Français." "There was so much sea that boats could not live in it." "The sea went so high," said O'Brien, "that no boats could come to my assistance." It was a marvel that so many lives were saved. Of the two unhappy French ships that went down in the heavy seaway, under the fire of the "Royal George" and the "Torbay," scarcely any of the crews survived. The crews of the other French ships, on the contrary, managed to reach land; and the escape of the people of "L'Héros," without being surrendered as prisoners who might be exchanged for some of the English from the two wrecked ships, formed the subject of an angry correspondence.

A reader acquainted with the subject might be surprised at the non-appearance in this place of the Despatch said to have been transmitted to the French Government by M. de Conflans, giving an account of his defeat with a plausible audacity which throws Napoleon's bulletins into the shade. It was printed by Campbell, Beatson, and other writers of the period, while Smollet scornfully threw the discredit of it on the shoulders of the French Government; but a note in the "Gentleman's Magazine" for 1781 declared the letter to be "spurious, being a *jeu d'esprit* of an officer of the 'Torbay'"; which is indeed by far the most probable account of it. It is a pity to load with further disgrace the memory of a man who is sufficiently condemned by his own countrymen. "This deplorable catastrophe," says M. Martin, "consummated the humiliation of France. The navy, whose honour had hitherto been intact, fell to the level of the land forces. The corruption, effeminacy, and selfishness of the Court now penetrated the military, and then carried away the naval, nobility." One of the three admirals, however, M. Du Verger, deserved to rank with the best officers; for he fought the "Formidable" against overwhelming odds, and fell at his post like a gallant Frenchman. Conflans had also hitherto proved himself one of the best men the French navy possessed.

If the naval Commander-in-chief did not shine upon this occasion, what shall we say of the commander of the forces? This was the Duc d'Aiguillon, one of the most notorious characters of the period. He was as yet rather favourably known to the English; for it was no business of theirs that he excited ridicule by witnessing, from the safe elevation of a distant windmill, the defeat of the English rear-guard at St. Cas by the troops he commanded—"*vainqueur malgré lui*"; and he had shown great courtesy to the officers who had been taken prisoners on that occasion. If he was nothing else, he was a man of the most imposing presence, and possessed of all the arts which found favour at the French Court.

On the present occasion Sir Edward Hawke had written to him, begging that he would cause enquiry to be made for the Lieutenant and boat's crew of the "Essex" who had been driven on shore, and for the men belonging to the "Resolution," who had deserted the ship on a raft,—in order that they might be exchanged with the prisoners he had taken in the "Formidable." Lord Howe had been the medium of communication, and everything was satisfactorily arranged; but when the English Admiral had sent his prisoners on shore on parole, he was surprised to find that no Englishmen were delivered up according to the agreement, especially as one at least of them was known to be imprisoned. Still further, more than a fortnight had elapsed, and none of the crew of "L'Héros," the ship which had struck to Howe, had been surrendered. Of this Hawke complained to the Duke, on December 8th, in the most courteous terms. In the meantime he had sent Captain Ourry, of the "Actæon" frigate, to recover the guns of "L'Héros"; and he, having been fired upon during the operation, had returned the fire, and burnt part of the town of Crozic. The Duke had replied on December 11th to Hawke's letter, justifying the action of his officers in firing on the ship, complaining of the fire being returned, and making the attempt to recover the guns an excuse for not complying with the terms agreed upon. This was too much for the Admiral, who replied with a severity far from undeserved, and in a style wholly foreign to his nature, but evidently assumed for the occasion :—

"ROYAL GEORGE,"
12th December, 1759.

I have the honour of your Grace's letter of the 11th inst. in answer to which I beg leave to acquaint you that Captain Ourry has acted entirely by my order, and that I approve of what he has done. His manifesto, of which your Grace has transmitted me a copy, is sufficient proof of his humanity and the tenderness of my orders, which were not to fire unless he should be fired upon.

Without further recollection I need only have recourse to my letter to your Grace of the 29th November by Lord Howe, with regard to the "Héros." My words are, "I therefore claim these officers and men prisoners, and expect from your Grace's known honour that they will be delivered up to me." The hull and guns were not mentioned; for the first I had set on fire, and the second I look on as in my own power to recover. Let me further beg your Grace to look over the agreement you signed with Lord Howe. Is the artillery so much as mentioned in it? No; every article I have strictly observed; exchanged seamen, released officers, soldiers, and militia, on the terms of the Cartel, and sent the Gardes Marines on shore on parole. I could not help being surprised that no notice was taken in that agreement of the claims of the "Héros'" officers and men, and was answered:—that matter belonged to another department, not to your Grace's, which occasioned my writing to you again on that subject. I can only further assure your Grace that had a captain of a British man-of-war under my command begged quarter and surrendered to the French, and afterwards run away with his ship, in open breach of the rules of war, I would have immediately delivered up the ship with the commander to have been treated as the forfeiture of his honour deserved. The same I should have expected from the Duc d'Aiguillon, if I did not consider him the subject of a State in which the will of the monarch constitutes right and wrong.

I assure your Grace, upon my honour, that I never heard of any memorial to be presented to the Admiralty of England, who have no concern in matters of this kind. By the bounty of the King British seamen are entitled to everything surrendered by, and taken from, an enemy in war. In their names, and for their benefit, I shall endeavour to recover the "Héros'" guns, as also those of the "Soleil Royal," which was deserted and left to our mercy. The delivery of the officers and men is all that depends at present on the honour of your Court; the artillery are within our reach. Our endeavours to take them away being justifiable, I was in hopes would not have been interrupted; but since your Grace and the Marquis de Broc have thought fit to fire on my ships, I shall take as severe a revenge as I can, as soon as I receive supplies from Britain.

For I came out near eight months ago, only furnished with orders to decide the fate of the two nations with M. de Conflans on the open sea; but when we met, as he did not choose to stay for me, he has thereby changed the nature of my military operations, and reduced me to the necessity—entirely repugnant to my natural disposition—of sending fire and sword into that country from whence your Grace, with forty battalions under your command, by the authenticated instructions of Marshal Belleisle, was to have spread the most dreadful calamities of war in Great Britain or Ireland.

I cannot persuade myself your Grace could be serious when you termed my enterprises irregular. It was merriment; and I shall not be surprised, if in the same *gaiété du cœur*, I should be accused of having acted irregularly in attacking M. de Conflans, after a chase of 20 leagues in the open sea, within your islands and on your coast, and in setting fire to the "Soleil Royal."

As an individual I honour and respect the Duc d'Aiguillon: as commander of a British squadron against a declared enemy I strictly obey the orders of the great King, my Master; only following my own judgment as circumstances may alter.

I have the honour to be, with the most profound respect and regard, your Grace's most humble and most obedient servant,

EDWARD HAWKE.[*]

It has been the more necessary to copy this letter, since, though correctly given in Beatson's collection (with a few slight verbal errors), there is another version among the Hawke MSS., which appears to have been circulated in English newspapers, and which, being apparently drawn from a confused memory, aided by a lively imagination, is a coarse and inferior production.

Of the Duke, when he became more known in later

---

[*] Hawke Papers.

years, there was, if we may trust the "Annual Register" and Walpole's works, but one opinion. He was an "undisguised profligate, proud, ambitious, vindictive, void of honour or principle." "His mal-administration of Brittany was an appropriate prelude to his career as President of the Council. In both offices he incurred almost universal hatred and contempt." His shocking treatment of the virtuous M. de Chalotais, and his close alliance with the infamous Du Barri, were perhaps the points which excited most indignation in England, but the above correspondence indicates with tolerable certainty the character of the man who was afterwards to display it on a larger scale.

Hawke's subsequent letters from Quiberon dwell on the failure of supplies of provisions and all necessaries from England, which was partly perhaps owing to the Easterly gales, but no doubt also to the neglect which had so often been exposed. He is obliged to remonstrate with the officer in charge at Plymouth for sending out several ships unfit for service, and on board of them

> fourscore of the "Ramilies'" company. These poor fellows had been cruising near seven months, and wanted rest and refreshment. I desire you will not break in upon her crew, as you must thereby disable her at a time when she is much wanted.

But by the error of the officer these men's lives were saved; for two months later the "Ramilies" was wrecked with nearly all hands. The distressing want of provisions here described, occurring so soon after a great victory, was the origin of the well-known epigram :—

> Ere Hawke did bang
> Monsieur Conflans,
>   You sent us beef and beer;
> Now Monsieur's beat
> We've nought to eat,
>   Since you have nought to fear.

Hawke's health was now failing. Writing on December 16th, he says :—

> I have now been thirty-one weeks on board, without setting my foot on shore, and cannot expect that my health will hold out much longer. I therefore hope to be relieved.

It will be remembered that he had already broken down more than once. It was not however till January 17th, 1760, that he returned to England with his victorious fleet. Meanwhile the most rapturous expressions of joy at the glorious conclusion of a long suspense which had sorely tried the English temper, had broken out, on the arrival of the good news, in every form of bonfire and illumination known to the age. No victory during the war came home to the people so much in the light of a deliverance as this: others had conquered, Hawke had saved. All their late alarms were forgotten; and perhaps till the time of Nelson (unless the rejoicings on Rodney's victory are to be excepted), no one more distinctly received the acclamations which answered to the military triumph of the Romans. The cases of Vernon and Keppel, who were the momentary idols of the mob, cannot be considered as exceptions: for the one lost his petty wreath of laurels as soon as he had gained them, and the feeling about the other was a mere personal and political enthusiasm for a favourite admiral, who was considered to have been persecuted by political opponents. Yet if we were to judge by the signboards still existing on public-houses, those are the only English admirals, besides Nelson, who have ever sustained the honour of their country. The first letter Hawke must have received was the following from Lord Anson :—

ADMIRALTY,

DEAR SIR EDWARD, December 1st, 1759.

I have the utmost satisfaction in assuring you that the arrival of Captain Campbell with the good news of the success and glory which has just crowned your long and worthy labours for the public service has given the most general joy and satisfaction here. His Majesty extremely approves every part of your conduct, and the behaviour of your whole fleet, and is fully satisfied that nothing was omitted which could be done to gain and improve the victory. It is his gracious intention to recompense a service of so much honour and importance. I am authorized by the Duke of Newcastle to acquaint you that a Grant is proposed and agreed to, of fifteen hundred pounds per annum, to you and your family for thirty-one years, the longest term the King can grant,* &c., &c.

This sum was increased to £2,000 a year, and assigned for the lives of the Admiral's two sons. On the 21st he was received at Court in the most marked manner, the King "meeting him as he entered the room, and thanking him for the services he had rendered his country." On the 28th he received the thanks of the House of Commons. The Speaker made use during his speech of the following expressions :—" Your expedition was for the nearest and most affecting

---

* Hawke Papers.

concern to us—the immediate defence of His Majesty's kingdoms against a disappointed and enraged enemy, meditating in their revenge our destruction at once. Your trust, therefore, Sir, was of the highest nature; but to which your characters of courage, fidelity, vigilance, and abilities, were known to be equal. You soon freed us from fears .... You have overawed the enemy in their ports, in their chief naval force; till shame or perhaps desperation, brought them forth at last. You fought them, subdued them, and in their confusion and dismay, made those who would escape to seek their security in flight and disgrace. Thus their long preparing invasion was then broken and dispelled; which cannot but bring to our remembrance the design and the fate of another Armada in a former age of glory, where defeat was at that time the safety of England, and the lasting renown of the English navy." Hawke replied in the usual modest terms. The following short note from the aged and famous Lord Granville, may perhaps have touched him as much as this expression of national gratitude:—

Lord Granville sends his compliments to Sir Edward Hawke, and congratulates him on his safe arrival after a long, laborious, glorious, and ever-memorable campaign, for which service his country cannot be too grateful.*

Another letter, a child's scrawl, written in pencil, and traced over in ink, has also been preserved:—

Sir Edward Hawke,

I hear you have beat the French fleet when they were coming to kill us, and that one of your Captains twisted a French

---

* Hawke Papers.

ship round till it sunk. I wish you was come home, for I intend to go to sea if you will take me with you.

I am Lord Granby's second son,

CHARLES MANNERS.*

It is curious that this charming letter should be signed by "Charles" Manners who was the eldest son, and became Duke of Rutland. The second son of the famous Lord Granby was Robert, who went to sea, and was killed in Rodney's action in 1782. He must have been the writer. Perhaps the boys quarrelled over the childish effusion; one wrote and the other signed; or possibly the tracing of the ink was in fault. The monument to the gallant Lord Robert and his comrades in Westminster Abbey is familiar to all Englishmen.

The subsequent grants of a Peerage to officers for services almost infinitely below those which Hawke had performed, made during the century and a quarter which has since passed, must naturally raise the question why nothing of the sort seems to have been thought of in this case. It could not be for want of precedents, when we consider the cases of Lords Torrington and Anson; nor for want of means to support the rank; for, highminded as Hawke had always proved himself, he had made some prize-money, had a fortune of his own, and the pension now assigned him went far in those days. We are driven to attribute what was certainly disgraceful to the Government, to Hawke's simple-minded abstinence from all political intrigue and self-assertion, on the

---

* Hawke Papers.

one hand, and to the enemies his straightforward conduct had made at the Admiralty and elsewhere, on the other. We have discussed his relations with Pitt, with whom he was certainly not a favourite; nor was Anson, after all that had passed, at all likely to be an ardent friend in a matter of this sort: and the excuse was at hand that Boscawen and Saunders might think themselves ill used if Hawke were made a peer. Yet he was not only their senior, but, as we have seen, their services could not be compared with his. It was not for seventeen years that the Government did at last what ought to have been done at first.

Two interesting circumstances are connected with the honours and the pension conferred on Hawke. The Address of the Speaker and the Admiral's answer excited such public interest that it was printed in the London newspapers. As the struggle for the publication of debates, the success of which formed the most useful result of all the confusion caused by Wilkes' turbulent career, had not yet commenced, and the House still jealously guarded its privileges, the printers of all these newspapers had to beg pardon on their knees at the bar of the House, and to pay their fees.

The other incident does credit to the Irish people, with whom Hawke had not the remotest connection except by his public services. The Pension had been assigned on the Irish Revenues; and it was thought appropriate because the invasion had been understood to be directed against that island, though some French authors believe that it was really intended for Scotland.

It was the only pension which had been granted on that establishment for several years that the Irish deemed founded on the claim of merit. Indeed they expressed themselves very fully on this subject on a subsequent occasion; for in a few years afterwards, when there was an enquiry set on foot respecting the pension-list, the most zealous promoters of it declared with one voice that the Pension granted to Sir Edward Hawke was clearly excluded from the object of their enquiry; agreeing that nothing gave them so much satisfaction as that it was in the power of their country to promote the domestic happiness of so distinguished a hero, to whom every part of the British Empire was under such infinite obligations. If we mistake not, when the Bill passed for laying a tax of four shillings in the pound upon pensions, that granted to Sir Edward Hawke was expressly excepted.*

It may also be mentioned that the City of Cork was the first to display its appreciation of Hawke's merits by presenting him, in March 1760, with the Freedom of the City in a gold box.

The whole conduct of this great admiral, in every step of the process which led to the Victory of Quiberon, has now come before us. Let us compare with the facts which have been presented the verdict of that admirable historian, the late Lord Stanhope, who (surely from the absence of any Life of Hawke) had formed an idea of our hero wholly below the true standard. That, in notices of him previous to this date, the historian should have failed to detect the elements of independent greatness in the Admiral would create no surprise,—for the general absence of such appreciation has been sufficiently accounted for in these pages. But for the purpose of glorifying

---

* "Westminster Magazine," November, 1781.

Pitt, the historian has not been justified, even by the opinions of contemporary admirers of that wonderful man, in merging the Admiral's share of the final victory in that of the Minister. We have seen how resolved Pitt was that Hawke should have his chance of destroying Conflans, but we have not seen the slightest indication that Hawke himself doubted for a moment that it was not only possible, but his duty, to keep the sea, even through the storms of winter, and that he should soon be able to "make downright work of it." His whole correspondence, as far as it bears on this subject, is before the reader: nothing has been concealed.

But what are Lord Stanhope's words? Describing the dangers of the French coast, and giving credit to the Admiral for braving them, he remarks:—

Had Sir Edward Hawke desired to retire without striking a blow, he would not have wanted strong arguments to justify his conduct, and no doubt, had there still been a Prime Minister like Newcastle [he *was* Prime Minister in name] there would have been no lack of admirals like Byng. But it is the peculiar glory of Pitt—and a praise which all parties have concurred in awarding him—that he could impress his own energy on every branch of the public service; that under his direction our chiefs, both by land and sea, viewed obstacles as he did—only as a spur to exertion, and as an enhancement of fame.*

On this it is a duty to remark that judging Hawke by the first battles he fought, in the earlier war, there is not the smallest reason to suspect him of requiring the "impression" of any other person's "energy" upon him; judging by his conduct in the Seven

---

* "History of England," vol. iv. p. 169.

Years' War, there is not the slightest evidence of any deterioration. He of all men least required any "spur to exertion," and least paid attention to any "enhancement of fame." It will not be open to any future historian to indulge in these depreciatory expressions.

No such remarks, it may be observed, accompany the notices of Hawke in Hervey's contemporary "Naval History," now a rare book. In speaking of the victory of Quiberon won by "this intrepid son of Neptune, the impetuosity of whose courage equals anything recorded of the boldest of our naval heroes," he says he was

perhaps the only commander that had been in the service of England since the days of Blake that would have engaged the French under the circumstances of situation and weather in which he then was.

And again :—

There was indeed something so bold and daring in his conduct that past times may be searched in vain to produce a like instance of heroism in a large fleet.*

And the contemporary historians not only tell us that this victory gave the finishing blow to the naval power of France during the remainder of the war, but describe its immediate effects—coming so soon after the Battle of Minden—on the whole position of France, how the public credit of the nation now collapsed, how the Court stopped payment of interest on twelve different branches of the National Debt, and how the ordinary necessities of Government were alone supplied by the contributions of plate and

---

* Vol. v. pp. 191, 581.

money procured from private individuals, very much after the manner of the old English "Benevolence."

In describing the part taken by our hero in the glories of 1759, the *annus mirabilis*, there must be no disparagement of his splendid band of colleagues, any more than of the great Minister without whose able combinations, spirit, and fortitude, these instruments could never have effected their great work of founding the Empire. It is a glorious galaxy, and the nation felt and appreciated its merits on the whole. Nothing shows the mind of the age more than its poems and ballads. This Chapter shall conclude with a selection from them. The first, in imitation of an Ode of Horace, is from the "Gentleman's Magazine" of 1760:—

> What glorious deeds Boscawen grace!
> And Hawke the ennobler of his race;
> Thy ships with boasted vengeance fraught,
> Through tempests he undaunted sought:
> See! See! those ships or fly or burn,
> Or shrink, Vilaine, within thy urn.

The second was composed by Paul Whitehead, and sung by Mr. Beard, at the Theatre Royal, Covent Garden, in the character of a Recruiting Serjeant, in December 1759.

> In story we're told how our monarchs of old
>   O'er France spread their royal domain,
> But no annals can show their pride laid so low
>   As when brave George the Second did reign.
>
> Of Roman and Greek let fame no more speak
>   How their arms the old world did subdue,
> Through the nations around let our trumpets now sound,
>   How Britons have conquered the new.

East, West, North, and South, our cannons' loud mouth
  Shall the right of our monarch maintain;
On America's strand Amherst limits the land,
  Boscawen gives law on the main.

Each port and each town we still make our own,
  Cape Breton, Crown Point, Niagar,
Guadaloupe, Senegal, Quebec's mighty fall,
  Shall prove we've no equal in war.

Though Conflans did boast he'd conquer our coast,
  Our thunder soon made Monsieur mute;
Brave Hawke winged his way, then pounced on his prey,
  And gave him an English salute.

At Minden you know how we conquered the foe,
  While homeward their army now steals,
"Though," they cried, " British bands are too hard for our hands,
  Begar, we can beat them in heels."

While our heroes from home, for laurels now roam,
  Should the flat-bottomed boats but appear,
Our militia shall show, no wooden-shoed foe
  Can with freemen in battle compare.

Our fortunes and lives, our children and wives,
  To defend is the time now or never;
Then let each volunteer to the drum-head repair:
  King George and old England for ever.

Of all the exploits which justified this and similar outbursts of national exultation, the Victory of Quiberon was by far the greatest. The author of the "Life of Lord Keppel," who was assisted by the experienced hand of the present Admiral of the Fleet, Sir Henry Keppel, G.C.B., observes that "all other achievements were eclipsed by Hawke's splendid action, by which the French maritime power was completely destroyed. Never had this country a prouder pre-eminence than at the period when George the Third ascended the throne." *

One more effusion of the period may conclude this Chapter. It has perhaps less claim to poetical merit than even the foregoing; but the circumstances of its composition must plead for its admission. It seems to have been circulated as a broadsheet of the day.

THE GREAT FIFTY-NINE:
OR,
ADMIRAL HAWKE'S VICTORY OVER THE GRAND FRENCH FLEET COMMANDED BY MARSHAL CONFLANS OFF BELLEISLE, NOVEMBER 20TH, 1759.

Written on board the " Royal George " at sea.

Ye stout British tars, ever firm in the wars,
   Your deeds shall in history shine;
For no annals can show a more glorious blow,
   Than brave Hawke's in the Great Fifty-nine.

All rivals for fame at so noble a game,
   Swift o'er the rough waves we advance;
Fresh laurels in view, with ardour we flew,
   To strike the swelled topsails of France.

See Keppel and Speke, toil and glory they seek,
   Resolved every danger to face;
Whilst Denis and Howe fearless rush on the foe,
   Hawke leading the spirited chase.

Now the culverins roar, re-echoed from shore,
   Fate waits on the dubious fray;
Our Rear, a bold train, every canvas they strain,
   To share the renown of the day.

---

* Vol. i. 296, 297.

Hostile rocks round us lay, yet we pressed on our prey,
  In so mighty a cause at a venture ;
They trembled with awe, as soon as they saw
  The famed " Royal George " * in their centre.

Conflans crowded sail, but it would not avail,
  His ship she lies blazing on shore ;
The Marshal's undone, and the proud " Royal Sun " †
  Is set, not to rise any more.

Away they all scout, 'tis a general rout,
  That ill with their vaunting agrees ;
Six capital ‡ sail, sad victims they fall,
  The rest fly dismayed o'er the seas.

Though the rude billows raged, yet so close we engaged,
  That rarely a shot was misplaced ;
The troops on the land, chill'd with horror they stand,
  To see the White Flag so disgraced.

No longer they'll boast of descents on our coast,
  The bright Queen of the Main to reduce ;
The fair English Rose, more lovely it blows,
  While droops the faint Flower de Luce.

Each generous heart played so gallant a part,
  That glory has crowned our endeavours ;
And what is still more, the lasses on shore,
  Will esteem us deserving their favours.

---

* Hawke's flag-ship.
† Conflans' flag-ship.
‡ " Capital " was the word used at this period to denote line-of-battle ships as distinguished from smaller vessels.

CHAPTER XIII.

LAST SERVICES.

THE remaining services of our Admiral during the war are void of any special interest. The consequences of his own victory left him no more to do than Nelson would have found had he survived Trafalgar. The runaway ships in the Vilaine had to be blocked up, as they could not be destroyed; and this work was assigned to Boscawen, while Hawke was allowed to remain at home for several months to recruit his health. Two or three characteristic touches alone require to be extracted from the correspondence of this period.

Professional readers may care to know that the Admiral, being called upon to report as to the performance, in the late battle, of the new locks and tubes supplied to guns, reports that

> in the engagement of the 20th of November I had demonstration of tin tubes being very pernicious things. One carried away two fingers of a man's hand in the "Royal George," and others penetrated far into the decks and beams over the guns in which they were used. Locks in my opinion do not answer in an engage-

ment though they may be of use in a chase. Flannel cartridges must be of the greatest utility, and also tin cases filled with shot of 6 or 8 oz. for Upper and Quarter Deck guns.

Here we see the progress of modern gunnery. The tin tubes had to give way to quill, and locks to become mechanically improved so as to be useful for something more than chase-guns. Canister shot and the flannel cartridges which it seems difficult to imagine as not having existed ever since bows and arrows gave place to artillery, now found their way into the service.

The "Ramilies," Hawke's old flagship, was lost in February, and we find him applying to the Admiralty for aid to

four poor, unhappy women, widows of warrant officers of the late "Ramilies." They are left destitute of everything, and both they and their children must infallibly starve unless the Board will commiserate their unfortunate situation.

A difficulty arises as to a Spanish ship which tried to break the blockade, and which, like the Dutch and Swedes, Hawke had ordered to be searched and sent off the coast. This, in the delicate relations existing at the moment with Spain, was a very different matter from the Dutch or Swedish difficulty, and the Admiralty were shabby enough, now the danger had passed away, to try and saddle their admiral with the responsibility. He writes on May 31st:—

As soon as I can get a little better health I intend going to Town, when I flatter myself that I shall convince Lord Anson that I did no more in this affair than what became an officer in my situation.

Once more he hoists his flag on board the "Royal George." This was in August, 1760. Soon afterwards he returns to the hard case of the Masters and their claim for Pilotage. He pleads " the great fatigue and pains which the Masters who conducted squadrons on that dangerous station" had undergone. No attention had been paid to his former application, nor is the provisioning of the fleet any better than ever, after all that had taken place.

On September 4th he once more arrives at Quiberon. The Government had now determined, not only to establish a permanent blockading force in those Roads, but to obtain possession of Belleisle itself. Pitt was bent on this acquisition. His real motive was to obtain a sort of perpetual trophy of the Victory of Quiberon, a convenient support for blockading fleets, and a set-off against Minorca whenever the Peace should be debated; but he treated it in the Council as a new method of making a diversion in favour of Frederick. Walpole asserts that both Boscawen and Hawke had this very year, successively, reported against the practicability of taking the island; but that seems unlikely, as Keppel, whom Pitt destined for the attack, was ordered to fit out a squadron for the purpose, and to place himself under Hawke's orders; and the following letter to Hawke from Anson, which contains the first intimation of Pitt's design, treats the Admiral with the most entire confidence in his approval: it is undated, but cannot be later than October, 1760 :—

SIR,
The situation of the King's affairs in Germany requiring a diversion to be made on the enemy's coasts, His Majesty's ser-

vants have considered which may be the properest place for that purpose, and examined Mr. Keppel who, having been lately in the Bay, had an opportunity of making the observations which I send herewith on part of the coast of the Isle of Belleisle, which 'tis thought may be attacked with the best prospects of success; and the King as well as his servants reposing great confidence in you, I have it in command to let you know that a very considerable body of troops, with a train of artillery, are collecting together, and transports ready to embark them whenever it shall be thought proper. Wherefore you are desired to use every means in your power to inform yourself how near ships can lay to batter the several works in the sandy bays of Belleisle mentioned by Mr. Keppel, and what depth of water there is close to the shore, and to ascertain the distance of the citadel from the said sandy bays. You will also inform yourself whether troops can be landed at Lomanie or any other part of the island besides those described in Mr. Keppel's paper, and how far they may be from the Citadel. . . . I hope it is needless for me to repeat the confidence that is reposed in you on this occasion, and the necessity there is for the strictest secrecy.*

It has been generally stated that the death of the old King, which took place on October 27th, put a sudden stop to these preparations; but it was in reality the lateness of the season. Among the Hawke Papers are the Secret Instructions transmitted to the Admiral by Pitt, and signed by the young King on November 17th, three weeks after he had ascended the throne. These Instructions require Hawke to afford every assistance to Keppel and General Kingsley in their attack on, and occupation of, Belleisle, to protect the expedition from annoyance by the enemy in any quarter, and to keep up a cordial understanding with the General. There was a difference here as to the

---

* Anson Correspondence.

relations between Keppel and his chief, which distinguishes the position from that which had in 1758, given such offence to Hawke in the case of Howe; though perhaps a distinction not so clear as he might have desired. These Instructions however came to nothing. The expedition was on the point of sailing, but was counterordered at the last moment, and broken up in December; nor was it resumed till March of the following year, when Hawke had left the station. There was no longer by that time any French force in the Vilaine, and nothing, therefore, to interfere with the brilliant success attained under the excellent joint combinations of Keppel and General Hodgson, creditable to both alike.

One concluding word is required as to this King, whose death carried with it great issues. Enough has been said above in relation to George the Second, and the personal influence he exercised in elevating his country out of the depressed state into which it had fallen in the first half of the century. So studiously has he been disparaged in modern times, chiefly in consequence of the publication of Lord Hervey's and Horace Walpole's Memoirs, that it is difficult to believe, when we turn to the pages of contemporary writers, that they are speaking of the same man with ourselves. Among the former there is one general echo of the praises of

"this great prince," and how "he lived to see the British name, under his auspices, advanced to the highest pitch of dignity and grandeur." He had "added to the Crown of Great Britain the riches of the American fisheries, the hostile territories taken from the French in North America, the sugar-islands of Guadaloupe and its dependencies, the gum trade of Africa, and the greatest and most improvable commerce in the Asiatic regions." "His conquests eclipsed those of our Henrys and Edwards."*

Even those who most praised the administration of Pitt, never allowed the merits of the King to be forgotten; nor should they be forgotten. Monarchy was a practical and operative fact in the last century; and the different fate of England and France was correctly typified by the different characters of George the Second and Louis the Fifteenth. In the morality of their private life there was not much difference; but in all that goes to make a useful head of a nation there was no comparison. The Sybarite who left his people to be governed by his mistresses and their minions deserved to fail; and his too-loyal subjects, treasuring up, however, the day of vengeance, were the sufferers. The punctual, business-like, courageous, straightforward Sovereign of a free people deserved to win. Private retribution did indeed follow private delinquencies. He paid the penalty of his immorality in the family troubles which never deserted his palace.

To the subject of our Memoir his death must have been the loss of a personal friend, or at least patron. Hawke had probably been pulled through more difficulties than he knew by the sense that was generally entertained of the old King's good feeling towards the man he is said to have called "my Captain." In the correspondence subsequent to the date of the King's death there is certainly an indication of a change in Hawke's rela-

---

* Entick's "History of the War," vol. v. p. 80.

tions with the Admiralty. His wishes about the relief of his ships, and the keeping up of their proper force, are no longer attended to. He detects a gross imposition in the sale of a French frigate to the Spaniards, but the Admiralty, no doubt for political reasons, do not support him. He is again thirty weeks out, and "his health is much impaired."* At last, on March 11th, 1761, he strikes his flag once more, and goes into the country "for the recovery of his health." The object of keeping so large a fleet in Quiberon Bay had passed away; for the few remaining ships which had taken refuge in the Vilaine in 1759, and not been broken up, escaped, by the advantage of a dark night and the blunder of the guard-ships which should have detected them, to Brest in January, 1761. The capture of the island of Dumet by Lord Howe, under Hawke's orders, is the only incident of this long and weary service noticed in the Despatches or contemporary books; and that was only of importance because it supplied the blockading fleet with water, and rendered it so far independent.

An absurd remark of Campbell's† on the "inactivity" of Hawke's squadron in 1761, has been sufficiently met by Charnock,‡ and scarcely requires notice in this place. He had no instructions to make descents

---

* " Sir Cloudesley Shovel said that an admiral would deserve to be broke who kept great ships out after the end of September, and to be shot, after the end of October. There is Hawke in the Bay weathering this winter, after conquering in a storm."—Walpole's "Letters" (Cunningham), Jan. 14th, 1760.

† " Lives of the Admirals," vol. iv. p. 180.   ‡ Vol. iv. p. 289

on the French coast, a policy which, though the French were forced to keep troops ready in case of such descents, Pitt had now relinquished; and the attack on Belleisle was, as we have seen, being a Commodore's command, placed in other hands. He performed the service on which he was sent. The "public" may or may not, as Campbell states, have felt "general surprise and indignation" at the return of the squadron; but his remark is unsupported, and it seems most improbable, since Hawke's orders were perfectly well known; nor was Keppel's appointment to attack Belleisle ever taken as a slur upon the Admiral. His rank entitled him to command against fleets, and there were none left to fight. We have seen that Hawke had enemies: they probably found access to Dr. Campbell. Perhaps the best answer to such remarks is that within a few weeks of the return which caused " surprise and indignation," Hawke was unanimously elected and sworn an Elder Brother of the Trinity House, and next month received the freedom of the City of Dublin in a gold box.

It remains to be said that the year 1760 afforded a remarkable contrast to 1759, and that this was the natural effect of the completeness of the conquests of the last-named year. Rodney, keeping watch over Havre, was successful in destroying the remainder of the flat-bottomed boats which had threatened the English coast; the conquest of Canada was assured by the capture of Montreal; and a few single actions of ships, like those which marked the expiring efforts of the French after 1805, served to display the spirit which had been so brilliantly exhibited in the battles of the previous years. France was completely exhausted; and in England the question of Peace was uppermost from the moment of the young King's Accession. From that moment the speculation, characterized by the phraseology which the new development of coal fuel suggested,—whether the machinery of government was to be supplied with Scotch coal, Newcastle coal, or pit-coal, whether the country was to be governed by Bute, Newcastle, or Pitt, was the leading feature of English politics, and it carried with it the question of peace or war. Neither France nor England were, however, perfectly serious in the diplomatic conferences which began to be held. The English were still under the magic influence of Pitt, and by no means felt their new empire secure. The French had one last card to play, and in 1761 they succeeded in playing it.

The war was in fact to end as it had begun in 1739. The Spaniards were once more to be principals. Spain, nearly at the end of her resources in 1748, had been glad to make peace at that date; and, though entirely sympathizing with the French when the war broke out afresh, and only restrained from trying her fortunes once more by the prudence of Wall, the Prime Minister, supported by the Queen who ruled Spain during the closing years of the imbecile Ferdinand the Sixth, she was now betrayed by the new sovereign into a further step towards ruin. This was the late King's half-brother, Charles the Third of Naples, who became at the death of Ferdinand, in 1759,

Charles the Third of Spain. His weakness in suffering his new kingdom to be made the catspaw of France—partly the result of gratitude for French assistance in re-arranging the Bourbon thrones in Italy, but still more of the festering grudge entertained ever since the summary proceedings of Mathews and Martin at Naples in 1742—proves how even a good and respectable King may be a *damnosa hereditas* to his subjects. His policy however fell in only too well with the passions of those subjects, and with the alarm they felt at the enormous progress which England had lately made, at the expense of France, in North America and the West Indies.

As to the character of Charles the Third of Spain, so much eulogised by Lord Stanhope,* there is much to be said on the other side, even in reference to his domestic Government. It is an immortal honour to have abolished torture, checked the Inquisition, and encouraged national enterprise; but a man whose overwhelming interests were centered in field-sports could not be expected to take a large view of affairs.† He

---

* " History of England," vol. iv. p. 184.

† In a trustworthy report of a conversation with Mr. Harris, afterwards the celebrated Lord Malmesbury, in 1777, that wise ambassador, who had recently left Madrid, described the Spanish King as follows :—

" He has no extraordinary reach of capacity, is no plotter against other people's peace or his own, but is decent in every department, with sense enough to fill all his public functions with a sense of dignity, yet entirely given up to field-sports, the ladies, and praying. In conversation he is affable, and even agreeable, but above all things, decent: nay, I may say that on

was no sooner seated on his throne than the full battery of Bourbon family influence was turned upon him, and the new Family Compact of 1761 was, after incessant efforts, the result.

The work of Cardinal Fleury was now completed. The brilliant prospects opened up by the acquisition of Lorraine, the settlement of the Bourbons on the Italian thrones, and the Family Compact of 1733, which was to ensure the salvation of Spain and her co-operation with France for ever,—so that, as Louis Quatorze once said, there should no longer be any Pyrenees,—were now crowned by a fresh and far more important Compact. But for Spain this was an anachronism; and the new King, who showed so many good qualities, would have served his country better had he possessed all the bad qualities in the world, and refused to listen to the Marquis de Choiseul. The two wars, culminating in 1759, had placed all parties in a totally different position from that which they had previously held. The Colonial Empire of France, which had been the grand object of the French in formerly coming to the assistance of Spain, had collapsed like a child's castle of cards; and the warriors formed under Pitt's administration were perfectly capable of adding to the British conquests the whole of what was left to Spain. That she saved any portion of the wreck was due to the intestine struggles which accompanied the accession of George

---

every occasion he conducts himself with the strictest propriety. He is remarkably fond of shooting, and will on no occasion sacrifice that amusement to business."—MS. *penes auctorem.*

the Third, and the remarkable forbearance which signalised the British negotiations for peace.

All through the year 1761 the armaments of Spain had excited the remonstrances of Pitt, and being perfectly assured that her fresh alliance with France was virtually formed, he insisted on a Declaration of War which might forestal her hostile action. The Bute interest prevailed against him; and in October he resigned. It soon transpired that the Spanish Court, as Pitt well knew, had only been waiting for the arrival of the galleons, and that the Compact, which it was vainly attempted to keep secret, had then been instantly signed. By the end of the year the breach between Spain and Great Britain was publicly declared; the Declaration of War had to be made in January 1762; and the designs of Spain upon Portugal, assistance in which had been the immediate bribe held out by France, were disclosed by a perfectly unjustifiable Declaration of War against that peaceable Power by the two Courts. The British forces were now to be ranged in defence of their faithful ally, and Hawke was called for the last time from his retirement.

Hoisting his flag at Spithead on April 27th, 1762, our Admiral's position seems to be very much like what it had been at the opening of the war in 1755. He is the visible representative of the Admiralty, arranging for the distribution of the home fleet, suggesting plans for blockading Dunkirk and Brest, providing convoys, expediting transports, and pressing seamen. The bustle all around him is not indeed so intense or so wild as at the former period, for there is no longer any confusion or alarm : but great armaments have been already despatched, and others are proceeding.

The resignation of Pitt had certainly not affected the vigour with which the new expeditions were planned or commanded; but then, as his friends maintained, they had all been originally planned by him, and the spirit which he had infused was that which animated the officers; the success of Rodney and Monckton in the West Indies was indeed directly due to his own administration. The capture of Havana by Lord Albemarle, Sir George Pocock, and Keppel, though obtained at a great cost of life, was one of the finest achievements of the war, and with the success of Draper and Cornish at Manilla, brought Spain on her knees. In the course of a few months her colonies had been shattered to pieces, nor had France, by her last efforts, gained anything but a partner in misfortune.

Hawke's personal share in the glories of this year was but small, though through the capture of some rich Spanish ships by his cruisers, he seems at last to have acquired wealth. He is stated in some accounts to have made a short cruise in May to look out for M. De Ternay who had escaped out of Brest with a small squadron; * but this is a mistake. He did not leave Spithead till June 25th, when, with the Duke of York as his Rear-admiral, in the "Princess Amelia"

---

* Charnock's "*Biog. Nav.*," vol. iv. p. 290.

(Lord Howe serving as the Duke's Flag-captain and dry nurse), he, in the "Royal George," proceeds at the head of a squadron of ten line-of-battle ships to cruise off the north-west coast of Spain. The object of this cruise was to protect Portugal from the ten Spanish line-of-battle ships lying in Ferrol; the land forces sent by England under Lord Loudoun, Colonel Burgoyne, the Count de la Lippe, and others, protected her from invasion by land. There is no truth in the statement that the Admiral was sent to Lisbon to the help of the Portuguese. Whatever the moral effect of his name might be, it was produced from his station between Capes Ortegal and Finisterre. The Spanish ships did not venture to come out; Lisbon was safe by sea; and the Portuguese troops, by the help of the English, were more than a match for the feeble levies of Spain.

Not the slightest incident deserving notice occurs in this cruise. The official letters of the youthful Rear-admiral are carefully preserved amongst the Hawke Papers; but the only one which shows any character is the first:—

Sir Edward,   Tuesday Evening.

I have this moment obtained the King's permission to hoist my flag under your command. I need not tell you how happy I am, nor how ready I shall be punctually to obey every order I receive. I am just setting out for Kew, and remain, your affectionate friend,

Edward.*

The services of an officer of such rank as Hawke

---

* Prince Edward, of whom something might have been made, had he lived, uniformly treated Hawke with proper respect.

on a station where nothing was likely to occur, were not required for any length of time. On August 24th his squadron puts into Torbay to refit, and the Admiral requests Lord Bute to let him haul down his flag. The notice of this return, in the "Gentleman's Magazine" of that date, is not a bad specimen of the small amount of information current on foreign affairs, even amongst cultivated society: — "The sudden return of this fleet without attempting anything occasions much speculation. It was fitted out at an immense expense, and great expectations were raised from the known courage of the commander: its return therefore seems the more extraordinary." There was nothing to "attempt"! To attack Ferrol had never been dreamt of. To blockade an inferior force of Spanish ships could be done by anyone; and the Peace was already as good as made.

The last letter of Hawke's official correspondence afloat is on the 26th, when he grants the Duke of York leave of absence for a few days. Sir Charles Hárdy, an excellent officer, and friend of Hawke's, takes the squadron, when refitted, under his command, and (the Duke still serving as Rear-admiral) continues the blockade. To this the negotiations for peace, which Lord Bute was now pressing with all his might, soon put an end. On September 3rd Hawke comes on shore; and his service at sea is closed.

It was probably during this last command, with his flag in the "Royal George," that the following incident occurred:—"Owing to a collection of soot in the funnel of the stove, the ship took fire in the great cabin. Sir Edward was at that time occupied in dressing himself; and when this circumstance, which to men less firm would have been of the most alarming nature, was discovered by him, he went out on deck, and taking the First Lieutenant aside, calmly said to him in a low tone of voice, 'Sir, the ship is on fire in my cabin; give the necessary directions to the people to put it out.' "* The "Royal George" was not built to be burnt. This is the ship which, after bearing Hawke's flag triumphant, sank in a moment at Spithead, when "Kempenfelt went down, with twice four hundred men." Has it ever been noticed how appropriate are the poet's words—"His fingers held the pen"? Kempenfelt was famous as a man of superior abilities and a taste for literature. He and Lord Howe share the honour of making the great improvement in naval signals which marked the close of the century.

Shortly before Sir Edward's last cruise the career of his old chief and friend, Lord Anson, had also terminated. He died suddenly on June 6th, 1762, at the age of 65. Notices of his services and character have formed a considerable portion of this book, and they will therefore require no further attention. It has not been found possible, under all the lights which the life of Hawke throws upon the period, to endorse the whole of the judgment which Sir John Barrow, forty-three years ago, passed upon his hero; but by

---

* Charnock's "*Biog. Nav.*," vol. iv. p. 292.

far the greater part remains. Few have served their country more honestly and efficiently. No department of the State required more reform than the Royal Navy at the time when he entered the Admiralty, and no one could have done more than he did, during the sixteen years of his administration, towards its regeneration. The reader has observed that there was yet much wanting in that administration to render it perfect; but allowance must be made for the times. Many years were to pass before the grossest abuses in the civil Government of the realm were swept away; but the Navy, under Anson, may be said to have led the way. At any rate merit was very generally rewarded, and honest, straightforward principles of regulating the service very generally adopted. The *matériel* of British fleets was at length raised to something like the level of that of their enemies, and the *personnel* was, at least in some degree, elevated beyond the low standard of preceding times. It was a grand thing for the Navy to have an honest man and a gentleman permanently fixed at the head of the profession through so many changes of Government; and we have seen that it was but in one instance, the case of the unhappy Byng, that any exception to this eulogy can be found.

Boscawen had also died before the war came to an end, and at an earlier age. He had not completed his fiftieth year, when he was carried off in January, 1761. Of him also we have observed sufficient marks both of character and services to enable us to appreciate his great merits. Virtuous like Anson and

Hawke, as brave and eager for employment and distinction as Nelson himself, and with every advantage of rank, he only wanted opportunity to have done the greatest deeds. Like Hawke and Anson he was most appreciated where he was best known; unlike his friends, he left behind him a wife whose great superiority of character reflected back a lustre on her husband to which the improved society of that period amply testifies. Among the revivers of literary taste and social religion, who were known by the nickname of "bas-bleus," hardly anyone held a higher place than Mrs. Boscawen, or carried her lofty rank better than the Admiral's daughter, the Duchess of Beaufort.

Of the merits of the Peace of Paris, the solid termination of the two wars which have been passed in review, this is not the place to speak. The balance of the numerous and heated arguments for and against, seems to incline towards a favourable view of it. Walpole's jocular remark upon its continental aspect was not far off the mark. "It includes Spain, saves Portugal, and leaves the hero and heroine of Germany to scratch out one another's last eye." * Its merits in the latter respect were as great as those of the Peace of Utrecht. Frederick and Maria Theresa found themselves, when left alone to fight it out, obliged to come to terms, much as the Emperor and the King of France had formerly discovered a similar necessity under similar circumstances; but this is not to say that the alliances and the wars into which

---

* "Letters to Mann," vol. iv. p. 120.

Great Britain had entered, had not been, till the objects of her own self-defence were obtained, both politic and necessary.*

It is more easy to find an author whose summing up of the history of these wars will be considered judicial, at least by Englishmen:—

"Once more," says Ranke, " in this world-embracing conflict between the two kingdoms, the internal superiority of the English was proved. In spite of an enormous debt the credit of England held good, and it was not necessary to lay on very excessive taxes: while the French Government had to resort to advances from those who rented State lands, and was obliged to increase by fresh imposts taxes which were already oppressive, so that it exhausted all its resources.

" We may regard this war as a continuation and completion of those great contests which came in with the Revolution of 1688. They were all directed against the predominance of France, and were at once Continental and maritime. . . . Less than ever was said about religious grounds. As a matter of historical fact, however, the religious motive was more conspicuous than before. The Protestant Powers were on one side, those of the [Roman] Catholic and Greek faith on the other.

" What a glorious Empire was it to the head of which George the Third came!—the product of one history, all of one piece, from the moment of the first Teutonic Settlement in Britain until the founding of its maritime dominion in both hemispheres. Through long centuries the logical and active mind of the people which rejected all that was foreign, and accepted only that which was akin to it, had worked at the great edifice which now was the strongest representative of the West among distant nations. The living elements of culture which the Empire included in itself worked in free movements, often opposed to each other, but for that very reason all the more strong and many-sided. Individual and corporate independence did not in the least disturb a united development of power."†

---

* For one of the best criticisms of the Peace of Paris see the " Annual Register for 1763," written by Burke.

† Ranke's " History of England," vol. iv. p. 420.

Contrast with this solemn, far-sounding strain the thought which Walpole communicated to his friend Mann, on the news of the triumphs of 1762:—

> Well! I wish we had conquered the world, and had done. I think we were full as happy when we were a peaceable, quiet, set of tradesfolks, as now that we are heirs-apparent to the Romans, and overrunning the East and West Indies.

But Walpole was the son of the man who was satisfied that the "tradesfolk" should be insulted and degraded; and how long their trade would have survived such treatment it required no prophet to foretell. It is true that the very colonies for which the mother country had been most concerned were the first to throw off a connection no longer vital, and that political faction vied with administrative imbecility in breaking up into fragments the Empire which had just been formed: but even so the grand inheritance was not dissipated, nor can its eventual issues be yet foreseen.

Of all the naval officers whose prime vocation ceased with the Peace of 1763, and whose high qualities, under the training they had undergone, would in a very few more years, had the Peace not intervened, realised to the letter Horace Walpole's hyperbole, there were now three, and three only, at the head of their profession; and there were three more, of a younger generation, perfectly fitted to take their places in another war. The first three were Hawke, Pocock, and Saunders; the second, Rodney, Keppel, and Howe. Hawke was considerably the senior, and it was under him that the three younger men had been mostly trained. Of these, the second had his opportunity in 1778, and lost it; the first and third were to hand down the lessons of the two Imperial wars to the Nelsons and Collingwoods of the next generation.

But though Hawke was a man of whom even Walpole could say that "he had as much merit in his profession and to his country as man could have,"* and though he had been Anson's righthand man for so many years, he was not asked to take Anson's place. The administration of the experienced admiral had turned the office of First Lord of the Admiralty into that of a director of routine, as long as peace might last; and there was no possibility of war for many years. Thus the place became one which anybody might be thought able to fill; and several civilians did fill it, during the ignoble and factious struggles which harassed the young King, for longer or shorter periods. Not one of them, George Grenville, Halifax, or Egmont, shewed any particular aptitude for the office, as Lord Sandwich (who himself held the post for a short time at this early period) did afterwards, and other civilians in later times. In the Rockingham Administration of 1765, Saunders and Keppel filled the posts of junior lords of the Admiralty. The two admirals having been deeply attached to one another in their professional service, the elder came to be entirely dependent on the younger, and the Board was really in their hands. When Pitt came back to

---

* "Mem. of Geo. III.," vol. ii. p. 398.

power in 1766, as Lord Chatham—full of the memory of Anson—he determined to have a naval First Lord. He did not, according to Walpole—and it is probable enough—wish to pass over Hawke or Pocock in favour of Saunders, their junior; but he did so for the following reasons. He discovered that Saunders, having already held an important position at the Board would retire if any other naval officer were placed over his head, and that his retirement would carry Keppel with it. The Board would be thus broken up: and besides he had taken a liking for Saunders ever since his ability had been displayed in the joint capture of Quebec along with Wolfe. That officer therefore became First Lord, but only for a couple of months; when he suddenly, along with Keppel, resigned his place, which, it is evident, he could not have much valued. Hawke was now instantly offered the post, which he accepted and held for the succeeding five years.

Walpole's account of this curious freak of Saunders is confirmed by an independent authority :—

"Saunders," says he, "a most gallant but weak man—[all naval officers are "weak" with this writer],—governed by Admiral Keppel and Lord Albemarle, had been persuaded by them to throw up his post of First Lord of the Admiralty, and join his old friends the Rockinghams."*

And in the "Selwyn Correspondence,"† "Gilly Williams" tells Selwyn :—

Your friend, yellow Saunders, gave up yesterday. He gave for

---

* "Mem. of Geo. III.," vol. ii. p. 398.
† Vol. ii. p. 91.

the only reason that at his time of life he could not think of living without the Keppels. (Keppel himself, it seems, resigned in order to mark his disapproval of Lord Chatham's dismissal of his friend Lord Edgcumbe from the post of Treasurer of the Household.)

Here ends the career of one of Anson's favourite pupils, of whose gallant conduct and generous spirit we have already heard. Sir Charles Saunders had no opportunity of commanding fleets in general actions; but the country thoroughly trusted him, and as we have seen, Pitt never forgot him. An incident connected with this appointment over the heads of Hawke and Pocock deserves notice, and may be inserted in the words of Charnock, who vouches for the truth of the anecdote:—

When Sir George Pocock was first made acquainted with the appointment of Sir Charles Saunders to the office of First Lord of the Admiralty, he immediately went to the late Lord Hawke, and complained to him in rather warm terms, of the indignity he thought offered on that occasion to the older flag-officers who had equally distinguished themselves. Sir Edward Hawke was at that very time on the point of going out in order to wish Sir Charles joy of his promotion; and when he informed Sir George of his intention, the opinion of that great and good man had such weight with him as not only to moderate his displeasure, but even to induce him to adopt a similar course himself. His disgust, however, though temporarily assuaged, was not effaced; and his former sentiments as to the public indignity offered to his contemporaries, and what he deemed private neglect to himself, induced him to persevere in his first resolution to retire from the service for ever.*

Here then, at the same moment with that of Saunders, the career of this fine officer came also to an end. His chief exploits had been performed in India, where he had displayed the greatest courage, but being

---

* "*Biog. Nav.*," vol. iv. p. 405.

matched against the ablest admiral the French possessed, and not always well supported, he was never able, though he fought no less than three pitched battles with him, to obtain any decisive success. Neither squadron ever took a ship from the other; but D'Aché was always driven off, and though the force of the English was decidedly inferior, suffered the greatest loss. It was this want of capacity for turning circumstances into account, so as to produce a decisive battle, which prevented Pocock from ranking with the great masters of naval warfare; but these Indian actions, taken along with his admirable behaviour at the capture of Havana, place him high in the second rank. Further, he seems to have been a man more than ordinarily fitted to inspire affection, and to influence his associates by examples of the highest kind. Amongst his other virtues, public and private, he is said "never to have been known to swear even on board his ship,"*—the abstinence on board ship being apparently an almost inconceivable mark of self-restraint, worthy of the angels to whom Hawke, in his emotion, compared his two victorious captains at Quiberon.

Lord Chatham's letter on Hawke's appointment has been preserved among the family papers, and may serve as a specimen of that great man's official style :—

BOND STREET,
Sir, Friday, Nov. 28th, 1766.
I am commanded by the King to acquaint you that Sir Charles Saunders and Mr. Keppel having come to a resolution

---

* Charnock's "*Biog. Nav.*," vol. iv. p. 467.

to resign their seats at the Admiralty, His Majesty has been graciously pleased to turn his thoughts to you, Sir, for the Head of that Board. I have the honour, in consequence, to propose to you in His Majesty's name that very important office.

Give me leave to assure you, Sir, that I have a particular satisfaction in executing the King's commands to me upon this interesting occasion, and allow me to add my sincere hopes that this letter may find you in as full possession of health as your country wishes you to be.

I have the honour to be, with most respectful esteem and consideration, Sir, your most obedient and most humble servant,

CHATHAM.

On December 2nd Chatham desires Hawke to be at the Levee next day to kiss hands.

Not much remains to us by which Hawke's tenure of this office may be illustrated. It was a period when statesmanship of every sort was at a low ebb. Chatham soon passed under a mental eclipse; Grafton was calling down on himself the not undeserved satires of "Junius"; Wilkes was making government impossible; not a single man of first-rate ability came to the front; and the young King was striving in vain to break through the fetters of a pampered oligarchy, which believed in nothing but itself as the representative of the Revolution families. Some stray hints, however, touching the administration of the Navy at this time, have survived.

One cardinal point at least of Hawke's Peace-administration deserves special mention. His practice gave rise to an authoritative maxim, always quoted in after times with the highest respect, just as in war he established for the first time the principle that the enemy must never be suffered to escape, but, in spite of all Instructions for keeping the line, must be engaged within pistol shot. Shortly after his death it was remarked in a pamphlet, styled "A Seaman's Remarks on the British Ships of the Line," and bearing all the signs of the highest authority, that the late Lord Hawke had laid it down, and during his whole administration acted on the maxim, in which Lord Sandwich had followed him:—"that our enemies being peculiarly attentive to their marine, our fleet could only be termed considerable in the proportion it bore to that of the House of Bourbon." In other words, the British fleet must always be kept in such a state that it would be a match for France and Spain combined, the only nations which could in that day be thought of as hostile maritime Powers. It would have saved England many millions if this maxim had not been constantly set aside when wars were over, and the supposed exigencies of the Chancellor of the Exchequer were brought to bear upon First Lords of the Admiralty. The writer goes on to prove his point. While Lord Hawke, he tells us, broke up 14 line-of-battle ships, he built 13, and left 15 on the stocks.* Thus he kept his country on a fair level with her rivals. The French had by no means given up the struggle, because they had been beaten. They had been steadily repairing their losses, and improving their resources, so that they had been known to have entirely built and completed a three-decker of 110 guns at Brest in 14 months, and a 74-gun ship was built, launched, rigged, and stored, at the same port in 95 days.

---

* See also "Life of Lord Keppel," vol. ii. p. 330.

Lord Sandwich, Hawke's successor, acknowledged his maxim; but was unable to comply with it as he wished. It was thus that Rodney, Howe, and Nelson found so much work cut out for them.

It is not till towards the close of Hawke's term of office that we hear of any attack upon his administration. Up to that time he was steadily working on the principle above mentioned, and, venerated by the whole service, was taking judicious care of the great interests committed to his charge.

It was under his auspices that in 1767 his old Captain, Augustus Hervey, succeeded in passing through the House a measure, which had been too long delayed, for improving the half-pay of naval Lieutenants by the addition of a shilling a day to the miserable pittance of two shillings, which they had hitherto received. His picture of their condition is distressing enough. The Lieutenants on half-pay—and they were numerous after such a war—"are now starving for want of subsistence, hiding themselves in the most remote corners of the country, some for fear of gaols, which their necessities and their misfortunes, not their faults, have reduced them to be afraid of; others to hide their wants from the world, being ashamed to appear where they cannot support that character which their long services, great merits, and delicate sense of honour entitled them to. These, Sir, in a few years must be all lost to the country. Already but too many of them have been obliged to seek, with their families, a settlement in America. Many are reduced to go as second mates in merchant ships: others have fixed themselves in trades." "He had the satisfaction of knowing that his measure had the good wishes of that great and brave admiral whom His Majesty has placed at the head of the naval service."* Hervey carried his point; it certainly was not much to ask.

The position held by the chief admirals of the day at this period may be here reviewed in a few words, since it is in connection with them that we find what distinctive notices of the First Lord occur. Keppel had a seat at the Board during a portion of the time his old chief was First Lord, and was regarded by Hawke and the service generally as the leading officer of the day, if active service was required. Thus when the preparations for war with Spain, in 1770, were made, he was at once designated for the chief command.

Rodney, Keppel's senior, was at the head of Greenwich Hospital, and at this period ruined himself by election expenses on the Tory side of politics. About the time when Hawke went out of office he became Commander-in-chief on the Jamaica Station, and on resigning his command, not being able to live in England, determined to economise in Paris; nor could he have returned to immortalise his name, and draw his country out of the abyss into which it had fallen in 1779, if it had not been for the generosity of a truly noble Frenchman, Marshal Biron, who had learnt to value his character.

Howe, who had held a seat at the Admiralty for a

---

* Parliamentary Debates.

short time under Sandwich and Egmont, had become Treasurer of the Navy; and when the expected war with Spain brought Keppel to the front, was nominated for the Mediterranean command.

"Sir Edward Hawke," says Barrow,[*] "incurred the censure of many for nominating so young an admiral to the command of so important a squadron; and he had an intimation of a motion intended to be made in the House for an Address to His Majesty to inform the House who had advised His Majesty to nominate Lord Howe, one of the junior rear-admirals, to such a command. The motion does not appear to have been brought forward, but Sir Edward Hawke declared he was perfectly ready to meet it; that he held himself responsible, as First Lord of the Admiralty, for the appointment recommended to His Majesty, and equally ready to declare that he did advise the King to sanction the one in question. 'I have tried my Lord Howe,' said Sir Edward, 'on most important occasions; he never asked me how he was to execute any service entrusted to his charge, but always went straightforward and performed it.'"

The reader has had opportunities of observing the truth of this generous testimony; but as we now part with his Lordship, it is time to sum up his career.

Much of Lord Howe's time seems to have been spent during this Peace in reading, and improving the education which he was taken from Eton too early to carry far. He recommenced his honourable career in 1776, when he took the American command, since which time his services have become a leading part of our later naval history. Even more than Keppel, he was Hawke's constant pupil, though not perhaps so intimate a friend; and in his noble character we see a true reflection of that of his master. In disregarding

---

[*] "Life of Howe," p. 79.

Howe's supposed disqualification for command on the ground of youth and rank, Hawke was strictly following Lord Anson's conduct in regard to himself. He began his own career as admiral at 42; Howe was nominated at 45. As it happened his best services had already been performed while under Hawke. When his time for great commands came, the long Peace seems to have rusted his original capacity. His career in America was not a distinguished one; it was thought by the best judges that he ought—though no doubt he suffered under great difficulties—to have done more with his fleet at the Relief of Gibraltar in 1782; and, in his famous Battle of the First of June, 1794, there is no doubt whatever that his great age alone prevented him from following up a victory which would have put nearly the whole of the enemy's fleet into his hands, if he had been a younger man. His final service to his country in the Mutinies of 1797 were considerable; but they also partook of the defects produced by age. Concessions of some sort were necessary; but Howe carried them so far that, had it not been for more vigorous officers, the country must have been ruined. If Howe is to be classed amongst the first rank of naval officers, it is not amongst the foremost occupants of that position that he should find his place.

In 1769 we find Hawke giving sensible advice to the Prime Minister on a point which, if the country had not been in a misgoverned condition, ought to have caused no difficulty at all. He was called upon in the House by Colonel Barré to give an account of the alleged concessions made to the French in a case where a French frigate, anchoring in the Downs, and refusing to salute the British flag, had been forced by a Lieutenant in command of an English frigate to lower her flag; and the French ambassador had demanded reparation. Every expedient failed to pacify the French; but at last they were silenced, by the advice of Hawke, on the ground that the Lieutenant had sailed for India, and could not be examined as to the truth of the matter till he returned, in about three years' time. This, which was a delicate affair under the circumstances, must have been well handled, since Hawke was able to tell Barré publicly that the French Ministry, "though they have complained, seem by no means disposed to carry things to extremities in support of their demand of redress, as they find no disposition in our Court to relax in the claim to that ceremonial of submission, the exacting of which was the occasion of the dispute."

It is from a speech of Hawke's in the course of this debate that we discover the fact that he made a visit to France in the summer of 1769, and was convinced by the observations he was able to make on that occasion "that the French were not in a condition to go to war." This conviction, which was perfectly just, served to tranquillize his own mind and that of his Government in view of the danger to be apprehended from the conduct of Spain in relation to the Falkland Islands. But it was not the duty of an Opposition to believe he was right.

This same year witnessed the opening fire of

"Junius" which had no little effect in shattering the Grafton administration of which Hawke formed a part. The first letter of the series contains a deadly atttack upon Grafton, North, Granby, Weymouth, Hillsborough, and Lord Mansfield. It was not likely that Hawke should escape. Junius dismisses him contemptuously enough:—"With respect to the navy I shall only say that this country is so highly indebted to Sir Edward Hawke that no expense should be spared to secure him an honourable and affluent retreat." It was not by such artillery that the Admiral was likely to be routed; but it was unfortunate for him that he did not resist Lord North's request to take his old post under the new *régime* of 1770. Very probably this request was backed by the King: but Hawke had been placed at the head of the Admiralty by Chatham, and with Chatham he should have retired. By too great facility in obliging the new Premier, who wished not only to make use of a great name, but to exhibit a Government as little changed as possible from the former one, Hawke found himself in opposition to his old, and feebly supported by his new, friends; and this at a moment when the threatened rupture with Spain laid a violent stress on his naval administration which he was quite unable to meet by himself, and which seems to have suddenly aged and worn him out, at least for a time.

The new Admiralty contained none but civilians: Saunders and Keppel were bound, as Whig partisans, to pick holes in the policy of Lord North, even though in so doing they had to attack their old chief; and Chatham himself, who had by this time nearly lost sight of all his old landmarks, condescended to vilify the Admiralty for not sending ships to sea, when the fact was that they could not be manned because Wilkes, emboldened by Chatham's own patronage, had exercised his whole influence in making impressment impossible. In vain the great orator expounded the law and custom of England; in vain he insisted upon the absolute necessity of the practice of impressment, if England was to hold up her head among the nations; the demagogue laughed in his sleeve. It was very well to scold all round; Chatham had become a privileged person.

Fortunately the firm attitude of the English Government in the matter of the Falkland Islands, as in the similar case of Nootka Sound, some years later, had a wholesome effect on the Courts of France and Spain. The fleets which were ordered to be equipped, and the names of the officers to be appointed in command, convinced these Powers,—which were not a bit better prepared than the self-abused English,—that the hour had not yet come; and they put the matter by till the Revolt of the American Colonies seemed to afford them the opportunity to recover the old position for which they panted. Very shortly after this date there appeared, in the saloons of Paris, the man destined to destroy all their hopes.

Hawke had demanded, previously to this quarrel with Spain, an increase of four thousand men for the navy. He did not get them. The supplies, under a series of weak Administrations had been cramped. It was with the utmost difficulty that he could keep the ships at their proper establishment. When the sudden strain came, some ships that would not in the ordinary course of things have been allowed to leave the home ports, were sent out as guardships to Gibraltar, and, from their unsafe condition, were obliged to return. None of the 16 ships which were to form Howe's fleet were of this class. The same thing had happened in 1747, when Anson was virtually First Lord under Bedford's administration, and Admiral Medley reported that no less than 8 of his ships were not in a condition to continue abroad;* and it was of frequent occurrence in the war.

This circumstance, however, which probably admits of some palliation, is sufficient to set Horace Walpole off in the following attack on naval administration generally, and that of Hawke in particular:—

The ignorance, blunders, and want of spirit in Newcastle, Lord Anson, and Lord Hardwicke, at the beginning of the Seven Years' war, made way for the predominant genius of Mr. Pitt. . . . The murder of Admiral Byng was to palliate the loss of Minorca, which had been sacrificed by the negligence of Lord Anson, and by the Duke of Newcastle's panic of an invasion. . . . The navy was in a wretched condition. Lord Egmont, while at the head of the Admiralty, had wasted between four and five hundred thousand pounds on pompous additions to the Dockyards. His successor, Sir Edward Hawke, though so brave and fortunate a commander, had never been a man of abilities, and was now worn out, grown indolent, and was almost superannuated, paying so little attention to the fleet that the ships were rotted in harbour, and of five ordered to Gibraltar, four had returned as being in too bad a condition to proceed, and the fifth was found rotten before it went to sea.†

---

* "Bedford Correspondence," vol. i. p. 286.
† "Mem. of Geo. III.," vol. iv. p. 204.

Anson's liability to this wholesale indictment has been noticed. Lord Egmont was no doubt perfectly right in enlarging the Dockyards to suit increasing demands for space; and as to Hawke, we may be sure this was the single fault which could be brought home to him, or we should have heard of more. His "abilities" as an officer we have gauged. Walpole would certainly have treated the Duke of Wellington with the same contempt. The charge of "indolence" is incredible, and wholly unsupported. Let us read it in the light of Keppel's statement which describes his chief's conduct at the Board.* "Worn out" he probably was; and at 66 might well be "superannuated." His health had however again broken down, as it often had before under unusual pressure, and in January, 1771, he sent in his resignation. That his colleagues did not see his services at the Board as Walpole did, may be judged by the following letter from Lord Palmerston, who was one of them:—

DEAR SIR,

    I did intend waiting on you this morning to have assured you in person how very sincere a regret I feel on hearing that your present state of health had made you determine to quit the laborious office you have held with so much advantage to the public credit and to yourself, and satisfaction to those who have had the honour of sitting with you at the Board.†

A month or two previously the celebrated Lord Shelburne ended a letter with the expression of his "unalterable respect and regard," which such a man would scarcely have used towards one who was occupying a post he could not properly fill.‡

---

* P. 80.   † Hawke Papers.   ‡ *Ibid.*

Lord Sandwich succeeded Hawke, and acted upon his plans; but fell short of the success Hawke had attained in keeping up the supply of new ships.* He failed to do so for the same reason that his predecessor had found himself on the eve of a war without a sufficient number in hand. Until the younger Pitt arose, no Government was strong enough to tax the country sufficiently to keep up a proper Peace-establishment. Eight years after Hawke had resigned, the tables were turned. Sandwich, for whom he made room, and whose bad moral character seriously impeded the exercise of his undoubted ability, found himself, during the strain of the new war, attacked much as Anson and Hawke had been attacked in their day. Augustus Hervey, now Earl of Bristol, Hawke's old trusted Captain, brought forward a motion, in 1779, to the effect that "the navy had rapidly decayed since the resignation of Lord Hawke, while its expense had increased." All that Sandwich could reply was that he was not solely, but jointly, responsible for the employment of the naval force, which was determined in the Cabinet, and finally sanctioned by the King: he was only answerable for the use or abuse of the means placed peculiarly in his hands. This excuse, though it is always in the power of a First Lord to resign (as some have, when their province has been egregiously interfered with by a Cabinet), was more to the purpose than the public knew. In some notes of Hawke's on his own resignation he

---

* "A Seaman's Remarks," &c., "Life of Keppel," vol. ii. p. 331.

remarks:—"The late Peace Establishment will not keep up fourscore ships of the line in perfect repair, especially when it is clipped ten or twelve thousand every year, by the Minister, of the Extraordinary Estimate." This explains the fact of the rotten ships, when there was a sudden call for the whole fleet.

Hawke's seat at the Admiralty brought him into contact with the King, and with his brother, the young Duke of Cumberland, all whose autograph letters have been preserved. Those of the latter do not indeed deserve much notice. They extend over the year 1769. This young officer, like his elder brother, the Duke of York, had been allowed to play at being an admiral, and his letters chiefly refer to claims for the promotion of some of his officers. About their services he speaks with the air of an experienced seaman, and he presses them on the First Lord with unbecoming importunity and some incoherency:—"You will be so good as to remember that when I paid you a visit at the Admiralty I then told you that your services entitled you to that respect which I would not show to any other First Lord at that Board, be he the first man in this country himself, to talk upon any business whatsoever, but go to the Fountain Head at first." Hawke seems to have reminded him of his elder brother's more respectful conduct, and the youth's next letter is slightly apologetic. Walpole's judgment on him is only too well confirmed by the above:—"He had neither the parts nor the condescension of York, familiarizing himself with bad company, and yet presuming upon a rank which he degraded, and, notwithstanding, made an annoyance."*

One of the King's letters refers to this brother, and is written with the view of preventing difficulties which might arise in the Mediterranean (where the Duke was cruising), from the French, who the King hears, "are uncivil to a very unwarrantable degree to every ship that comes near to Corsica." Another refers to Captain Wallis' famous voyage of discovery:— "He seems to have shown great assiduity in this service, and appears very worthy of reward." The third is as follows:—

RICHMOND LODGE,

SIR EDWARD HAWKE,   October 13th 1770.

      The great spirit shewed by the officers of the Navy on this occasion [the threatened war with Spain] makes me desirous of contributing as much as possible to their encouragement. I therefore think the promotion of Flag-officers, including Lord Howe, would be properly timed. If you are of that opinion I shall be desirous of seeing you with the list, and those you may judge best suited for the superannuated list. I cannot conclude without acquainting you that Sir Charles Knowles desired Lord Rochford to acquaint me that he had received an offer to go into the Russian service, where he is to receive an allowance of £2,000 per annum. I said I should willingly consent to what was so much for the Admiral's advantage, but thought he could not in that case remain Rear-admiral of the Fleet, though perhaps he might be permitted to remain in the list of Admirals, but that I should, with regard to this affair, talk with you before I gave any positive answer.

GEORGE R.

A good deal has been said about the King's bad spelling. The above letter is copied precisely from

---

* "Mem. Geo. III.," vol. ii. p. 105.

the original in every respect, and there is not a word ill-spelt in it. Perhaps the instances which occur in the Letters to Lord North may betray the stealthy footsteps of the disease which so often incapacitated the King, and may have made him at times careless and forgetful of common things.

We may complete our conspectus of the way in which Hawke's tenure of his seat at the Admiralty was regarded, by referring to two anonymous letters which appeared in the "Gentleman's Magazine" for 1770. It was not to be expected that he should escape scurrilous attacks; and the sting of the first of these letters lies in the imputation of avarice as the ground for his not having resigned his seat. It was an easy charge to make, but it is left unsupported by the writer in any single respect. He was answered in the following month by one who was equally opposed to Hawke's politics, and equally bitter against Lord North. He demands, however, fair play, and reminding his opponent that he has not substantiated his charge, bids him remember that Sir Edward Hawke's having "rescued three kingdoms from the immediate danger of foreign invasion, and perhaps from total destruction, is known to the whole world." He then draws a favourable comparison between him and a former First Lord of the Admiralty :—" You cannot say of him that he is proud, imperious, and inaccessible, that his servants must be bribed to gain admittance, even for a Memorial, &c. . . . . If Sir Edward Hawke errs, 'tis not from insolence; if he cannot do right, it is want of power in his office. . . . . Let us separate the Admiral from the Commissioner. While we look at one with honour and esteem, 'tis difficult to behold the other with disgust. Sir Edward Hawke is a character ever to be admired as a brave and gallant seaman. Politics may not be his *forte*; and surely he has not yet offended past redemption. Let us awhile suspend our judgment of this truly great man; and let us remember that he was as much a favourite with his late Royal Master for the goodness, as for the bravery, of his heart."

Hawke's services as First Lord of the Admiralty, taken along with Chatham's appointments, require a word, at the conclusion of this Chapter, on the vexed question whether naval men or civilians make the best First Lords. Sir John Barrow, in his "Life of Lord Howe,"[*] has argued it with much ability, and sums up in favour of civilians. This he does upon two main grounds, the certainty that naval First Lords will show a partiality to those who have served under them, and their want of the general knowledge necessary for a mixed position, half naval, half civil. The civil First Lord, assisted by naval men, is his ideal; and the custom of successive Governments has followed that direction.

Taking the subject in its general aspect, it will not be found easy to dispute his position; but it requires a Proviso. To place a civilian at the head of the Admiralty, is an artificial and unnatural

---

[*] Pp. 175, 193.

expedient, and should therefore not be too rigidly applied. If an Anson or a Hawke can be found, he should take precedence of any civilian. The same may be said of a Howe or a St. Vincent, who were First Lords. Rodney, Collingwood, and others might be named who, if placed in that position, would probably have governed the Navy better than any civilian. Lord Barham was one of the best First Lords, though, unlike the others named, he was scarcely at the head of his profession.

The naval First Lord should be the acknowledged head, a man who has shown first-rate ability all through a distinguished career, a man who has seen war-service and made opportunities, and who has acquired the tact and "general knowledge" which is not so rare among naval officers as the late Secretary of the Admiralty supposed. In times of peace it will of course be difficult to find the right man; nor is it of so much consequence; but in periods of war, if the triumphs of Lord Chatham are to be repeated, it may be well to remember his opinion as to the proper method of governing the Navy. Is it impossible that the compromise, often suggested, may yet be found the best, viz., that of placing a naval Commander-in-chief exactly in the same position as that held by the head of the Army? Thus the inestimable advantage would be gained of a permanent head of the Navy independent of the changes of Government, an end by no means obtained under the present system of a Permanent Secretary. The Army and Navy are machines of a wholly different description from other Public Departments. The only real difficulty would be that of superseding this great officer when he became too old; but this might be met by proper regulations.

CHAPTER XIV.

PEERAGE, RETIREMENT, AND DEATH.

WHEN Hawke resigned his seat at the Admiralty on the ground of health, he must have been flattered at the following kind expressions from Lord Rochford, the Secretary of State, dated, January 11th, 1771 :—

> I was favoured with your letter last night, and was extremely unhappy to have a letter of that sort from you to lay before the King, for no one can have a higher opinion than I have of the able and disinterested manner with which you have served the King so faithfully for so many years. When I had the honour this day to acquaint the King with your intentions, His Majesty was pleased to express in the strongest terms how sensible he was of the loss of so able and so gallant an officer, and regretted very much the bad state of your health which obliged you to come to this resolution.

But how came the grant of a Peerage, which was not conferred till 1776, to be again neglected? The retirement of the victor of Quiberon, now growing old and worn out, after five years' service at the head of the Admiralty, and accompanied by the sincere regrets of a Sovereign who honoured and trusted him, might seem to have been the most natural occasion in the world for conferring such a distinction. There were no doubt two reasons. The Swathling monument suggests one. Hawke never asked, nor desired anyone to ask, for such a favour. It was his character through life. He never even asked a favour for his officers unless they were the senior of their rank, or on some such irresistible ground. It was not his way. Perhaps there was some pride at the bottom of it. At any rate there was a great deal of dignity, and it was exceedingly rare. Distinguished officers like Amherst did not feel this compunction. Even the highminded Lord Howe is found haggling for offices and favours.*

Nor could political services be obtained without the bribe of peerages. What was the King, in the extremity of his early difficulties, to do? He fought manfully against the pressure put upon him, and only succumbed when he was driven to bay. In 1766 he attempted to obtain the Duke of Bedford's aid towards forming a Government, offering to call his eldest son to the Upper House, and to appoint Lord Gower to office. So exorbitant, however, were the demands of the "Bloomsbury gang" for Garters, peerages, and places that the King with good reason declared their demands to be too extravagant, and the negotiation was accordingly broken off. Walpole tells us, in 1768, that when Amherst asked for a peerage he was told that the King was so teased for them that he had given orders "none should be mentioned more,"† and in 1776, that "the King had involved himself in so

---

* "King's Correspondence with Lord North," p. 133.
† "Mem. Geo. III.," vol. iv.

many promises, and so many coronets had been asked, that for some years no peers had been created." *

This, then, was the second reason. Not only did the modesty of the hero stand in the way, but the King could not afford to make peers. At last he found himself able to break through his self-imposed restrictions, and bestow the rewards which are due from a Sovereign to real and distinguished merit. Even Walpole, on that occasion, finds no fault:— " Sir Edward Hawke was one of the principal heroes of the last war."† It was an "unsolicited peerage." We have no record of how it affected the old man. Probably he had ceased to care about it, if he ever had cared at all.‡

But Lord Hawke had not ceased to care for the fortunes of others. The only notice preserved of the Admiral's retirement, from 1771 to his death in 1781, is the extraordinary interest he took in Keppel's Courtmartial. What were his feelings about the American War which broke out so soon after he retired from office, we have no means of judging; but when France and Spain joined in the fray, it had no doubt aroused all his patriotic feelings. As the colleague of Chatham and Keppel he must have

---

* "Last Journals," vol. ii. p. 35.

† *Ibid.*

‡ As we have now arrived at the end of Lord Hawke's services, it may be mentioned that he became Vice-admiral of Great Britain in 1765. It should have been mentioned in its place that he attained the rank of Admiral in February 1757.

observed with pain the processes by which the country had drifted into the colonial quarrel; but when the old enemies, whom his own arm had humbled in the dust, came forth once more, and, taking advantage of the civil contest in which Great Britain was engaged, again threatened to invade her inviolable shores, the old man's blood rushed back with its youthful velocity, and his spirit stirred with every pulse of the popular emotion. His old friend and pupil, Keppel, personally pressed by the King, though a member of the Opposition, had been called to the front in the national emergency, and placed at the head of such a fleet as Sandwich could muster. It was inferior to that of France under D'Orvilliers, but Keppel's popularity with the service stood the country in good stead when ships had to be manned; and in June he found himself blockading the enemy off his old station at Brest.

It is unnecessary to give a detailed account of the famous incidents of this naval campaign. The subject of our memoir was only indirectly concerned in it through the Memorial to the King, which he signed at the head of a body of twelve distinguished admirals: there is no obscurity in the affair, except so far as it is cast around us by the partisan spirit in which it was regarded both at and since those times: and further, in so popular a book as Lord Stanhope's "History of England" will be found a concise and impartial summary, quite sufficient for all who are not called upon to make a complete investigation of the subject. But it so happens that among the Hawke

Papers are preserved two very interesting letters which it would be a pity not to publish, from Keppel himself, and from Lord Rockingham; and these will necessitate a few remarks which might otherwise have been avoided.

Excellent officer as Keppel was, he set out from the very first with what many people have considered a mistake. Soon after he arrived off Brest, finding, on board a frigate which he had seized, papers giving the strength of the enemy as far superior to his own, he at once, without further investigation as to the genuine character of the papers, or calling a Council of War, returned to Portsmouth for reinforcements. This created a bad impression upon friends and foes. At home it was held to be a retreat, and compared with Byng's. It might however be defended on the ground of the responsibility attaching to the commander of England's only fleet—for such it was,—and of obedience to the spirit, if not the letter of the Instructions he had received. Nothing more would have been heard of it, had the battle which ensued on July 27th been decisive. But when the fleets met off Ushant they were now nearly equal; indeed the English, from having cut off two ships, were a little superior, and victory was expected, as a matter of course, under such circumstances. As it was, the battle was just as indecisive as Pocock's or Hughes' actions in the Indian Ocean; and Keppel was fairly outmanœuvred by an enemy who had been beaten, as usual, when any ships got near enough to practise old English tactics. It is scarcely fair to blame this brave officer for not doing what a Hawke or a Rodney would most certainly have done. The prudence which he evinced in trying to keep his fleet together must have been painful to such a man; but he lost his opportunity by contenting himself with cannonades on opposite tacks, in line.

All this however might have been retrieved had it not been for one of those mistakes to which sea-fights are liable, and which was aggravated by the time lost in sending messages which the existing signals were not adequate to convey. Keppel's two gallant Vice-admirals, Harland and Sir Hugh Palliser,* had been engaged in the thickest of the fight; after which the first was still in a condition to understand and obey his chief's signals for drawing the whole fleet together for a final combat; the second was not. But curiously enough neither did Palliser make his crippled position known to the Admiral by signal; nor did Keppel, while keeping his general signal flying, and making the pendants of other ships to draw attention to it, do the same to Palliser; nor did any message reach the latter officer till late in the evening. The result was a misunderstanding, without heinous fault on either side; but it led to the failure. Keppel could not close with the French because his fleet was not in hand; and he hoped for better luck in the morning. When morning

---

* He spelt his name "Pallisser"; but as all the world has conspired to call him "Palliser," it is of no use to try and stem the tide.

broke, the French were found to have made off to such a distance that Keppel decided not to pursue them.

Still, in a sense, it was a victory. The alarm of a hostile fleet in the Channel was dissipated for the present; the English force had driven off the French one, only a little inferior to itself, with loss; and such a favourite as Keppel could hardly do wrong. His Despatch was somewhat obscure; and as it failed to notice the important events of the afternoon of the 27th, it was misleading; but it did not at first attract much attention. What turned out unfortunately for Keppel afterwards, was that he said at the end of this document :—" The spirited conduct of Vice Admiral Sir Robert Harland, Vice Admiral Sir Hugh Palliser, and the Captains of the fleet, supported by their officers and men, deserves much commendation."

When the period of Courtsmartial arrived, it seemed that this praise was given with a mental reservation; for the battle before the Courts raged over the accusation of Keppel that Palliser's misconduct was the cause of the failure. Yet it seems clear by the following letter to Lord Hawke that Keppel had not felt this at first, but thought of nothing else in the matter beyond the villainous trick of the enemy in leading him to believe that the battle was to be renewed, when he only meant running away. Hawke, blinded a little, we must suppose by friendship, seems to have written—his letter is not preserved—to congratulate Keppel on his engagement and his arrival at Plymouth. The following reply is among the Hawke papers:—

MOUNT EDGECUMBE,
August 11th, 1778.

MY LORD,

I received the honour of your Lordship's letter of the 7th inst., from Sunbury, this day. Believe me your approbation of my conduct conveys to me more satisfaction than I can express, as it confirms me in the zeal I ever hope to shew in the support of the honour of the flag, and particularly in continuing in the good opinion of one whose example is ever before me, and with whom I served so much of my time in my younger days. I flatter myself if the French had not run off in the night, my finishing the following day would have been more brilliant and decisive. The French accounts value themselves upon the afternoon of the battle. Indeed their behaviour operated so strongly with me that I had not a doubt of their fighting me fairly the next day, which I expressed in my public letter. If they were as stout as they pretend to be, it is certain they might have begun again in the afternoon, but I believe what I have said, that they were so beaten that this plan was merely bravado and trick to get away in the dark, which they did at midnight, leaving two frigates and a ship with lights to deceive us. They have dared to assert the English fleet put out their lights, a lie that everybody in the fleet can contradict. It is not my business to follow every falsity they spread, but to get again to sea with as little loss of time as possible. Admiral Campbell is sensible of your kind notice of him, and is proud of it. I shall make your compliments to Sir Robert Harland and Sir Hugh Palliser. The Captains will, I know, be thankful for your just opinion of them. They are indeed fine officers, and the ships are fine. Some of them indeed want more experience in discipline to do all that can be expected from them, but a complete fleet cannot be formed in a day. Our greatest want is petty officers, and that deficiency is general. I must once more thank your Lordship for the handsome attention you have so obligingly shown me. It is a certificate that I much value myself upon.

I am, &c.
A. KEPPEL.

The grateful feeling shown in this letter was no

doubt enhanced by the murmurs which had begun to rise. Those murmurs gathered strength after the fleet had again sailed, and had looked about for the Frenchmen in vain. The opportunity was gone; and the national spirit which had been fed so high in the previous war, expressed itself in every form of annoyance and disappointment. Whose fault had it been? Why was there no enquiry? Terror added to these feelings its peculiar vehemence and injustice; and party spirit, now at its extreme height, fanned the fuel into a flame. After such a different result of a naval battle from those which had of old crushed the enemy, would not even Spain venture forth once more?—as she soon did. With the whole of the national resources expended on the American War, in which the best commanders were making shipwreck of their reputation, how was the country to stand up against France and Spain? The country had indeed backed the King and the Government in the new civil war, but all the oratory was against them, all the active forces of the national intellect were on the other side. The effect of Chatham's dying words, beseeching the country never to surrender its rights over its colonies, had already passed away, and the people were beginning to realise, under the prospect of an immediate struggle for existence, what a task they had undertaken. Keppel had been the strongest Whig politician the Navy had ever sent to Parliament; and, as Burke's splendid panegyric, in his "Letter to a Noble Lord," abundantly shows, the adored favourite of his political friends, quite as much as of the seamen of the fleet. The Keppels were famous for their delightful manners; and the Admiral's deeds truly deserved admiration. It was clear that whatever else happened, he must be pulled through.

Fortunately for the Admiral there was a scapegoat. Sir Hugh Palliser, an officer of gallantry and distinction, but of a reputation far below that of Keppel,— for though an older man, he had not been brought forward early in life,—was a Lord of the unpopular Admiralty over which Sandwich presided, and a Tory Member of Parliament. He had however always been a friend and admirer of Keppel, and the latter appears to have owed his command of the fleet to Palliser's own strong recommendation.* He had fought with the utmost courage in the battle, his ship having been very severely handled; and, though he had made a mistake, as we have seen, had no idea, especially after the Admiral's Despatch, that he deserved anything but praise. When the fleet returned again in the autumn, what was his astonishment to find that the popular indignation had already turned against himself instead of Keppel!

The interval had been diligently used. The favourite's failure had been a trick of the Machiavellian Admiralty. Palliser had been sent out expressly to prevent a victory. What could be more clear? Had he not held back at the critical moment when the signal to join the Admiral had been flying for hours? This became the established theory of the battle. It

---

* Charnock's "*Biog. Nav.*," vol. v. p. 489.

was not surprising that a man of a somewhat proud and overbearing character like Palliser should refuse to bear such imputations, and he made the mistake of defending himself in a public newspaper, instead of instantly demanding an enquiry into his own conduct. Keppel, when called on to confirm his subordinate's statement of the circumstances, declined. Palliser now made another mistake; and after an unseemly altercation in the House of Commons with his chief, demanded a Courtmartial on *him*, and brought forward a series of most damaging charges. This was felt to be a high-handed use of his position as a Lord of the Admiralty, and Keppel at once became a martyr. He had run a narrow risk of being condemned like another Byng; he now figured as another Vernon. The King and the Government, North, Sandwich, and Palliser, shrank up into dwarf-like dimensions. The small form of Keppel swelled into the proportions of a giant. The Tories were silenced: the Whigs filled the whole air.

There was in truth a great deal to be said against Palliser's course of proceeding, and this it was which brought Hawke on the stage. The Memorial to the King, begging him to interpose and stop the Courtmartial now demanded, would have carried little weight except for his great name. It was an unprecedented step, and, though it failed of its immediate object, it influenced opinion. The last paragraph alone need be printed in this place: it sums up the rest:—

We therefore humbly represent, in behalf of public order as

well as of the discipline of the navy, to your Majesty the dangers of long concealed and afterwards precipitately adopted charges, and of all recriminating accusations of subordinate officers against their Commander-in-chief, and particularly the mischief and scandal of permitting men who are at once in high office and subordinate military command, previous to their making such accusations, to attempt to corrupt the public judgment by the publication of libels on their officers in a common newspaper, thereby exciting mutiny in your Majesty's navy, as well as prejudicing of those who are to try the merits of the accusation against the said superior officer.

This Memorial was signed by "the revered" * Hawke, Moore, the Duke of Bolton, Graves, Pigot, Harland, the Earl of Bristol, Young, Barton, Geary, Lord Shuldham, and Gayton. Most of these were Hawke's old followers, and some of them Tories. It will be observed that, though Lord Hawke did, as a matter of fact, approve of Keppel's conduct, neither here (nor in any other part of the paper) is there any expression of opinion on the questions to be tried. It was a protest against a line of action which the Memorialists rightly judged to be *pessimi exempli*, and in that respect was valuable for the future. As the two Courtsmartial, on Keppel and Palliser, ended in the acquittal of both, it might seem that it was a pity Hawke's advice was not followed, and a great scandal prevented: but in truth such a course was now impossible. It was necessary for the reputation of two gallant commanding officers at the head of a fleet, and therefore for the whole service and the country at large, that both should be tried.

* "Annual Register," 1780.

. But it was unfortunate for the cause of justice that party feeling was now transported to such an extraordinary pitch of intensity that Keppel's trial was in reality a farce. Admiral Montagu, one of the members of the Court who took the lead, was a rough and violent seaman, who had seen very little active service against the enemy, and was an extravagant friend of Keppel's. This man browbeat the adverse witnesses without mercy; and the whole Court was as much dominated by the enthusiasm in favour of Keppel as the Courts which condemned Mathews and Byng were by the popular feeling of their respective times. A special Act of Parliament was passed to allow the Court to be held on shore at Portsmouth instead of on board ship, its proper place; and thus noble lords and ladies were able to enjoy the excitement without any danger of sea-sickness. The grim old garrison town was turned into a Bath or Tunbridge Wells. Princes of the Blood, in the persons of the Dukes of Gloucester and Cumberland, ex-Prime Ministers, like the Marquis of Rockingham, leaders of the House of Lords like the Duke of Richmond, statesmen like Fox and Burke, came down and sat in Court for whole days, persuading themselves that they were come to stand by their martyr and idol when he was to be shot like Byng by a tyrant Admiralty.* When we read the excited letters from these personages it sounds like a joke. If ever a man's head was safe, Keppel's was.

---

* See Burke's "Letter to a Noble Lord."

The Marquis of Rockingham was, however, so considerable a person that his letter to Hawke, preserved among the Hawke papers, may at least amuse, and may possibly interest, some readers :—

My Lord,

The very noble part which your Lordship has acted in stating your opinion to the Crown on the odiousness and impropriety of a Courtmartial having been ordered on Admiral Keppel in consequence of charges and accusations made against him under the circumstances and in the manner they were, occasions my venturing to intrude a letter upon you, as I am sure the account it will give your Lordship will afford you much satisfaction.

The Courtmartial has now had four sitting days. Each day produced circumstances that must give pleasure to every one who honours Mr. Keppel. The accusations and the accuser are continually meeting with disappointments and discomfitures. Your Lordship, I imagine, will have heard of the events and proceedings on three of the former days. On this day Captain Digby was called as a witness by Sir Hugh Palliser. It has been understood that Captain Digby's evidence would be much in support of the accusations. In my mind it has proved entirely otherwise. He hesitated indeed, and did not give a direct and positive answer to the first question put by Admiral Montagu after his examination by Sir Hugh Palliser, but yet his answer was such as I think no man could give who thought Admiral Keppel guilty of that part of the charge.

Admiral Montagu's first question (which is understood to be a question from the whole Court) amounts to requiring the opinion of the evidence whether Admiral Keppel on the day of the action had been guilty of any neglect in not doing his utmost to burn, sink, and destroy, &c., the French, or had conducted himself in an unofficer-like manner. Captain Digby said—"he had long highly honoured and esteemed Admiral Keppel as an officer, and he *did so still*." He added that he declined giving any further opinion, for that as an evidence he had stated facts *on which* he thought it was not for him but for the Court to judge.

Admiral Montagu then put a question to Captain Digby—just reading to him the charge where Admiral Keppel is accused of having fled from the French fleet. The question he put was—"Did Admiral Keppel *run away* from the French fleet." Captain Digby answered without hesitation, "No." Tuesday night.

I was prevented from sending this letter to your Lordship last night [Tuesday]. Captain Digby was examined again this morning. Admiral Keppel put several questions to him,—many very material ones,—and I am happy to say that I do not think that *any one* of Sir Hugh Palliser's five charges against Admiral Keppel has received support from Captain Digby's evidence. Captain Windsor of the "Fox" was the next witness called. I enclose to your Lordship a printed copy of Sir Hugh Palliser's letter, (which was published in November in the "Morning Post"). I also enclose to your Lordship a minute of Captain Windsor's evidence. Your Lordship on comparing them will be astonished.

Wednesday night.

I was too late to send this letter last night [Wednesday], so that it is now Thursday night. Captain Hood was examined to-day. He began by a long speech, particularly relative to the alterations in his Log-book. That matter rests at present till Admiral Keppel cross-examines him, which I suppose will be to-morrow. There are some matters in Captain Hood's evidence which may require answers, or rather which Admiral Keppel on cross-examining him will overset. The material part relates to the signals made early in the morning on the 27th, *by which* Captain Hood in part asserts that the fleet was *dispersed* and *scattered*. In regard to many of the charges Captain Hood's evidence contradicts them, particularly Sir Hugh Palliser's assertion that the "Formidable" was left unsupported. Captain Hood says his ship, the "Robust," the "Terrible," "Worcester," "America," "Elizabeth," and the "Egmont"—he doubts in regard to the latter,—these five or six ships were *astern* of the "*Formidable*" *when she passed along the French line in action*. Admiral Montagu put two questions to Captain Hood: I enclose to your Lordship the minute of them, and shall only express my satisfaction in remarking that the assertion of Admiral Keppel's flying from the French fleet is too difficult a matter for evidence to be got to swear to.

I really must apologize for troubling your Lordship with so long a letter. I confess that I feel so much joy every day with what passes at the Courtmartial that I could not refrain from communicating some circumstances to your Lordship, who, I was sure, would feel much satisfaction, pleasure, and comfort in hearing them. It is too with great satisfaction that I can inform your Lordship that so far from this business creating a *disunion in the fleet*, it will have *quite the contrary effect*. Naval honour and naval integrity never shone brighter than they do at this moment here. The zeal in behalf of Admiral Keppel and the indignation against the attack and attackers seem to occupy the minds of all the best and ablest officers, and to extend itself through all the different ranks.

Captain Hood will be examined again to-morrow, as Sir Hugh Palliser had not finished to-day all that he intended to ask him. Admiral Keppel will then cross-examine Captain Hood, and all the business of the Log-books will be the part whereon he will first commence.

Admiral Keppel is in good health and good spirits. He conducts himself with so much propriety and dignity, and with such ability, as wins upon the minds of all his hearers.

I have the honour to be, &c., &c.
Portsmouth, Thursday night,   ROCKINGHAM.
January 14th, 1779.

The great Whig ladies accompanied their relatives at this interesting scene, which lasted, with all its exciting circumstances, thirty days. Lady Rockingham, an excellent person, writes thus:—

When I met you in the street I was just returned from Admiral Keppel's trial. . . . I went to that place in great anxiety at such an event as a Court Martial, appointed, in such haste, on so meritorious and beloved a friend; but I went in much resignation of mind and the fullest trust in the Almighty Defender of injured innocence; and I hope I returned with the strongest sense of gratitude.*

It will be observed from Lord Rockingham's letter that the special Act which allowed of the Court

---

* Letter to the Rev. John Burrows, *penes auctorem*.

being held on shore was scarcely needed. It was passed on the ground of the Admiral's bad health. He was subject to gout; but we see he was " in good health and good spirits." For the further explanation of the details mentioned in the letter the reader is referred to the Proceedings of the Courtmartial. Nor will any elaborate discussions be in place here. Suffice it to say that the painful and gratuitous charge against the Admiral for " running away " grew out of the scattered state of the English fleet on the afternoon of the 27th, when the French drew up in good order, and ready to fight. Finding only twelve ships at hand to renew the combat, Keppel hauled down the signal to engage, and made one for line of battle. He then ordered Sir Robert Harland, who was to windward with his division, to run down and form line astern of him. This gave the appearance of retreat, but was really part of the process of getting the fleet together, which was frustrated by Palliser's crippled condition, as mentioned above; while the action of the French in " standing after the British fleet," however strange a sight to Englishmen, could not be helped, their numbers being at the moment so superior.

As opinions of every kind have been freely hazarded on this celebrated Courtmartial, it is not of much consequence whether one more should be given. But, judging by the light of the Trials which have been already noticed in this book, it is hardly possible to avoid the conclusion that Keppel committed certain errors in judgment both at first and at last. Of these it has been held that his failure on the 28th to pursue the enemy, who were still visible from the mast head, was one; and, even giving so experienced an officer, charged with so heavy a responsibility, the benefit of the doubt on that point, some notice should surely have been taken of the failure to bring the enemy to a decisive action on the 27th. As it was, he got off with all the glory which could possibly have been acquired by the most successful officer; and that was certainly no advantage to the service. He supported himself, in one portion of his defence, by the example of "that truly great officer, Lord Hawke, who, rejecting all rules and forms, grasped at victory by an irregular attack," but dispassionate observers could hardly avoid the reflection that it was precisely because Keppel had only learnt part of his lesson, that he failed.

Palliser's charges were condemned by the Court as "malicious and ill-founded." Perhaps they were; they were certainly ill-judged; but on his Court-martial that officer escaped almost as well as his chief: indeed, his conduct was declared to have been "in many respects highly meritorious and exemplary."

The extravagant burst of joy at Keppel's acquittal in which Lord Hawke could not resist the temptation to join, though he must surely have had his own ideas as to Keppel's conduct, has been already noticed, and will be found concisely described by Lord Stanhope. Palliser was burnt in effigy, and his house sacked. "Perhaps," says Lord Stanhope, "no man was ever more cruelly used by the public through a virulent party spirit." Nor was Lord Rockingham right in prematurely asserting that the struggle had done no harm. It may have been necessary; but it produced insubordination, and even mutiny. Violent and unmeasured denunciations of an Administration, in which naval officers were drawn up in opposing ranks, and in which the populace were invited to take part, could not but leave a mark. Neither officer was again employed at sea; which was indeed their own desire. Keppel ended his public career as First Lord of the Admiralty under his friend Lord Rockingham; and the rank of Viscount could only be grudged to so fine an officer, even though he failed to be a first-rate admiral, when judged by the niggard recompense doled out to Hawke; Palliser retired to the Government of Greenwich Hospital.

A last, but most suggestive specimen of the aged Admiral's character comes before us in connection with one of the consequences of the Keppel Courtmartial. As that officer declined to serve the Government any longer, though at its greatest need, the command of the fleet had to be entrusted to one of Hawke's old friends, Sir Charles Hardy, and, on his death, to another—Admiral, afterwards Sir Francis, Geary. The Spanish having joined the French in 1779, the combined squadrons were able to muster 66 line-of-battle ships against Hardy's 36, and to insult the British coast with impunity. Hardy was not justified by the traditions then dominant in doing more than keep them at bay; and this he did with admirable skill. The enemy, however, ill-found and disunited, soon dispersed of his own accord, and Hardy, too old for so trying a responsibility, soon afterwards died. When Geary was appointed to command, and sent to blockade Brest in May, 1780, his old chief, now 75, wrote him the following letter, and, in August, another. Both must be inserted. If betraying some marks of fond old age, they at least display much amiability, and some touches of the old fire :—

My dear Sir,   June 6th, 1780.

      This is principally to thank you for the favour of your letter of the 3rd instant, and for all the kind acts you have been able to do for my parson, which was doing everything in your power. . . . I find by the papers that you are getting ready for sea with all the despatch that is possible, and that you will sail the instant that it is in your power: and though I could wish this could get to your hands first, yet the times are so very pressing from many unfortunate events, that I think the sooner you can get to my old station off Brest the better it will be for my country. When you are there, watch those fellows as close as a cat watches a mouse; and if once you have the good fortune to get up to them make much of them, and don't part with them easily.

Forgive my being so free: I love you. We have served long together, and I have your interest and happiness sincerely at heart. My dear friend, may God Almighty bless you, and may that all-powerful hand guide and protect you in the day of battle; and that you may return with honour and glory to your country and family is the sincere and faithful wish of him who is most truly, my dear Sir, your most obedient and most humble servant,

                                                             Hawke.

Again :—

                          Sunbury,

My dear Sir,   26th August 1780.

      I am greatly obliged to you for the favour of your letter of the 20th on your arrival at Spithead; indeed, it was more than

I expected, well knowing the hurry and bustle you must be in on your first coming into port. I do not wonder at the men being sickly upon so long a cruise: six weeks is long enough in all conscience; any time after that must be very hurtful to the men, and will occasion their falling down very fast. I hope in God they will soon recover, that you may be enabled to proceed to sea immediately, for by all accounts the enemy is out, so that nothing can well stir from home with safety. I wish the Admiralty would see what was done in former times; it would make them act with more propriety, both for the good of officers and men. I take it for granted that the great ones will let you have no rest till they get you out to sea again.

Although I am in a good deal of pain, and much in the invalid order, yet I cannot refuse myself the pleasure of wishing you all imaginable good fortune when you go out again; and I trust in God your next cruise will prove to be a happy and glorious one, both for your country and yourself. My good friend, I have always wished you well, and have ever talked freely and openly to you upon every subject relative to the service. Recollect some of these passages; and for God's sake, if you should be so lucky as to get sight of the enemy, get as close to them as possible. Do not let them shuffle with you by engaging at a distance, but get within musket-shot if you can; that will be the way to gain great honour, and will be the means to make the action decisive. By doing this you will put it out of the power of any of the brawlers to find fault. I am fully persuaded you will do your part; therefore hope you will forgive my saying so much on the subject.

I find the Russians are gone from the Downs, so you will have no trouble about them. My good friend, God bless you. May the hand of Providence go with you and protect you in the day of battle, and grant you victory over our perfidious enemies; and may you return with honour to your country and family again! These are the sincere and hearty wishes of him who is most truly and faithfully, my dear Sir, your most obedient and most humble servant, HAWKE.

Charnock, by whom these letters were given,* tells us that, in a postscript to one of his letters, Hawke

---

* Vol. v. p. 187.

tells Geary:—"I am glad you have got so excellent an officer with you as I am convinced Kempenfelt is: he will be of great service to you."

Geary is again mentioned in the following letter to the Hon. Admiral Barrington, with whom Hawke is about to send a young friend to sea :—

SUNBURY, June, 1780.

Permit me, my dear Sir, to wish you joy of your new Commander-in-chief [Geary]. I take him to be a good seaman, and believe he is a brave, honest, good-tempered man. I am only afraid of his being too easy, and that he will subject himself to be blamed, as Sir Charles Hardy was, for letting the discipline of the fleet come to nothing. I hope—for I wish him well—he will support the dignity of his high station in a proper manner, and that he will not let himself down, and make himself too cheap with the little people of the service.

What you say is too true. I am afraid our superiors have not their King and country so much at heart as they ought to have, otherwise they would think and act in a different manner to what they do. That pride, conceit, and folly in not consulting good men of the profession must of course throw everything into disorder and confusion; and the thinking all men are alike in the service must bring the navy to destruction at last, unless Sir George Rodney, General Vaughan and Sir Hugh Palliser will take us under their protection. You see what great things are done, and how greatly represented. Whatever you shall be concerned in I am convinced you will represent in a just and honourable manner, in its own fair and natural colours.

May the hand of Providence protect you in all your undertakings; and may your cruise prove as fortunate as your own heart can desire.*

Thus the old man keeps up his last connection with his beloved profession. The words in which he begs his friend "never to let the enemy shuffle off, but get as close to them as possible" were a legacy to the

---

* Hawke Papers.

service, and they were not forgotten. They came with weight from one who had taught the navy how to put them in practice. The letter to Admiral Barrington, above quoted, betrays the heaving of the political swell which succeeded the storm of the Keppel Courtmartial. Palliser and Rodney were at the head of the naval Tories, as Hawke and Keppel were of the naval Whigs. But let us remember what was the exceeding bitterness of the political conflict which raged from 1770 to 1784, when at last the time came, and the younger Pitt broke upon the world, and we shall understand that no one in a high position could possibly have kept himself entirely free from it. Not that party strife became any the less pronounced at the later period: but order and prosperity then began to reign in a manner which no one could have foreseen when our veteran left this last, almost despairing, letter for a future generation to unearth from its recesses. Rodney's despatches from the West Indies at this period are remarked upon by other writers as somewhat boastful; and there were plenty of people to expose any defect, jealous as they were in the highest degree, even in that hour of difficulty, of a Tory success. It required the brilliant victory of the Twelfth of April, 1782, to extinguish all such petty feelings, and restore its old tone to a profession which had grievously suffered by the events of the previous twenty years.

It is to be regretted that so few of Hawke's private letters have been preserved. We should probably have found in them many expressions of the same hearty, affectionate nature as in the foregoing. But without such help, we have seen enough to convince us that this great admiral learnt the road to success as much by his good heart as by his clear head, and lofty character. He was a man of principle, and his principles were derived from the highest source.

On October 16th, 1781, the "Annual Register" has the following entry:—" Died, at Sunbury in Middlesex, Lord Hawke, Vice Admiral of Great Britain, Admiral of the Fleet, President of the Maritime School, and an Elder Brother of the Trinity House." On the 18th, Walpole writing to Mann, and forgetting that "Hawke had never been a man of ability," remarks: —" Lord Hawke is dead, and does not seem to have left his mantle to anybody." If we had not already found it necessary to use Walpole's remarks with caution, this of itself would show him to be but little acquainted with affairs. Within six months of his use of this expression Rodney had won the only battle that could be ranked by the side of the victory of Quiberon since the days of Blake. Lord Sandwich knew better. A few weeks later he had written to Rodney :—" The fate of this Empire is in your hands, and I have no wish that it should be in any other." * By that victory off Dominica the labours of Chatham, Hawke, and Wolfe had been crowned; Great Britain shook off all the enemies that were furiously crowding and fastening upon her, the King's splendid patriotism was rewarded, the Peace of Versailles made possible,

---

* Mundy's "Rodney," vol. ii. p. 282.

and the breathing period of the next ten years granted, during which the son of Chatham might regenerate his country, and prepare her for the mighty task which yet lay before her Imperial path. Lord Hawke had lived at Sunbury for some years, but his grave was to be by the side of that of the beloved wife who had died at Swathling five and twenty years before.

The history which has been here given scarcely requires any recapitulation. It comes out clear and sharp in connection with one great and formative period, the twenty-three years during which the aggresive conduct of France and Spain forced England into the defensive war which led to the acquisition of her present Empire. Before that time we know but little of the Cornish barrister's son who married the young Yorkshire heiress. At the end of it he is at the head of his profession, and has established his position as the greatest officer that had appeared in the modern navies of Europe. Checked by many a stroke of bitter trial, we never find him failing in any work which he was given to do, except in the case of Rochefort, where we have seen he was not, and was held not to be, responsible; and we have had the means of forming some opinion as to the reasons why he was what Horace Walpole called "fortunate." We have watched his modest demeanour in prosperity, and his manly fortitude in adversity; and this not only in military but civil affairs. If a senior is promoted before him he is the first to wish him joy. If honours and rewards are showered upon the unworthy, it makes no difference to him, though he must have known he was worthy of them. At the end of his life the Peerage which should have marked the victory of Quiberon, or if not, the close of the war, or if not then, the retirement from the Admiralty,—comes at last. Then men seem to discover that they have a hero among them, and call to mind his surpassing services. He is "the great and good," the "revered Lord Hawke," the "father of the navy," the last of a great race, the prophet whose mantle there is no one to take up. Amongst his negative merits it may be observed that he never once in his long career found himself called upon to deal with mutiny in his ship or fleet. Seamen and officers knew him too well.

Like all great men, he formed a school. In this respect he was a partner with Anson, of whom the same thing may be said. But it is assuredly true in a far greater degree of Lord Hawke. Most of the officers who, after the Peace of Paris, rose to distinction, had served under him; and some of them owned their debt. They carried on the traditions which he had planted, down to the present century. Especially was this the case, as has been pointed out in Chapter III., in the matter of decisive engagements. It was here that the transformation of naval warfare displayed itself, and it is in this vital point that all succeeding transformations will culminate in future times. Perhaps even Nelson, who was a Post-Captain when Hawke died, caught more of his own noble spirit from the maxims and exploits of "the father of the navy" than he himself knew.

In the belief that the lineaments of such a man should not be suffered to remain any longer in obscurity, and that not only the Royal Navy but the whole British people cannot but feel some sort of shame that such obscurity should have existed so long, the writer of these pages, while profoundly regretting that he has been unable to do full justice to such a theme, and especially that more private letters have not escaped the ravages of time, presents this imperfect sketch to his readers, and claims their indulgence.

INDEX.

N.B.—The rank assigned to British Officers is, as far as can be ascertained, that at which they finally arrived.

A.

Abercrombie (or Abercromby), General, 359.
Albemarle, 2nd Earl of, 215.
Albemarle, 3rd Earl of, 442, 451.
Alberoni, Cardinal, 17, 328.
Ambrose, John, Admiral, 148, 161.
Amherst, Lord, 289, 338, 339, 340, 360, 361, 427, 473.
Anne, Queen of England, 5, 11, 12, 15, 29, 35, 58, 80.
Anson, Lord, 56, 65, 72, 73, 74, 76, 77, 82, 86, 87, 95, 98, 106, 125, 128, 130, 138; Chap. VI. to Chap. XIII. *passim*; 432, 445, 446, 447, 450, 451, 452, 459, 463, 464, 465, 470, 497.
Argyll, 5th Duke of, 236, 238.
Arnold, Thomas, Captain, 100.
Arnold, Dr. (of Rugby), 100.
Atterbury, Bishop, 51.

B.

Baird, Patrick, Captain, 405.
Balchen, Sir John, Admiral, 82.
Balfour, Captain, 385.
Barham, Lord, Admiral, 470.
Barnard, Sir John, M.P., 43, 46, 49.
Barnett, Curtis, Captain, 143.
Barré, Colonel, M.P., 459, 460.
Barrington, Hon. Samuel, Admiral, 292, 365, 385, 493, 494.
Barrow, Sir John, 87, 106, 130, 253, 256, 365, 445, 458, 469.
Barton, Matthew, Admiral, 483.
Beatson (historian), 412.
Beaufort, Duchess of, 447.
Bedford, 4th Duke of, 77, 170, 191, 199, 208, 216, 463, 473.
Belleisle, Marshal, 56, 248, 416.
Benbow, Admiral, 30.
Bentley, Sir John, Admiral, 182, 405.
Berkeley, George, Captain, 148.
Biron, Marshal, 457.
Bladen, Catharine Maria, 119.
Bladen, Elizabeth, 109, 124.
Bladen, John, 121, 122, 123.
Bladen, Martin, Colonel, 77, 110, 112, 118, 119, 120, 122, 123, 132.
Bladen, Thomas, Colonel, 110, 122.
Bladen, Thomas, Dr., 110.
Bladen, William, 110.
Blake, Admiral, 4, 60, 62, 75, 94, 259, 401, 425, 495.

500 INDEX.

Blakeney, Lord, General, 249, 268.
Blane, Sir Gilbert, M.D., 89.
Blayney, 2nd Lord, 110.
Bligh, General, 285, 357, 358.
Bolingbroke, Lord, 10, 12, 49, 216.
Bolton, Duke of. (See Powlett, Lord Harry.)
Bompart, M., Admiral, 368, 379, 380, 382, 387, 388, 390.
Borough, Sir John, 103.
Boscawen, Hon. Edward, Admiral, 65, 99, 106, 108, 109, 171, 172, 173, 175, 202, 203, 204, 220, 225, 227, 230, 231, 234, 240, 264, 276, 288, 289, 338, 339, 340, 341, 342, 360, 378, 379, 422, 426, 427, 430, 432, 446, 447.
Boscawen, Hon. Mrs., 447.
Boys, William, Commodore, 377, 378.
Braddock, General, 222, 283.
Bradstreet, Colonel, 359.
Brett, Sir Peircy, Admiral, 171, 377.
Brodrick, Thomas, Admiral, 288, 291, 306, 312, 317, 318, 329, 379.
Brooke (poet), 50.
Brooke, Catharine. (See Lady Hawke.)
Brooke, Humphrey, 119.
Brooke, Walter, 119.
Buckle, Matthew, Admiral, 806.
Burgoyne, General, 443.
Burke, Edmund, 3, 8, 14, 48, 49, 53, 54, 55, 57, 79, 480, 484.
Burnaby, Sir Wm., Captain, 206.
Burrish, George, Captain, 135, 136, 148, 161.
Bute, Earl of, 438, 441, 444.
Byng, Hon. Edward, Colonel, 252.
Byng, George, 1st Viscount Torrington, 66, 71, 72, 80, 81, 86, 100, 142, 169, 220, 421.

Byng, Hon. John, Admiral, 98, 102, 108, 124, 125, 163, 219, 220, 221, 222; Chap. VIII. *passim*; 280, 283, 327, 371, 424, 446, 463, 476, 482, 484.
Byng, Hon. Robert, 125.
Byron, Hon. John, Admiral, 82, 292, 306, 365.

C.

Calder, Sir Robert, Admiral, 304.
Campbell, Dr. (historian), 326, 412, 436, 437.
Campbell, John, Admiral, 388, 407, 410, 479.
Campbell, Thomas (poet), 4.
Canterbury, Thomas, Archbishop of, 236, 238.
Carteret, Lord Granville, 49, 216, 217, 236, 238, 420.
Cavendish, Captain, 259.
Cavendish, Mr., 123.
Chambers, William, Admiral, 198.
Charles II., King of England, 33, 35, 60, 64, 94.
Charles III., King of Naples, 26, 189, 438.
Charles III., King of Spain, 488, 489.
Charles VI., Emperor, 126.
Charnock (biographer), 114, 162, 206, 220, 436, 452, 492.
Chatham, Earl of, William Pitt, 8, 9, 10, 12, 24, 39, 53, 55, 79, 205; remainder of book *passim*.
Chesterfield, Lord, 191, 211, 216, 380.
Choiseul, Marquis de, 440.
Clarke, Colonel, 290, 313, 320.
Clerk (Author of "Naval Tactics"), 70.
Clive, Lord, 204, 222, 282, 383.

INDEX. 501

Cochrane, Earl of Dundonald, 345, 346, 353, 401.
Cock, Mr. Joseph, 386.
Codrington, Christopher, Lieut., 275.
Cole, Mr., 152.
Collingwood, Lord, Admiral, 392, 404, 450, 470.
Collingwood, Thomas, Captain, 276.
Compton, Major, 122.
Conflans, Marshal and Admiral, 79, 370, 372, 378, 382, 387, 388, 390, 391, 395, 399, 404, 405, 406, 407, 412, 413, 416, 418, 424, 427, 429.
Conway, Marshal, 78, 285, 290, 291, 300, 305, 311, 312, 319, 320, 321, 327, 330.
Cook, Captain, 89, 259.
Cooper, Thomas, Captain, 148, 151, 161.
Corbett, Mr. (Secretary to the Admiralty), 123.
Cornewall, James, Captain, 148, 149, 150, 166.
Cornish, Sir Samuel, Admiral, 442.
Cornwallis, Hon. Edward, General, 286, 291, 300, 320, 327.
Cotes, Thomas, Admiral, 181, 186, 382, 383, 387.
Coxe (historian), 8, 27.
Cromwell, Oliver, 38, 60, 62, 94, 229.
Cumberland, Henry, Duke of, 466, 467, 484.
Cumberland, William, Duke of, 236, 238, 239, 241, 281, 283, 284, 330.

D.

D'Aché, Admiral, 97, 359, 360, 453.
D'Aiguillon, Duc, General, 382, 413, 414, 415, 416.

D'Amblimont, M., Captain, 182.
Darcy, Lord, 119.
De Beaufremont, M., Admiral, 370, 406, 407, 409.
De Broc, Marquis, 415.
De Chalotais, M., 417.
De Court, Admiral, 132, 145, 146, 150, 196.
De Fromentière, M., Captain, 182.
De Grasse, Comte, Admiral, 79, 97.
De L'Angle, Merrick, Captain, 148.
De la Bédoyère, M., Captain, 182.
De la Clue, M., Admiral, 378, 379.
De la Jonquière, Admiral, 170, 172, 213.
De la Lippe, Comte, General, 443.
Denis, Sir Peter, Admiral, 171, 172, 292, 306, 365, 381, 405, 407, 409, 410, 428.
De Roquefeuil, Admiral, 82, 137, 139, 140.
De Saint George, Commodore, 171, 172.
De Ternay, M., Commodore, 442.
De Vaudreuil, Comte, Captain, 182.
Devonshire, 4th Duke of, 259.
Digby, Hon. Robert, Admiral, 365, 385, 485, 486.
Dilke, William, Captain, 148, 151, 161.
Dorset, Duke of, 236, 238.
D'Orvilliers, Admiral, 475.
Douglas, Sir James, Admiral, 306.
Draper, Sir William, General, 442.
Drummond, Charles, Admiral, 148.
Du Barri, Madame, 417.

502 INDEX.

Dubois de la Mothe, Admiral, 193, 230, 231, 288, 289, 324, 338.
Duchaffault, M., Captain, 182.
Duff, Robert, Admiral, 365, 369, 382, 383, 384, 388, 390, 397, 405, 408.
Duguay, Comte, Captain, 182, 195, 235, 243, 245, 289.
Dupleix, M., 171, 212, 213, 222.
Durell, Philip, Admiral, 182, 300.
Durell, Thomas, Captain, 41, 115, 126.
Durouret, M., Captain, 182.
Dury, Alexander, General, 358.
Du Verger St. André, M., Admiral, 370, 405, 413.
Duvignault, M., Captain, 182.

E.

Edgcumbe, 1st Earl of Mount Edgcumbe, 365, 368, 374, 452.
Effingham, Lord, 297.
Egmont, 2nd Earl of, 450, 458, 463, 464.
Eliott, Lord Heathfield, 23.
Elliot, John, Admiral, 377.
Elizabeth, Queen of England, 28, 50, 68.
Entick (historian), 85, 323.
Essex, 4th Earl of, 110.
Eugene, Prince, 15.

F.

Fairfax, Sir William, 110.
Falconer (poet), 391.
Falmouth, 1st Viscount, 203.
Fanshaw, Captain, 92.
Ferdinand, Prince, of Brunswick, 360.
Ferdinand VI., King of Spain, 438.

Fleury, Cardinal, 11, 14, 24, 26, 138, 139, 440.
Forbes, General, 359.
Forbes, Hon. John, Admiral, 148, 149, 166, 175, 264, 265.
Foster, Captain of privateer, 273.
Fowke, General, 250, 268.
Fox, Charles James, 10, 484.
Fox, Stephen, 1st Lord Holland, 219, 236, 238, 239, 242, 257.
Fox, Thomas, Admiral, 178, 181, 182, 183, 184, 188, 189, 194.
Frederick the Great, King of Prussia, 108, 188, 225, 257, 281, 282, 290, 332, 333, 334, 336, 337, 348, 359, 447.
Frederick, Prince of Wales, 216.
Frederick, Sir Charles, 389.
Frogmere, Rowland, Captain, 148, 161.

G.

Gabaret, M., Commodore, 147.
Galissonière, M., Admiral, 213, 251.
Galway, Ruvigny, Earl of, 15.
Gambier, Lord, Admiral, 345, 346.
Gascoigne, John, Admiral, 148.
Gayton, Clark, Admiral, 483.
Geary, Sir Francis, Admiral, 364, 381, 382, 383, 387, 391, 488, 490, 491, 493.
Geddes, Alexander, Captain, 107.
George I., King of England, 13, 17, 18, 28.
George II., King of England, 106, 108, 191, 237, 266, 280, 296, 328, 331, 332, 334, 367, 426, 427, 432, 434, 435.
George III., King of England, 76, 106, 428, 440, 448, 450, 454, 461, 467, 472, 473, 474, 475, 482, 495.

INDEX. 503

Gloucester, William Henry, Duke of, 484.
Glover, Richard, 21, 49, 252.
Godolphin, Earl, 10.
Gower, 2nd Earl, 478.
Grafton, Duke of, 454, 461.
Granby, Marquis of, 421, 461.
Granville, Earl. (See Carteret.)
Graves, Samuel, Admiral, 310, 346, 483.
Grenville, George (Prime Minister), 450.
Grenville, Thomas, Captain, 171, 236, 238.
Griffin, Thomas, Admiral, 229.
Grotius, 80.
Gybbon, Mr., M.P., 122.

H.

Haddock, Nicholas, Admiral, 82, 83, 84, 132.
Halifax, Montagu, Earl of, 214, 450.
Halifax, Saville, Lord, 10.
Hammonds of Scarthingwell, Towton, &c., 119.
Hanway, Thomas, Captain, 171, 181, 186.
Hardwicke, 1st Earl of, 215, 236, 238, 239, 242, 254, 259, 265, 277, 463.
Hardy, Sir Charles, Admiral, 82.
Hardy, Sir Charles, Admiral, 364, 391, 406, 444, 490, 491, 498.
Harland, Sir Robert, Admiral, 181, 183, 186, 477, 478, 483, 488.
Harrison, Robert, Admiral, 176, 181.
Hawke, Catharine (daughter of Lord Hawke), 124.
Hawke, Edward (father of Lord Hawke), 109.

Hawke, Edward, 1st Lord, Admiral, 3, 4, 53, 56, 60; remainder of book *passim*.
Hawke, Frances (sister of Lord Hawke), 122.
Hawke, Lady, 119, 120, 121, 122, 123, 124, 190.
Hawke, Martin Bladen, 2nd Lord, 124.
Henri IV., King of France, 104.
Henry VIII., King of England, 63.
Herbert, Earl of Torrington, Admiral, 64, 80.
Hervey, Lord, 434.
Hervey, Augustus, 3rd Earl of Bristol, Admiral, 365, 370, 371, 372, 375, 384, 385, 456, 457, 465, 483.
Hervey, The Hon. William, Captain, 92.
Hillsborough, 2nd Viscount, 461.
Hobbs, James, Lieutenant, 244.
Hodgson, General, 484.
Holburne, Francis, Admiral, 227, 230, 231, 288, 332, 349.
Holderness, Lord, 290.
Hood, Alexander, Lord Bridport, Admiral, 486, 487.
Hosier, Admiral, 19, 21, 23, 84.
Howard, Colonel, 292, 320, 322, 327.
Howe, Earl, Admiral, 70, 79, 97, 99, 107, 285, 292, 302, 310, 319, 346, 348, 350, 352, 353, 354, 356, 358, 360, 365, 366, 367, 381, 391, 392, 401, 405, 407, 409, 410, 414, 415, 428, 434, 436, 443, 449, 456, 457, 458, 459, 463, 467, 470, 473.
Hughes, Sir Edward, Admiral, 476.

J.

James I., King of England, 98, 108.

James II., King of England, 60, 94.
Janssen, Sir Theodore, 110.
Jenkins ("fable" of ear), 14, 31.
Johnson, Doctor, 49, 50.
"Junius," 13, 454, 461.

K.

Keene, Sir Benjamin, 39, 40.
Kempenfelt, Admiral, 445, 493.
Keppel, Viscount, Admiral, 76, 78, 79, 80, 90, 92, 95, 99, 199, 204, 205, 248, 249, 260, 265, 278, 292, 302, 359, 360, 365, 403, 405, 407, 409, 410, 411, 418, 427, 428, 432, 433, 437, 442, 449, 450, 451, 452, 453, 457, 458, 461, 464; Chapter XIV. *passim.*
Keppel, Sir Henry, Admiral, G.C.B., 427.
Kingsley, General, 433.
Kingston, Duchess of, 365.
Knowles, Sir Charles, Admiral, 108, 175, 190, 203, 290, 291, 302, 304, 305, 307, 311, 316, 329, 339, 467.

L.

Lally, M., 213.
Lawrence, Colonel, 222.
Lawson, Sir Wilfrid, 3rd Baronet, M.P., 42.
Leake, Sir John, Admiral, 14.
Legge, Hon. Edward, Commodore, M.P., 185, 186, 192, 199.
Lendrick, John, Captain, 372, 385, 386.
Lestock, Richard, Admiral, 82, 84; Chapter V. *passim*; 221, 285.

L'Etendueère, Admiral, 181, 182, 188.
Ligonier, Lord, General, 290, 296.
Lingen, Joshua, Admiral, 148.
Lloyd, James, Captain, 148, 151, 161.
Lloyd (Lieutenant of "Berwick"), 153, 155, 156, 165.
Long, Robert, Admiral, 148.
Loudoun, Lord, 332, 448.
Louis XIV., King of France, 5, 15, 16, 27, 33, 56, 58, 61, 64, 94, 212, 440.
Louis XV., King of France, 5, 139, 485.
Lovett, John, Captain, 148.
Lyttelton, 1st Lord, 102.

M.

McKinley, Lieutenant, 296, 297.
Macnamara, M., Admiral, 230, 231.
Mallet (poet), 50.
Malmesbury, 1st Lord, 439.
Mann, Horace (Minister at Florence), 140, 248, 265.
Manners, Lord Charles, 421.
Manners, Lord Robert, 421.
Mansfield, Murray, Earl of, 257, 265, 461.
Maria Theresa, Empress, 188, 226, 272, 447.
Marlborough, Charles, 3rd Duke of, 236, 238, 324, 356, 357.
Marlborough, John, 1st Duke of, 10, 12, 15, 18, 94, 110, 111, 203.
Martin, M. (historian), 413.
Martin, Sir William, Admiral, 108, 189, 489.
Master, Streynsham, Captain, 100.

Mathews, Admiral, 56, 71, 72, 78, 82, 84, 95, 100, 106, 131; Chapter V. *passim*; 205, 221, 229, 251, 264, 283, 286, 371, 439, 484.
Maule, Henry, Bishop of Dromore, 122.
Maurice, Prince, 94.
Medley, Henry, Admiral, 463.
Midwinter, Captain, 185, 186.
Mirepoix, Duc de, 230, 232, 285.
Mirepoix, Madame de, 215, 230.
Mitchell, Cornelius, Commodore, 168.
Monckton, General, 442.
Monk (or Monck), General, Earl of Albemarle, 62.
Montagu, Duke of, 199.
Montagu (or Mountagu), 1st Earl of Sandwich, 62.
Montagu, John, Admiral, 484, 485, 486.
Montagu, Hon. William, Captain, 171, 172.
Montcalm, Marquis de, General, 332.
Moore, Sir John, Admiral, 180, 181, 185, 433.
Mordaunt, Sir John, General, 284, 285, 290, 291, 292, 293, 296, 300, 304, 306, 307, 311, 312, 315, 316, 318, 319, 320, 321, 323, 324, 325, 326, 327, 330, 356.
Mostyn, General, 65.
Mulgrave, 2nd Lord, Captain, 77.

N.

Napier, Sir Charles, Admiral, 353.
Napoleon, Emperor, 69, 377, 401, 412.
Narborough, Sir John, Admiral, 63.

Navarro, Don J. J., Admiral, 146, 154, 157.
Neilson, Thomas, Lieutenant, 398.
Nelson, Earl, Admiral, 4, 60, 71, 75, 79, 87, 88, 91, 98, 100, 116, 285, 353, 392, 401, 402, 404, 411, 418, 419, 430, 447, 450, 456.
Newcastle, Hollis, Duke of, 205, 210, 216, 217, 218, 223, 230, 286, 238, 239, 253, 257, 259, 271, 279, 327, 389, 419, 424, 438, 468, 497.
Norris, Harry, Admiral, 176.
Norris, Sir John, Admiral, 80, 81, 82, 163.
Norris, Richard, Captain, 148, 157, 158, 161, 163, 164, 165, 166, 220.
North, Lord, 461, 468, 482.
Nugent (poet), 50.

O.

O'Brien, Lucius, Admiral, 411, 412.
Ogle, Sir Chaloner, Admiral, 82, 85, 86, 115, 117,
Onslow, Speaker, 48.
Osborn, Henry, Admiral, 148, 151, 154, 166, 249, 338, 360.
Ourry, Paul Henry, Captain, 414.

P.

Palliser (or Pallisser), Sir Hugh, Admiral, 76, 163, 477, 478, 479, 481, 482, 483, 485, 486, 488, 489, 490, 493, 494.
Palmerston, 2nd Viscount, 464.
Parry, William, Admiral, 385.
Pelham, Henry, Prime Minister, 76, 210, 211, 216, 217.

Penrice, Sir Henry (Judge of the Admiralty Court), 196.
Perrie, Mr., 200.
Peter the Great, Czar of Russia, 82.
Peterborough, Mordaunt, Earl of, 15.
Pett, Peter, 93.
Pett, Robert, Captain, 148, 161.
Peyton, Edward, Commodore, 167, 168.
Peyton, Sir Yelverton, Captain, 92.
Philip V., King of Spain, 85, 86.
Pigot, Hugh, Admiral, 483.
Pitt, William (son of Lord Chatham), 10, 79, 465, 494, 496.
Plumer, Mr., M.P., 46.
Pocock, Sir George, Admiral, 65, 97, 186, 204, 859, 860, 442, 449, 451, 452, 458, 476.
Pope, Alexander (poet), 49, 50.
Potter, Mr. M.P., 330.
Powlett, Lord Harry, Admiral, 245, 488. (See Duke of Bolton).
Prideaux, General, 861.
Pulteney, Earl of Bath, 12, 43, 46, 49, 50, 216.
Purvis, Charles, Admiral, 148.

R.

Ranke, Leopold von (historian), 25, 157, 448.
Reynolds, John, Admiral, 872.
Richelieu, Cardinal, 108.
Richelieu, Marshal, 252, 830.
Richmond, 3rd Duke of, 484.
Robins, Major, 87.
Robinson, Sir Thomas, 236, 238, 239.
Rochford, Earl of, 236, 238, 472.

Rockingham, Marquis of, 476, 484, 485, 487, 490.
Rockingham, Marchioness of, 487.
Rodney, Lord, Admiral, 4, 28, 60, 69, 70, 71, 79, 97, 99, 182, 186, 187, 189, 192, 194, 204, 292, 316, 329, 377, 401, 418, 437, 442, 449, 456, 457, 470, 477, 493, 494, 495.
Rooke, Sir George, Admiral, 14, 18, 80.
Ross, of Bladensburg, General, 110.
Rowley, Sir Joshua, Admiral, 405.
Rowley, Sir William, Admiral, 82, 84, 146, 148, 150, 151, 154, 155, 156, 157, 163, 164, 166, 167, 265.
Royston, Lord, 271.
Rupert, Prince, 94.
Rushout, Sir John, 122.
Russell, Earl of Orford, Admiral, 64, 80.
Russel, John, Captain, 148.
Ruthven, Colonel, 110.
Rutland, 3rd Duke of, 286, 238.

S.

Sackville, Lord George, General, 824, 856.
Sanderson, Sir Thomas, 48.
Sandwich, 1st Earl of. (See Montagu.)
Sandwich, 4th Earl of, 170, 211, 224, 450, 456, 458, 465, 475, 481, 482, 495.
Sandys, Mr., M.P., 122.
Saumarez, Philip, Captain, 171, 172, 182, 184, 186, 189.
Saunders, Sir Charles, Admiral, 77, 181, 186, 189, 192, 194, 204, 268, 2750, 289, 856, 411, 422, 449, 48, 451, 452, 458, 461.

INDEX.   507

Saxe, Marshal, 59, 82, 139, 140, 248.
Sclater, George, Captain, 148, 161.
Scott, Arthur, Commodore, 181, 186.
Selwyn, George, 451.
Shelburne, 2nd Earl of, 464.
Shovell, Sir Cloudesley, Admiral, 63, 81, 436.
Shuldham, Lord, Admiral, 483.
Smith, Mr. Joseph, 347.
Smith, Sir Sidney, Admiral, 358.
Smith, Thomas, Admiral, 102, 108, 260.
Smollett (historian), 118, 206, 412.
Somers, Earl, 9, 12.
Southey, Robert (historian), 87.
Speke, Henry, Captain, 405, 407, 410, 412, 428.
Stanhope, 1st Earl, 15, 17.
Stanhope, 5th Earl (Lord Mahon), 9, 258, 428, 424, 439, 475, 489.
Stanhope, Sir Thomas, Captain, 185, 405.
St. John, General, 110.
St. Vincent, 1st Earl, Admiral, 392, 470.
Steevens, Charles, Admiral, 182, 244.
Stepney, George, Captain, 148.
Storr, John, Admiral, 405.
Stuart, Lieutenant, 397.
Sully (the French Minister), 108.

T.

Taylor, Robert, Lieut., 369.
Taylor, Wittewronge, Captain, 391.
Temple, 1st Earl, 264, 266.
Tencin, Cardinal, 59, 138, 140, 377.

Thackeray (author of the "Life of Chatham"), 289, 388.
Thames, Mr., 293, 294, 295.
Thierri (French pilot), 290, 301, 311, 848.
Thompson (poet), 49, 50.
Thurot, M., Captain, 377, 378.
Torrington, Viscount. (See Byng.)
Townshend, Hon. George, Admiral, 148.
Towry, John, Captain, 148.
Tyrawley, Lord, General, 268.
Tyrrell, Richard, Admiral, 384, 385.

V.

Vauban, Marshal, 310.
Vaughan, General, 498.
Vernon, Admiral, 20, 21, 22, 49, 55, 82, 84, 85, 86, 87, 101, 107, 115, 125, 148, 173, 203, 206, 207, 285, 418, 482.

W.

Wager, Sir Charles, Admiral, 80, 81, 118, 148.
Waldegrave, Hon. John, General, 324, 356.
Waldegrave, 2nd Earl, 218, 238, 289, 241, 258, 259.
Wall, General (the Spanish Minister), 438.
Wallis, Samuel, Captain, 467.
Walpole, Horatio, Lord Walpole of Wolterton, 24.
Walpole, Horatio, 4th Earl of Orford, 56, 65, 77, 78, 140, 159, 173, 202, 203, 222, 223, 252, 258, 259, 260, 265, 266, 267, 330, 338, 365, 398, 408, 417, 432, 434, 447, 449, 450, 451, 463, 464, 466, 473, 474, 495, 496.

Walpole, Sir Robert, 1st Earl of Orford, 8, 9, 10, 13, 17, 19, 21, 24, 27, 30, 32, 41, 42, 43, 45, 49. 51, 52, 54, 55, 76, 81, 83, 84, 110, 115, 122, 139, 210. 217.

Warren, Sir Peter, Admiral, 73, 107, 171, 172, 173, 174, 175, 176, 177, 178, 179, 180, 190, 193, 197, 198, 201, 202, 203, 208, 209, 340.

Washington, General (President of the United States), 222.

Watson, Charles, Admiral, 97, 148, 181, 186, 192, 193, 204, 222.

Watson, Thomas, Captain, 101.

Wellington, Duke of, 393, 464.

Wentworth, General, 283, 285.

West, Temple, Admiral, 148, 151, 161, 171, 235, 264, 265, 268, 269, 288.

Weymouth, 3rd Viscount, 461.

Whitehead, Paul (poet), 426.

Whitwell, Matthew, Admiral, 385.

Williams, Edmund, Admiral, 148, 161.

William III., King of England, 5, 12, 25, 29, 58, 64, 80, 94, 104.

Wilkes, John, 88, 422, 454, 462.

Wilmington, Lord, 122.

Windsor, Captain, 486.

Wolfe, James, General, 282, 289, 300, 303, 310, 311, 314, 316, 320, 326, 327, 338, 339, 340, 341, 353, 360, 361, 362, 366, 367, 451, 495.

Wright, Fortunatus, Captain of privateer, 274.

Wright, Mr., Surgeon, 385, 386.

Wyndham, Sir William, M.P., 43, 45, 46, 49, 216.

Y.

Yonge, Professor, 259.

Young, James, Admiral, 365, 397, 483.

York, Duke of, Edward, 107, 365, 366, 367, 368, 374, 391, 442, 443, 444, 466.

ERRATA.

Page 107, line 25, *for* "With the exception" *read* "Except in the case."
" 173, 202, 203, note, *for* "vol. i." *read* "vol. ii." (These references are to the 2nd Edition.)
" 259, note, *after* "Mann" *insert* "vol. iii."
" 265, line 1, *after* "say" *insert* "but."
" 292, line 18, *for* "General" *read* "Colonel."
" 297, last line, *for* "regiments" *read* "regiment."
" 323, last line, *erase* "as."
" 336, note, *for* "24" *read* "240."
" 397, line 4, *erase* "who."
" 436, transfer note * to page 418.
" 459, line 5, *for* "best" *read* "most complete."
" " line 18, *for* "service" *read* "services."
" 464, line 1, *after* "Anson's" *read* "limited."
" 467, note, *for* "vol. ii." *read* "vol. iii."
" 470, line 16, *for* "is" *read* "are."
" 473, line 28, *for* "given orders none should be mentioned more" *read* "forbidden Grafton 'to name a peerage for any man.'"
" " note, *erase* "p. 133," *and for* "vol. iv." *read* "vol. iii. p. 239."

LONDON : PRINTED BY W. H. ALLEN AND CO., 13, WATERLOO PLACE.